BUSINESS ETHICS AND INDIAN VALUE SYSTEM

(Text and Cases)

ANAND SINGH
Assistant Professor,
Institute of Management Sciences,
University of Lucknow, India.

ISO 9001:2008 CERTIFIED

First Edition : 2011
Reprint : 2017

Published by : Mrs. Meena Pandey for **Himalaya Publishing House Pvt. Ltd.,**
"Ramdoot", Dr. Bhalerao Marg, Girgaon, Mumbai - 400 004.
Phone: 022-23860170/23863863, Fax: 022-23877178
E-mail: himpub@vsnl.com; Website: www.himpub.com

Branch Offices :

New Delhi : "Pooja Apartments", 4-B, Murari Lal Street, Ansari Road, Darya Ganj, New Delhi - 110 002. Phone: 011-23270392, 23278631; Fax: 011-23256286

Nagpur : Kundanlal Chandak Industrial Estate, Ghat Road, Nagpur - 440 018. Phone: 0712-2738731, 3296733; Telefax: 0712-2721216

Bengaluru : Plot No. 91-33, 2nd Main Road Seshadripuram, Behind Nataraja Theatre, Bengaluru - 560020. Phone: 08041138821, Mobile: 09379847017, 09379847005.

Hyderabad : No. 3-4-184, Lingampally, Besides Raghavendra Swamy Matham, Kachiguda, Hyderabad - 500 027. Phone: 040-27560041, 27550139

Chennai : New No. 48/2, Old No. 28/2, Ground Floor, Sarangapani Street, T. Nagar, Chennai - 600 012. Mobile: 09380460419

Pune : First Floor, "Laksha" Apartment, No. 527, Mehunpura, Shaniwarpeth (Near Prabhat Theatre), Pune - 411 030. Phone: 020-24496323/24496333; Mobile: 09370579333

Lucknow : House No 731, Shekhupura Colony, Near B.D. Convent School, Aliganj, Lucknow - 226 022. Phone: 0522-4012353; Mobile: 09307501549

Ahmedabad : 114, "SHAIL", 1st Floor, Opp. Madhu Sudan House, C.G. Road, Navrang Pura, Ahmedabad - 380 009. Phone: 079-26560126; Mobile: 09377088847

Ernakulam : 39/176 (New No: 60/251) 1st Floor, Karikkamuri Road, Ernakulam, Kochi – 682011. Phone: 0484-2378012, 2378016 Mobile: 09387122121

Bhubaneswar : 5 Station Square, Bhubaneswar - 751 001 (Odisha). Phone: 0674-2532129, Mobile: 09338746007

Kolkata : 108/4, Beliaghata Main Road, Near ID Hospital, Opp. SBI Bank, Kolkata - 700 010, Phone: 033-32449649, Mobile: 07439040301

DTP by : **Bright Computer Systems, Gayatri Nagar, Sitapur Road, Lucknow, Mobile: 9450614766, 9793630385**

Printed at : Shri Krishna Offset Press, Delhi.

DEDICATION

Dedicated to my parents Smt. Jayanti Singh and Shri Krishna Pal Singh whose blessings and prudence nurtured me to become an able learner.

I also wish to express my gratitude to those scholars who have laid foundation of ethics in the modern world and my special praise to those whom I have quoted in my book. My special thanks to my students whose trust, faith & belief in me has always encouraged me to contribute in the field of academics.

The effort of Mr. B.C. Pathak in typing the manuscript is duly acknowledged & special thanks to Himalaya Publishing House for publishing this book. Finally a request to the readers to express their views as well as their suggestions for improvement of the book.

ANAND SINGH

Lucknow

CONTENTS

CHAPTER–I : RENAISSANCE & EMERGENCE OF MODERN WORLD ... **1**

Scientific Development ... 2
Growth of Literature ... 3
Art, Sculpture & Architecture ... 4
Ethics and Virtues of Renaissance ... 6
Modern Industrial Revolution ... 7
Features of Industrial Revolution ... 9
Development of Textile Industry ... 9
Steam Engine ... 10
New Methods of Transport ... 10
Development of Iron Industry ... 12
Management Ethics and Ethical Problems of Industrial Revolution ... 12
Factory Systems ... 13
Was India the First Coloniser ... 14
Colonial System ... 14
Neo-colonialism ... 16
Weber's Protestant Ethics & Rise of Capitalism

CHAPTER–II : WESTERN ETHICAL THEORIES, APPROACHES AND ITS CONTRIBUTION IN MANAGEMENT ... **20**

Characteristic of Ethics ... 20
Economic Ethics ... 22
Dialectic and Theory of Knowledge ... 24
Hierarchy of the Sciences ... 25
Doctrine of Ideas ... 25
Cosmology ... 26
Ethics ... 26
Politics ... 27
Philosophy and the Sciences ... 28
Voltaire ... 31
Political Theory ... 34
Marx's Political Economy ... 35
Meteorological Climate Theory ... 36

The Utilitarianism of John Stuart Mill ... 36
Inductive Inference ... 37
Emile Durkheim (1858 – 1917) ... 40

CHAPTER–III : ROLE OF INDIAN ETHICS IN MANAGEMENT ... 44

Dharma as a Strategic Intervention Tool ... 46
Internal Conflict Management ... 47
Doctrine of *Karma* as a Management Technique ... 47
Dharma as a tool of Anger Management ... 48
Time Management ... 48
Purushottama – A Model of Leadership ... 49
Team Management ... 50
Characteristics of Indian Ethos ... 50
Traditional Economic Ethics ... 56
Rural Economy ... 57
Urban Economy ... 58
Sri Madbhagvadgita and Modern Management ... 62
Buddhist Economic Ethics ... 66
Buddhism and Globalization ... 74
Jainism and its Economic Values ... 78
Kautilya's Economic View ... 82
Kautilya's Financial Measures ... 85
State Trading ... 87
Budget, Accounts and Audit ... 88
Income, Expenditure and Balance ... 88
Accounts ... 89
Proper Maintenance of Account Books ... 90
Financial Discipline ... 91
Manu's Artha-Dharma ... 92
Vivekananda's Socio-Economic Ethics ... 97
Moral Laws of Gandhi ... 102
Cult of Non-Violence ... 104
Techniques of Social Revolution ... 104
Concept of Democracy & Society ... 107
Economic Ideas ... 108
Trusteeship Theory ... 110

CHAPTER–IV : CORPORATE SOCIAL RESPONSIBILITY & CORPORATE GOVERNANCE **112**
Social Responsibility versus Social Responsiveness ... 113
Arguments For & Against Social Responsibility ... 114
Social Responsibilities of Business Towards Different Groups ... 115
Corporate social responsibility : initiatives and examples ... 118
Corporate governance ... 121
Corporate Governance in Industrially Developed Countries ... 122
German – Japanese Model ... 123
Corporate Governance in India ... 123
Corporate Governance in the Public Sector ... 124
Code of Conduct for Corporate Governance ... 125
Measures to Improve Corporate Conduct ... 126

CHAPTER–V : ETHICAL MANAGERIAL PRACTICES **... 128**
Ethics in Marketing ... 128
Definition of marketing ethics ... 128
Importance of Marketing Ethics ... 129
Scope of Marketing Ethics ... 130
Key Ethical Issues in Marketing ... 130
Recent Trends in Ethical Marketing ... 133
Ethical Norms and Values for Marketers ... 134
Ethics in Finance ... 136
Theoretical assumptions ... 136
Importance of Ethics in Finance ... 138
Ethical Issues in Finance ... 138
Conclusion ... 139
Ethics in Human Resource Management ... 141
Stakeholder Theory and Ethical HRM ... 142
Significance of Ethics in HRM ... 143
Key Ethical Issues in HRM ... 143
Ethical HR Practices ... 145

CHAPTER–VI : STRESS **... 147**
What is Stress ... 147
Types of Stress ... 148
Constructive and Destructive Stress ... 148
Episodic and Chronic Stress ... 149
Sources of Stress ... 149

Personal Factors ... 150
Organisational Factors ... 151
Role Ambiguity ... 152
Environmental Factors ... 154
Emotional, Physiological and Behavioural ... 155
Burnout ... 155
Studying Stress: Focus on Physiology ... 155
Selye's General Adaptation Syndrome ... 155
Coping ... 157
Astanga Yoga ... 160

CHAPTER–VII : GLOBALIZATION AND ITS IMPACT **164**

Features ... 166
Effects ... 167
Globalisation of Markets ... 168
Globalisation of Production ... 169
Globalisation of Investment ... 170
Globalisation of Technology ... 172
Globalisation and Global Institution ... 173
Declining Trade Barriers and Globalisation ... 174
Average tariff rate on manufactured products ... 174
Globalisation and National Sovereignty ... 174
Advantages and Disadvantages of Globalisation ... 175
Globalisation in India ... 176
Anti-Globalisation ... 177
World Trade Organisation ... 180
Regulation of International Trade ... 180
Structure of WTO ... 182
Objectives of WTO ... 183
Functions of WTO ... 183
WTO Agreements ... 183
Free Trade versus Protection ... 185
Trade Barriers ... 187
Non-tariff Barriers (NTBs) ... 187
WTO – Current Issues ... 188
Floating Exchange Rates ... 188
International Capital Movement ... 189

UNO & Its Ethics	...	190
The important articles of United Nations charter	...	192
Indian Constitution as a Source of Ethics	...	196
Right to Equality	...	197
Right to Freedom	...	198
Directive Principles of State Policy	...	200
Fundamental Duties	...	202
CHAPTER–VIII : INDIAN SOCIAL SYSTEM–AS A SOURCE OF ETHICS	...	**204**
Varna System	...	206
Caste	...	216
Features of Caste System	...	216
Merit of Caste System	...	217
Demerits of Caste System	...	217
Changes in the Caste System	...	218
Samskaras	...	220
The Ashramas	...	228
Brahmacharya Ashrama	...	228
Grhastha Ashrama	...	230
Vanaprastha	...	231
Sannyasa	...	232
GUILD (SHRENI) ORGANISATION	...	234
Origin & Development	...	234
Structure	...	235
Functions	...	236
Special Feature	...	237
Guild and State	...	238
Liability and Relevance	...	240
Hindu, Buddhist And Jaina System of Education (Ancient India)	...	243
Takshasila University	...	247
Islamic System of Education	...	249
British and Modern Education	...	252
Sir Charles Wood's Despatch on Education, 1854	...	255
The Hunter Education Commission, 1882-83	...	256
The Indian Universities Act, 1904	...	257
The Sadler University Commission, 1917-19	...	258
The Hartog Committee, 1929	...	260

Sargeant Plan of Education ... 260
Radhakrishnan Commission, 1944-49 ... 260
University Grants Commission ... 261
Yashpal Committee ... 261
Development of Women Education ... 263
Right of Children to Free and Compulsory Education ... 265
CHAPTER–IX : MODERN SOCIAL INSTITUTIONS IN INDIA ... **267**
General Characteristics of the Family ... 267
Forms of the Family ... 268
Changing Pattern of Family ... 271
Future of Indian Family ... 273
Status of Women ... 275
Models of Social Change ... 286
Sanskritisation ... 286
Westernisation ... 287
Modernisation ... 288
CHAPTER–X : OVERVIEW OF CROSS-CULTURAL MANAGEMENT ... **292**
Anthropological Meaning of Culture ... 292
Universals of Cross-Cultural Business ... 294
Protestant ... 299
Cross-Cultural Diversity ... 303
Indian Panorama ... 303
Cross-Cultural Business Pattern ... 304
Cross-Cultural Business Zones ... 305
Exhibits and Case Studies ... 310
Index ... 320

1 CHAPTER

RENAISSANCE & EMERGENCE OF MODERN WORLD

The intellectual awakening which heralded the beginning of the modern age of the Europe received a strong impetus by the fall of the Constantinople in the hands of Turks in 1453. It forced the Greek scholars to seek asylum in Italy. These scholars were mainly responsible in stimulating the interest of the European scholars in classical literature which encouraged a new movement known as "Renaissance". The word renaissance literally means rebirth signifying the decline of feudalism, the rise of nation states and the beginning of modern sciences etc. The movement specifies two factors. "The discovery of the world" and "The discovery of man". The discovery of world indicates the geographical discoveries of the fifteenth & sixteenth centuries which facilitated trade across the Atlantic, the Pacific and the Indian Ocean, as well as discovery of the new world of America, South Africa and Australia. The discovery of man means the phase of society which discarded the medieval papal monarchy and relied on progressive and independent ideas.

Renaissance literally means rebirth signifying the decline of feudalism, the rise of nation states and the beginning of modern sciences etc. The movement specifies two factors.

The origin of Renaissance movement could be traced from 'Crusades' i.e. military expedition undertaken in Europe between 11th to 13th century to recover the Holy land Jerusalem from Seljuk Turks. Because of these crusades the Europeans came into contact with enlightened people of East. The intellectual horizon of crusades had broaden up because of interaction of Indians, Arabs and Chinese. The crusaders helped in ending the European segregation from rest of the world. Aristotle's scientific works, Indian (Arabic) numerals, Algebra, Mariner's compass and Chinese paper making technique reached Western Europe through crusaders. The crusaders had business links with eastern nations and many traders settled in the courts of kingdoms of Asia. So there was a tremendous increase in economic prosperity which fostered the spirit of Renaissance.

'Crusades' i.e. military expedition undertaken in Europe between 11th to 13th century to recover the Holy land Jerusalem from Seljuk Turks.

The chief characteristic of Renaissance is 'humanism'. The humanists dreamt of an integrated personality of man who possessed a fascinating body and fine feelings. The secularism was the key characteristic of it. They accepted that the good of life and happiness of common people are more important instead of serving the God or demonstrating spiritual hegemony. The chief character of Renaissance could be seen in the field of science, art, architecture and literature.

Scientific Development

The planet theory of Pope was based on Ptolemy who asserted in second century that earth is the centre of the Universe but Copernicus, the scientist of Poland ridiculed it.

The hallmark of scientific revolution of renaissance was the knowledge gained by means of observation and experiment. The planet theory of Pope was based on Ptolemy who asserted in second century that earth is the centre of the Universe but Copernicus, the scientist of Poland ridiculed it in the sixteenth century and explained that earth is a planet which rotates around the sun. Since this theory was against the Biblical idea so he was compelled to stop the propagation of his discovery by the order of Pope. Copernicus theory generated the idea that the world is infinite and the earth is a small part of it. His work *'De Revolutionibus Orbium Coelestiurm'* started a new scientific era. The Italian scientist Giordano Bruno (1548 – 1600) improved the theory of Copernicus. He declared that the universe is infinite, limitless and unfathomable. Neither the sun nor the earth is in the centre of the universe. The universe is a constellation of innumerable stars and each star is far away from the other. He emphasized that the earth revolves around the sun and is flat at poles. His discoveries were declared anti Christian and he had to struggle with dogmatic Christian inquisitions. According to the verdict of the priests he was burnt alive on 16th Feb. 1600. Several of Bruno's ideas were authenticated by Danish scientist Tycho who built a modern observatory with the help of king of Denmark Brauhe. The german astronomer Johann Kepler postulated in his book *'Mysterium – Casm Ographian'* that the planets revolve around the sun and their orbits are not circular but elliptical. Galileo Galilei, the imminent scientist of Italy invented telescope and observed that there is no heavenly conceptions of medievalism. He observed that moon is not totally spherical but has hills and seas. After observing spots on sun he declared that the sun rotates on its axis. He published his scientific observation in his book *Sidrius Nontius.* In his another publication *Dialogue concerning the two chief systems of the world – Ptolmic and the Copernican* was published in 1632. In it he ridiculed Ptolmy's Cosmology. The church prosecuted and compelled him to retract his ideas at the age 70. Galileo also discovered that falling masses depend upon the distance travelled by them and not on their weight which refuted the doctrine of Aristotle. Leonardo da Vinci was supposed to be first modern scientist who ridiculed the hypothesis of Catholics. Before Copernicus, Leonardo says that the sun does not revolve around the earth and the earth is a planet like the moon. He also like Galileo says that distance accelerates the speed of a falling object. He also developed a hydraulic and some new phonetics. He said that sound travels in waves. From the phenomenon of thunder-light he deduced that the speed of light is faster than that of sound. He also invented a huge crane to lift the heavy load and manufactured a steam operated piston and a bicycle type chain having ball rollers structure. He declared that the energy might be produced by way of the force of air and also built a two mast warship which because of its inner mast could float even when its outer structure was wrecked. Leonardo also excelled in Aerodynamics.

The Catholic superstitions were also shattered by the medical inventors. The pathologist Grirolamo Fracastoro found that causes of disease is not only the deficiency of the body fluids but there may be outward factors. He wrote a book on contagious disease and discovered the cause of syphilis. His discovery on contagious disease led to development of bacteriology. Another biologist William Harvey (1518-1658) of England has discovered the route of blood circulation and compared the body by hydraulic machine. Harvey's discovery paved way for a systematic Physiology. Robert Boyle discovered that the volume of gas is inversely proportional to the pressure and stipulated that there are certain elements which combined together to make other objects. He is credited with the development of modern chemistry. The British scientist Francis Bacon in his *Novum Organum* stressed that a person must apply his wisdom and reason in search of truth and make experiments to acquire sound knowledge. The French scientist Rene Descartes explored the application of Algebra in geometry and made significant contribution in the field of philosophy. He refused the doctrine of Aristotle and emphasized upon logic as means of seeking true knowledge. Isaac Newton (1642-1727) was born in England and revolutionized the science. Newton through his new discoveries reaffirmed the Copernicus thought. Newton in his work *Principia Mathematica* postulated that the nature affects on the Laws of Universal Gravitation which explain why heavenly bodies move downwards instead of upwards. He revealed that how the gravitation maintains the existence of cosmos. Newton also discovered the method of infinitesimal Calculus and with the help of it he formulated the Laws of Motion. The scientific work was also accelerated by the Royal Society of London AD (1662) and the French Royal Academy AD (1666). All these development led to tremendous growth of science and industry which shattered the ancient, inveterate and dogmatic beliefs. This scientific revolution led to development of modern industrial world based on the idea of democracy, liberety and equality.

Newton in his work *Principia Mathematica* that the nature affects on the Laws of Universal Gravitation which explain why heavenly bodies move downwards instead of upwards.

Growth of Literature

The development in the field of literature started when Gwarino Da Verona brought 50 Greek and Latin manuscripts to Italy in 1409. At that time a Humanist Academy was established. Slowly a lot of literatures were produced in the native languages which led to development of Italian, French, Spanish, Portuguese, German, English, Dutch and Swedish languages. The Renaissance literature emphasised upon human life and their characteristics. The renowned writers like the English dramatist Shakespeare, the French satirist Rabelais and the Spanish poet Cervantes did not choose religious themes and endeavored to describe the simple ideas of humanity. The prominent writers of Italy were Dante (1265-1321), Francisco Petrarch (1304-1374) and Giovanni Boccaccio (1313-1375). Dante has been compared to Homer. His *Divine comedy* deals with his imaginary journey through hell, purgatory and paradise. In his book *The* Monarch Dante said that the sovereign should be supreme in non religious matters. Petrarch was more moderate and scientific in his approach. He undertook long voyages and added the different ideas in his manuscript. He was appointed as teacher in Paris University and was also invited to deliver lecture by the King of Naples. In his interpretation of the works of antiquity from which the word 'humanism' is derived Boccaccio, a disciple of Petrarch wrote *Decameron* in which he has projected a new style of humorous stories. He highlighted the moral degradation that prevailed among the elites of the Italian society. Some other Italian scholars like Ariosto, Tasso and Cellutani also made their contributions to Italian literature. Machiavelli (1469-1527) lived in Florence and his famous contribution was *The Prince.* He propounds that religion is a weakness of the state. He was censored by the Pope. Marcigleo (1275-1343) in his writing Defender of Peace criticized political intervention of the Pope in European nation states.

Rabelais (1495-1553) and Montaigne (1553-1592) were prominent scholars of France. Rabelais raised slogan against religious fanaticisms and orthodoxy. He has written in Satiric and his slogan was *Thirst for intelligence, morality, experience and truth.* His famous books are *'Pentagrule'* and *'Gargantua'.* Montaigne a renowned essay writer had reputed place in the french society. He raised his pen against the prevailing chaotic rule and medieval anarchy. The title *First Modernist* was given to him.

Renaissance also revolutionized English literature Geoffrey Chauser (1340-1400) is known as father of English poetry. His work *Canterbury Tales* reflects the impact of *Decameron.* He also invented Sonnet. Thomas Moore (1478-1539) in his book *'Utopia'* visualised the social evils and economic disparities of English society. Fransis Bacon (1561-1626) was a politician, advocate and a philosopher. His essays show a poetic style. The greatest contribution during renaissance was made by William Shakespeare (1564-1616) who contributed famous comedies and tragedies. His most significant contributions are: *Merchant of Venice, Romeo and Juliet, Hamlet, King Lear* and *Macbeth.* Hobbies was another prominent writer of England.

Some other European countries like Holland, Germany, Spain and Portugal also contributed in the field of literature. The Dutch scholar Erasmus became a great humanist and scholar. In his *"In the Praise of Folly"* he satirized the hypocritical and superstitions life. Miguel de Cervantes (1547-1616) of Spain wrote *Don Quixote.* He criticized the feudal society of the world. Later on he was burnt down by order of priests.

Art, Sculpture & Architecture

The art and architecture during age of renaissance were based on humanism displaying the harmony of art and beauty. It accommodated the sentiments of common people.

Painting

The remarkable progress was made in the field of painting. The new style of painting was first developed in Italy. Fra Angelico and Massoccio were few of the early painters who initiated the new style of Renaissance. But unprecedented contribution was made by three prominent painters of Italy: Leonardo da Vinci (1452-1519), Michaelangelo (1425-1564) and Raphael (1483-1520).

Leonardo was a scientist, musician and a philosopher.

Leonardo was a scientist, musician and a philosopher. At the age of 15 he became a disciple of famous painter Varragenio and rivalled him. He made a deep study of human anatomy and physiology in order to bring reality to his paintings. He painted number of sketches of common life. The *Last Supper* and *Monalisa* are his world famous paintings.

He made a deep study of human anatomy and physiology in order to bring reality to his paintings.

Michaelangelo was a painter, sculptor, and an engineer too. On the ceiling of Sistine chapel in Rome, he has painted fresco scenes from Biblical stories. *'The Last Judgement'*, is his most famous painting completed by him in eight years. '*The Fall of Man*' is his another famous painting. Raphael also occupies a famous place in society of painters. He beautifully painted the emotion of affection and motherhood. His greatest contribution is *Madona*.

Some other famous painters of Europe during this age are: Lucas, Duirer and Henis Dalven in Germany, Degavallis Kaith in Spain and Van Eyek brothers in Holland.

Michaelangelo was a painter, sculptor, and an engineer too. On the ceiling of Sistine chapel in Rome, he has painted fresco scenes from Biblical stories.

Sculpture

Lorenzo Gipperti (1378-1455), Donatello (1386-1466) and Michaelangelo were prominent sculptors of the age. Lorenzo Gipperti built ornamental and beautiful doors for the cathedeal of Florance. These doors were made of bronze and stories of old testaments were carved out on them. The large size statue of saint Mark in Venus was a masterpiece of Donatello's sculptor. He translated the magic of innocence in his statues. Michaelangelo carved out statues for Cathedral of Medici. Two of his famous sculptors are: (i) *Pieta* – 16 feet high statue made in Rome and (ii) the statue of David which was carved out of the citizen of Florence. There sculptors also influenced the art of England, Germany, and France. The tombs of Isabella and Emperor Ferdinand in Spain show such influence.

Architecture

In the medieval age the gothic architecture dominated by catholic superstitions prevailed all over Europe. Renaissance produced new style of architecture in Europe. It was a combination of Greek, Roman and Persian style which laid great stress on technique and ornamentation. The round and horse shoe arches were introduced in structures first in Italy then in other European nation states, Filippo Brunilleschi (1377-1446) was architect of this new style. Michaelangelo with Raphael built the St. Peter's Cathedral in Rome. It is famous for its magnificent and massive dome. Lubre's Palace in Paris, St. Paul's Cathetral in London and Escorial palace in Spain were splendid monuments of the renaissance architecture.

In the medieval age the gothic architecture dominated by catholic superstitions prevailed all over Europe. Renaissance produced new style of architecture in Europe. It was a combination of Greek, Roman and Persian style which laid great stress on technique and ornamentation.

Music

The protestant movement ushered in a new era for music. In the protestant religion there was a lot of scope for songs and prayers. The great reformer Martin Luther introduced songs in the protestant prayers and himself compiled religious songs. Givovann Palestrina (1524-94) was a famous Italian composer. In 1554 he published a book on Chorus. Markendas was another famous composer of renaissance age. Instrumental music gained credence in common society. The old ribic was replaced by violin. The Harpsichord another famous instrument was developed which later evolved as Piano.

Ethics and Virtues of Renaissance

The ethics of renaissance manifest the influence of scientific outlook and intellectual enquiry collectively called 'enlightenment'. The slogan of intelligentia class of this age was reason, tolerance and humanity. The impact and influence of science and logic on the thinking and outlook of the masses was so much that this age was known as the age of Intellectual Revolution.

Instead of superstitious rituals and divine interference, emphasis was laid on all human activities for making the human destiny.

During the age of enlightenment man was the centre of activities and thought. Instead of superstitious rituals and divine interference, emphasis was laid on all human activities for making the human destiny. This phase established human privileges, human rights and human ideals.

The renaissance rejected the traditional economic and social institutions like feudalism, fiefdom etc. and people tried to learn the reality by examining the system through science and logic. The intellectual of this age focused attention on the shortcomings of administration and economic institutions, social disparity as well as degenerating economic condition and thought of new institution which could give them bright future.

The intellectuals of this age thought that world is like a machine which functions according to some natural laws which are eternal and everlasting. It is good for human being if he discovers natural laws and acts according to them instead of violating them. The natural laws could be understood only by means of intellect and reasons.

The people of this age thought that main cause of disparity among the society is that everyone does not get equal opportunity of education and welfare schemes. The literature of this age shows liveliness and boldness in order to awaken the contemporary society which ignites creative thought in the society. The literature also condemned the ancient conventions and the order which were degenerating the society. They fostered the humanism which gives priority to human civilization and preferred human prestige, rights and ideals.

MODERN INDUSTRIAL REVOLUTION

The global expansion of trade and commerce during renaissance age consolidated the position of trading community who succeeded in driving the feudal forces out of office. By the end of the eighteenth century, the urban middle class had completely redeemed themselves from the feudal forces. They started investing money in industries to earn profit and because of it the feudal economy was transformed into industrial and capitalist economy. Advanced technology introduced by experimental science brought about tremendous changes in the process of production. This phenomenon is known as Industrial Revolution.

First of all it originated in England and then gradually expanded in the other parts of the world. In the period between 1750 to 1850 steam based production system was introduced in England. Domestic and overseas businesses increased due to development of modern transportation and the nature of economy was completely overhauled. Industrial revolution originated in consequence of growth of three inter connected fields – economic organization, technology and business structure. Economic organization means access to excessive capital and growth of native and foreign markets for the procurement of raw materials and the sale of machine made goods. Technology has been defined as maximum use of machines for production and minimum use of human labour. The business structure deals with skills for use of land, labour and capital. The overall changes of industrial revolutions can be categorized under following categories:

Industrial revolution originated in consequence of growth of three inter connected fields – economic organization, technology and business structure.

1. Growth of engineering and technology
2. Revolution in manufacturing of iron and steel
3. Use of steam and hydropower in textile industry
4. Development of chemical industry
5. Discovery of coal mines
6. Development of the modern transport system

Because of industrial revolution following change occurred in the European society:

1. The feudal system of governance and economy became outdated and new economy emerged based on steam operated machines.
2. Initially hydropower, then steam power, electricity and later on natural oil were used to operate plants and machines.
3. Agriculture was mechanized and extensive farming started based on new technology and tools.
4. Steel plants were opened to develop infrastructure.
5. The capital was used to earn profit.
6. International trade started and colonial system developed.
7. Phenomenal changes in transport due to steam engine and machine based ships.

The Industrial Revolution which started in England in 1760, later on covered all the European Nations, USA and Japan. The effect of this revolution can be categorized under four fields.

1. Demographic Revolution : Due to sufficient food production the population of Europe increased stupendously since 1750 and contributed to the rapid growth in human labour. With increase in population the demand and prices of commodities increased which encouraged the manufacturers to increase their production and introduce technological improvements.

Agricultural Revolution and Industrial Revolution in England and other European countries have been closely associated with each other.

2. Agricultural Revolution : Agricultural Revolution and Industrial Revolution in England and other European countries have been closely associated with each other. Because of modern inventions and decline of feudalism new structure of agriculture emerged in Europe which had following attributes:

(*i*) In place of open and scattered agricultural fields, the cultivation of industrial phase developed on consolidated fields on large scale.

(*ii*) Modern researches were utilized in it and because of it animal husbandry and other associated sectors of agriculture developed as industry.

(*iii*) Income in agriculture sector increased and also per capita productivity.

(*iv*) In agriculture sector a new class of agricultural laborers emerged and later on these laborers left their agricultural jobs and joined industries.

3. Commercial Revolution : The machine based production and consequential demand of raw materials and market for machine made goods compelled England and other European Nations to develop colonial system of trade with foreign colonies. It had following features:

(*i*) Industrial revolution could not bank upon the limited developed market for its growth so trade relations with foreign countries were developed which later on turned into colonial system.

(*ii*) With the help of the foreign trade these nations developed many of their industries by importing cotton and other raw materials from foreign nations.

(*iii*) On the strength of profit gained from foreign trade, essential capital was obtained for development of agriculture, mine technology and industrial development.

(*iv*) Certain new institutions like insurance companies, banking system etc were developed which augmented domestic as well as foreign trade. The East India companies of England, France and Holland initially thrived on loans provided by banks and their respective governments.

(*v*) With the growth of trade and industry the urban industrial centres and cities were developed and expanded. The cities like London, Liverpool, Manchester, Birmingham etc. made considerable progress during this age.

4. Transport Revolution : Due to innovation of modern technology the transportation system was revolutionized. Roads, canals, ports, bridges and railway were rapidly developed in England, France, Holland, Germany etc. Modern transport system led to tremendous growth of capital in these nations.

Features of Industrial Revolution

1. Change in Agrarian System : To meet the demands of growing industry and population new techniques were introduced in the agrarian system to produce more grains and cotton. A number of scientific methods and more advanced type of tools were invented. A British landlord Jethro Tull invented a machine called Drill by which seeds should be sown in fixed rows. Another landlord Town discovered the advantage of rotation of crops. In 1770 Robert Bakewell of England adopted professional method to earn profit from animal husbandry. He adopted artificial insemination in breeding the sheep and succeeded in breeding cattle which yielded enough milk and meat. An English farmer Arthur Young (1741-1820) visited England, Ireland and France to survey the contemporary agricultural system. After it he recommended the making of large agricultural farms out of small fields. He also published a journal *'Annals of Agriculture'*. In order to introduce these scientific technologies large agricultural farms were developed by merger of several small fields and making an enclosure around them. For that purpose 956 enclosure acts were passed between 1792 and 1815 in England only. This left lot of people landless who moved to industry. By the end of 1840 a German Chemise Justin Von Leebing proved that the fundamental diet for plants is Potash, Nitrogen and Phosphorus. Because of the use of these organic fertilizers the productivity increased many folds. In 1793, an American Whitney invented a threshing machine and in 1834 Cyrus H. Machornic invented mowing machine. All these inventors and power driven machines brought revolution in agriculture which fulfilled the growing demands for commodities and encouraged growth in production.

Development of Textile Industry

Up to early eighteenth century the cotton industry of England and other European countries were mainly dependent on import from India and other South East Asian countries. Because of these technical revolution of machine made textiles developed in Europe.

Evolutionary Chart of Textile Industry

S.N.	Year	Inventor	Invention	Result
1.	1733	John Kay	Flying Shuttle	Increased the speed of weaving
2.	1764	James Hargreaves	Spinning Jenny	Made it possible to spin yarn on & spindles at a time.

3.	1769	Arkwright	Water Frame	A weaving machine which worked with water power. It had several rollers and contributed to the establishment of large factories.
4.	1779	Samuel Crompton	Mule	Combined the mechanism of spinning jenny and water frame and made a new machine called the 'mule': It increased the speed of spinning and made the production of fine yarn and fine fabric possible.
5.	1785	Cartwright	Powerloom	It could he operated both by steam power and water power. It accelerated the speed of weaving cloth.
6.	1793	Whitley	Cotton gin	It could separate cotton fibre from the seeds quickly.
7.	1825	Richard Roberts	Weaving machine	It accelerated cloth weaving.
8.	1846	Alias Hobbe	Sewing machine	It revolutionized cloth stitching.

In 1733 John Kay invented a 'Fly Shuttle' by which weaving could be done faster. In 1764 James Hargreaves invented 'spinning Jenny' which span eight yarns at a time. The chain of inventions continued up to nineteenth century. The large scale production of cotton led to colonization of India, South East Asia and Africa which became exporter of raw cotton and market for produced goods of the west.

Steam Engine

During industrial revolution machines based on water and wind power had limitations. So better replacement was contemplated which could run new machines smoothly. In 1712 an Englishman Thomas Newcomer invented a steam engine to drain water with technology but it was not fuel efficient. In 1769 James Watt amended Newcomers engine and invented a new steam engine. His engine was used in textiles industry which was trendy and fuel efficient.

New Methods of Transport

Due to ever increasing trade and industry means of transport also increased. In eighteenth century a Scottish engineer Mc Adam developed new technique of road making which was durable and less costly than earlier roads. For domestic as well as foreign trade canals were dug. During eighteenth century major cities of England were linked with big canals which facilitated the transport of the heavy goods from one place to another. In 1869 a French engineer Ferdinand de Lesseps completed the construction of Suez Canal which connects the Mediterranean Sea with the Red Sea. With the construction of Suez Canal the distance between India and Europe was reduced to the one third of the earlier distance. An American Hobert Fulton invented a faster sea boat which was developed as steamers. In 1838, a steam boat crossed the Atlantic Ocean for the first time in eighteen days. The invention of railway engine revolutionized the land transport system George Stephenson invented his famous engine Rocket in 1814 and first railway train was run between Manchester and Liverpool in 1830. The invention of petrol engine in 1880 was another remarkable step in the field of transportation. Motor car factories were opened in USA, France, Germany and England. In 1839 Charles Good Year discovered that the process of vulcanization to harden the rubber: The Rubber Tyre made journey faster and comfortable.

Remarkable improvement was also made in the field of communication. In 1840 blind Englishman Roland Hill started a system through which anybody could send a letter to any place in Great Britain by offers of a one pence stamp on the letter. Other countries followed this system soon. In 1844 Samuel Morse invented telegraph machine. In order to connect two continents water telegraphs was introduced and cable was established between North America and Europe known as 'Atlantic Cable'. In 1876 Graham Bell invented telephone which revolutionized the communication at that time. A few scientists such as Farade, Bunsen, Siemens, Ampere and James Young led many inventions which become advantageous for industrial growth.

Inventions Benefitting Industrial Revolution

S.N.	Invention	Inventor	Country	Year
1.	Road Building Technique	McAdam	Scotland	-
2.	Steam Engine	Thomas Newcomen	England	1712
3.	Canal Building Technique	James Brindley	England	1761
4.	Steam Engine	James Watt	England	1769
5.	Technique of Making Pure Steel	Henry Court	England	1784
6.	Steam Boat	Robert Fulton	America	1807
7.	Steam Engine (Rocket)	George Stephenson	England	1814
8.	Rubber Tyre	Charles Goodyear	America	1839
9.	Telegraph	Samuel Morse	America	1844
10.	Technique of Steel Making	Henry Bessemer	England	1856
11.	Atlantic Cable	Cyrus Field	America	1866
12.	Suez Canal	Ferdinand de Lessepes	France	1869
13.	Telephone	Graham Bell	England	1876

Development of Iron Industry

In the eighteenth century new type of furnaces for melting iron were built and modified and hard steel was manufactured. In 1704 Henry Court invented the technique of pyddling by which the standard quality of steel was manufactured. It brought about revolutionary changes in the production of steel. An English engineer Henry Bessemer discovered the processes of steel making by blasting through molten pig iron in a large container. It facilitated the production of steel on large scale.

Management Ethics and Ethical Problems of Industrial Revolution

The industrial revolution ushered in remarkable effect on economic ideology. The role of liberalism based on the principle of individual liberty prevailed all over Europe.

The industrial revolution ushered in remarkable effect on economic ideology. The role of liberalism based on the principle of individual liberty prevailed all over Europe. It promoted constitutionalism, supremacy of public, equality before law, religious tolerances and understanding of nationalism. It also encouraged principle of non interference by the state in economic affairs. Adam Smith propounded principle of Laissez Faire which says that state should not control trade and commerce. David Ricardo says that every national economy is based on certain natural laws and the "Iron Law of Wages" is one of them. According to this law it is not possible for a worker to earn more than his livelihood.

The spirit of public welfare and efforts for improving the condition of workers gave birth to Socialism.

The economic system based on the capital growth and Capitalism was opposed. The system of Capitalism led to misery of workers. Some scholars of England and France demanded improvement in the economic condition of the workers. The spirit of public welfare and efforts for improving the condition of workers gave birth to Socialism. The ultimate goal of Socialism was to eliminate the class discrimination. The socialists demanded a just distribution of money and maintained that all factors of production should belong to all human society. To counter it an industrialist of England Robert Owen established co-operative institutions for workers in his factories and made arrangements for their lodging, recreation, adequate wages and their children's education. William Thomson, Thomas Hudskin and John Gray were prominent socialists who spoke for workers. Saint Simon and Faurriae asserted same views in France. Louis Blanc demanded the 'Right to Work' for workers and justified the establishment of 'national factories' to protect the interest of workers. Karl Marx gave a practical and dynamic shape to socialism. The leadership and ideas of Karl Marx and Engels gave birth to Scientific Socialism or Communism.

The industrial revolution strengthened the middle class values in the European societies. With the advent of factory system joint family system was eroded. The struggle between workers and factory owners, exploitation of labour, growth of population in industrial cities and certain problem related to health, hygiene developed. The workers had to dwell in the slums and had to work for 14 to 16 hours every day. Women and children also worked for long hours but received less wages than men. The problems like unemployment and deterioration of public health system increased. To counter these problem numbers of legislations were enacted which made specific provisions for the fixation of working hours, minimum wages etc.

Industrial revolution created wealth and resources which concentrated privilege and power in few hands and on the other hand worker were compelled to live under pecuniary subjugation. The industrial workers were compelled to organize themselves in trade unions for the redressal of their grievances or redemption of carnalities inflected upon them.

Industrial revolution created wealth and resources which concentrated privilege and power in few hands and on the other hand worker were compelled to live under pecuniary subjugation.

The revolution encouraged the tendency to establish colonies by holding political and economic control of underdeveloped countries. England, France, Holland, Spain, Beligium extended their colonial empire in Asia and Africa. Because of colonial and commercial competition the European nations started fighting amongst themselves that led to increased international tension which created circumstances responsible for World Wars.

Factory Systems

In the eighteenth century the new mode of production was developed in Europe. The new system was known as 'Factory System'. Initially the representative of a trade company was called a 'Fectors' and his workshop or warehouse was known as a factory. But during Industrial Revolution the prevalent meaning of factory changed and it was given a capitalist orientation. Now the factory came to be known as a place where workers produced goods on large scale with help of machines. This production was meant for profit. In the beginning of Capitalism, production mainly depended on 'pulling out' system. In this system the capitalist supplied raw materials to the workers who manufactured goods at their residence with their own tools. The capitalists or traders collected these finished goods and sold them in markets for profit. The advantage of this system was that the capitalists could have goods manufactured by the workers who will spread far and wide and they were not concerned with the personal problems of the workers. The traders needed a lot of time in calling on the workers to collect the finished products. It was difficult to maintain the quality of the products and it was also doubtful that a particular worker would complete his assignment in time. A unique method was evolved to overcome all these problems to assemble all the workers at one place and to manufacture the goods there. The first necessity was the construction of structure for a factory and then to bear all the expenses of buying machines and tools. It was also felt necessary to appoint supervisors to look after the process of production. In 1700 Christopher Palhan of Sweden opened a factory with 100 workers for manufacturing utensils and found that the cost of production had come down.

Was India the First Coloniser?

Colonial system generally defines economic relations between one or more countries in which the mother country purchased raw materials from dependent country and in return sells their produced goods. It not only lead to de-industrialization of dependent country but it also acts as potential market for industrialized countries. But earliest protestant economy was not based on such ideals. India was first such country who expanded her trade and commerce with China, South, East and Central Asia. The economic and cultural relations were so strong that still in more than 25 Asian nations Indian culture and religions have strong influence. In the early centuries of the Christian era economic activities and religious missionaries penetrated to Mynmar, Srilanka, Indonesia etc. The earliest Indian settlements in Java were established in AD 56. In the second century of the Christian era several small Indian principalities were set up. There states flowered into the kingdom of Sri Vijaya. In Indo-China which is presently divided into Vietnam, Cambodia and Laos, Indian set up kingdoms of Kamboja and Champa. These Indian settlements in the Indian Ocean flourished till the thirteenth century and slowly intermingled with local culture. The continuous mingling of people gave rise to a new type of art, language and lifestyle. It shows happy blending of Indian and indigenes style. The great Buddhist temple is not found in India but in Borobudur in Indonesia. The Hindu temple of Angkorvat in Cambodia is larger & than that.

So the trade led not only to exchange of goods but also of elements of culture. India set up their own colonial set up but this system was not based on exploitation, hatred and violence. In 1000 years, of cultural reciprocation there is only one evidence in 1025 when Rajendra Chola used force in South East Asia to protect the mercantile interest of Indian traders. The economic profit was the main motive but Indian contribution seems to be more important in art, religion, scriptune and language. Such type of trade relation could be the best model for future global trade.

Later on a new system of production was devised in which the process of production was divided into several smaller segments and one group of workers performed only one process. The foundation of industrial production in the eighteenth century was based on this new organization. For the punctuality of time the workers were trained. They had to cultivate the habit of standing at one place and attending to one mechanical process all through. Initially the factory workers led a very sad and miserable life and towns expanded haphazardly and slums multiplied like mushrooms. These towns arose mostly in the eastern parts of Europe. Because of the new structuring of town emerged in Europe *i.e.* the residents of eastend (poor) and the residents of west end. The unhygienic conditions in town provided a fertile ground for epidemic. Typhus fever broke out in Glasgow for first time in 1810 and all the industrial towns in Europe came under grip of epidemic of typhoid between 1831 and 1832. Slowly reforms started and modern factory system came to be established.

Colonialism is a process whereby the sovereignty over the colony is claimed by the other nation and the social structure, government and economy within the territory of the colony are monopolized by the colonists.

Colonial System

Colonialism is a process whereby the sovereignty over the colony is claimed by the other nation and the social structure, government and economy within the territory of the colony are monopolized by the colonists. Colonialism is a certain set of unequal relationships between colonists and the indigenous population. The reasons for the practice of colonialism may be:

1. The profits to be made by system of exploitation
2. To expand the power of the industrialized nation by means of possession of colonies.
3. To spread the colonists way of life including religion and political philosophy through administrative interference.

The term colonialism represents process of European settlement and political control over the rest of the world, including America, Australia and parts of Africa and Asia. Colonialism is a relationship between an indigenous majority and a minority of foreign invaders. The fundamental decisions affecting the lives of the colonized people are made and implemented by the colonial rulers in pursuit of interests that are often defined in a distant country. Rejecting the cultural compromise with the colonized population, the colonizers are convinced of their own superiority and their ordained mandate to rule.

There are two forms of colonialism, mainly based on the number of people from the colonizing country who settle in the colony:

1. Settler colonialism involved a large number of colonists, typically seeking fertile land for agrarian economy.
2. Exploitative colonialism involved fewer colonists, typically interested in extracting resources to export to the mother country. This category includes much larger colonies where the colonists would provide much of the administration and own much of the economic resources and rely on indigenous people for labour.

The colonialism has a long history. Colonies in antiquity were built by the Egyptians, Phoenicians, Greeks, Roman and Indians. The word colony comes from the Latin word colonia – a place for agriculture. The first phase of colonialism took place between (250 BC – 480 AD) during classical antiquity when the Greco Roman empire actively engaged in politico cultural and socio-economic expansion. The second phase of colonialism or modern colonialism started with the Age of Geographical Discoveries between the fifteenth and twentieth centuries and was more focused on European powers competing with each other for acquisition of new territories rather than alliance building in the discrete sense as was commonly done in the classical era. It could be said however that there was an unspoken alliance between all these respective European powers when it came to spreading the influences of empire hereby establishing rather sophisticated imperial networks globe-wide. During this time Portugal and Spain discovered new lands across the oceans and built trading posts. For some people, it is this building of colonies across oceans that differentiated colonialism from other types of expansions. These new lands were divided between the Portuguese Empire and the Spanish Empire. The seventeenth century was the creation of the British Empire, the French Colonial Empire and the Dutch Empire. It also saw the establishment of some Swedish Overseas Colonies and a Danish Colonial Empire. The spread of colonial empires was reduced in the late eighteenth and early nineteenth centuries by the American Revolutionary War and the Latin American wars of independence. However, many new colonies were established after this time, including the German Colonial Empire and Belgian Colonial Empire. In the late nineteenth century, many European powers were involved in the Scramble for Africa. Empire of Japan modeled itself on European colonial empire. The United States of America gained overseas territories after the Spanish-American War and the term American Empire was coined.

Neo-colonialism

The term neo-colonialism has been used to refer to a variety of things since the decolonization efforts after World War II.

Rather colonialism by other means – residual effects or aftershocks of old colonialism or a contemporary extension.

The term neo-colonialism has been used to refer to a variety of things since the decolonization efforts after World War II. Generally it does not refer to a type of colonialism but rather colonialism by other means – residual effects or aftershocks of old colonialism or a contemporary extension thereof in more subtle and seemingly unobtrusive ways. The relationship between stronger and weaker countries is similar to exploitative colonialism. Such accusations typically focus on economic relationships and interference in the politics of weaker countries by stronger countries. Colonialism may be a form of Capitalism which enforces exploitation and social change. Working within the global capitalist system, colonialism is closely associated with uneven development; Marx says that it is an 'instrument of wholesale destruction, dependency and systematic exploitation producing distorted economies, socio-psychological disorientation, massive poverty and neo-colonial dependency'. Colonies are constructed into modes of production. The search for raw materials and the current search for new investment opportunities have been the result of inter-capitalist rivalry for capital accumulation.

Weber's Protestant Ethics & Rise of Capitalism

- Max Weber (1864-1920) was born in Germany. He provided the method of Verstehan (sympathetic understanding) and ensured scientific rigour through his ideal method and considered sociology as an interpretative understanding of social action.
- He defined legitimacy based on the types of social action as charismatic, traditional and legal rational and provided first systematic study on bureaucracy, though he was equally critical of it. His major works are:
  1. Protestant Ethics and Spirit of Capitalism (1930)
  2. The City (1958)
  3. Economy and Society (1958)

German sociologist Max Weber developed the protestant ethics in 1904-05. The English translation of his thesis appeared in form of a book *The Protestant Ethic and the Spirit of Capitalism* in 1930. Weber in thesis propounded that protestant movement especially Calvinist was seed bed of character traits and value that developed the modern Capitalism.

Max Weber says that in pre protestant society business had been strictly limited to traditional way of life, the traditional rate of profit and the traditional amount of work. So in this phase the Capitalism was not possible. The protestant movement suddenly destroyed the traditional structure of economy and ushered in the era of Capitalism into a rational and unashamed pursuit of profit for its own sake. In the age of reformation, contrary to medieval belief religious vocations were no longer considered superior to economic vocations and only personal faith mattered with God. Martin Luther (1483-1546) was a pioneer of this idea but he did not pursue this potential revolution further because he was bound to traditional static view of economic life.

John Calvin (1509-1564) transformed this idea for more practical purpose, Calvin mixed core theology with Human Psychology. He propounded that grace is free gift something that the giver must be free to bestow or withhold. Under this definition sacrament, good deeds, contrition, virtue, etc. could not influence God. Such absolute divine freedom from mortal man's perspective seemed unfathomable. Thus whether one was among those saved (the elect) become urgent question for average reformed churchman. Weber says uncertainly about salvation had the psychological effect of producing a single minded search for certainty. Although one could never influence God's decision to extend or withhold election, one might still attempt to ascertain his or her status. If one glorified God and confirmed to what was known of God's requirement for this life then that might provide some evidence of election. This upright living which could not earn salvation, returned as evidence of salvation. Thus the Calvinist living was thoroughly rationalized in this world and dominated by the aim to add to glory of God on the earth. Such a life became a systematic living out of God's revealed will. This singleness of purpose left no room for diversion and according to Weber it created an ascetic character. No leisure and enjoyment but only activity serves to increase the glory of God. Only in a calling this focus finds full expression. A man without a calling lacks the systematic, methodical character which is demanded by worldly asceticism. A calling represented God's will for that person in the economy and society.

Calvin mixed core theology with Human Psychology. He propounded that grace is free gift something that the giver must be free to bestow or withhold.

Such emphasis on a calling was first step for a full fledged capitalist spirit. Weber says that idea of profit is taken from it and shows that one of his elect has a chance of profit and he must do with a purpose. This providential interpretation of profit making of justified the activities of the businessman and led to the highest ethical appreciation of the middle class, self made man. A sense of calling and an ascetic ethic applied to the labour is as well as the entrepreneurs and businessman. The Capitalism requires reliable, honest and punctual labour which did not exist in traditional societies. The free labour will have to submit to the systematic discipline of work under Capitalism. It requires an internalized value system that is provided by Calvinism.

So Weber's ascetic Protestantism has been an all encompassing value system that shaped one's whole life and not merely ethic or job. Life was to be controlled better to serve the God. Impulse and those activities that encouraged impulse such as sport or dance were to be shunned. External enjoyments and ornaments tried to turn attention away from inner character and purpose. The simple life was accepted as best. The protestant ethic orders life according to its own logic and also according to needs of Modern Capitalism.

Weber's protestant ethic is critised on the basis that some of the Modern Capitalism and economy have arisen before the reformed Protestantism. It is found that Calvinism emerged

Weber's protestant ethic is critised on the basis that some of the Modern Capitalism and economy have arisen before the reformed Protestantism.

later than Capitalism suggesting no cause and effect relationship. The reformation contributed to the development of Capitalism only as a matter of circumstances. For example in Holland Capitalism preceded Calvinism and in Switzerland it lagged by too long a period to suggest causality. Even sometime catholic country like Beligium developed Capitalism about the same time as the protestant countries. Weber says that traditional Capitalism which was distinct from Modern Capitalism. He says that the traditional Capitalism could have emerged first but the Calvinism created the modern Capitalism. The protestant ethics points out the congruency between culture's religion and its economic system. The cultural values are instrumental in economic developed of a country. There recent studies shows that the cultural values may not be religious but its secular ideals are a binding force for economic growth of a country.

Capitalism

Adam Smith in his Wealth of Nations propounds the policy of Laissez Faire i.e. free competition, a competition with almost no government intervention. Laissez Faire implies that market dominates. This essence of Laissez Faire is carried forward today by Capitalism. The term and the system is of very recent origin. It is only after industrialization that we see Capitalism in its full sway.

There does not seem any inherent problem with Capitalism. Infact, Max Weber related it to the Protestant Ethics. Here the spirit of Capitalism is seen as a calling. But Marxist interpretation of the term holds it as an exploitative mechanism. Infact Marx saw this arrangement also as exploitative. He elaborated the following sequence of evolution of societies:

1. Primitive Communism
2. Ancient Society
3. Feudal/Asiatic Society
4. Capitalism
5. Socialism/Communism

According to Marx classes, i.e. the people with the same relationship with means of production do exist in every society. Thus, two dictiotomous classes i.e. one of haves and the other have-nots is the reality in every phase of history. But in the earlier phases this exploitation of have-nots by haves, was under a paternatistic veil. In Capitalism there is no such veil as the relationship between haves and have-nots just based on wages. So, the class dictiotomy is most apparent in Capitalism and so is exploitation. According to Marx the economic relationship is bound to reflect in other domains also like religion, education, law, system of government etc. In todays context there is a clear triumph of Capitalism. The counter view point of state intervention, is no long so dominant. The advent and advancement of Capitalism is now seen as globalization, which also means liberalisation and privatization.

Suggested Question

1. Scientific inventions, art, literature, architecture etc. have changed the feudal and stagnant society of Europe into vibrant and Capitalist Society. Explain with suitable example.
2. What are the important features of Industrial Revolution? How has it affected the economic structure of the world?
3. Neo-imperialism can be compared with the colonial systems. Verify the statement with suitable examples.

References

1. Fisher H.A.L. *A History of Europe,* Vol. I & II, 1981, Delhi.
2. Bhattacharya Haridas Ed. *The Cultural Hesitage of India,* 1937, Calcutta.
3. Weber *Max*
   (*i*) *The Protestant Ethics & Spirit of Capitalism*, 1930, New York
   (*ii*) *The Theory of Social & Economic Organization,* 1947, Oxford.
4. Durkheim Emile
   (*i*) *Division of Labour in Society* (1893), Gleincoe
   (*ii*) *The Elementary Forms of the Religious Life* (1912), London.
5. Carpentor, J.E., *Theism in Medievalism India*, London.
6. DasGupta, Surendranath, *A History of Indian Philosophy*, Cambridge.

2

CHAPTER

WESTERN ETHICAL THEORIES, APPROACHES AND ITS CONTRIBUTION IN MANAGEMENT

'Ethos' means customs, usages or habits.

The word 'Ethics' is derived from the Greek word 'ethica' which originates from the substantive 'ethos'. 'Ethos' means customs, usages or habits. Literally 'ethics' means the science of customs or habits of men. It is the science of the habitual conduct of men. Ethics is the science of character and conduct. It evaluates the voluntary and habitual actions of a person and analyses whether it is right or wrong. It evaluates the character of a person and considers its virtuousness.

Ethics is the science which evaluates, that, the conduct is appropriate or not. Conduct is a purposive action, which involves choice and will. Ethics is the science of human character as expressed in right or wrong conduct. Appropriate conduct refers to the good deeds, which are essential for an ideal human life. Thus Ethics is the science of Goodness. It is the science of morality.

It is concerned with the evaluation of conduct with reference to an ideal. It seeks to determine the supreme ideal involved in human conduct. Ethics is the science of the ideal involved in human life. Further it tries to explain the appropriateness of human actions. The ideals involved in human life includes truth, good and beauty. Ethics is the science of the moral good of a man.

Ethics, a normative science –is a systematic body of knowledge. It deals with human conduct together with the inner volitions and their motives systematically.

Characteristic of Ethics

Ethics, a normative science –is a systematic body of knowledge. It deals with human conduct together with the inner volitions and their motives systematically. It depends upon observation, classification, and explanation of human conduct with reference to an ideal.

But Ethics is not a positive science. A positive, natural or descriptive science deals with facts and explains them by their causes. It tries to know what a thing really is by discovering its relationship to other things, especially its causal relation. Ethics is not concerned with the nature, origin and growth of human conduct. It does not explain human actions by means of certain laws. It is not concerned with conduct as a fact or event in space and time, determined by an antecedent event and determining a succeeding event. It is concerned with judgment upon conduct, its rightness or wrongness. It passes judgment of value upon human actions with reference to the moral ideal.

A normative science is also called a regulative science. But normative sciences are not concerned with actual facts or their laws, but with norms which regulate human life. Normative sciences seek to determine norms, ideals, or standards. There are three ideals of human life, viz. Truth, Beauty and Goodness. These are the supreme values in human experience. They correspond to the three aspects of our conscious life – knowing, feeling and will. Logic is concerned with the general conditions involved in the pursuit of Truth. Asthetics is concerned with the creation and appreciation of Beauty. Ethics is concerned with what is right in human action in the pursuit of good.

Ethics is not a practical Science which teaches to know, and an art to do. It merely tries to ascertain the moral ideal but does not lay down rules for the attainment of it. It does not teach how to live a moral life. It is the business of a normative science to define an ideal, not to lay down rules for its attainment. The study of ethics has a bearing on our moral life. It is a morality and theory which is bound to act on practical life.

Ethics is not an art and cannot be regarded as a practical. It determines the nature of right and wrong with reference to the supreme good. But it does not teach the art of living a moral life. It does not lay down moral precepts. It does not teach how to control our passions, resist temptations, strengthen our will and cultivate a virtuous life.

It deals with the whole of human experience, but only from the point of view of will and activity. It considers man as doing or pursuing an end, but not as knowing or feeling. It observes and classifies moral phenomena and explains them by the moral ideal. It distinguishes moral judgments from logical and asthetic judgements and culminates them to a system. Ethics is particularly concerned with man. It is the business of ethics to determine what is human good and not what is cosmic good. But metaphysics investigates the nature of the universe and the cosmic good or the goal of the universe. So ethics is not a part of metaphysics.

Ethics, seeks to define the moral ideal. Ethics must enquire into the nature of the off springs of actions, motives, intentions, voluntary actions, and non-voluntary actions and so on. The fundamental problem of ethics is the nature or the moral ideal or standard with reference to which we pass moral judgements.

When an action conforms to the moral ideal, it is said to be right; when it does not conform to it, it is said to be wrong. Right actions are said to be duties. The end which is served by the moral laws is said to be good. Ethics is concerned with the highest or absolute good. Thus, the fundamental notions of ethics are right and good.

Our right actions have merit and our wrong actions have demerit. Ethics enquires into the criterion of merit and demerit. It tries to find out what makes an action meritorious. Ethics assumes the freedom of the will. It discusses the nature of human freedom. Ethics enquires into the nature of responsibility. Criminals are responsible for their crimes. So they ought to be punished. Ethics gives the moral justification for punishment. Ethics determines the nature and kinds of right, duties and virtues determined by the ultimate moral standard. Virtues and vices come within its scope.

The aim of the ethics is to define the highest good of man as a member of the society. It investigates the nature of the *Summum Bonum* which is the highest personal good and the highest social good. Ethics is the theory of morality. It converts moral faith into a rational insight. It analyzes the common notions of morality and discovers the rational and essential elements in them.

Ethics are criticism of common sense. It exposes the defects and inconsistencies of the social customs, usages, social, political, and religious institutions, and gives a real insight into the nature of the moral ideal. This criticism is to dispel many erroneous notions and to remove many inconsistencies in popular beliefs. Ethics attacks the basis of popular morality, purges its errors and inconsistencies, and places on a secure footing all that is valid and essential in morality. It separates the essential from the nonessential, the permanent from the transitory, the spirit from the form of social or moral institutions and rationalizes our notions of right and wrong. Moral insight into duties makes their performance possible. Theory inevitably acts on practice. Theoretical ethics is the secure foundation of practical or applied ethics. The concrete duties of life should be determined with reference to the moral ideals. Knowledge is a condition of virtue.

Man is a social being. He cannot live apart from society. He owes the major portion of his mental and moral development to society. The individual imbibes his notions of right and wrong, good and evil, from the customs and manners prevailing in a society. Being apart from a society is an abstraction. Again social progress depends upon the morals of individuals. The vision of the moral reformers determines progress of the society. Thus the individual and the society influence each other. Ethics is the science of morality of the individual. Social ethics is the science of the structure, origin, and development of human society. It is the natural history of social groups. It studies the origin, growth and development of social groups through modification of customs and institution. Thus ethics is closely connected with it. Social ethics investigates the habits, manners, customs, and institutions of human society in all its stages of development from the savage state to the civilized. It tries to discover the origin and development of social institutions through different stages to their present state. It further investigates the nature, origin, and development of habits, customs, manners and institutions of social groups without reference to any moral standard. It does not consider their moral worth.

Economics is the science of goods which satisfy human wants. Economics aims at relative goods.

Economic Ethics

Economics is the science of goods which satisfy human wants. Economics aims at relative goods. Economic goods should be considered in relation to the highest good. Their ultimate worth is determined by their moral worth. Food, clothing, shelter, money and the like are good because they lead to development of persons. Economic goods have no intrinsic worth in themselves. They are instrumental values. Thus economics is closely connected with ethics.

Economics is the science of wealth. But wealth is not an end in itself. It is a means to human welfare. Production, distribution and consumption of wealth should be so arranged as to contribute to the realization of the greatest welfare of humanity. They should be subordinated to the moral end, viz., the development of personality of each member of the commonwealth of humanity. Economics should not be divorced from ethics. They should be brought into close relationship to each other. At present economists tends to treat economics as a science of welfare rather than of wealth. Economic phenomena should be controlled in such a manner so as to contribute to the general social welfare. Ethics are closely connected with each one.

Economic ethics deals with the facts relating to production, distribution and consumption of wealth and generalizes from them the economic laws, with a view to increasing the material prosperity of the people. Ethics investigates the moral ideal which would regulate production, distribution and consumption of wealth. It is concerned with wealth and material prosperity. Material prosperity should be subordinated to moral welfare. Physical enjoyment should be subordinated to virtuous life.

The rights to property depend on the moral rights to personality. Property is indispensably necessary for the development of personality. Property and personality go together. The rights of exchange and distribution of property also are derived from the moral rights of personality.

Plato

Plato was born in 427 BC., He first studied music, poetry, painting and became a pupil of Socrates in 407. He traveled to Egypt, Asia minor, Italy and lived for a time at the court of Dionysius I, the tyrant of Syracuse, who became his enemy and sold him into slavery as a prisoner later on he founded a school 'the academy', where he taught mathematics and the different branches of philosophy. His death occurred in 347 BC. He was an aristocrat by birth and by temperament, an uncompromising idealist, hostile to everything vulgar. The writings transmitted under his name (35 dialogues, 13 letters), most of the letters and all of the definitions are considered to be spurious, although it seems that several of his letters are genuine.

Plato's system incorporates and transforms the doctrines of his predecessors. Plato shares the skepticism of the sophists regarding knowledge of sense appearances, and agrees with Socrates that genuine knowledge is always attained by concepts. He accepts that the world is in constant change, but restricts its application to the world of sensuous appearances. He agrees that reality is manifold.

How true concepts and judgments may be obtained? His chief object is to obtain them and to know reality in all its phases – physical, mental and moral and to comprehend it in its unity and completeness.

Plato did not explicitly divided philosophy into: (1) logic, or dialectic (including theory of knowledge); (2) metaphysics (including physics and psychology); and (3) ethics (including politics), but such a division is implicit in his work.

Dialectic and Theory of Knowledge

Plato clearly understood the great importance of the problem of knowledge and argued that there can be no genuine knowledge. Sense perception does not reveal the true reality of things, but gives mere appearance. Yet opinion may be true or false; even when it is proved true, it rests on persuasion or feeling and hence has no value. Genuine knowledge which is based on reason can authenticate itself.

The advance from sense perception and opinion to genuine knowledge cannot be accomplished unless we have a desire for truth. The love of truth impels us to be dialectic; it impels us to rise beyond sense perception to conceptual knowledge of the idea from the particular to the universal. The dialectical method consists, first, in the comprehension of scattered particulars into one idea and the division of the idea into species.

To Plato, the concept or idea of justice does not have its origin in experience; it does not derive by abstraction from particular cases of justice. These are merely the means of clarifying and making explicit the concept of justice which already existed obscurely and implicitly in the soul. Man is indeed the measure of all things, of all truth, in the sense that universal concepts, ideas, the principals lie imbedded in his soul and form the starting point of all his knowledge.

Knowledge is the corresponde nce of thought and reality,

Knowledge is the correspondence of thought and reality, knowledge must have an object. If the concept is to have any value as knowledge, something real must correspond to it then it must, for instance, be pure, absolute beauty corresponding to the concept of beauty and realities must exist corresponding to all our universal ideas.

Plato's theory of knowledge is divided into four segments. The lowest segment represents conjecture, a kind of sensuous knowledge conversant with image, shadows, reflections, dreams etc. Conjectural knowledge is mere guesswork and is at best probable. The second segment of the divided line represents belief, the knowledge of sensible objects, whether material objects such as trees, mountains, rivers etc., or human artifacts such as houses, tables, works of handicrafts. The source of belief is sense perception and although it is more reliable than conjecture, it likewise is only probable knowledge. Conjecture and belief are grouped together by Plato under the heading opinion, which embraces all sense-derived knowledge. The third segment of the line represents discursive intellect, or the understanding which occupies itself not with sensuous particulars but with mathematical entries such as numbers, lines, planes, triangles and other arithmetical and geometrical objects. This form of knowledge is hypothetical in that it proceeds deductively from definitions and unproved assumptions. Plato clearly anticipated the modern postulation and interpretation of mathematics when he suggested that mathematics rests on assumptions or suppositions rather than on self evident principles or axioms. The highest segment represents rational insight, the objects of which are the forms or ideas and the method by which such knowledge is achieved is dialectic. Dialectical knowledge rests on categorical principles, not on hypotheses and dispense entirely with sensible.

Hierarchy of the Sciences

Plato's hierarchy of the sciences, have been explained in his *Republic*. Each of the abstract sciences are discussed beginning with arithmetic and concluding with dialectic. Arithmetic he describes as an abstract science of number and of numerical relations. Its theoretical value consists in the fact that it liberates the intellect from sense and thereby promotes abstract thought. After arithmetic, he mentions plain and solid geometry. Though his primary concern is theoretical, with the ability of abstract geometry to draw the mind towards the eternal forms, he does not ignore the application of geometry to warfare, architecture, land measurement, etc. Astronomy by which the means the science of solid bodies in motion is the next. Astronomy is not the descriptive science of the motion of the heavenly bodies. The chief value of such knowledge is that it directs the mind of celestial motion and thus paves the way for the dialectical study of the harmony of the eternal forms. Harmonics is the study of the motions of the bodies which produces harmonious sounds. Like astronomy, it directs the mind to ideal harmony scheme and is the science of the principal of harmony. Dialectic is the coping stone of the sciences concerned with the forms in their organic unity. In its theoretic aspects, dialectic is the completion and fulfillment of scientific inquiry; on its practical side it serves as a guide for morals and statecraft, and for the other humanistic pursuits.

Doctrine of Ideas

The idea or concept comprehends or holds together the essential qualities common to many particulars. There are ideas of things, relations, qualities, actions and values; ideas of tables and beds and chairs; of smallness, greatness, likeness; of colors, odours, and tones; of health, rest, and motion of beauty, truth and goodness. The ideals or archetypes, though numberless are not disorganized and chaotic. They constitute a well ordered world or rational cosmos. The ideal order forms an interrelated, connected organic unity. The ideas are arranged in logical order and subsumed under the highest idea and which is the source of all the rest. The truly real and the truly good are identical; the idea of the good is the logos, the cosmic purpose.

Plato's theory of ideas is his most original philosophical achievement. The essentials of the theory are clearly delineated in the Platonic dialogues. Forms or ideas, defined as the objects corresponding to abstract concepts are real entities. There is a great variety of forms, including the forms of classes of things – house, dog, man etc. of qualities – fairness, roundness; of relations etc. of values, goodness, beauty etc. The forms belong to realm of abstract entities a 'heaven of ideas', separable from concrete particulars in space and time. The separation of the forms and their exemplifications is commonly referred to as the platonic dualism. The forms are superior to particulars in degree of reality and value. The form is a model or archetype of which the particular is a copy. The forms are non mental and subsist independently of any knowing mind. Since they are non temporal as well as non spatial, they are eternal and immutable. The forms are logically interrelated and constitute a hierarchy in which the higher forms communicate with the lower or subordinate forms. The supreme form in the hierarchy is the form of the good. The forms are apprehended by reason, not by sense though sense may provide the occasion and the stimulus for finally the relation between a particular and the form which it exemplifies is called 'participation'.

Cosmology

Plato's cosmology is permeated with many mythical elements and often contradicts his other teachings. The Demiurge or creator fashions the world after the pattern of the ideal world. He is guided by the idea of the good and forms as perfect a universe. The demiurge is not really a creator, but an architect and the two principles, the ideal and the material, are already in existence. They are not created by the demiurge. The function of the demiurge is to impose the forms on a pre-existent material or receptacle. The world so generated is composed of the four material elements; earth, air, fire, water and an animating soul, the world-soul. This world soul is compounded of the indivisible and the divisible, of identity and the change, and is thus able both to know the ideal and perceive the corporeal. It has its own original motion, which is the cause of all motion. The world would be an intermediary between the world of ideas and the world of phenomena. Plato's cosmology is a teleological world view clothed in mythical garb.

The world so generated is composed of the four material elements; earth, air, fire, water and an animating soul, the world-soul.

Plato's cosmology may be considered as an attempt to differentiate the 'causes' or creative factors of the actual world. The four factors in creation enumerated in the Timaeus are: (1) The Demiurge or God, the active and dynamic cause of the world. (2) The pattern as archetype of the world. Demiurge, in the creation of the world, was guided by an eternal and pre-existing model which resided in the world of forms. (3) The receptacle. The principle provides the locus and matrix of creation. It is the source of the indeterminacy, the brutal factuality, the disorder and the evil of the world. (4) The form of the good. This principle functions in Plato's cosmology as the source of the purposiveness of things, of the teleological and valuational aspects of nature and mind.

Ethics

Ethics is based on Plato's metaphysics. The universe is basically a rational universe, a spiritual system. The material phenomena around the world are mere fleeting shadows of eternal and never changing ideas. Since they are transitory and ephemeral so have no absolute worth. Reason, which alone is conversant with the highest good, has absolute worth. Hence the rational part of man is the true part, and man's ideal must be to cultivate his reason, the immortal side of his soul.

The individual is wise in whom reason rules over the other impulses of the soul knowing what is advantageous for the whole inner economy and for each member of it. Reasons take counsel and the spirited faculty fights the battles of reasons. It gives effect to its counsels by its bravery. An individual, therefore, is brave when the spirited part holds fast through pain and pleasure. He is temperate when spirit and appetite yields to reason and submit to its authority. Temperance, or self control, is mastery over certain kinds of pleasures and desires. When these three inward principles are in tune, each doing its proper work and the man is just. The just and honorable course is that which a man pursues in this frame of mind and he has achieved the ethical attitude when he is wise, brave and temperate. Such a man would not repudiate a deposit, commit sacrilege or theft, be false to friends, a traitor to his country, or commit similar misdeeds. Justice is the supreme virtue, and any soul in which it dwells is incapable of any sort of wrongdoings.

Politics

Plato's theory of the state, which is set forth in the *Republic*, is based on his ethics. The mission of the state is to promote virtue and happiness and its laws is to bring about conditions which will enable as many men as possible to become good. The state should be organized like the universe at large and the individual virtuous soul; should be in the ascendency.

There are as many classes in society as there are functions of the soul, and the harmonious relations of these classes to each other correspond to those obtaining in a healthy soul. Those who have philosophical insight embody reason and ought to be the ruling class. The members of the warrior class possess the spirited element and their task is defense. The agriculturists, artisans, and merchants represent the lower appetites, and do the production of material goods. Justice is realized in a state in which each class, the industrial, military and guardian does its own work and attends to its own business without meddling in the task of the other classes. A state is temperate and brave and wise in consequence of certain affections and conditions of these same classes. Every individual ought to have some occupation in the state.

The ideal society forms a complete unity, one larger family hence, Plato opposes private property and monogamous marriages, and recommends, for the two upper classes, who are to be supported by the workers, communes and the common possession of wives and children. Among his other recommendations are supervision of marriages and births, exposure of weak children, compulsory state education, education of women for war and government, censorship of works of art and literature. Plato did not have high opinion of art. Plato thought that it could be made to contribute to moral culture.

The state is an educational institution, the instrument of civilization. The state shall undertake the education of the children of the higher classes, following a definite plan of instruction, which shall be the same for the citizens of both sexes during the first twenty years of life. A selection of the superior individuals shall be made from the ranks of the greatest ability in their studies, in military affairs, and in their other activities will study dialectic for five years. They will be put to the test of holding military commands and subordinate civic. At the age of fifty, those who have shown themselves worthy will devote themselves to the study of philosophy, until their turn comes to administer the higher offices for their country's sake.

Plato's *Republic* is the depiction of a perfect state, the dream of a society embodying the principles of justice.

Plato's *Republic* is the depiction of a perfect state, the dream of a society embodying the principles of justice. It is frequently spoken of as utopian, and indeed, Plato's philosophy is rationalistic in the sense that it holds rational knowledge of the universe to be possible. His philosophy is realistic and it affirms the existence of extra mental realities of forms or ideas. Its ethical theory is anti-hedonistic, intuitionistic, and idealistic, a version of the self realization theory. Its political theory combines aristocratic with socialistic and communistic elements. The platonic system, by combining apparently incompatible doctrines into the unity of the great creative synthesis, escapes the radical incoherence and inconsistency of philosophical eclecticism.

Aristotle

Aristotle was born in 384 BC. At the age of seventeen he entered Plato's Academy, where he remained for twenty years as student and teacher. After the death of Plato (347 BC), he visited to Assos, Mysia, then to Mitylene, and is said to have returned to Athens to open a school of rhetoric. In 342 BC he was called by King Philip to direct the education of his son Alexander. He opened a school in the gymnasium dedicated to the Lycean Apollo, from which the school received its historic name, the Lyceum. It also been called the Peripatetic School, because of Aristotle's habit of walking while giving instructions. After the sudden death of Alexander in 323 BC, the philosopher was accused by the anti Mecedonian party at Athens and compelled to flee to Euboea, where he died in 322 BC.

Andronicus, who published an edition of his works between 60 and 50 BC. places the number of books written by Aristotle at 1000.

Philosophy and the Sciences

Aristotle says that the universe is an ideal world, an organic whole of interrelated parts, a system of eternal and unchangeable ideas or forms. These are the ultimate essences and causes of things, the directing forces or purposes that makes them what they are. The ideas are not detached from the world immanent in it. Our world of experience is not an untrustworthy appearance, but is a reality. Experience is the basis of knowledge. Starting from experience one rise to the science of ultimate principles. Genuine knowledge does not consist of mere acquaintance with facts, but in knowing their reason or causes. Philosophy or science in the board sense, embraces all such reasoned knowledge. It includes mathematics and the special sciences. The science or philosophy which studies the ultimate or first cause of things is called by Aristotle the first philosophy - metaphysics. Metaphysics is concerned with being qua being; the different sciences. The special sciences or philosophies are named second philosophies.

He arranged the sciences as follows: Logic, which elaborates the method of enquiry employed in all the other sciences. Theoretical sciences, which are concerned with pure abstract knowledge. The theoretical sciences enumerated by Aristotle are: mathematics, physics, biology and psychology and first philosophy or what is now known as metaphysics. Practical sciences, in which knowledge is pursued as a means to conduct rather then as an end in itself. The practical sciences are ethics and politics.

Aristotle is the true founder of logic in the sense of a scientific treatment of the valid forms of reasoning. Logic as formulated by Aristotle has dominated, to an almost unbelievable extent, the thought of later times. There have been only two major revolts against the traditional logic in modern times. The first was led by Francis Bacon in his advocacy of the inductive method; and the second is the one carried on at the present time by the mathematical logicians. Aristotle considers it an important instrument for the acquisition of genuine knowledge, and holds that we should not proceed to the study of the first philosophy, of the science of the essence of things, until we have familiarized ourselves with the principle of logical thought. It is an elaboration of the method employed in the pursuit of all knowledge and is therefore antecedent to all special inquiries. In this sense it may be described as 'the science of sciences'. Aristotle regarded his logic as a tool or instrument of scientific research to be applied in every sphere of knowledge.

The Aristotelian logic defines with precision the prerequisite of genuine scientific knowledge. Scientific truth is characterized by strict necessity. The concepts do not receive exhaustive treatment in Aristotle's logic. Aristotle's primary concern is with the logic of judgments or propositions. He discusses the nature and different kinds of judgments, the various relations in which they stand to one another, and the different kinds of demonstration.

Aristotle treats at great length the nature of demonstration, the process of elaborating the derivative propositions from the original truths. His demonstration or deduction always takes the form of a syllogism or series of syllogisms. He was the first to discover in the syllogism a basal form in which all though moves, and to give it a name. Valid or scientific demonstration is always in the form of the syllogism. It is syllogistic and deductive. The ideal science in Aristotle's day was mathematics, and the use of mathematics as a model explains the important role deduction plays in his logic. His aim was to attain in other sciences the demonstrative certainty of mathematics. The system of scientific knowledge rests on certain axioms or basic truths which neither admit of nor require proof. They are the basis of all truth, and as such are indemonstrable. The axioms are thus the first links in the long chain of our reasoning. The basic truth are known by intuition, e.g. by the immediate and direct insight of the reason. Intuition is the apprehension of the universal element in particular.

Our knowledge always begins with the sense perception, and rises from particular facts to universal concepts. Introduction is a preparation for deduction. The ideal of science must always be to derive particulars from universals, to furnish demonstration or necessary proof. This cannot be done until introduction has done its work, until experience has aroused the knowledge of the universal lying dormant in our reason.

Logic concerns itself with the thought forms, with the moulds to which our thinking must conform if it is to achieve certain truth. The famous Aristotelian theory of the categories included among his logical doctrines, is also a part of his metaphysics. The categories are the fundamental and indivisible concepts of thought. By the categories, Aristotle means the most fundamental and universal predicates. It may be a thing what it is (man: substance), how it is constituted (white: quality), how large it is (two yards long: quantity), how related (greater, double: relation), where it is (in the Lyceum: space), when it is (yesterday: time), what posture it assumes (lies, sits: position), the condition it is in (armed: state), what it does (burns: activity), and what it suffers (is burned: passivity). All this means that the objects of our experience exist in time and place and can be measured and counted. These are related to other things and have essential and accidental qualities.

The Four Causes

The causal concept is much wider in its application for Aristotle than modern science. It designates any condition requisite to the occurrence of something. Aristotle recognizes four principles operative in any process (1) the material cause, by which he understands the crude and relatively undifferentiated stuff. It was this type of cause which was introduced by the Milesian nature philosophers in their attempts to explain the world by means of water, air or some other material substratum. Aristotle illustrates the material cause by the formless bronze from which the sculptor plans to fashion its statue. (2) The formal cause is the pattern or structure, which is to become embodied in the thing when it is fully realized. The formal cause of a statue is the general plan or idea of the statue as conceived by the sculptor. It is the Aristotelian counterpart of the platonic form. (3) The efficient or moving cause is the active agent which produces the thing as its effect. It is that through which the thing is produced. This type of cause corresponds closely to cause in the modern scientific sense. The efficient cause of the statue includes the chisels and other instruments used by the sculptor in his work. (4) The final cause is the end or purpose towards which the process is directed. In sculpturing, it is fully realized and completed statue.

Theology

Aristotle's metaphysics culminates to theology. The eternal motion on the part of matter, an eternal unmoved mover, something that causes motion, without moving itself.

Aristotle's argument from motion to the unmoved cause of motion is perhaps the first complete formulation of what has come to be known as the cosmological argument for God's existence. The production of motion by that which is unchangeable and devoid of motion is a metaphysical enigma which Aristotle seeks to resolve by suggestion that God induces motion in other things in a fashion similar to that in which a fixed ideal or object of desire moves the human will to act. God acts on the world, not by literally moving it, but as a beautiful picture or an ideal act on the soul. Expressed in other words, God is the final cause of all that occurs. He is the highest purpose or highest good of the world. All beings in the world, plants, animals, man desire the realization of their essence because of this highest good.

The Aristotelian view of God is reflective thought. He is free from pain and passion, and is supremely happy. He is everything that a philosopher longs to be.

Ethics

The highest good for man is self realization. It is not interpreted as a selfish individualism. A man realizes his true self when he loves and gratifies the supreme part of his being. It is rational when he is moved by a motive of nobleness. Aristotle's books on friendship and justice appreciates the exalted altruistic spirit of his teaching. The virtuous man will act often in the interest of his friend and of his country.

The highest good for man is self realization. It is not interpreted as a selfish individualism.

Justice is a virtue implying a relation to others. It promotes the interests of another whether he be a ruler or simply a fellow citizen. Justice is taken in two senses, lawfullness and fairness. Laws pronounce upon all subjects with a view to the interest of the community as a whole, or of those who are its best or leading citizens, whether in virtue or in some other respect.

Man is a social being who can realize his true self only in society and the state. Families and small communities are prior in time to the state. The constitution of the state must be adapted to mould character and requirements of its people. It is just when it confers equal rights on the people as they are equal and unequal rights in so far as they are unequal. Citizens differ in personal capability, in property, qualifications, in birth and freedom, and justice demands that they be treated according to these differences.

There are good constitutions and bad ones. The monarchy, the aristocracy, and the polity, a form in which the citizens are nearly equal being good forms, and the tyranny, oligarchy, and democracy are bad. Aristotle advocates a city state in which only those are citizens whose education and position in life qualify them for active participation in government. He justifies slavery on the ground that it is a natural institution.

VOLTAIRE

Voltaire was the most honourable person of his period. Voltaire's father admitted Voltaire in the aristocratic Jesuit College "Louis-La-grand". When Voltaire was a clerk in the court, he wrote his first drama "Oedipus" which satirized despotism and orthodoxy. It broke all previous records of the theatre in which it was staged.

He was a great writer, poet, philosopher, journalist, critic and above all the satirist. He had to bear the great trial of imprisonment, beating, book burning and frequent exiles. In dozens of his novels, historical books, letters, essays, plays and poems, he condemned the corruption in the church, the privileges of the aristocrats, censorship, slavery and war. He earned fame at a very early age. In reality, he was only ten when people were attracted towards his extraordinary abilities. Chief goal of his life was to expose superstition and injustice and dispel them. Voltaire's entire literature is a mirror of his strong opposition to the Roman Catholic Church. In the matter of politics, he wished that the honest, generous and emancipating the rule of Frederick. The eighteenth century and the French revolution were swayed by his wit and satire, clarity of his language and his humanistic appeal.

Voltairie's famous book '*Letters on English*' published in 1733 in which he has narrated the experiences of his stay in England. Very candidly and boldly he compared the prevalent conditions of France with British institutions, religion and the spirit of freedom of expression. The French government banned the book but it kindled a strong desire among people to read it.

Voltaire considered Newton to be greater than Caesar and Alexander. Voltaire was a great exponent of individual freedom and the natural rights of man.

Voltaire considered Newton to be greater than Caesar and Alexander. Voltaire was a great exponent of individual freedom and the natural rights of man. Frederick, the Great of Prussia was Voltaire's ideal. Voltaire stressed the constitutional monarchy. He supported the view that the interests of the governed masses should he kept in view while making laws for them. He held that punishment should commensurate with crime and should be awarded only when there is full evidence against a criminal.

In his famous book entitled *The Age of Louis XIV*, Voltaire not only wrote about the achievements of Louis XIV but expatiated upon the intellectual trends vividly and vigorously by way of commenting upon the meaningful contributions of contemporary thinkers, writers and artists. In another book *Treatise on Tolerance* published in 1763, Voltaire called intolerance not only undesirable but also a blemish on human behavior. 'Has God given us hands and heart to kill other people and to think of murder? Are the Christians not murderers of their own brethren although Christianity preaches to love even enemies?' Such questions are raised in that book.

Voltaire struggled hard for sixty years to pull Europe out of the marshes of medieval parochial thoughts. He fought a creative and effective war against cruelty, rigidity, privileges and religious orthodoxy. He fomented more than any indefatigable critic the social fevour which ultimately culminated into the French revolution. He has the credit of diffusing knowledge, intelligence and principle of nature not only in France but in the entire Europe, Voltaire's writings proved to be very effective in inclining people towards intellectualism and new ideas. He prepared a background for the freedom of ideas and ventilated his strong feelings for a change very impressively and boldly.

Rousseau

Rousseau was the philosopher of France. He was born in Geneva in 1712. Living in the jaws of abject poverty, he passed his life with great hardship without education and later on educated himself by means of his own experiences gathered in his life. His personal and family life was a great failure. He was a true lover of nature and believed in refining one's internal beauty under its influence.

In his essay *Discourses on Science and Arts*, Rousseau criticized modern civilization and professed that material happiness does not indicate progress. Modern progress is leading man to his downfall. True progress is connected with moral development. In modern society, morality is replaced by disparity, corruption, cruelty and jealousy. Such an adverse behavior will lead to terrible condition. In 1754, he published another essay entitled *Discourse on the Origins of Inequality*. He explained how vain pride, greed and selfishness overcame the hearts of simple people and led them as prey; how the powerful people created a terrible condition by building strong boundaries around their fields and coercing the poor to become their slaves.

He concluded that to a large extent inequality breeds social evils. He clarified that there are various types of inequalities in human society: firstly, the natural inequality in the sense that some people are passive and some active; some people are dull and some intelligent; secondly, there is an inequality created by society in the way that the privileged section of society has the right to get a good job but the weaker section does not. The natural inequality may be tolerated as it is beyond control. But social disparities must be removed. Rousseau justified a revolutionary change in social institutions.

Rousseau maintained that the most ideal time the human beings had was when there was no concept of private property. Property has bred greed, corruption and narrow ambition in society. It creates war. So he was against economic disparity. In his book *'Emile'* he stressed that children should be encouraged to express their thoughts and feelings freely. According to him, the development of moral values should be given top priority in education. He held that children should be educated in accordance with their tastes. Education should be utilitarian so that children get benefit out of it rather than forget what has been taught to them. He objected to the study of ancient languages like Latin and Greek. He did not favour religious education for children.

Rousseau's most famous book entitled *Social Contract* (1762) opens with this sentence: *Man is born free but he is everywhere in chains.* As man became civilized, he made a contract to consolidate power and gave birth to state. In fact, the growth of property necessitated the origin of state. The office of the king was set up in order to meet the demands of administration. According to Rousseau, state originated with a contract for power to be enjoyed by the creators of state. Therefore, Rousseau asserts that the public is empowered to change all those representatives who interfere in the maintenance of freedom, equality and fraternity. He held that democracy is the ideal form of government.

Rousseau's most famous book entitled *Social Contract* (1762) opens with this sentence: *Man is born free but he is everywhere in chains.*

He advised all people to a return to simple life. On the one hand Rousseau directed the attention of people towards social discontent caused by the aristocrats and on the other, to the strength of his enchanting and impressive words, he inspired people to win their rights. Rousseau may be criticized that he lived in imagination and lacked rationality to perceive but he stirred the orthodox society. He paved way for it by rejecting contemporary institutions and systems. He expressed his great faith in the potentialities of man rather than in any individual institution or a particular person. He held that all people are equal and free. The slogans of equality, liberty and fraternity during the French Revolution were inspired by his ideas. His ideas left an indelible effect upon the French Revolution. Napoleon has truly stated that "If Rousseau had not taken birth, the emergence of French Revolution would have been impossible".

Montesquieu

Charles de Secondat, baron de Montesquieu was born in 1689. He was a French political thinker, who is famous for his theory of separation of powers. He was largely responsible for the popularization of the terms feudalism and Byzantine Empire. After having studied at the Catholic College of Juilly Louis de, he achieved literary success with the publication of his Lettres persanes (Persian Letters, 1721), a satire based on the imaginary correspondence of a Persian visitor to Paris, pointing out the absurdities of contemporary society. He next published considerations sur les causes de la grandeur des Romains et de leur decadence (Considerations on the Causes of the Grandeur and Decadence of the Romans, 1734), considered by some scholars a transition from The Persian Letters to his master work. De l' Esprit des Lois (The Spirit of the Laws) which was originally published anonymously in 1748.

Montesquieu's work remained a powerful influence on many of the American founders, most notably James Madison of Virginia, the "Father of the Constitution".

Political Theory

Montesquieu's *Spirit of the Laws* is the first consistent attempt to survey the varieties of human society and to classify and compare them.

Montesquieu was among the first to extend comparative methods of classification to the political forms in human societies. Montesquieu's *Spirit of the Laws* is the first consistent attempt to survey the varieties of human society and to classify and compare them. Its aim is to study the inter-functioning of institutions. Montesquieu's political anthropology gave rise to his theories on government.

Montesquieu's most influential work divided French society into three classes (trias politica): the monarchy, the aristocracy, and the common. According to Montesqieu two types of governmental power existed: the sovereign and the administrative. The administrative powers were the executive, the legislative, and the judicial. These were separate forms and dependent upon each other so that the influence of any one power would not be able to exceed that of the other.

There were three main forms of government, each supported by a social "principle": monarchies, which rely on the principle of honor; republics which rely on the principle of virtue; and despotisms, which rely on fear. The free governments are dependent on fragile constitutional arrangements.

Montesquieu was ahead of his time in advocating major reform of slavery. In *The Spirit of Laws* he firmly accepted the role of a hereditary aristocracy and the value of primogeniture. He endorsed the idea that a woman could head a state and held that she could be as effective as the head of a family.

Meteorological Climate Theory

In his meteorological climate theory, which holds that climate may substantially influence the nature of man and his society. By placing an emphasis on environmental influences as material condition of life, Montesquieu prefigured modern anthropology's concern with the impact of material conditions, such as available energy sources, organized production systems, and technologies, on the growth of complex socio-cultural systems. He asserts that certain climates are superior to others, the temperate climate of France being ideal. The climate of middle Europe is optimal.

Karl Marx

Karl Heinrich Marx (1818-1883), a German Jew was born on 5 May 1818 in South-East Germany. He quarreled with German officers in connection with the publication of a newspaper and went to Paris. In Paris he met Friedrich Engles who became owner of a cotton mill and settled in England. Marx and Engles worked together to achieve their identical goal. The French government exiled Marx from Paris. Marx was greatly shocked by the events which occurred in 1848, the year called an era of revolutions. With Engels he issued a declaration in German.

He pursued his writing work with Engles in Brussels. The "Communist Manifesto" was published in 1848. By means of this manifesto both Karl Marx and Engles stirred workers to unite, to achieve political power and to do away with the sovereignty of the middle class. The publication of the manifesto demonstrated the prospective power of socialism. Marx came to London in 1848 and lived there as an expatriate till his death (1883).

After settling in England, Marx persevered to seek solid thoughts and objectives in order to make his communist revolution a great success. Meanwhile, he continued his creative role in the activities of the Communist League of London. He contributed 500 articles to a daily paper the "New York Tribune". Making a good use of the British Museum Library, he started writing his great work 'Das Kapital' and its first volume was published in 1867.

Marx's *Political Economy*

Marx argued that alienation of human work (and resulting commodity fetishism) functions precisely as the defining feature of Capitalism. Prior to Capitalism, markets existed in Europe where producers and merchants bought and sold commodities. According to Marx, a capitalist mode of production developed in Europe when labor itself became a commodity. When peasants became free to sell their own labor power, and needed to do so because they no longer possessed their own land. People sell their labor power when they accept compensation in return for whatever work they do in a given period of time. In return for selling their labor power they receive money which allows them to survive. Those who must sell their labor power are 'proletarians'. The person who buys the labor power is generally someone who does own the land and technology to produce, is a 'capitalist' or 'bourgeois'. The proletarians inevitably outnumber the capitalists.

Marx distinguished industrial capitalists from merchant capitalists.

Marx distinguished industrial capitalists from merchant capitalists. Merchants buy goods in one market and sell them in another. Since the laws of supply and demand operate within given markets, a difference often exists between the price of a commodity in one market and another. Merchants, then, practice arbitrage, and hope to capture the difference between these two markets. According to Marx, capitalists, take advantage of the difference between the labor market and the market for whatever commodity the capitalist can produce. Marx observed that practically in every successful industry input unit costs are lower than output unit prices. Marx called the difference 'surplus value' and argued that this surplus value had its source in surplus labour, the difference between what it costs to keep workers alive and what they can produce.

Capitalism can stimulate considerable growth because the capitalist can, and has an incentive to reinvest profits in new technologies and capital equipments. Marx considered the capitalist class to be the most revolutionary in history because it constantly improved the means of production. But Marx argued that Capitalism was prone to periodic crises. He suggested that over time, capitalists would invest more and more in new technologies, and less and less in labor. Since Marx believed that surplus value appropriated from labor is the source of profits, he concluded that the rate of profit would fall even as the economy grew. When the rate of profit falls below a certain point, the result would be a recession or depression in which certain sectors of the economy would collapse. Marx thought that during such an economic crisis the price of labor would also fall, and eventually make possible the investment in new technologies and the growth of new sectors of the economy.

As he wrote in his *'Critique of the Gotha Program'*, between capitalist and communist society there lies the period of the revolutionary transformation of the one into the other.

Marx believed that increasingly severe crises would punctuate this cycle of growth, collapse, and more result in growth. Moreover, he believed that in the long scene this process would necessarily enrich and empower the capitalist class and impoverish the proletariat. He believed that if the proletariat were to seize the means of production, they would encourage social relations that would benefit everyone equally, and a system of production less vulnerable to periodic crises. He theorized that between Capitalism and the establishment of a socialist system, a dictatorship of the proletariat – a period where the working class holds political power and forcibly socializes the means of production – would exist. As he wrote in his *'Critique of the Gotha Program'*, between capitalist and communist society there lies the period of the revolutionary transformation of the one into the other. Corresponding to this is also a political transition period in which the state can be nothing but the revolutionary dictatorship of the proletariat. While he allowed for the possibility of peaceful transition in some countries with strong democratic institutional structures such as Britain, US and Netherlands, he suggested that in other countries with strong centralized state oriented traditions, like France and Germany, the 'lever of our revolution must be force'.

The Utilitarianism of John Stuart Mill

John Stuart Mill (1806-1873) was the son of James Mill. The elder Mill introduced him to the philosophy of the eighteenth century, and Hartley's psychology and Bentham's ethics. Hartley's doctrine of the association of ideas became the guiding principle of Mill's psychology and kindred studies. In 1823, after a few years spent in travel and in the study of law, Mill entered the service of the East India Company, where he remained until its abolition by Parliament in 1858. He was elected to Parliament as a Liberal and served for three years, but his greatest influence on the political life of his country was exercised through his writings Logic, Principle of Political Economy, Utilitarianism

The idea of social and political reform gave direction to Mill's intellectual labors. He shared the eighteenth century's enthusiasm for progress and enlightenment, and believed in the supreme efficacy of education. In order to bring about reforms, knowledge is necessary, knowledge of the right is the ends and the means of realizing them. In order to reach knowledge, correct methods must be employed, and to the study of these Mill addressed himself in his Logic. The wonderful progress of the natural sciences suggest an examination of scientific methods and their application in the mental or moral sciences – psychology, ethics, economics, politics and history. The investigation of methods of knowledge could not be carried on successfully without a consideration of the general principles of the theory of knowledge.

Inductive Inference

Mill's entire logical theory is based on the laws of association. The child infers that the fire will burn because fire and the burn came together before; the inference, in this case, is from one particular to another and not from the universal to the particular, nor from the particular to the universal. This is, indeed, the elementary form of all inference. It makes no difference whether one infers from the fact that Peter died the death of Paul or the death of all men: in the latter case we can simply extend the inference to an indefinite number of particular cases instead of only to one. We have passed from the known to the unknown in both cases, and the same process of inference is involved. The conclusion in an induction extends what is observed in certain particulars to one or more similar particulars and thus embraces more than is contained in the premises.

The syllogistic process – e.g., all men are mortal, Paul is a man, hence he is mortal is not a process of inference, because it is not a progress from the known to the unknown. In every syllogism, considered as an argument to prove the conclusion, there is a begging of question: the proposition, Paul is mortal, is already contained in the general proposition, all men are mortal. The major premise of a syllogism does not prove the conclusion. The inference is finished when we have asserted that all men are mortal; the major premise is established by the particular instances: it is a concise or compressed form of expression of the results of many observations and inferences. It tells us in effect what has already been found, registers what has been inferred, what events, or facts, have gone together and were, therefore, inferred to belong together and gives directions for future inductive inferences.

Ethics

In his ethical theories Mill follows, the traditional English hedonistic school, the most important representatives of which are Locks, Hutcheson, Hume and J. Bentham (1748-1832). Mill regarded the reading of Dumont's *Traite de legislation*, an exposition of Bentham's principle speculations, as an epoch in his life, one of the turning points in his intellectual history. In his Utilitarianism, he agrees with Bentham that happiness, or the greatest good of the greatest number, is the *summum bonum* and the criterion of morality. He differs from his master, however, on several important points. According to Bentham, the value of pleasures is to be measured by their intensity, duration, certainty or uncertainty, propinquity or remoteness, purity and extent (the number of persons affected by them). No difference is to be made in quality; other things being equal, 'push-pin is as good as poetry'.

Mill, on the other hand, teaches that pleasures also differ in quality, that those which go with the exercise of intellectual capacities are higher, better, than sensuous pleasures, and that persons who have experienced both prefer the higher pleasures. 'No intelligent person would consent to be a fool; no instructed person would be an ignoramus,' no person of feeling or conscience would consent to be selfish or base. You would not exchange your lot for that of a fool, dunce, or rascal, even if you were convinced that a fool, dunce, or rascal is better satisfied with his lot than you are with yours. 'It is better to be a human being dissatisfied than a pig satisfied better to be Socrates dissatisfied than a fool satisfied'. The fool and the pig may think otherwise, but that is because 'they only know their side or the question', the fool's and the pig's. Bentham and Mill also agree that we ought to strive for the greatest happiness of the greatest number; but Bentham justifies this on the ground of self interest, while Mill bases it on the social feelings of mankind, the desire for unity with our fellow creatures. He tells us that utilitarianism requires a man to be as strictly impartial between his own happiness and that of others as if he were a disinterested and benevolent spectator. 'In the golden rule of Jesus of Nazareth, we read the complete spirit of the ethics of utility. To do as one would be done by, and to love one's neighbor as oneself, constitute the ideal perfection of utilitarian morality'. Indeed, the greatest happiness principle is a mere form of words without rational significance, unless one person's happiness – on the assumption that it is equal in degree and that proper allowance is made for kind – is of exactly as much importance as another's; Bentham's dictum, 'Everybody to count for one, nobody for more than one', may be considered an explanatory commentary on the principle of utility.

Mill's utilitarianism, vacillates between opposing views; in addition to the empirical association psychology with its hedonism, egoism, and determinism, one find leanings towards intuitionism, perfectionism, altruism, and free will. The very inconsistencies of the theory, however, made it attractive to many minds, and there is much in it with which the opposing schools may agree. As Green pointed out, Mill's version of utilitarianism was of the greatest significance in practice; it substituted a critical and intelligent conformity to conventional moral precepts for a blind and unquestioning one. The theory of the greatest happiness of the greatest number has tended to improve human conduct and character. It has helped men to expand their ideals in a manner beneficial to a wider range of persons; and it has done this, we may add, not because of its hedonistic elements, but because of the emphasis which it placed on universalism; for after all, what the utilitarian's were aiming at was the realization of a better social life, in which each man should count for one and no one for more than one. Mill in particular became the philosophical spoke man of liberalism in England, and fought the intellectual battles of democracy. In his works on Liberty and the Subjugation of Women he insisted on the fullest possible individual rights, because he regarded social well being as inevitably bound up with individual well being. He pointed out 'the importance, to man and society, of a large variety in types of character, and of giving full freedom to human nature to expand itself in innumerable and conflicting directions', and he regarded the repression of women as a greater loss to the community than to women themselves. In the first edition of his *Political Economy* (1848), he favored economic individualism, but in time his '*ideal of ultimate improvement went far beyond Democracy*' and brought him close to socialism.

Immanuel Kant

Immanuel Kant was born in Konigsberg in 1724. At the Collegium Fredericianum, where he prepared for the university, he was chiefly interested in the Roman classics; at the University of Konigsberg he studied physics, mathematics, philosophy and theology. In 1755 he received an appointment as special lecturer (privat dodent) at the University and lectured on mathematics, physics, logic, metaphysics, ethics, physical geography, anthropology, natural theology and 'philosophical encyclopedia'. In 1770 Kant became professor of logic and metaphysics, a position which he held until 1797, when his feeble physical condition made it necessary for him to retire. He died in 1804.

The Problem of Knowledge

Knowledge always appears in the form of judgments in which something is affirmed or denied. But not every judgment is knowledge; in an analytical judgment the predicate merely elucidates what is already contained in the subject. All bodies have specific gravity. Not all synthetic judgments, however give us genuine knowledge; some are derived from experience.

Kant's claim; then, is that knowledge consists of synthetic a prior judgments. Synthetic a posteriori judgments add to our knowledge, but are not sure; the knowledge they yield is uncertain and problematic.

He accepts the existence of universal and necessary knowledge as an established fact; hence he does not ask whether synthetic a priori judgments are possible, but only how they are possible. The theory of knowledge is a strictly demonstrable science, a priori or pure science, one that bases its truths on necessary principles a priori. His method is not psychological, but logical or transcendental. There can be no synthetic judgment without a synthetic mind, no spatial judgment without a space perceiving mind, no causal judgment without mind thinking in terms of cause and effect. In employing this method Kant is, of course, employing human reason with all its categories; he is taking for granted the possibility and validity of knowledge.

He accepts the existence of universal and necessary knowledge as an established fact;

Ethics

Kant's moral philosophy, which he present in his Foundations of Metaphysics of Morals, Critique of Practical Reason and Metaphysics of Morals, may be regarded as an attempt to settle the quarrel between intuitionism and empiricism, idealism and hedonism. His fundamental problem is to discover the meaning of goodness, right and wrong, and duty, and the implications of our moral knowledge; how shall we define duty and what follows from man's moral nature?

Kant had learned from Rousseau that nothing is absolutely good in this world or out of it except a good will. To this, Kant added that a will is good when it is determined by respect for the moral law, or the consciousness of duty. An act that is done from inclination, say from self love or even sympathy, is not moral. How right or wrong an act is does not depend on its effects or consequences; it is immaterial whether happiness or perfection results, so long as the motive of the agent is good. Pure respect for the law is the sole motive of genuine morality. The moral law is a categorical imperative; it commands categorically, unconditionally. Kant's ethics, extols duty for duty's sake. It does not concern itself with particular acts or even with general rules, but lays down a fundamental principle. This law is the supreme test of what is right and wrong.

Categorical imperative is a universal, necessary law, a priori, inherent in reason itself.

Categorical imperative is a universal, necessary law, a priori, inherent in reason itself. Its claim is recognized even by the common man; though he may not be clearly conscious of it, it governs his moral judgments; it is his standard or criterion of right and wrong.

The rational will imposes upon itself universal laws, laws that hold for all and are acceptable to everybody obeyed the law of reason, a society of rational beings would result, a kingdom of ends, society organized by rational purposes. The categorical imperative, implicitly commands a perfect society; it necessarily implies the ideal of a rational realm of spirits. Therefore, every rational being ought to act as if he were by his maxims, his universal principles, a legislating member of a universal kingdom of ends. He is both sovereign and subject; he both lays down and acknowledges the law. By virtue of his moral nature, he is a member of a spiritual kingdom; in recognizing the authority of the law over him, he recognizes the ideal world as the highest good.

A man who is governed by the moral law and not by his impulses, his selfish desires, his appetites, are free. The brute is the play ball of its wants and instincts; through the knowledge of the moral law within him, man can resist his sensuous appetites, all of which aim at selfish pleasure. And because he can suppress his sensual nature he is free: he ought, therefore he can. The moral imperative is the expression of man's real self of the very principle of his being. It is his innermost self that expresses itself in the moral law; the moral law is his command in so far as he is a rational being. He imposes the law upon himself, and this is his autonomy.

The moral imperative insures the freedom of the will. If it were not for our moral nature, or practical reason, a proof of free will would be out of the question. Our ordinary perceptual and scientific knowledge deals with appearances in the spatio temporal order, where everything is arranged according to necessary laws.

Emile Durkheim (1858 – 1917)

Emile Durkheim was born in 1858 in France. His early contact with the disastrous Franco Prussian war made a major impression on Durkheim which is reflected in his constant fascination with the study of group solidarity. Durkheim was an agnostic. His fellows used to call him metaphysician.

In 1887, he was appointed to the faculty of the University of Bordeaux where the first course in social science in all of France was created for him to teach.

Major Contributions:

1. Division of Labour (1893)
2. The Rules of Sociological Method (1895)
3. Suicide (1897)
4. The Elementary Forms of Religious Life (1912)

Durkheim died in 1917. He established the priority of society rather than individual. His focus remained on social order, integration and cohesiveness.

Professional Ethics

The society today is marked by high division of labour. The old scenario of simple societies with just a few types of occupations is giving way to the world of specialization. For any society it is necessary that it must ensure some integration. In the simple society this integration is achieved by the commonness in the problems and challenges that the members have as the society is simple. But with the high division of labour the integration can only be ensured through interdependence. If the various professions do not regulate their members then high division of labour is sure to create a state of confusion. The nature of man is marked by an uncontrolled appetite or greed so we need to check it through ethics. Thus, Durkheim relates 'Professional Ethics' with 'Civic Morals'. Civic Morals are related to the very existence of society for examples. Let us suppose that there is villages with one single well and there are 200 families in the village with each family having 5 members. So the rush on the well will be 200x5=1000 members, if we ensure division of labour that only one member from one family is responsible for fetching water then is rush is of just 200. So, division of labour ensures survival and saves us from the competition of all against all. Thus, increasing division of labour is synonymous with more freedom and happiness. But if the increasing professions do not control themselves by ethics and morals then this high division of labour will turn into an anomie or anomic division of labour. Anomie is the state of normlessness. It is the state where a person do not get proper guidelines from society and is confused.

1. A similar explanation as regards relevance of ethics in professions is given by Anthony Giddens. In his book *'Consequences of Modernity'* Giddens show that in this age of modernity we are heavily dependent on experts, on account of specialization. It's hard to think, as the thinking gets fragmented. So, confusion and meaninglessness prevails.
2. As different from normal, layman meaning the term profession implies a calling. To be professional does not imply to be inhuman. it is rather to serve for the interest of the society and for all.

Any profession is a specialization and hence it call for certain ethics to ensure the utility of that specialization for the service of all. Durkheim saw a number of problems arising from specialization in industrial society but believed the promise of the division of labour outweighted the problems. He outlined his views in *"The Division of Labour in Society"*, first published in 1893. He saw a fundamental difference between pre-industrial and industrial societies. In the former there is relatively little social differentiation, the division of labour is comparatively unspecialized. Social solidarity in pre-industry societies is based on similarities between individual members. They share the same beliefs and values and, to a large degree, the same roles. This uniformity binds members of society together in a close knit communal life. Durkheim refers to unit based on resemblance as 'mechanical solidarity'.

Any profession is a specialization and hence it call for certain ethics to ensure the utility of that specialization for the service of all.

Solidarity in industrial society is based not on uniformity but on difference. Durkheim referred to this form of unity as 'organic solidarity'. Just as in a physical organism, the various parts are different yet work together to maintain the organism, so in industrial society occupational roles are specialized yet function together to maintain the social unit. Durkheim believed division of labour could increase the interdependence of members of society and so reinforce social solidarity. In order to produce goods and services more efficiently, members of industrial society specialize in particular roles. Specialization requires cooperation. The interdependence of skills and the exchange of goods and services are, in themselves, insufficient as a basis for social solidarity. The specialized division of labour requires rules and regulations, a set of moral codes which restrain the individual and provide a framework for cooperation. The exchange of goods and services cannot be based solely on self interest, 'for where interest is the only ruling force each individual finds himself at war with every other'. Durkheim saw the development of contract as a beginning of the moral regulation of exchange. Two parties enter into a legal agreement based on a contract for the exchange of goods and services.

Durkheim believed that the specialized division of labour and the rapid expansion of industrial society contained threats to social solidarity. They tend to produce a situation of 'anomie' which, literally translated, as normless. Anomie is present when social controls are weak, when the moral obligations which constrain individuals and regulate their behavior are not strong enough to function effectively. Industrial society tends to produce anomie for the following reasons. It is characterized by rapid social change which disrupts the norms governing behavior. In Durkheim's elegant phrasing, 'The scale is upset; but a new scale cannot be immediately improvised. Time is required for the public conscience to reclassify men and things'. In particular Durkheim argued that the customary limits to what people want and expect from life are disrupted in times of rapid change. In industrial society men become restless and dissatisfied since the traditional ceiling on their desires has largely disintegrated. Increasing prosperity resulting from economic expansion makes the situation more acute. Durkheim states, 'With increase prosperity desires increase. At the very moment when traditional rules have lost their authority, the richer prize offered these appetites stimulates them and makes them more exigent and impatient of control'. A new moral consensus about what men can reasonably expect from life is required. This will involve the regulation of competition in the exchange of goods and services.

Durkheim believed that the solution to anomie can be provided within the existing framework of industrial society. Self interest which dominates business and commerce should be replaced by a code of ethics which emphasizes the needs of society as a whole. In Durkheim's words 'economic activity should be permeated by ideas and needs other than individual ideas and needs'. He sees occupational associations as the means to subject economic activity to moral regulation. Various industries should be governed by freely elected administrative bodies on which all occupations in the industry are represented. These bodies would have the power 'to regulate whatever concerns the business relations of employers and employed – conditions of labour – wages and salaries – relations of competitors one to the other and so on'. Such associations would solve the problem of anomie in two ways. First, they would counter individualism by reintegrating individuals into a social group which would re-establish social controls. By establishing consensus about the rewards various members of society could reasonably and justifiably expect, normative limits would be placed on individual desire. In particular, Durkheim believed that inheritance as a mechanism for distributing property would gradually die out because of its 'fundamental injustice'. Property would be owned by occupational associations and exchanged by means of contracts. Economic rewards would be based on the contribution of the services of various occupations to the well being of the community. 'The sole economic inequalities dividing men are those resulting from the inequality of their services'. Durkheim envisaged a delicate balance between the state and occupational associations.

The voluntary associations which administer the practice of professionals such as doctors and lawyers. In professional associations, he saw many of the features that were lacking in industry and commerce. These included a clearly established code of conduct which is binding on all members and a sense of duty, responsibility and obligation to the community as a whole. Durkheim saw professional ethics as the key to a future moral order in industrial society.

Adam Smith

Adam Smith was a Scottish moral philosopher, Smith is the author of "*The Theory of Moral Sentiments* and *An Inquiry into the Nature and Causes of the Wealth of Nations*". Smith is widely cited as the father of modern economics.

Smith studied moral philosophy at the University of Glasgow and the University of Oxford. In his later life, he took a tutoring position that allowed him to travel throughout Europe. Smith returned home and spent the next ten years writing "The Wealth of Nations", publishing it in 1776. He died in 1790

He considered freedom of business essential for the prosperity of a nation. He stated that businessman should be permitted to do any trade and labourers should have the freedom to do any job. Price and quality of things should be determined by competition in business instead by government rules. Smith influenced the principles of economics so much so that he is called the father of modern economics. His policy of *'laissez-faire'* gained enormous popularity among businessmen in the eighteenth century. The desire of businessman to get rid of government control on business was a significant cause of both the American and French revolutions.

Suggested Question

1. Define Ethics. What are the important characteristics of western ethics which influenced the modern trade and commerce?
2. Durkheim was one of the first thinkers who introduced idea of capitalism in his theories. Explain
3. Adam Smith's Lassie Faire criticized the feudal economy and encouraged modern industrial system. Comment.
4. Explain the virtues and ideas of Voltaire, Rousseau and Montesquieu. How they influence the ideas of the existing world?

References

1. Pangle, Thomas, *Montesquieu's Philosophy of Liberalism*, Chicago, 1989
2. Beck, Lewis White, *Early German Philosophy: Kant and his predecessor*, Harvard University Press, 1969
3. Rawls John, Lectures on the History of Moral Philosophy, Cambridge, 2000.
4. Shackleton, Robert, Montesquieu A Critical Biography, Oxford, 1961
5. Isaiah Berlin, Karl Marx, His Life & Environment, Oxford, 1963
6. Wokler, Robert, Rousseau, Oxford, 1995
7. Gay Peter, Voltaire's Politics-The Poet as Realist, Yale University, 1988.
8. Thiley Frank, A History of Philosophy, Allahabad, 1984

3

CHAPTER

ROLE OF INDIAN ETHICS IN MANAGEMENT

The Indian ethical values profusely propound the set objectives for human beings to make significant contributions in their own field of operation. The Indian ethos set the agenda of professionalism with a cause. It has a significant impression in the area of professional management. The people who relish their assigned work are destined to perform better and the resistance to work and dislike for the authorities diminishes the output and quality. The Indian religious scriptures emphasise that all the acts or *Karma* how so ever difficult should be performed with ease. It improves work environment and impress those who witness such actions. It creates wider acceptance, appreciation and also reduces the work tension and negative approaches. So it offers a great opportunity to management professionals for stress free performance.

***Dharma* says that in this *Samsara* the work is as vital to all the human beings as food, shelter and material prosperity.**

The *Dharma* says that in this *Samsara* the work is as vital to all the human beings as food, shelter and material prosperity. The type of work may differ from person to person but its significance is same. Irrespective of one's origin or place in social stratification, one is to engage in some productive work. It is necessary to maintain balance of body, mind and living environment. In *Mahabharata* Lord Krishna advises not only about the performance of action in the right direction but also encouraged the spirit of such actions. The total commitment to action seeks no reciprocation for such actions are the key words in the Indian ethos. Irrespective of the nature of work the involvement of person in it and degree of their commitment are the basis of *Karmayoga.* The conscious avoidance of action or half hearted involvement are not desirable. The most important task for modern professionals is to train oneself for their assigned works. The right work approach is the vital part of *Karmayoga.*

Assessment of reality or facts is an important management tool. Whether it is necessary to proceed in a pre-set direction and alter the course of action to avoid failure is critically significant. The business leaders should have unique capacity for quick and correct assessment of reality and assume corrective line of action. The *Bhagvadgita* guides the managers decision making ability if any unpalatable decision becomes necessary under challenging situations. It must be taken promptly without fear of criticism. The long range validity of decision is more important than its immediate perception by the people. The Indian scriptures like *Ramayana, Mahabharata* and leaders like Buddha, Mahavira set the example of charismatic leadership and led the people and disciples through their own illustrative actions. The management professionals could learn something from them and utilize it in business. These fundamentals are:

- Knowledge and expertise are necessary for any efficient managers
- Preaching without practice is not advisable
- An example set by a leader has multilateral utilities
- Humility despite knowledge and prowess are essential for harmonious working environment and co-existence
- The managers should precisely learn the *Prakriti* of his key people or their action.

The Indian ethos also preaches to avoid negative actions. The ideal *Purshottama* or Lord Rama and Krishna and *Uttamapurusha* or Buddha are the manifestation of positive energies and its basic elements being goodness, justice and empathy, application of which in any human endeavour, business, governance invariably lead to better work environment and enhanced productivity. The policy of righteousness, capability based work assignment, performance based rewards, training for settlement and emphasis for non-material motivation as preached by sages of India are highly productive in promoting greater flow of positive energy in an organization. The *Bhagvadgita's* technology of manpower management can be highly beneficial in improving corporate performances in the competitive work environment. For any collective exercise the people constitute the most important component. The success of the organisation depends upon the quality of people selected and the way they are managed. A good practitioner of management is the most important aspect of collective human action irrespective of work relevant. A management *guru* should perform this function. Lord Krishna shows his ability to manage the leades in eighteen days of Mahabharata War. Krishna's method of sharp observation, decisive analysis, productive engagement, active monitoring has valuable relevance in corporate organizations.

The value of commitment has great significance in human relations. In corporate organisations commitment adherence is as valuable as in the field of intellect and spirituality. It leads to the long term dependability of a business manager and the ability of followers to accept these values. The value of commitment accelerates further when comes to a person who is holding more responsibility in an organization. In India our Gods, like Krishna, Rama and enlightened beings meticulously fulfilled all the commitments irrespective of cost involved. Commitment adherence has been the diverse way of attracting or aligning the forces of righteousness for fight against evil. It has been applied as an modern management tool. The professionals are expected to delegate part of their responsibility and have to monitor the status of various projects. The intervention at the right time known as strategic intervention is necessary if undesired results are to be avoided.

In *Ramayana* Rama has intense rapport with his fellows. He took active support of Hanumana, Jamwant and others to defeat the evil of Ravana. The same thing happened with Arjuna and Krishna. The productive relationship always preludes to:

(*i*) Instant co-operation and eventual performance excellence

(*ii*) Total fulfillment of objectivity without creation of feelings of obligation

It is also vital for human resource management in assignment of works as per their capabilities and training and guidance for sharpening their potentials to relinquish the forces of negation and retardness. Indian scriptures explain the three modes of human nature *(Gunas) Sattva, Rajas and Tamas.* Through three attributes the human consciousness manifests itself into diverse characteristics apparent to world. Because of it no two persons will have the same attributes as the interplay of the *Gunas* makes a different variety possible, such as the three brothers Ravana, Vibhisana and Kumbhakarna though born of same mother but different in nature and consequent actions. Similarly in professional environment, assignment of work and placement of workers should be done in accordance with their *Prakriti.*

The ethical values illustrate the principle of time management accessibility to pay performances and its utility in discharge of a professional's responsibility. The kindness *(metta),* compassion *(karuna)* and caring *(maitri)* are positive human values. The action rich in these virtues have great power for release of positive energy to create goodwill in a business environment. Thus the management performance is thought to be centric and karma centric. Its relation with Indian thought process can be elaborated under following constituents.

Dharma as a Strategic Intervention Tool

The *Mahabharata* mention such strategic intervention necessary. The timing and extent of intervention should be measured in right quantum and just in time.

The intervention at the right time is known as strategic intervention. The professionals are expected to delegate their power of their subordinates and intervene in the business when it demands intervention. The *Mahabharata* mention such strategic intervention necessary. The timing and extent of intervention should be measured in right quantum and just in time. Krishna's role as a charioteer of Arjuna in the *Mahabharata* war has provided him a great opportunity for strategic intervention. When the Pandavas faced wrath of Karna who has deputed as commander of Kaurava forces, Krishna used his celestial powers and sunk the chariot deeply into ground to avoid the dreaded weapon of Karna. Similarly Krishna's strategic intervention could be seen when Arjuna failed to kill Jayadratha. In modern economic organizations it can be used as management tool to take appropriate decisions. These strategic interventions can be positive as well as negative. When business is growing and the opportunities are exhausting for further acceleration, the intervention could be in the form of reward, citations and other benefits. It will encourage the employees to be more committed to the organization. At the time of failure such interventions come in form of sanctions. The business leaders using his skills and experience trances in policies and practices the overcome to problems. Such examples are also found in early India when the *Shrenis* (Guilds) were given special protection by the state, but the state interferred in the policies when their standard of business started deteriorating.

Internal Conflict Management

All sort of organisations possess some kind of internal conflict. It is human nature or *prakriti* to have differences and the intra-organisational conflict is an inherent character of an association. In corporate environment, efficient conflict management play pivotal role and thus corporate professional could learn a great from skillful employment of mythical inner-conflict management technology. The numerous God incarnated on earth to eliminate the evil forces. The jobs of these incarnations were not just to manage the evil forces but to wipe it out from the universe. Rama and Krishna killed numerous demons to establish dharma in the *Samsara*. The God with their charming personality, divine aura controlled and managed the unavoidable internal conflicts in the *Jambudvipa*. They as a man of celestial wisdom employed a divine technology and acted as a magician by using the technique of manpower management. The chief components of this management are leading by example, active appreciation and merit, non material motivation, supervised delegation and management of mind as mean of superior control. So it can be a unique methodology for intra-organisational human resource management and can yield for better dividends for promotion of co-operation.

Doctrine of *Karma* as a Management Technique

Corporate organizations represent working organization and its people. The divine doctrine of *Karma* can play constructive role in improving corporate work culture. The necessity of action as propounded by Vasudeva to Arjuna in *Geeta* has substantial implication in the corporate governance. One can acquire superior knowledge of one's assigned area and becomes a specialist. The *Karma* principle says that (i) Action is worship (ii) Act should not be bound by its results *(Niskam Karma)* (iii) Selfless work is the essence and the *Karma* is the force of creation. All these attributes of *Karma* may inspire workers. The *Karmayoga* is a system of righteous work based on ethic and religion. A little effort toward making work little selfless at the part of doer can substantially reduce the negative energy and boost to immense initiative and innovation. Many corporate managers do not perform their best in their particles, assignment under the uncertainty of results and fear of criticism. They prefer to select the route as directed by their bosses or withhold the implementation. So the process of imitation unnecessarily blocks innovation. The managers often restrain from giving constructive suggestions as they are afraid of the results. The extensive concern for fruit of work became a major obstacle in progress. The *Karmayoga* also leads to completion and creates output differentiation. The *Karmas* have characteristics of *Karmic* interaction, *Karmic* accumulation and Karmic balance. All these features have

The extensive concern for fruit of work became a major obstacle in progress.

active relevance in the field of corporate environment. The various models of Krishna as a *Karmayogies* can be taken as a example for corporate governance.

(*i*) Krishna had leadership quality. He himself adopts a method before advocating its practice by others. He was a man of action and never hesitated to take any sort of work.

(*ii*) Despite threat to his life he went to Kaurava court to make out a amicable settlement and later on become charioteer of Arjuna to overcome the difficulties of Mahabharata war.

(*iii*) The unpleasant potentialities did not deter him to do unpleasant works. To establish the peace he killed kamsa and fought for Arjuna.

Dharma as a tool of Anger Management

Anger is the exhibition of negative authoritative manifestation by a person in a position. It encourages emotions to lose the perceived path and manifests reaction. In business organizations some authorities do it as an expression of right and they are most frequent vehicle of anger manifestation. Sometime trivial matters became the cause of outburst when the juniors fail to perform the expected targets or in a reactive response avoid to do the needful. While the authority may mistake his anger expression as a tool of persuasion, the workers normally perceive it as unfair treatment. Anger is a form of negative characteristic and to be an essential evil or unavoidable part of human interactions. Negative aspects of anger manifestation mostly develop from the fact that under influence of anger one loses his capability of logical thinking which results into imbalance of expressions as well as the decision making. The *Bhagvadgita* says thert *from anger comes delusion and from delusion loss of memory. From loss of memory comes the ruin of discriminative power and from ruin of discrimination the person perishes.* It further says that the *absence of anger is a moral quality and the gateway to hell is lust, anger and greed. Therefore one should avoid these three.* In corporate work culture indiscriminate use of negative energy by the bosses lead to jeopardize the conducive work tradition. Its indirect impact is more injurious and persistent than the direct and immediate which generating silent resistance to suggestions, co-operation, initiative and innovation. The holy teachers of India suggested that there should be only constructive and measured expression of protest rather than action in support of what is correct or in the opposition of what is incorrect. Buddha also given his view on anger. He never reacted on his opponents but silently listened them and opposed their futile ideas with his calms and virtues.

Time Management

In modern business organization there are wider dissatisfaction with the outcome of their efforts towards efficient time management. Stress and friction within the work structure are such that the efforts of any kind of time management do not bring adequate results. In Indian perspective time *(Kal)* is accepted as celestial source and the ordinary approach is bound to bring only ordinary results. Krishna in *Bhagvadgita* employed the principles of *Karma and*

Dharma to reduce the excessive concern for results and to augument the righteousness content of actions. Once the over engagement with result is reduced and righteousness is increased and the stress in work environment will diminish substantially. Such condition will sprout cooperation and initiative. The resultant positivity of thought and action is bound to produce greater productive interaction within a organization and with such phenomenal development greater work performance and output will flow effortlessly. Krishna delivered the importance of time in *Bhagvadgita* in respect to individuals, organization, kingdom and all that falls under umbrella of universe. He emphasized the importance of time and its all pervading influence on all happening and occurrences. Krishna says that the wheel of time *(Kal-Chakra)* always moves and it has been never static. Time makes the circle of life and it influence everything in perpetual motion. Time governs response of man to various situation – *dharma* and *adharma* action and inaction. It is the celestial tool that manages everything in the universe. The characteristic of its omnipresence lies behind the idea that the modern business organization adhering to time management.

Purushottama – A Model of Leadership

The *Purushottama* is a symbol of positive response of energy and it exhibits *Karuna, Maitri, Metta, Ahimsa, Asteya* etc.

The *Purushottama* is a symbol of positive response of energy and it exhibits *Karuna, Maitri, Metta, Ahimsa, Asteya* etc. All these elements are necessary organs of business organization which invariably leads to better work. Its positive energy destroys the negative approach to work and inculcate positive forces which brings immense dividends to an organization. Indian religions such as Hinduism, Buddhism, Janism manifest that the world has been created as a play ground for humans. These divine leaders are role models who fought arduous battles against the enemies of virtue and helped the common people by establishing *Dharma* in the universe. Lord Rama incarnated as *Purushottama* to kill Ravana. Buddha achieved *nirvana* to stop futile sacrifices and to preach *ahimsa.* These *Purushottamas* have shown the high level of positive energy full of *Sattavic Prakriti.* They observed *Dharma* and protected the people from persons of *Tamsika Pravritti.* It gives lesson that negative leadership manifestation in the corporate world could dilute the commitment appreciation and impartiality of the organization. By incorporating the ideals of *Purushottama* a corporate leader can avoid certain negative manifestations such as:

(*i*) Partiality in selection and placement

(*ii*) Discrimination on account of caste, religion or birth

(*iii*) Gender discrimination and exploitation

(*iv*) Unproductive criticism

(*v*) Reluctant to share information and opposing new ideas

(*vi*) Senior subordinate conflict and non co-operation

(*vii*) Unjustified re-allocation of work assignments and transfers

Rama as Aryan king of kosala went in exile accompanied by Lakshmana and Sita. To kill Ravana, he went to Rameshwaram and organized the force dominated by Dravidian elements. His orgnising capacity was so illustrious that the local people were ready to sacrifice everything for him. Because of his leadership quality he was able to kill Ravana. Similar instances could also be taken also for Buddha. Buddha with is charismatic leadership established the Buddhism not only in India but also abroad. In recent days more than twenty five Asian nations follow Buddhism and it is one of the fastest growing religions of the world.

Team Management

The recruitment and management of good team is an essential requirement for a business leader to give desired result. The energy required for performance and action could only be acquired with team only. Such managements can be found in the great epics of Ramayana and Mahabharata. Rama went to forest with Lakshmana and Sita. When Sita was abducted by Ravana. Rama organized formidable force to kill Ravana and devised action and unique leadership for that. Krishna in the *Mahabharata* war shows such skills. He become the charioteer of Pandavas who were only five but Krishna solicited the support of various things to defeat Kauravas. Following components could be faced by team management skills of these leaders.

(*i*) Active identification of resource person

(*ii*) Training and canvassing for strategic movements

(*iii*) Superior guidance and active mentoring

(*iv*) Protection of privileges and assign appropriate duties to the team managers.

Such judicious and rewarding methodology for efficient team management could be thought provoking. The *gurus* of modern management can learn some techniques from managerial skills of these mythical heroes.

Characteristics of Indian Ethos

In Indian context it has been generally admitted that ethics begins when the freedom of the individual will is conceded. It has been tried by the critics of Indian moral theories that, there cannot be any science of ethics in India, especially in brahmanical literature because of certain philosophical presuppositions. There is other objection that the admission of the law of *Karma* as governing force for human actions seriously imperils the freedom of the will. It interprets that the past lives of any individual have a determining force in controlling his actions of the present life. The actions, that a man is capable of doing, depend not only upon what he wishes but also upon the moral results of the actions of his previous lives. But Indian philosophical systems are more intellectualistic than moralistic in their outlook, and its aim is not a purification of the will but a clarification of the understanding. In India the Socratic identification of virtue with knowledge was more widely practiced than anywhere else in the world. Manu, forbids the imparting of instruction to persons swayed by passions, and the *Gita* promises knowledge to the man of faith *(Sraddha)*. Morality, was regarded as a necessary ground of philosophical competence *(adhikara)*. India with its belief in castes *(jati)* and classes *(varna)* and stages of life *(asrama)* had directed its moral philosophy to the realities of a social situation which is to be found nowhere else in the world. Its classification of duties and virtues was naturally influenced by its social organization and no one who is not familiar with its social life is likely to have an intimate knowledge and appreciation of its ethical code. There are transcendental considerations that have a bearing upon man's conduct. Belief in God, departed ancestors, and future life would naturally dictate certain types of conduct, and ethics would have some reference to the unseen universe with which man has to hold contact.

The Vedas were regarded as the ultimate source of all *dharma*. All other sources of *dharma* such as the *Smrti* (legal literature), *sadachara* (the pattern of good conduct and *svasya atmanah priyam* (actions pleasing to individual conscience), were ultimately based upon the mental and moral equipment of the Vedic scholars. The Vedas *Rigveda, Yajurveda, and Samaveda* enunciated that the universe was governed by moral order *(rita)* and truth *(satya).* The Vedic speculation went to the length of supposing that the first products of the divine creation *(tapas)* were these two *(rita and satya)*, which means that before beginning of cosmos, there must be regularity in the behavior of things. The God obeys order *(ritavart)* and are protectors of law *(ritasya gopa)* and fixed ordinances (*dhrtavrata).* The supreme importance has been attached to law and law of Karma in its various forms, as adopted by Brahmanism, Buddhism, and Jainism. It is quite possible that the Vedic Aryans, who had to regulate their life, whether nomadic or settled, by the observation of certain cosmic phenomena that came to a very early understanding of the laws governing the nature.

The Vedas were regarded as the ultimate source of all *dharma.* All other sources of *dharma* such as the *Smrti* (legal literature), *sadachara* (the pattern of good conduct and *svasya atmanah priyam* (actions pleasing to individual conscience), were ultimately based upon the mental and moral equipment of the Vedic scholars.

The continuity of the moral tradition was the recognition that the bond between man and the higher powers was broken by the invasion of sin. Number of words in the Vedas signifying wrong doings which shows that the religious minds were keenly aware of lapses in their moral conduct and were solicitous about re-establishing their moral relation with the God through appropriate means. The genuine repentance, unconnected with physical lust, is frequently met with in the Vedas and it was widely believed that human conduct was subject to the constant scrutiny of overseeing powers and that sins could not be hidden from their gaze. The God with whom morality was specially associated was Varuna and to a lesser extent Brhaspati. The righteous were assured of a good reward for their rectitude and has been promised the fruit of their charity, benevolence, and sacrificial acts *(istapurta).* The broken link between God and man could be repaired by recourse to confession and penance, and continuance in sin entailed not only failure in life, but also physical ailment which could be removed only by proper prayer to the God and the abandonment of the immoral life. There was a subtle relationship between acts and their fruits. The change of attitude towards the function of the God in joining merit to get fruit was responsible at a later time for the enunciation of the doctrine that there were certain mystic forces in the world.

The Upanishads constitute a landmark in the development of Indian spirituality and the belief in the doctrine of Karma. In Buddhism and Jainism the God of the Vedas either disappear altogether or continue in colourless subsidiary. The austerities hardened and renunciations are more insistently demanded. The attachments of all kinds are denounced in gradually stronger language. It is obvious that substitute for faith in divine pleasure was found in the belief in the efficacy of moral life, and those who did not subscribe the dogma that pious souls go to the eternal heavens of merciful and pacified God could still believe that spiritual advancement was possible by ethical actions alone. Preachers inclined to the view that perfection *(shreyas)* was to be preferred to pleasure *(preyas).*

The scripture may direct that certain actions should be performed. They would be obligatory simply because the scripture has said though no reward has been promised and no reason assigned. The non performance of such actions would entail sin. These are called *nitya karmas* (duties of perfect obligation). But the scriptures may sometimes be more kind and specific about what benefit would accrue to the performer of actions. There would be *kamya karmas* or duties of imperfect or contingent obligation (one is not obliged to perform them if one has no desire to have the fruits thereof). For instance, only those who aspired to go to heaven or to attain mundane objectives like the birth of a son or the attainment of wealth were under an obligation to perform relevant sacrifices. Besides these, there were other duties that were contingent in the sense that their performance depended upon certain specific things happening, but they were obligatory in the sense that if those things happened, the relevant actions had to be performed *(naimittika karmas).* Thus various sacraments associated with certain happenings like birth, death, etc. had to be performed when those events occurred.

The heterodox systems formulated their moral law without a theistic basis. The Buddhism and Jainism conspired together to establish firmly the self sufficiency of the moral law and to lay the basis of the classical doctrine of *Karma* according to which moral actions produced their own fruit without reference to any kind of divine dispensation. The others endowed God with all auspicious qualities, including the capacity of cancelling evil and human imperfection. God not only possesses knowledge and power but is also forgiving, compassionate, and indulgent towards the weak. These attributes will have no meaning if God cannot come to the help and rescue of sinners and out of his superabundant grace take back to his heart the penitent sinner. The Mimamsakas admitted the existence of *nisedhas* or negative injunctions. The moralists thought that the first necessity of a moral life was resistance to evil solicitations. Social justice and social harmony would demand forbearance from certain types of acts which were anti-social or subversive of social discipline. Hence it was felt that prescriptions must be supplemented by prohibitions and incentives by restraints. If man was supposed to be evil by nature and morality to be a constant restraint to suppress the evil that is in man. It was held that man had an innate goodness which turned into evil on account of the obscuration of his intellect. Hence, virtue is knowledge and the proper means of making men virtuous is to give proper enlightenment to their soul.

The principle of moral obligation in Brahmanism rested upon a recognition of specific duties attached to each caste and in each stage of life. Society is composed of all sorts of people in mutual interaction and is not a homogeneous fraternity of persons belonging to the same caste or profession. Hence there must be certain duties which cut across all sectional divisions and are necessary for maintaining the strength and progress of the social organism. There are transcendental matters towards which all people must bear the same type of attitude. The abjuration of the six deadly sins – lust, anger, greed, infatuation, pride and jealousy – is a human obligation which all must fulfil. The distinctive Indian contribution to this list is the renunciation of excessive attachment and hatred of all kinds. The ultimate ideal being the securing of justice in society. They advocated resistance to evil in the interest of the greater good to the world at large. The Brahmanical theory of God descending on earth not only to succor the righteous, but also to put down the unrighteous. Human objectives were divided into four categories – moral action *(dharma),* economic activity and statecraft *(artha),* propagation of the race *(kama)* and emancipation *(moksha).* It was taken for granted that the rules of morality and the rules of the state would not always tally and it was conceded that certain actions that would not be permissible in furtherance of private interests were allowed for the safety of the state. Murder, for instance, would be a heinous private offence, but a just a war might be a moral duty of the state, although every war would involve the killing of enemies. The art of government *(dandaniti)* was generally conceived in human terms and spirituality had a large share in determining the state policy. It is acknowledged here that the condition of the body has some hand in determining the state of the mind, and hence prescriptions cover not only the discipline of the mind, but also the control of the body. Cleanliness, steadiness, concentration of the sense organs, withdrawal of the same from unholy and unseemly objects, regulation of the breath and assumption of characteristic bodily attitudes were also pressed into the service of controlling the mind, dissipating wayward thoughts, and bringing about a meditative pose. The objective always was to make the body an ally instead of an enemy. The four positive attributes are friendliness *(maitri),* compassion *(karuna),* sympathetic joy *(mudita),* and ignoring of human frailties *(upeksa).* The rules of health must be obeyed if the spiritual aspirant is to keep under sufficient control his flighty thoughts and impulsive propensities. Ablution and other types of cleansing were ordained because they helped to bring in a helpful mental attitude. The practice of austerity, might bring in a propensity towards spiritual outlook, and *tapas*, e.g. mortification of the flesh could be defended on the ground that it enabled the soul to gain control over the body.

The materialists like the Carvakas did not recognize the reality but prescribed a code of duties as positive which constitute the entire body of moral truths. And if people do agree to put up with some inconveniences and pains, it is because they would be assured of enjoyment of pleasures. The conduct of the good is imitated by the people at large, as customs vary from place to place and from time to time, in certain matters at least ethical relativity was inevitable. In any matter of doubt one would not commit any wrong if one were had to follow the customs of one's own locality *(desachara),* community *(lokachara)* or family *(kulachara).* If the ultimate object of moral conduct is to maintain the social equilibrium and ensure social peace, then obviously nothing that disturbs them should be practiced. Buddha or Mahavira has laid down the law of moral life for his followers that constitutes the ethical code. By their strenuous moral life and their perfect intelligence these prophets have peered into the realm of truth and because they have the good of the people at heart and are moved by compassion at the sight of their misery. They have spread the truths of moral life as perceived by them and enabled them to ford the stream of *samsara.* But Hinduism says that the omniscience belonged only to God and freedom from all disturbing elements was only a divine prerogative. The eternal, omniscient Being who has never been infected by any kind of ignorance, sin, or incapacity can alone lay down the laws of moral life. Hence morality is a divine prescription and human endeavour should be directed to discovering and following the moral prescriptions of God.

There is fundamental similarity in respect of certain moral duties and wide divergence in respect of others, A moral prescription of one religion would be considered as grossly immoral in another theological presuppositions and obviously a large hand in determining change in moral attitude. Brahmanism in its institution of castes and stages of life *(varnasrama)* made it possible to recognize relativity in moral duties of the different sections of the people in their different stages of spiritual life. Similarly, each stage of life had its own special duties, though here again certain universal duties were also present. The philosophers of India improved upon this conception by linking moral obligation with the stage of spiritual attainment.

The question arose about the types of actions in which men indulge and the results of such actions *(karmas)* are divided into good *(sukla)*, bad *(Krishna)*, mixed *(suklakrshna)*, neither good nor bad *(asuklakrshna)*.

The question arose about the types of actions in which men indulge and the results of such actions *(karmas)* are divided into good *(sukla),* bad *(Krishna),* mixed *(suklakrshna),* neither good nor bad *(asuklakrshna).* The different theories of heaven and hell to be found in Brahmanism, Jainism and Buddhism that took effective note of the different destinies of the good and the evil. A distinction was drawn between modes of existence which were merely meant as punishments or rewards of actions done *(bhogabhumi)* and modes of existence in which fresh accumulation of merit and demerit might take place *(karmabhumi).* The heterodox systems practically limited the field of moral activity to this mundane world and extolled human life to the extent of supposing that salvation could come to man and man alone. The Brahmanical view that salvation was possible through ethical behavior in other realms also as found in the Vedantic theory of progressive salvation *(kramamukti).* It says that spiritual progress could be attained even by God who are supposed to be already half way towards salvation through their earlier ethical activities. But heaven and salvation were not identical. The Samkhya describes the gift to the sacrificing priest *(dakshina)* as a kind of bondage *(bandha)* and says that the sacrifices which lead to heavenly existence *(svarga)* simply postpone the attainment of salvation *(moksa).* It had to be effected by effort along a very slippery path of which the spiritual novice was asked to beware. Minute prescriptions were laid down in Buddhism, Jainism and Brahmanism about attaining the different stages of this ascent of the soul *(bhumi, gunasthanaka),* and warnings were sounded about the lurking dangers of each stage and also the powers *(rddhi, vibhuti)* and insights *(abhijna).*

The *Madbhagvadgita* made a notable departure from the beaten track by denying that *Karma* could be avoided at any time. It discusses the various types of actions and points out that as not being, even God not excepted, could be entirely free from action. The spiritual act is not exclusive of the performance of the ordinary duties of life, but is a transformation of the same. This theory of *karmasannyasa* presupposes a belief that ultimately the finite beings are to consider themselves as tools for the working out of divine plans. Injury *(himsa)* is a bad a subjective feeling, but may be God as an objective fact needed to redress iniquity and outrage done by the evil. Krishna's exhortation to Arjuna to fight the unrighteous Kauravas cannot be justified on any other ground. It is not an incitement to violence but an exhortation to fulfil the obvious duty of a Kshatriya to keep all evil in the state in proper check. The *Gita* with its Samkhya-*Yoga* leanings could also exploit the theory of the *gunas* in the interest of ethics. There are some attributes which are essentially good and spiritual *(sattvika),* others which are active and somewhat spiritually indifferent *(rajasika),* while there are still others which are lethargic and prone towards evil *(tamasika).* Obviously, the incentives and restraints would not be identical in the cases of these three.

It has been charged against Indian ethics that it lacks the crusaders zeal for improving the world. It prescribes methods of self improvement, without reference to social duties. This charge is difficult to maintain, in view of the fact that again and again it has been repeated that without performing the duties of one's own station, one cannot remedy the spiritual myopia that blurs one's vision for truth, without which spiritual illumination and final deliverance are not possible. The five great sacrifices *(mahayajnas)* were ordained to fulfil one's duties not only to the self, but to the entire creation and even to God and manes. The universe was regarded as a unitary whole, composed of different types of beings, all of whom shared in the gifts of man. Hospitality at tending the sick, and providing food were regular features of a householder's life. Duties to relations did not mean only showing respect, friendship, or affection but also supporting them in distress and maintaining cordiality of social relationship by a system of give and take. *Dana* understood in a comprehensive sense as including not merely gifts to Brahmanas and priets, but also scattering bounty all around in the form of planting trees, building highways, digging wells and tanks, and providing places of shelter and treatment, of which all persons and even animals might avail themselves. The Brahmancial and Buddhist literature mention passages expressing sentiments, prayers and resolutions instead of getting any temporal power or personal pleasure or even final liberation one might be given, opportunities of serving humanity at large. Whether Brahmanical or Buddhist, the code of ethics proceeded on the assumption that in spite of their differences all souls were at bottom swayed by the same feelings and tendencies and yearned after pleasure. The identity of the human race was further accentuated by the Vedantic theory of the identity of all souls through Brahman. Men were advised to practice the golden rule and not to treat others as they did not like to be treated themselves.

The kingly acts of Rama, the brotherly affection of Laksmana and Bharata, the chastity of Sita, Savitri, and Damayanti, the generosity of Karna, the compassion of Sibi and Jimutavahna, the truthfulness of Yudhisthira, the steadfast vow of Bhisma, the devotion of Dhruva and Prahlada, and the sacrifice of Dadhichi, have served as beacon lights through the ages and illumined the path of conduct of commoners and wanderers. Through countless tales of courage, forbearance, nobility and character the three great religions of India have tried to impress upon the minds of people, the necessity of following moral ideals through all hazards in order to achieve that spiritual perfection without which final liberation is impossible. India still holds the world's record in religious toleration is due to the fact that forcible conversion and oppression of the heretics were not counted among the moral virtues. The benediction of peace *(santi, svasti)* should be uttered at the end of all religious ceremonies.

India recognized like international relations could not be fully governed by the laws of private morality. Evolved a science of statecraft *(arthasastra)* in addition to a scheme of salvation *(mokshasastra)* and kept apart these four objectives of human life *(catur-varga)* – morality or sacrificial duty *(dharma),* earthly prosperity including economy and statecraft *(artha),* conjugal necessity *(kama),* and emancipation *(moksha).* The king had many duties to perform like, maintain order and discipline in the state and while the objective of a righteous war *(dharmayuddha)* was steadily kept in view and humane treatment of enemies and criminals was recommended. Injustice and wanton oppression were not allowed to go scot free and a king not punishing a criminal incurred moral guilt as not performing an appointed duty. Supporting the virtuous and weeding out the vicious were laid down as equal moral obligations. But unpleasant duties were not to be performed in a spirit of anger or vengeance, and the reformation of the character of evil-doers was a primary duty to be attempted with kindness and patience. It preached the necessity of keeping in constant remembrance the solidarity of the human race, task of self discipline, and the spiritual basis of all moral activity. Indian thinkers commonly speak of two functions of knowledge – one which is theoretical, i.e. revealing the existence of some object *(artha-paricchitti)* and the other which is practical, i.e. affording help in the attainment of some purpose in life *(phala-prapti).* The results of these two functions of knowledge are what adherence to fact and value.

Traditional Economic Ethics

Indian thinkers divided knowledge *(sastra or vidya)* into four branches *(i) anviksiki, (ii) trayi, (iii) varta and (iv) dandaniti.*

Indian thinkers divided knowledge *(sastra or vidya)* into four branches *(i) anviksiki, (ii) trayi, (iii) varta and (iv) dandaniti,* which may be broadly interpreted respectively as (i) philosophy (ii) three Vedas (iii) economics and (iv) polity. The word *varta* primarily represents *vrtti* or means of livelihood. *Varta* according to Kautilya dealt with agriculture, cattle breeding and trade. Later on, money-lending or usury was included under *varta* by the *Bhagavata Purana, Sukra-Nitisara,* etc., and the *Mahabharata* included *vividhani silpani* (arts and crafts). Thus, in modern nomenclature, *varta* dealt with the economics of agriculture, trade, banking and industry, which shows that consumption, distribution and taxation, forming part of modern economics were left out of the scope of *varta.* These latter topics were included in the works on Arthasastra. The Arthasastra, covers a wider field than *varta.* It has been called *Arthaveda.* The Indians fully recognized the importance of economic science. The root ideas of the early Indian conception of wealth to be its material quality, its appropriability, its being the result of acquisition, its not being quite identical with gold, its consumability and its attractiveness due to scarcity. The Arthasastra, the Epics, the Smrtis and other works on ancient Indian economics knew the importance of wealth in the scheme of life for gaining the *purusarthas* (ends of human life), and were fully conscious of the depressing influence of poverty. Wealth was never regarded as an end in itself but as a means to an end.

Rural Economy

Indian economists give predominance to rural economics because agriculture has been the occupation of the population throughout the ages. Along with cattle breeding and dairy farming, agriculture constituted the most important part of *varta.* Land, labour, capital and organization appear to have been the four agents of production according to ancient Indian economists. The creation of proprietary interests in land and the laying down of elaborate rules for the survey and demarcation of individual holdings, since the days of Kautilya, indicate the recognition by ancient Indian economists of the property in dealing with agriculture. The creation of a beneficial interest by law in favour of the person who first cleared the forest or reclaimed waste land facilitated the clearing of jungles and bringing of waste land under cultivation. The great advance in agriculture and the thorough knowledge of the minute details of agricultural pursuits are seen not only in the treatises of Kautilya followed by Sukra but also in the Smrti literature. The fact that the following principles and practices, the interdependence of agriculture and cattle farming, the use of fertilizers, the rotation of crops, the relative advantages of extensive and intensive cultivation, the evils of fragmentation of holdings, the relative advantages of large and small scale farming according to the crops cultivated, the adjustment of crops to soils and *vice versa,* the wisdom of carefully selecting seed grains, the value of forest conservation, the use of fallow land; the value of even inferior land in the vicinity of centres of population, irrigation by rain, rivers, tanks, reservoirs and mechanical agencies, agricultural drainage, prevention, correction and eradication of numerous risks, such as rain, drought, ravages of locusts, pests, mice, birds and wild pigs etc were known to people. Highly beneficient agricultural administration and a good knowledge of rural economics are seen from Kautilya's Arthasastra. The members of a village were held jointly liable for keeping their roads, water channels and tanks in efficient repair, which ensured perfect maintenance of irrigational works. Any damage to such works of public utility was to be urgently rectified even from the resources of temples. Special facilities were to be given to those who constructed tanks, dams, and roads out of piety, so that the state might receive co-operation from individuals in providing irrigation works. Fixing fair prices for agricultural products at frequent intervals served the interest of the people as producers and consumers. In order to meet the menace of famine, different parts of the kingdom were to be provided with granaries capable of holding grain sufficient to meet the normal requirements of three years. The interests of the cultivators were guarded against distraction or nuisance by banning the intrusion of actors, dancers, singers, drummers, and wandering minstrels into villages. The officers and servants of the king had to live outside the limits of the village, apparently to save the villagers from oppression. The soldiers also were prohibited from entering villages except on the king's business, and even then they were not to oppress cultivators or have any dealings with them. The Indian ethics advocated an uninterrupted pursuit of agriculture even in times of war and the accounts of foreign travelers confirm that agriculturists were unaffected by the march of armies. The economic interests of cultivators were safeguarded by fixing fair prices.

Labour was an important factor of production. Kautilya and Sukra permit the employment of women in state factories and agricultural operations. According to Sukra, the remuneration of a labour should be proportionate to his productivity and qualification and the wages should be sufficient to maintain the labourer and his family in tolerable comfort. Sukra's rules, which provide leisure hours, leave, and bonus for domestic servants and workmen's insurance in sickness, old age, or accident, show the actual practice. The labour or servant, on the other hand, had to pay penalties for breach of contract in addition to being liable for damages caused by his neglect. Further, strikes of workmen to raise wages were declared illegal. Making a distinction between pure and impure types of labour, the test of purity lying in the nature of the occupation and the material employed. Kautilya, Kamandaka, Sukra and others say that hired labour cannot be abolished and the efficient labour results from training. The competent supervisory authority is necessary for getting work done and a proper output can be ensured only through payment by results. Economists visualized the importance of capital to industry and other productive undertakings. The normal aim of our ancient financiers to budget for heavy and recurring surpluses resulted in swelling the state hoard. The inference about the scarcity of private capital, or about its falling far short of the demands for it is also implied by the evidence in the Mahabharata, which advocates that the state should advance cash grants and seed grain to agriculturists and run a large number of industrial concerns.

Urban Economy

In the India, valley civilization (2600 BC – 1900 BC), the trade was organized and probably guilds were responsible to facilitate the trade. Their contribution in early Indian economy is not known because their scripts are still not deciphered. The organization of guilds after decline of Indian valley civilization started towards the end of the Vedic period, and Panini refers to the *gana, puga, vrata and sangha*. The word *gana and sangha* were used to denote any corporation or union for political or economic purposes, while *puga and sreni* signified corporations of merchants, artisans, or others whose principal object was to gain wealth by trade or industry. The *Dharma Sutras* indicate that the chief industries were all organized in guilds i.e. *Sreni, naigama (or nigama), pasanda, samuha.* The workers or craftsmen's guilds correspond to the modern labour organizations while merchants' guilds approximate to the Guild Merchant of mediaeval Europe. The *Dharma-Sutras* recognized the validity of the laws and customs established by the guilds of cultivators, traders, usurers, herdsmen, artisans, craftsmen etc., whose headmen occupied a high place in the royal tribunal. Manu and Yajnavalkya compare the customs of the *srenis* and analogous bodies with legal authority. The law books recognize the binding force of the agreements with the *sanghas* and breaches of which were dealt severely. The punishments ranged from heavy fine or imprisonment to confiscation and banishment. Kautilya's elaborate treatment, demonstrates the important role played by the guilds in the economic system of the Mauryan and post-Mauryan age. They effectively controlled local sources of production, arts and crafts and trades and industries served as an important link between the central authority and the several economic units in the country.

Trade as an important form of economic activity existed even protohistoric times in India, and its indispensable accessories money, currency, credit, exchange and banking were developed at very early age. Kautilya advocates considerable state control both in trade and industry. It was obligatory on traders to get a licence while foreign traders required a passport. According to both Kautilya and Sukra, the two factors to be considered in fixing value or price are the cost of production and demand for the article. Wholesale prices for goods were fixed by the Superintendent of Commerce. A margin of profit was allowed to retailers. The consumers and customers were protected by the state which employed an army of spies and market inspectors against unauthorized prices and fraudulent transactions. The goods had to be sold at fixed market places and the dealer had to specify particulars as quality, quantity and price, which were scrutinized and recorded in official books. The duties of the Superintendent of Commerce (Panyadhyaksha) included not only the prevention or minimization of the chances of deceit, or of undue advantage being taken by the seller over the buyer but also ensuring that the prices were not exorbitant.

To encourage, promote and facilitate trade both inland and foreign, were enjoined to improve and increase means of communication and transport. They had to also secure new markets for the surplus products of the country. The rest-houses and store-houses were to be provided for traders for whose protection proper police escorts were also recommended. The river boats and ocean going ships were to be pressed into service. As a compensation for the taxes paid by the trade the government granted it security against thieves, forest tribes, wild forest folk, etc. Several facilities were afforded to encourage foreign trade. Foreign merchants could sue in Indian courts, and were protected from being harassed.

Localization of industry and creation of local markets for the sale of products resulted from the caste and guild organizations. Elaborate rules were framed for the organization, establishment and management of markets. The speculation, smuggling, adulteration, cheating and dishonesty were punishable, according to the gravity of the offence with fines, or imprisonment or even mutilation. Kautilya advocates state monopoly of industries on the basis of risk, cost or rarity. The state was advised to become both the manufacturer and trader, and to sell articles through departmental agency. The mines of gold, silver, diamonds, gems, precious stones, copper, lead, tin, iron and bitumen, which provided the main source of state revenue, were nationalized. The Pearl, conch shell, coral, etc. were explored from ocean mines, and it was a state concern. The ores provided minerals, while *rasas* like mercury came from oil fields. Salt manufacturing was a state monopoly for which licences were granted to private entrepreneurs. There was also state monopoly of armament industry, coinage and ship-building; further, the state controlled the manufacture and sale of wines and liquors. *Kusida* is the term used for the lending of money on interest and the early *Dharma-Sutras* display a strong prejudice against usury. Money lending or usury *(kusida)* came to be recognized as one of the four divisions of *varta* and interest came to be regarded as a normal share of the national dividend. There are different rates of interest for loans with or without pledge. Fifteen percent per annum was the normal rate of interest, but it could be higher according to the security given, the nature of the risk involved and other factors. The welfare of the debtor was safeguarded by forbidding compound interest, interest above the normal customary rate, accumulation of interest exceeding the amount of the principal or personal service in lieu of interest.

Some kind of banking may be inferred from the literary evidences and inscriptions regarding loans, deposits, interests. Guilds, partnerships and joint stock organizations must have helped the evolution of the system of group credit. The *Jatakas* and the *Arthasastra* testify to the existence of instruments of credit, promissory notes or debt sheets and banking pledges and book credits. The banks could perform not only economic functions but also religious activities. A person could invent money with the guilds and the guilds could invent such money in trade. The profit earned on such investments could be spent for welfare and religion causes. Such investments were known as *Akshyanivi.*

Though the bulk of retail transactions was conducted by barter on account of the scarcity of currency and the low prices of products, the use of coins was also in evidence. The coins originated and developed in India before foreign contact. Indian coinage, comprising *punch-marked* silver and copper coins, goes back to about 600 BC. The earliest coins were based on the weight system of which the unit was *raktika (rati or gunja* berry). *Suvarna* was the standard gold coin of eighty ratis, while the copper coin of the same weight was called *karsapana,* though a copper *pana* of a hundred *ratis* was also known. *Purana* or *dharana* was a silver coin of thirty two *ratis.* The guilds and even merchants issued these coins duly stamped with their symbol, signifying correctness of weight and purity of the metal. Under the *Arthasastra* scheme, coinage was a state monopoly and officials under the Mint Master *(laksanadhyaksa)* received bullion from the public to be struck into coins on payment of some charges.

Kosa (treasury), as one of the seven constituents of the state and had supreme importance along with army. The *Arthasastra,* the *Mahabharata, Kamandaka Nitisara, Visnudharmottara Purana* say that the king depends on the treasury or the treasury is the root of the state. The head of the treasury department was known as *Kosadhyaksa.* A large portion of the state revenue was collected in kind and the proper keeping and periodical renewal of the collected stock rendered the task of the treasury department in ancient India arduous. They insist on a full and flowing treasury for the state by appropriating a large portion of the state revenue for the creation of a reserve fund or treasury, which is not to be touched except on occasions of grave calamity. Provision had to be made against famines which necessitated the maintenance of the treasury and gold hoards. Richness of the treasury depended on the surplus of revenue over expenditure. The elaborate rules were laid down for the efficient accounting of public receipts and expenditure and their auditing. Sukra emphasizes the keeping of daily, monthly and annual accounts and the entering of the several items of income on the left side of the accounts and those of the expenditure on the right. Somadeva recommends the appointment of auditors when there is discrepancy in the items of income and expenditure.

Kautilya classifies that sources or items of revenue differently at different places. Two important classifications are *ayasarira* (body of income) and *ayamukha* (source of income), each being subdivided under seven heads. *Ayasarira,* which refers to the convenient centres of collection, comprises *durga* (fortified cities), *rastra* (rural areas), *khani* (mines), *setu* (irrigation works), *vana* (forests), *vraja* (herds) and *varipatha* (river borne trade routes). The *Bhaga* (royal share), *vyaji* (compensation), *parigha* (gate duty), *klpta* (fixed tax), *rupika* (premia on coins) and *aiyaya* (money fine) are the subdivisions of *ayamukha.* Another classification is *anyajata* (accidental revenue), *vartamana* (current revenue) and *paryusita* (outstanding revenue). Kamandaka enumerates eight principal categories *(astavarga)* of filling the treasury through the heads of departments, viz. agriculture, trade routes (both land and water), the capital, water embankments, catching of elephants, working mines and collecting gold etc., levying wealth (from the rich) and founding towns and villages in uninhabited tracts. The principal source of revenue in ancient India was taxation. In the financial theories of the *Arthasastra* and allied works, the ruler's right to levy taxes and contributions and the people's obligation to pay them arise from an implied contract between the state and its subjects. The principles that guided the state in matters of taxation show the solicitude of the economists for the welfare of the community. Taxation was to be reasonable and equitable and is the criterion of judging its equitableness consisted in the feeling of the state on the one hand and that of the agriculturists and the trades on the other, that they have received adequate and reasonable return for their mutual services. Any increase in taxation, if unavoidable, was to be gradual. Additional taxation was an exceptional measure to be resorted to only under grave national emergency in the absence of any other alternative. An article was to be taxed only once. Net profit and not gross earning was the basis for taxation of trade and industry.

Kautilya maintains resentment among his subjects and their possible migration to another country appears to have worked as a deterrent on kings taxing their subjects beyond their means. In a similar vein the *Mahabharata* states that "the Vaisyas, if neglected, would disappear from the kingdom and would reside in the forest". Yajnavalkya points out that the king who extracts taxes by unjust means not only loses his wealth but also goes to destruction along with his relatives. Religious beliefs as well as humanitarian ideas of the age were responsible for exempting from taxation certain classes of people like learned Brahmanas and Bhiksus. The dumb, the deaf, the blind, students studying in a Gurukula, and hermits were also not taxable. The infants, women or destitute, poor widows and people otherwise helpless were also tax free. Military villages were exempted from taxation. Untaxable property included articles required for sacrifice, earnings of craftsmanship, receipts from alms and articles worth less than a copper coin. Regarding the proportion of revenue to expenditure Sukra, one sixth of the income should go to saving and one half should be spent on the army; and one twelfth each of charity, ministers, inferior officials and the Privy Purse. The *Manasollasa* recommends that ordinarily three fourths of the revenue should be spent and one fourth should be saved. Megasthenes along with Kautilya's regulations indicate that this head of national defence absorbed a considerable portion of the revenue. The other items on the expenditure side answered the several obligations of a welfare state, which included the king's privy purse; his ministers and officers; police and other protective establishments for citizens, merchants and travellers; legal, judicial and punitive departments, granaries and *gosalas,* grants to local governments; roads and other equipment with bridges, rest houses, trees and watering places, ships and ferries; irrigation works; maintenance of mines, forests, forts, public factories, mints, store houses and palaces, religious and charitable endowments like temples, hospitals, schools and universities.

SRI MADBHAGVADGITA AND MODERN MANAGEMENT

The *Bhagavad-Gita* calls itself a *Yoga-sastra.* Yoga used in it is a positive expression. It connotes the positive aspect of *moksa,* as it means union with the Infinite. Its message is termed as *yoga,* the *avatara* who delivers the message is designated Yogesvara, and the ideal man to whom the preaching delivered is called a *yogin.* The word *Yoga* is not used in the *Gita* in any narrow or technical sense of thought control as in Patanjali's *Yoga-Sutra.* It is used here in its primary sense of union or fellowship with God. The *Gita* teaches the way of union or fellowship and that union has to be achieved through right effort, right devotion, and right knowledge. The *Bhagavad-Gita* knows limitations, nor rigid distinctions. It speaks also of *Buddhi-yoga*, *Dhyana-yoga* and *Sannyasa-yoga.* The discipline of our will and call is *Karma-yoga,* the discipline of our emotions and call is *Bhakti-yoga,* and the discipline of our understanding and call it *Jnana-yoga.* Spiritual life is a whole and it involves the direction of the whole mind, our will, our emotions and our understanding. The path of light begins with right discrimination, goes through obedience to the law and moral action and thence through self forgetting love and service and ends in spiritual freedom where the individual realizes that he is part and parcel of all the embracing spirit. The *Gita* treats *yoga,* which stands not only for the goal of spiritual life but also for the way leading to it, as one of exposition. They are only means to an end and the end is *yoga.* True *dharma* is that which is ever in vital connection with *yoga.* All rules of *dharma* are dissolved at last in the fruition of *yoga.* The *Gita* says, Surrendering all rules of *dharma,* come to me alone for shelter. Do not grieve. *Yoga* in the *Gita* involves and transcends *dharma,* as religious life involves and transcends moral life. It stands both for the way and for the goal.

Karma-yoga was regarded as the solvent of *karma bandha* or the so-called law of *Karma.* The *Gita* does not deny that *jnana* is a solvent, but reaffirms that *Karma-yoga* is also an equally efficient solvent. The whole *Gita* is a long and sustained protest against the dangers of quietism. In evolving its doctrine of *yoga* with its well-balanced emphasis on *karma, bhakti and jnana,* the *Gita* begins with the preliminary discipline of the mind, known as *Buddhi-yoga.* The *Gita* gives *buddhi* a very high place in its analysis of human personality. It says, 'The senses are said to be great, the mind is greater than the senses, and the understanding is greater than the mind, but greater than the understanding is He (the *Atman*)'. The *Buddhi* or understanding is thus next only to the *Atman* in man. The rational element is next only to the spiritual element. It is by exercising reasons fully, that a man can rise to the level of the spirit. It is a necessary for *Karma-yoga* and *Bhakti-yoga* as for *Jnana-yoga. Buddhi-yoga* implies equanimity or evenness of mind, and attitude of detachment, freedom from error or delusion and ability to rise above the mere letter of the law. It is the preliminary discipline of the mind indispensable to every kind of life – whether it is *Karma-yoga, Bhakti-yoga, Dhyana-yoga* or *Jnana-yoga.* The importance of *buddhi* is thrown by the distinction which the *Gita* seems to draw between *jnana* and *vijnana* i.e. between intellectual enlightenment and spiritual realization. Realization is never complete without the enlightenment of the understanding. *Jnana* is obviously connected with *buddhi.* The awakening of *buddhi* leads to *jnana,* as the awakening of the *Atman* leads to *vijnana* (Spiritual realization). It speaks of three types of *buddhi.* The understanding which, being enveloped in darkness, regards wrong as right and which reveres all values. Thus the great scripture has no patience with those who are intelligent but devilish in character. Without a disciplined mind, *Karma-yoga* would result only in rash action, *Bhakti-yoga* in superstitious worship, and *Jnana-yoga* in vague abstractions. The *Gita* is a theistic gospel and its object is not to bring to the feet of God a rash or a sentimental or an anemic soul but a fully integrated, dynamic soul.

Karma-yoga means performance of actions without caring for their fruits and the goal from the outside world to our own inward self it cares only for the spiritual value of actions and not for their material consequences. Because of it the chaos of our mental life is reduced to order and harmony. The *Gita* says, 'the resolute mind has a single aim; but the thoughts of the irresolute are manifold and endless.' The single aim not money making or pleasure seeking or anything of the kind. All the given conditions of life will then be looked upon as only machinery for shaping the soul. They are not at all ends in themselves, but only means to an end. There comes the realization that there is really no such thing as failure in life. When our aim will be something inward like the improvement of the self, there can be no failure whatsoever. For every righteous act or noble feeling or kind thought automatically exalts the soul, whatever may be its consequence in the outer world. Here success is in own hands and is not subject to chance, uncertainty, or fear. As the *Gita* says, 'In this no effort is ever lost and no harm is ever done; even a little of this law saves a man from great fear'.

With the realization that the kingdom of God is within us, to be traversed day by day with pure thoughts and noble deeds, one cease to expect too much from the world. If human beings would not work ceaselessly for improving the conditions of the society the evil will remain in the world for all time to come. Once the human being resolutely shift their aim inwards, it seems to touch the core of reality amidst a thousand transient things. Everything falls into its place. It is the beginning of a happiness which grows day by day'. The *yogin* begins to feel that experience, of which the scripture speaks so often. *Karma-yoga* does not mean that the *yogin* reaps no fruits. He reaps a hundredfold. Only they are the invisible fruits of the spirit, far more lasting and valuable than the tangible fruits of the world.

Karma-yoga is only the method of our work. It lays down only the manner in which one should discharge their duties. The *Gita* connects *svadharma* with *svabhava,* one's duties with one's nature. Better is one's own duty, though imperfectly done, than the duty of another done perfectly. He who does the duty imposed on him by his own nature incurs no sin. It is one of the remarkable features of the *Bhagavad-Gita* that strikes an extraordinarily modern note in its clear and unmistakable recognition of the influence of natural dispositions on the individuality of man. The almost overpowering influence of natural dispositions on of man indicated by classification of men into two types – the godly and the ungodly. The division is everywhere based on the three supposed fundamental qualities of Nature – *sattva, rajas and tamas.* Man thus belongs to two worlds – the natural world and the spiritual world. He has a body and a mind which belong to the former, and a soul which belongs to the latter. *Yoga* is not for him who eats too much, nor for him who eats too little. It is not for him, O Arjuna, who sleeps too much, nor for him who keeps vigil too long. But for the man who is temperate in his food recreation, who is restrained in all his actions, and who has regulated his sleep and vigils. The *yoga* puts an end to all sorrows.

The natural man should neither be indulged nor suppressed but wisely directed. The *Gita's* solution of the problem is contained in its doctrine of *svadharma*. *Svadharma* in its ultimate analysis means the law of one's own being. Every man has first of all, to be true to himself, to the law of his own being. He has to achieve the best, he is capable of by perfecting his own natural endowments and by making the most of the circumstances in which he is placed. It is only then that he will become an efficient member of society. An action which is not done with perfect, ease is not the best action. And an action which is really beyond one's capacity and which is undertaken only through ignorance and rashness is the worst. The *Gita* divides all actions into three classes. Under the first class come those actions which are organically related to the nature of the man who performs them; under the second, those which involve great strain and under the third, those which are undertaken by a man without regard to his own capacity and the consequences. The *Gita* says that one should discharge their duties, as a tree discharge its duty of putting forth flower and fruit with perfect ease and spontaneity. Man should play his part in the world consciously and voluntarily as animals and trees play their part in nature unconsciously and involuntarily. Therefore an ideal society is that in which all men are assigned the duties which they are most fitted to discharge, in which every man's *svadharma* is based on his *svabhava*. The *Gita* is holding that every person's individuality is sacred and precious and all that an educator has to do is to make every child, who is urtrusted to his care, discover his *svadharma* and allow him free play to develop along his own natural lines. It says that all our varied individualities find their fulfillment only in service to God.

The originality of the *Gita* is seen not only in the formulation of the doctrine of *Karma-yoga*, but also in the illustration of it in which God works in nature and in history. It accepts of *Isvara* Himself as a great *karma-yogin*. He makes nature to produce every day, every moment, innumerable forms of life. He makes the sun rise every morning and set every evening. He makes the wind to blow. He sends down rain and dew. He is seated in the hearts of all creatures, making them breathe, live, think, forget and remember. He works incessantly and selflessly not caring for the fruits of his action. The final step in the exposition of *Karma-yoga* taken by *Gita* is the supreme *karma-yogin*. He is eternally quiescent; and as *Isvara*, the Creator, Protector and Destroyer. He is always and everywhere active. The absolute emerges from the prism of time, space and causality as creator and a world of creatures. The *Gita* draws from the mystery of the divine being is that man also should reconcile within himself activity and rest. He should find rest in work and work in rest. He, who sees no work in work and work in no work is wise among men. He is a *yogin* and has accomplished all work. A wise man should work ceaselessly and yet remain unaffected by every moment the results of his work. This is possible only when he eradicates the notion that he is a separate, self with interests of his own and allows the universal spirit to work through him.

A man should give up not only the fruit of action, but also the agency of action, lies in the germ of *Bhakti-yoga*. The *Bhagavad-Gita* traverses the whole range of *bhakti* from the crudest kind of worship practiced by the ignorant to the highest kind of contemplation on the impersonal absolute, of which only the most advanced souls are capable. It's exposition of *Bhakti-yoga*, in of rituals, sacrifices, worship, surrender, meditation, contemplation and realization is original. Bhakti-yoga is a marvelous expansion of the various kinds of *upasanas*. The *avatara* of Krishna has become the highest ideal of love and beauty and the religion of love that he taught became so extensive and refined. In all ages and countries the heart of man longed for God, his love expressed itself through some kind of symbolism. When it is conceived as a place, the worshipper looks upon himself as a pilgrim on the way to it. When it is conceived as a person, various kinds of emotional relationship has been established between the worshipper and the worshipped. The human being accepts God as a master and look upon himself as a servant or he may think of him as a friend and look upon himself as a comrade. When the ultimate reality is conceived as a spirit either immanent or transcendent, the worshipper becomes either a seer or a thinker, and this gives rise to what has been called nature mysticism in one case and philosophical mysticism in the other. When the ultimate reality is conceived as a state of consciousness, the worshipper looks upon himself as a sleeper awakened. In the *Bhakti-sastras* of later days various conceptions of God are there and when he speaks of it's as a place, he uses the terms *loka, sthana, pada, gati and dhaman*, when accepted as a person the terms *Purusa, Isvara* etc are mentioned.

The intensive phase of *Bhakti-yoga* is called *Dhyana-yoga*. It consists of moments of intense rapture when the soul is lifted to the heights of the eternal being. The final stage in the path of light which leads to union with God is called *Jnana-yoga*. The word *janana*, is knowledge. It means, much more than ordinary knowledge. It comprises both knowing and being. The word *jnana* is also often used in other sense. It means metaphysical knowledge and not spiritual realization. The *Gita* explains to *jnana* a metaphysics as well as religious experience. *Jnana-yoga*, means not only knowledge of God but of his several manifestations, and also the realization of the soul's union with him. It includes also the experience of the mystic unity of all things.

There is a fundamental difference between the conception of God implied in *jnana* and that implied in *bhakti*. In the exercise of *bhakti* God has been accepted as a being, outside ourselves, possessing in perfection all those spiritual values. Human conceptions of justice, mercy, love, goodness, etc. are such poor things that it is ignoble to clothe the Supreme Being with them. Descriptions of *jnana* are the highest moral qualities mentioned, but also unswerving devotion to God. That is why the *Gita* speaks only of the two paths of *Karma-yoga* and *Jnana-yoga* and not of the three paths, of *karma, bhakti and jnana*. The unique feature of *jnana*, as taught in the *Gita* is that is never divorced from service to society. The teaching of the *Gita* is that starting with our natural endowments; that are is live in the material world doing duty to society in a spirit of detachment.

BUDDHIST ECONOMIC ETHICS

Buddhism

Gautama Buddha was born in 563 BC in Lumbini forest of Tarai region. His father Suddhodhan was chief of Shakya clan of Kapilvastu. At the age of 29 Gautama took *Mahabhinishkramana* (renunciation) to attain knowledge. At age of 35 he achieved *nirvana* (salvation) in Bodh Gaya. For next 45 years he wandered from place to place and delivered his discourses. His first discourse at Sarnath is known as *Dhammachakkpravartana* (turning the Wheel of Law) in which he deliver his message of *Chararyasatya* (four noble truth). He died in 483 BC at Kusinagar. Buddhism is widely popular religion today. In more than 25 countries of Asia, it has a enormous influence and in Europe and USA, it is the fastest growing religion.

Buddhism is a pragmatic teaching which starts from certain fundamental propositions. It teaches that it is possible to transcend this sorrow-laden world of experience and is concerned first and last with ways of achieving that transcendence.

Buddhism is a pragmatic teaching which starts from certain fundamental propositions. It teaches that it is possible to transcend this sorrow-laden world of experience and is concerned first and last with ways of achieving that transcendence. It uses ethics and meditation, philosophy and science, art and poetry to point a way to this Wisdom. In the past two hundred years society in the West has undergone in a more fundamental transformation than at any period since Neolithic times in terms of technology or the world of ideas. In the West it is creating problems and perceptions to which Buddhism seems particularly relevant. The historic task of Buddhists in both East and West in the twenty first century is to interpret perennial Buddhism in terms of the needs of industrial man and woman in the social conditions of their time, and to demonstrate its acute and urgent relevance to the ills of that society.

MIDDLE PATH: A GOLDEN WAY TO LIFE

Buddha's *Majjhimamarga*, (the middle path) is accepted as the golden mean of Aristotle. In his *Dhammachakkapravartana* at Sarnath he delivered his first sermon Chararyasatya or four noble truth. Buddha in his very first sermon recommended avoidance of extreme rigidities of life. He condemned the inordinate sacrifices and excessive rituals of Brahmanical religion as well as denounced rigrous practices of Jainism and Ajivikas. The four noble truths are:

(*i*) There is suffering (*dukkha*). It says that life is full of misery and pain. Poverty, disease, old age, death, selfishness, greed, anger, hatred, quarrels etc are the sufferings.

(*ii*) There is cause of suffering (*dukha-samudaya*). Buddha says that everything depend upon its causes. Everything in this world is conditioned and relative. Suffering must be based on cause.

(*iii*) There is a cessation of suffering (*dukha-nirodha*). If the cause being removed, the effect ceases to exist. Everything being conditional and relative is necessarily momentary and what is momentary must perish.

(*iv*) There is way leading to cessation of suffering *(dukkha nirodhagaminipratipat). This ethical path is known as the 'Noble Eight Fold Path (Astangikamarga).* It is also known as *Majjhimamarga* or middle path. It consists of eight steps. (1) Right Faith *(Samyak drshti)* (2) Right Resolve *(Samyaka Samkalpa)* (3) Right Speech *(Samyaka vak)* (4) Right Action *(Samyaka Kamma)* (5) Right Living *(Samyaka Ajiva)* (6) Right Effort *(Samyaka Vyayama)* (7) Right Thought *(Samyaka Smriti)* (8) Right Concentration *(Samyaka Samadhi).* Buddha says that this middle path leads to enlightenment and knowledge.

Buddhism rejoices the possibility of a true freedom as something inherent in human nature. For Buddhism, the ultimate freedom is to achieve full release from the root causes of all suffering: greed, hatred and delusion, which clearly are also the root causes of all social evils. Their grossest forms are those which are harmful to others. To weaken, and finally eliminate them in oneself and as far as possible, in society is the basis of Buddhist ethics. The experience of suffering is the starting point of Buddhist teaching and of any attempt to define a distinctively Buddhist social action. The Pali word *dukkha* arises from poverty, war, oppression and other social conditions.

This struggle may not be so desperate in certain countries which enjoy a high material standard of living spread relatively evenly throughout the population. Nevertheless, the material achievements of such societies appear somehow to have been 'bought' by social conditions which breed a profound sense of insecurity and anxiety, of restlessness and inner confusion. Lonely, alienated industrial man has unprecedented opportunities for living life in the context of equipment. He has a highly valued freedom to make meaning of his life from a huge variety of more or less readily available forms of consumption or achievement – whether career building, home making, shopping around for different world ideologies or dedicated social service. In developing countries to live thus, in the context of equipment, has become the great goal for increasing numbers. Thus, from the experience of social conditions there arises both physical and psychological suffering. But more fundamental still is that profound sense of unease, of anxiety which arises from the very transience (*anicca*) of life (*viparinama-dukkha*).

Buddhism offers to the individual human-being a religious practice, a way, leading to the transcendence of suffering. The secular humanistic activist sets himself towards the endless task of satisfying that desire, and perhaps hopes to end social suffering by constructing utopias. The Buddhism is concerned with the transformation of desire. He contemplates and experiences social action in a fundamentally different way from the secular activist. Through Buddhist realism does not believe in the Golden Age of a perfect society, or in the permanence of social conditions, yet Buddhism strongly believes that social imperfections can be reduced, by the reduction of greed, hatred and ignorance, and by compassionate action guided by wisdom. *"He, who has understanding and great wisdom does not think of harming himself or another, nor of harming both alike. He rather thinks of his own welfare, of that of others, of that of both, and of the welfare of the whole world. In that way one shows understanding and great wisdom".*

Human societies, too, suffer the round of birth and rebirth, of revolution and stability. Each age receives the collective *karmic* inheritance of the last and has been conditioned by it, and yet also struggles to refashion it. And within each human society, institutions, social classes and subcultures, as well as individuals, all struggle to establish their identity and perpetuate their existence. Capitalist industrial society has created conditions of extreme impermanence, and the struggle with a conflict-creating mood of dissatisfaction and frustration. In these conditions, egotistical enterprise, competitive conflict and the struggle for status become great social virtues, while, in fact, they illustrate the import of the three root-causes of suffering-greed, hatred, and delusion.

These cravings have become cemented into all forms of social structures and institutions. People who are relatively successful unaccumulating goods and social position, wish to ensure that they remain successful. They reward and encourage greed, selfishness, and exploitation rather than love, sharing and compassion. Certain people's life styles, characterized by greed and over-consumption, become dependent on the deprivation of the many. The present generations are living in this world under great pressure, under a very complicated system, amidst confusion. Everybody talks about peace, justice, equality but in practice it is very difficult. This is not because the individual person is bad but because the overall environment, the pressures, the circumstances are so strong, so influential. Buddhist social action simply concerned with relieving suffering; ultimately, in creating social conditions which will favour the ending of suffering through the individual achievement of transcendent wisdom.

Political power may manifest and sustain social and economic structures which breed both material deprivation and spiritual degradation for millions of men and women. In many parts of the world it oppresses a wide range of social groupings – national and racial minorities, women, the poor, homosexuals, liberal dissidents, and religious groups. Political power finds its most terrible expression in war, which reaches now to the possibility of global annihilation. For both, the oppressors and the oppressed, *karmic* delusion is deepened. Each group or nation emphasizes its differences, distinguishing them from its opponents; each projects, its own short comings upon them, makes them the repository of all evil, and rallies round its own vivid illusions and blood warming hates. Crowned with delusive idealism, it is an awesome and murderous folly. And even when victory is achieved, the victors are still more deeply poisoned by the hate that carried them to victory. Buddhism's "Three Fires" of delusion *(moha),* hatred and ill will *(dosa),* and greed and grasping *(lobha)* surely burn nowhere more fiercely. Otherwise political power may be used to fashion and sustain a society whose citizens are free to live in dignity and harmony and mutual respect, free of the degradation of poverty and war. In such a society of good heart all men and women find encouragement and support in making, if they will, the best use of their human condition in the practice of wisdom and compassion will came out. This is the land of good *karma,* not the end of human suffering, but the beginning of the end, the bodhisattva-land, the social embodiment of *sila*. Political action thus involves prejudice, power conflict, social oppression and social in justice. These social and political conflicts are the great public *sansaric* driving energies of our life to which an individual responds with both aggression and self repression. The Buddha Dharma offers the possibility of transmitting the energies of the individual into wisdom and compassion.

Buddhists are concerned with political action, firstly, in the direct relief of non-volitionally, caused suffering now and in the future, and, secondly, with the creation of social *karmic* conditions favourable to the following of the way that leads to the cessation of volitionally caused suffering and the creation of a society of a kind which tends to the ripening of wisdom and compassion rather than the withering of them. Evil springs from delusion and it takes the characteristic forms of hatred, aggression and driving acquisitiveness. In Buddhism the cultivation of *sila* (habitual morality) by attempting, to follow the precepts is an aspiration towards breaking this *karmic* cycle. It is a first step towards dissolving the egocentricity of headstrong willfulness, and cultivating heartfelt awareness of others. The *karmic* force of violent behavior will be affected by the circumstances in which it occurs. The great evil of violence is its separation into death of us and them, of my righteousness and your evil. If you counter violence with violence you will deepen that separation is through thoughts of bitterness and revenge. Buddhist non-violent social action *(avihimsa, ahimsa)* seeks to communicate, persuade and startle by moral example. *"One should conquer anger through kindness, wickedness through goodness, selfishness through charity and falsehood through truthfulness"*

Buddha intervened personally in the battle field as in the dispute between the Sakyas and Koliyas over the shares of the Rohini. Since that time, history has provided us with a host of examples of religiously inspired non-violent social action, skillfully adapted to particular situations. These are worthy of deep contemplation. Well known Mahatma Gandhi's non-violently struggle against religious intolerance against British rule in India, and also the Rev. Martin Luther King's black people's civil rights movement in the United States. Finally there is a type of situation in which the truly massive folly of the conflict and of the contrasting evils may leave nothing to work with and there is a space left only for personal sacrifice to bear witness to that folly. Such was the choice of the Buddhist monks who burnt themselves to death in the Vietnam war surely one of the most savage and despairing conflicts of modern times. The Buddhist with its compassion, its equanimity, its tolerance, its concern for self reliance and individual, responsibility is the most promising of all the models for the new Society. It helps people to overcome ego-centredness, through co-operation with others, in place of either subordination and exploitation or the consequent sense of righteous struggle against these things. It offers to each a freedom conditional only upon the freedom and dignity of others, so that individuals may develop a self reliant responsibility rather than being the conditioned animals of institutions. The emphasis should be on the undogmatic acceptance of a diversity of tolerably compatible material and mental ways, whether of individuals or of whole communities. There are no short cuts to utopia, whether by social engineering or theocracy. The good society should simply provide a means, and environment, in which different ways, appropriate to different kinds of people, may be cultivated in mutual tolerance and understanding. The good society will concern itself primarily with the material and non material production. Nothing wrong with material progress is provided to man to takes precedence over progress. The keynote of Buddhist economic is simplicity and non violence. From an economist's point of view, the marvel of the Buddhist way of life is the utter rationality of its pattern-amazingly small means leading to extraordinarily satisfying results. It suggests some kind of diverse and politically motivated society with co-operative management and ownership of productive wealth. It would be conceived on a humanity and complexity of organization or of environmental planning, and would use modern technology selectively rather than being used by it in the service of selfish interests. It is a question of finding the right path of development, the Middle Way, between materialist heedlessness and traditionalist immobility.

In the philosophy of the Buddha, an analytical study of ethical concepts and theories as well as positive recommendations to lead a way of life regarded as "the only way" *(ekayana magga)* for the attainment of the *summum bonum* or the highest Good. This way of life is considered both possible and desirable because man and the universe are just what they are. It is justified in the light of a realistic account of the nature of the universe and of man's place in it. While this way of life in its personal dimension, as it were, helps us attain the highest Good, it also has a social dimension insofar as it helps the achievement of the well being and happiness of the multitude or of mankind as a whole *(bahujanahita, bahujanasukha)*. The well being and happiness of mankind considered to be of supreme and this well being and happiness is conceived of as both material and spiritual welfare.

Buddhist ethics has a close connection with a social philosophy. This social philosophy is also fully developed. There is an account of the nature and functions of government, the form of the ideal social order and how it is likely to be brought about. The Dharmmapada says that *"Not to do any evil, to cultivate the good and to purify one's mind-this is the teaching of the Buddha"*. If all our present actions, choices and decisions were strictly determined by our psycho-physical constitution-which is partly hereditary, by our environmental influences, by our psychological past, or by all together-how is it possible for us to refrain from evil or do good? The very possibility of our reframing from evil and doing good, therefore, it depends on the fact that our choices and decisions are not strictly and wholly determined by such factors and in this sense are "free".

Our decisions, which result in right or wrong acts, make a difference to our nature and future. They have their own personal reactions in this life as well as in lives to come. These three facts, as often emphasized by the Buddha namely freedom *(kiriyavada)*, survival *(atthi paro loko)* and moral causation *(hetuvada)* make moral responsibility a reality and self development a practical possibility as well as a dire necessity. What we do by way of our mental, verbal and bodily acts makes a difference to our nature and regulates our future development. The *Dhammapada* says that *"By oneself alone is evil done and by oneself alone is one saved (lit purified). Salvation and damnation depend on oneself (paccattam) no one can save another"*. So the teaching of the Buddha can help us only if we decide to follow it: "You yourselves must make the effort," "the transcendent Ones are only teachers; those who follow the path and meditate are delivered from the bonds of Mara". This moral and spiritual development is not an unending process for its goal is *Nibbana,* the ultimate good or the ethical ideal according to Buddhism, a goal which may be achieved by some in this life itself.

According to Buddha, it is the motive and intention, which ought to be a primary determining the rightness or wrongness of an action. Mere good intentions are not enough. The act must be performed as well before we can say whether a right action has been done. Besides, for the action to be a skilful, the act itself must be appropriate. Viewing the individual and the social goods separately, a right action is, therefore, one which tends to bring about one's own ultimate good as well as contributes to the weal and welfare of society. The ten right actions *(dasa kusala kamma),* which have these characteristics are stated as follows: (1) He refrains from killing and full of mercy to all beings (2) He refrains, from stealing and is honest and pure of heart (3) He refrains from sexual misconduct and does not transgress the social mores *(csaritta)* (4) He refrains from lying and is devoted to truth. On being summoned as a witness before an assembly or a court of law, he claims to know what he knows, he does not claim to know what he does not know, he claims to have seen what he saw and does not claim to have seen what he did not see; he does not utter a conscious lie for the sake of himself, for the sake of others or for some gain (5) He refrains from slander and holds himself aloof from wrong doings. (6) He refrains from harsh speech and uses language that is civil and pleasant to hear (7) He refrains from idle gossip and speaks at the right time in accordance with facts, which is meaningful, righteous and in accordance with the law (8) He refrains from covetousness, does not covert another's property (9) He refrains from ill will (10) He refrains from holding false views and holds the right philosophy of life, believing in the reality of this world and the next.

Right actions are, therefore, which are instrumental in bringing about the ultimate good of one and all. Since happiness is one of the basic characteristics of this ultimate good, right actions are those which tend to promote the happiness of oneself as well as of others. But this happiness is not to be considered in isolation from moral perfection, realization or knowledge regarding the nature of things, emancipation of mind, perfect mental health. Another account of right actions from the standpoint of the individual ultimate good as the goal is the noble eight-fold path, consisting of right beliefs *(samma ditthi).* Right efforts *(samma vayama)* is involved in trying to give up false beliefs. In dispelling these wrong beliefs and consciously adopting right beliefs as a basis for action, one is led by right awareness *(samma sat).* The right beliefs, right effort and right awareness help in the cultivation of the other factors of the path. Thus, right beliefs help in the cultivation of right aspirations, which in turn promote right speech and right action. Right action is mades for a right mode of livelihood. This helps in right effort, which in turn further provide right awareness or right mindfulness, which results in right meditation until eventually they culminate in right understanding *(samma jnana)* and right emancipation *(samma vimutti).* So we see that right actions are right *(samma)* in being the efficient means for the realization of the good. Wrong the other hand, constitute those that prevent the realization of the goal on the part of oneself and others *(attavyabadhaya samvattati paravyabadhaya samvattati).*

Right motives are a necessary conditions of right action, they are included in the eight-fold path as right aspirations *(samma sankappa)*, so that all right actions could be defined as, what are instrumental in bringing about the ultimate good. Since right actions constitute a middle path *(majjhima patipada)* between two extremes, these extremes constitute wrong means for the attainment of the goal. The actions constituting them are, wrong actions. A set of wrong actions consists of causing pain to oneself *(attantapa)* or others *(parantapa)* or both. The ascetics who mortify the flesh, hunters, fowlers and robbers, who cause pain and suffering to others, kings who practice penance and burden their subjects with the performance of wasteful and cruel sacrifices, all fall into the category of people who do these wrong actions by causing pain to oneself, others or both.

In the other extreme are those who recommend free indulgence in one's desires, saying, for example "there is nothing wrong in indulgence in sensual pleasures" *(natthi kamesu doso)*. Buddha says, enjoy limited pleasures in the present but because of their failure to see that indulgence gives diminishing returns by way of pleasure and results in our becoming slaves to our undergo suffering . The Buddha says that those whose desires are strong are likely to achieve happiness in due course by restraining and curbing their desire in the present even at the cost of a little unhappiness. Right actions are right because they are based on a realistic understanding of man and nature, an awareness of the goal of human endeavour and of the correct means to realize. Their rightness is to be judged by the nature of their motivation as well as the nature of their consequences. These consequences may be psychological or social and experiencable in this life or in future lives. The desire for fame or happiness in this life or the desire to be born in a better state in the next life could provide the initial incentive for betterment. Buddha points, truth is not always pleasant and it is sometimes necessary to state unpleasant truths or remind ourselves of them in order to arouse others or emerge from our state of smug satisfaction. The mind, according to Buddhism, has a prior origin to our present human. Its judgement, as to the rightness or wrongness of our actions, is not to be ignored though it cannot always be trusted.

Buddhism, includes human actions not due to economic determinism or God's will. Economic factors, no doubt affect and condition human behavior. And according to the Buddhist philosophy of society, the economic factor constitutes one of the predominant factors (along with the ideological factor) in bringing about social change. It is not the only factor. Nor does it strictly determine human behavior. Hereditary, environmental and psychological factors condition man's actions according to the Buddhist account of conditioned genesis *(paticcasamuppada),* but still, man has within himself an element of initiative *(arabbha-dhatu)* or free will *(attakara),* by the exercise of which be can make decisions, which make the future (including his own) different from what it would otherwise be.

The factor of freedom, along with human survival after death, and the correlation between moral acts and consequences (the good acts tending to bring about pleasant consequences and the evil acts unpleasant consequences) make individual moral responsibility a reality. Without survival and this correspondence between acts and consequences a religious ethic promoting moral and spiritual development would be impossible. Buddhism gives a positive account of the ends, both social and psychological, worth attaining and of the means of attaining them. The Buddhist ethical theory is also based on its theory of reality. Buddhism says that since human freedom is a fact, along with such other facts as survival, *kamma* and *Nibbana,* moral propositions are significant. The ethical theory of Buddhism presupposes its theory of reality. But this theory of reality is independently established in the light of verifiable evidence. Obscure metaphysical presuppositions do not come into the picture. "It states that one should first try to better oneself before working for the general good." The *Dhammapada* states: "One should not, hinder one's own welfare at the cost of serving others; perceiving one's own welfare, one should devote oneself to the sake of the general good". The Buddha also recognized the fact that conventions differed in different countries or under different social systems. This was why he permitted that the minor rules of the order may be interpreted in different social and historical contexts, so moral conventions may differ from time to time or from country to country. As long as the general principles of morality were not violated, these variations in mores do not seriously alter the basic values observed. Relativism is recognized and not considered as undermining the objectivity of values. But, on the other hand, there could be "unrighteous epochs" or "unrighteous social orders" which in varying degrees violate the principles of morality, due to ignorance of the true nature and significance of moral values. Life is those social orders, which violate the principles of morality, would involve a greater degree of unhappiness according to the degree to which such principles have been violated. The Buddhist theory appears to be teleological rather then deontological. It determines the nature of right and wrong actions in terms of motives and consequences rather than, on the basis of their being done out of a sense of duty, regardless of consequences. This does not, mean that it ignores duties and consequences. Buddhist ethical theory considers it the fundamental duty of man to strive to attain the ultimate good and a persons who has attained it is seemed to have discharged all his obligations (*katakaraniya*).

Man in society has various duties to perform towards the various classes of people, with whom he is involved. The state, likewise, has certain duties to discharge towards its subjects, who are ultimately responsible for it. But all these duties become duties by virtue of the fact that they are the right actions, which promote the "welfare and happiness of the multitude" *(bahujanahitaya bahujanasukhaya),* Yet they, too, should be performed not out of a cold sense of duty but as far as possible out of a desire for selfless service, love (compassion) and understanding. This is not to deny that actions done with goodwill and with no expectation of reward are seemed to be better than those performed with the hope of egoistic rewards in this life or the life to come. Ultimately, the perfect persons act out of a spontaneous sense of selflessness, love and understanding and not out of any sense of duty or expectation of earthly reward or divine. So the ethical theory of Buddhism is one of ethical universalism, which recognizes the relativity and the subjective reactions regarding moral values without denying their objectivity, to be measure in terms of the motives with which the acts are done as well as their psychological, social and karmic consequences.

Man in society has various duties to perform towards the various classes of people, with whom he is involved. The state, likewise, has certain duties to discharge towards its subjects, who are ultimately responsible for it.

Ethical propositions are of various sorts. According to the Buddhist analysis, such propositions would have two components, a factual component and an emotive-prescriptive component. The factual component would be primary importance since the validity of ethical propositions would depend on the truth or falsity of the statements comprising this component. The emotive prescriptive component would only have a secondary significance. "*Nibbana* is the ultimate good", the factual component consists of a statement of the characteristics (such as supreme happiness, moral perfection, ultimate realization, utter freedom etc.), whose co-presence justifies the use of the epithet "the ultimate good" for *Nibbana*. However, stating the factual component does not exhaust the meaning of the word "good". There is an emotive prescriptive component. The Buddhist ethical theory gives a naturalistic analysis of ethical propositions, while asserting that such an analysis does not fully exhaust the meaning of ethical propositions, since they contain emotive prescriptive components as well.

Buddhism and Globalization

The term 'Globalization' has earned wide prominence because of growing interdependence of cultures and economies through increasing cross-cultural transactions in goods and services and rapid diffusion of technology. The cultural proximity and assimilation of cultural traits grow through globalization as ideas, spiritual values etc. reaching through trade, travel and media around the world at lightning speed. In cultural context the process of globalization encourages close contact and intermingling of people between various parts of globe with possible increasing personal exchange of ideas, mutual understanding and efforts to create the global village.

Buddhism has been instrumental to diffuse culture from one part of the world to another. Its spiritual ideas, manners, customs were transmitted from one region to other transgressing political boundaries.

Buddhism has been instrumental to diffuse culture from one part of the world to another. Its spiritual ideas, manners, customs were transmitted from one region to other transgressing political boundaries. It played influential role in integration of culture of different nationalities. During this process it adopted regional character because of group psychology of pre-conditioned tendencies and the native genius of the people. The sending of dharmma missionaries to different places in the Indian subcontinent and the other parts of Asia in order to propagate the message of Buddha in third century B.C. has been the most representative example of Buddhist globalization in historical perspect. Buddhism acted as social agency to cultivate the standard cultural pattern and virtues which are conducive to peace. It also preaches harmony and goodwill in the world unsettled and prone to outbursts of cruelty and violence. It is oriented to whole society i.e. *Bahujana*. In his first exhortation to the monks he enjoined them to propagate the welfare message amongst the masses. Buddhism is not a mere creedal faith but an ethical agency to set the standard of social behaviuor and virtues to encourage the peace and goodwill in the society. The aim of an ordained monk was to make efforts through teaching of Buddha to help the people. Buddha instructed the monks that 'Go forth, O bhikśus, on your wandering, for the welfare of the masses. Let not two of you should go the same way. Proclaim the dharmma which is beneficent at the beginning, beneficent in the middle and beneficent at the end for the divine and human.' Thus samgha became a spiritual preceptor, the personal counselor and the educator of the society with which it lived.

The globalization has also led to social and cultural crisis, poverty and powerlessness in some pocket of the world. It has eroded the traditional community structure and accelerated the depletion of natural resources. The third world economies have virtually succumbed to intensive consumerism mainly those produced by the transnational corporations. The people have been induced to abandon their traditional way of life and culture evolved over thousands of years and, was most suitable to their local conditions and environment. The labourers are compelled to sacrifice their services at low wages in the name of industrialization. The peasantry has been displaced for the sake of large infrastructure projects. The people are taught to compete and indulge in excessive consumerism which encourages greed, violence and delusion in the society. It is the globalization of tan.hā or craving. It may be craving for the gratification of passions or of eternity or for the success. The vast chunk of the population who are lured by the consumer oriented mercantilism will never have the means to acquire the commodities portrayed to them. So they consider themselves inferior and culturally backward. The globalization brings about certain groups of people who are not currently capable of coping with the increased competitive pressure to compete with the rest of the world. By economic hegemony the dominant nations control the political institutions and economy of the dependent nations who need their financial and economic support. Such bondage leads to enormous debts and erosion of traditional institution for the underdeveloped nations. The principle of interdependence may be a positive step aimed at curbing this deep rooted problem. It encourages the principle of equality and justice together with rule of law for all the nations. The paticca samuppada explains that 'every existing thing is both conditional and conditioning and that nothing can exist independently. Everything depends in some way or the other conditionally on one-another. It recognizes the existing reality of a thing, a person or a nation. It always tends to make a greatly united world in which all the people regardless of nation, religion, culture etc. can co-exist and live independently and harmoniously. In the context of globalization the interdependence also means that whatever principles, policies and actions taken should have positive impact. The Buddhist teaching of non-discrimination and equality are related to this understanding. It recognizes the complexity of causation that produces conflicts and suffering and clarifies the issues that leads to reconciliation and solution to the problems. The mindset of Buddha was to establish equalitarian ethos which could cut across the tribalism and the distinction of race or religion He asserts that 'lineage does not enter into man's being either good or bad, nor do good look or wealth.' It provides a new way of thinking for current situation and act as potential and competent force for the process of globalization to cope with international competitiveness and challenges to meet global demand as well as develop co-operative working environment.

The Buddhist ideals constantly put forth the society are reasoning, moderation, and harmony, a constant awareness of the primacy of Buddhist teaching, charity as a way of life, compassion and wisdom. The society is conceived as universal and distinguished from discriminating society. It is a community of righteousness anywhere and everywhere uncensored by the rules of regional or national affiliation. It is on vissāsa (mutual trust and co-operation in place of conflict and acquisitiveness), ahasa (non-violence), samata (equality of all human beings) etc. In the era of globalization people are becoming more aware about the rights and privileges. Because of mutual hostilities and competition there is growing sense of deprivation, intolerance, aggression, revenge etc. Buddhism can play an optimistic role in keeping the direction of the globalization in such a way that it helps to maintain and protect the cultural identity of a nation, at the same time revolutionizing the system in terms of globalization. The society is preoccupied with the things that leads to strife, exploitation and imbalance. Buddhism has no place for poverty and exploitation and has to adjust with the harsh reality of the society with moderation. Buddhism tries to enhance appreciation of life and overall improvement. Buddha says that who does not wish for his own prosperity by unfair means is wise, virtuous and religious. The ideal society envisaged by Buddha is in which the state has responsibility to wipe out discrimination and ensure the full employment for all sections of society. It repudiates vision of future based on the notion of progress as an unlimited growth leading eventually to destructive consumerism and strives for a just world order which will end hegemony and all other forms of hostilities. The person who carries out his purpose by violence is not a right person. Those who know the advantage and disadvantage of their doings are wise. The role of dharmma is to act as custodian of moral and cultural values and to be all pervasive force. The growing economic, interdependence, increased cultural reciprocation, rapid advancement in information technology and geo-political challenges are binding people and bio-sphere more tightly in a single global system. This process also sprouts differences everywhere fuelled by regional, ethnic diversity and disparities. The ideological and religious conflict is taking heavy toll on human lives. The dharmma preaches that greediness is the worst disease and the contentment is the greatest wealth and trust is best relationship. It gives the notion of desirability of evolving a culture prelude to modern social, economic and administrative institutions and formulates the most consistent theory of human suffering known to mankind. It ridicules an unbridled materialism and mundane passions.

In the age of globalization, development will have to be defined in cultural and ethical terms and not merely in terms of material wealth. The people's participation will require decentralization of power, distributive justice, egalitarian ethos and material security. The underdevelopment within a nation is characterized not only by the production of pseudo-use values and non use values but also by mal-distribution of genuine use values. Their over-consumption by the privileged class goes hand in hand with their under consumption by the masses. The materialism is engulfing each and every society of the world and is eroding their vibrant cultural values. In the present globalize world, to gain wealth, power and to fulfill the insatiable sensual pleasure through undesirable means are becoming the most domineering values. The people are obsessed with packaged food and standardized products sponsored by transnational organizations, especially the younger generation of eastern nation is more addicted to western variety of foods like hamburger, pizza and unhealthy soft drinks in place of traditional healthy and hygienic food products. The food items are now not preferred by their intrinsic value of nutrition but on basis of their multinational logo and advertisements. The sustainable and traditional patterns are fast changing. In the east, the traditional joint family structure is on the verge of collapse and the nuclear family structure is becoming the norm of the society. The monoculture of globalization has been promoting a system totally at odd with the existing values of the traditional societies. It encourages to negative direction of karma leading to unemployment, disintegration of traditional family and community structure and imbalance in ecosphere. When the society is facing such kind of difficulties motivated by unwholesome and evil roots, it will loose the healthy structure and will not be able to survive. Buddhism states such implications. The monks are sometimes entrusted to interfere with states activities for just cause. The approval and disapproval of their policies was to articulate the voice of the people and has considerable impact on state policies. In Sri Lanka when any state policy went wrong the monk could seek protest with the act of 'turning down the bowl'. Even in recent Thawang visit of venerable Dalai Lama the monks protested against China by the turning the bowl act. The economic growth of a nation depends upon economic efforts or their people and each country has its own history, religion and tradition. Any economic development scheme cannot be planned without paying attention due this factors. A nation has to make a serious effort to carve out both an alternative vision of the modern society and an indigenous path leading to it. In India and China much of these traditional knowledge and expertise have been lost in the name of modernity and science, depriving common people everywhere of help in the time of need. Recently China has restored her traditional expertise with the help of a genuine scientific attitude. The commentarial and exegetic literature of. Buddhist apologetics are helpful in this rectification. Buddhist in China is not a replica of Indian Buddhism but it was developed in the trends of Chinese mind so it is a signified Buddhism. It helped China to globalize its economy. The laughing Buddha, Chinese martial art and paintings etc. are common features of European and American societies. Buddhism is a popular subject of Hollywood movies. The Hollywood actor Richard Gere not only became an ardent follower of Buddhism but also a brand ambassador to spread the message of Buddha in Europe and America.

The idea put forward by Buddhism before the society is of general applicability cutting across the divisive tendencies and provide social adhesive to fuse the diverse ethnic cultural elements into harmonious social groups based on certain homogeneous and egalitarian principles. Buddhism considers the society as universal and distinguished and brings in the vision of an alternative society. Its functions are not like a religion, but like a social agency and preaches goodwill and harmony. The dhamma says:.

"Making the money like the bee
Who does not harm the flower
Such a man makes his pile
As an ant-hill gradually;
The man grows healthy,
Thus, can help his family,
And firmly binds his friends to himself"

So the role of Buddhism in era of globalization is the custodian of values of society that led to co-existence, harmony and peace. It boosts refinement and moderation in life and sets aside the brutalities and hostilities away from the nations and the people.

JAINISM AND ITS ECONOMIC VALUES

Jainism

Jainism is supposed to be one of the earliest religions of India. Tradition says that it was founded in the Indus Valley civilization. The movement was in reality started by Parsvanath, in the twenty third *tirthankara* who was born in 9th century BC in Kasi. He first propounded the *Chaturyama* principle i.e. *Satya, Ahimsa, Asteya and Aparigraha.* But the real expansion of Jainism was laid by Vardhamana Mahavira. He was born in 540 BC in Vaishali. He attained *Kaivalya* (salvation) at age of 43 and popularised Jainism in north India. He added fifth principle of celibacy (Brahmacharya) in the *Chaturyama* of Parsvanath.

The *sastras* that form the fundamental basis of Jainism are based on the teaching of Parsva and Mahavira. Their teaching was first imparted to *ganadharas,* who were the chief disciples of *jina* or *tirthankaras.* According to Jainism, then, everything that there is, was, or ever will be, has been classified as either animate *(jiva)* or inanimate *(ajiva)* and has been defined as that in which there is Origination, Destruction and Permanence. This division of the universe, according to the Jaina metaphysics, into two everlasting, uncreated, coexisting but independent categories – the living *(jiva)* – also used to connote life, vitality, soul or *consciousness,* non living *(ajiva)* – is, according to the Jainas, a perfect division. The *ajiva* is further divided into *dharma, adharma, akasa, pudgala* and to these some also add *kala.* The *jiva* or the soul, except in its final state of liberation *(kaivalya)* has been always in combination with *ajiva,* and thereby brings into existence a kind of energy which is known as *karma* and which cannot conduce to freedom, perfection or peace. These *karmas* or deeds of the soul, beginningless time. The natural qualities of the soul are thus more or less obscured and consequently various conditions of weal *(punya)* and woe *(papa)* are experienced.

Anuvrata of Jainism – A Global Ethic

The Jaina *Samgha* consists of Bhikshus, Bhikshunis and Lay followers. Here the monks lay followers are organically connected and the difference in them is only of degree and not of kind. There is only one fivefold spiritual discipline of Jainism. In case of monkhood it is extremely strict and puritanic, while in the case of lay life it is modified. The five vows monks are called 'Great Vows' *(Maha-Vrata),* while those of laity are called 'Small Vows' *(anu-vrata).* These five vows are (1) *Ahinsa* or non-injury in thought word and deed (2) *Satya* or truth in thought and deed (3) *Asteya* or not to steal i.e. not to adopt it in thought and deed (4) *Brahmacharya* i.e. abstention from self indulgence by thought, speak or action (5) *Aparigraha* i.e. non possession of material wealth. In case of monks three rules are to be followed in a rigrous way but in the case of lay followers these rules are moderated such as *Brahmacharya* is restricted as chastity and *Aparigraha* as contentment. The *Aparigraha* has been accepted as role model for trader community to earn and thrive. It does not stop the earning but restrict the saving up to some extent. So by help of *Aparigraha* flow of money could be maintained in the market. Similarly by following the Jains Creeds the disparities between developed and developing would be minimized.

In *punya* include those matters that are connected with the soul and are the result of good and virtuous actions. Those that are contradictory to these are called *papas. Punya* is the meritorious kind of *karma,* while *papa* is the sinful kind of it. When the soul is thus striving under such auspicious *(subha)* and inauspicious *(asubha) karmas* it is helped by the activity of the mind, speech and body, which fact either helps the inflow of such *karmic* matter and thereby the soul gets bound to them, or acts as a bar to it. It is here that we get *asrava, samvara* and *bandha.* The activity of the mind, speech and body which makes the inflow of *karmic* matter into the soul possible is technically called *asrava,* while the same sort of activity which acts as a bar to such an inflow is called *samvara.* The actual investing of the soul by this matter is called *bandha.* Thus according to the Jaina it is we who are responsible for our own condition. In whatever degree we are ignorant, in pain, unhappy, unkind, cruel or weak, it is because, since birth and even previously in the infinite past, we are and have been acquiring and incorporating into ourselves *(asrava, bandha)* – by the attraction and assimilation of subtle, unseen, though real physical matter *(pudgala)* – energies *(karma)* which clog the natural wisdom, knowledge, blissfulness, love, compassion and strength of the soul, and which excite to unnatural action.

The Jaina *sastras* say that by means of a strict religious life and austerities all these *karmas* can be destroyed, and the soul can ultimately achieve its natural state in *moksa.* Thus the purging of the *karmas,* or rather their destruction is called *nirjara,* and the utter annihilation of all *karmas* or the complete freedom of the soul from *karmic* matter is called *kaivalya.* Thus *nirjara* is possible by a change in the soul or by reaping the effects of *karmas,* or by penances before their time of fruition. *Jiva,* deluded by the *karmic* forces, experiences ignorance, misery and wretchedness in this world. Such a revolving of *jiva* in this phenomenal world is called *samsara,* and to get free from this *samsara,* which is the result of the delusion of the soul, is to achieve *moksa,* or final emancipation. *Moksa* is a state in which the soul is quite free from all karmic forces. *Karmas* are like clouds to it, and when it gets absolved from them perfectly pure spirit shines with all its luster, like the open sun, and this is *moksa.* When *kaivalya* is achieved the pure and free *atma* gets to its own natural state, liberated from the material body and its veils. The way to *kaivalya* is naturally revealed by *jina.* It lies through the *ratnatraya,* or "The Three Jewels" of *samyak-darsana* (right belief), *samyak-jnana* (right knowledge) and *samyak-caritra* (right conduct).

Samyak-darsana wants to achieve is that "instead of being blinded by cold logic and cunning sophistry, or eaten away by the corrosion of skepticism, it may grow into the tree of knowledge and fructify into the world blessing fruit of righteous conduct". Right knowledge enable to examine in detail all that the mind has inculcated through convictions. In short it gives a right and clear insight into the same *tattvas.* Right conduct consists in the strict observance of all the precepts laid down by *jina,* through which *nirvana* is attained. In practical life this practice of right conduct is divided into two broad divisions: *sadhu-charitra,* or the conduct of a *sadhu* and *grhastha-charitra* or the conduct of a layman. On the whole the rigour of Jaina discipline anticipates a great amount of strength of will and character.

Beginning with the five great vows of non killing *(ahimsa)*, truth *(satya)*, non stealing *(asteya)*, chastity *(brahmacharya)* and non attachment *(aparigraha)* and the three-fold restraint of the mind, speech and body Jaina discipline goes to the final stage of a man's spiritual career when he desires neither life nor death and when he may take up the vow of *anasana*, which in a stricter sense means "fasting which precedes and ends with death".

Once the soul, overpowered with the four *kasayas* (passions) – anger, vanity, intrigue and greed – and the senses, and perforce kept away from its natural state by good and bad energies called *karmas,* gets free from all such obstructive and foreign forces, it is said to enjoy all the attributes of God. *Tirthankara* is a peculiar term of Jainism. *Tirthankara* is he who sheds spiritual rays which bathe the ocean of this phenomenal world in a pure light, and it is through this that one is enabled to reach the heights of spiritual well-being. These *tirthankaras,* by endowing fresh vigour, and giving new light and revival to *dharma,* bless the world. There were twenty four *thirthankaras* life to the Jainas is governed by the immutable law of cause and effect. Not only is man endowed with *jiva* but also all creatures, including plants, animals, birds, insects and even atomic and invisible beings, like the smallest particles of the elements of the earth, the fire, the water and the wind are endowed with the soul *(jiva).* According to the Jainas life in all its forms is sacred and as it moves towards the same goal it is not to be disturbed or disintegrated any kind of violence. This is the rationale underlying the most dominating characteristic of Jainism i.e. the principle of *ahimsa.*

To a *mank* he must carry three articles with him – a straining cloth for his drinking water, a broom and a veil before his mouth lest he might unconsciously swallow or crush any invisible animalcule. A layman also observes so many precautions in daily life; but something which is rather striking is not to eat and, if possible, not to drink after sunset, that he might not swallow insects through mistake. The Jaina *ahimsa* is not the *ahimsa* of a weak but that of a brave soul which is or wants to be above all the evil forces of this world. *Himsa* or injury to a certain extent is inevitable in human life and hence a daily confession and a day to day consciousness of sins or wrongs committed during the course of the day is a necessity for the ultimate goal to be achieved. *Samayika* and *pratikramana,* the two disciplines which have directly resulted from it, play a very important part in the lives of both the clergy and the laity.

Samayika follows take vow that he will renounce all sinful activities. Till he live, with mind, speech and body, neither will he do nor will he make others to do them. That (sin) O Lord! he will revert from them; he will condemn them in the presence of my spirit and preceptor and he will vow to keep my soul free from such actions. The vow of *samayika* who has attained the attitude of equality which makes him look at all kinds of living beings as he looks towards himself. *Padikamanum,* or Sanskrit *pratikramana,* is a frank confession of sins and sincere desire for their forgiveness. It is repentance for faults that already attach to the soul. When engaging in *pratikramana – i.e. confession* the *Jainas* think of the sins that they may have committed against any being possessing any *indriya* and ask forgiveness. This is the natural outcome of a teaching that encourages civic and philanthropic virtues born out of the principle of *ahimsa,* which in its active form means helping humanity.

Doctrine of *syadvada* or *anekantavada* of the Jainas or the doctrine of *nayas* standpoints a peculiar feature of the Jaina logic. Jaina metaphysics starts with a dualistic division of the universe into *jiva* and *ajiva,* and that in them lies the *tripadi* of *utpada, Vyaya and dhruva,* respectively meaning Origination, Destruction and Permanence. Here origination means no new creation, because to the Jaina mind the whole universe of being has existed from all eternity. *Guna* of origination *(utpada)* is just to show that in a permanent universe, meaning having no origin. There is always origination of its modes of manifestations. Thus everything that is *sat,* or the conception of being is neither the absolutely unchangeable, nor the momentary changing qualities or existences, but involves them both. This is the theory of indefiniteness *(anekantavada).*

The innumerable qualities of a thing cannot be predicted in one statement, but they are all implied by any statement which predicates one of the qualities of a thing. Everything has to be considered in four different aspects: the matter *(dravya),* space *(khsetra),* time *(kala),* and nature *(bhava).* The doctrine of *syadvada* holds that since the most contrary characteristics of infinite variety may be associated with a thing, affirmation, made from whatever standpoint *(naya),* cannot be regarded as absolute. It is the method of knowing or speaking of a thing synthetically. *Syadvada* it the science of "the assertion of alternative possibilities". The *syadvada* doctrine is not a doctrine of doubt. It enables a man to look at things with a wide and liberal view. It teaches us how and in what manner to look at things of this universe. The dynamic character of reality consists only with relative or conditional predication. It does not deny the possibility of predication. It is the use in seven different ways of judgment which affirm and negate, severally and jointly without self contradiction, thus discriminating the several qualities. Answering the seven questions from the seven points of view is called *saptabhangi-naya,* or pluralistic arguments.

The various possibilities were classed under seven neads *(sapta-bhangi)* each beginning with the word *syat,* which is combined with one or more of these terms: *asti* (is), *nasty* (is not), and *avaktavya* (cannot be expressed). Thus you can affirm existence of a thing from one point of view *(syat-asti),* deny it from another *(syat-nasti),* and affirm both existence and non existence with reference to it at different times *(syatasti-nasti).* The thing cannot be spoken of *(syat-avaktavyah).* Similarly, under certain circumstances, the affirmation of existence is not possible *(syat-asti-avaktavyah)* and also both *(syat-asti-nasti-avaktavyah).* What is meant by these seven modes is that a thing should not be considered as existing everywhere at all times, in all ways and in the form of everything. It may exist in one place and not in another and at one time and not at another. *Syadvada* is a unique feature of the Jaina philosophy. *Syadvada may* be described as the central and unique feature of Jaina metaphysics. Mahavira's ideals were lofty and holy and that his message of equality of mankind and all living beings proclaimed to the caste stricken and *yajna* ridden people of India was large hearted and benevolent.

KAUTILYA'S ECONOMIC VIEW

Kautilya was born in fourth century B.C. After completion of his study he was appointed as Chancellor of Takshsila University. Here he trained Chandra Gupta Maurya in ethics and warfare Chandra Gupta Maurya was instrumental in deposing the last Nanda king Dhanananda. After accession of Chandragupta Maurya, Kautilya or Chankywa was appointed as Prime Minister of Magadha. In Magadha he evolved the state policies and its pragmatic theories. His policies are elaborated in his book *'Arthasastra'*. The original manuscript of *Arthasastra* was discovered in 1909 by R. Samsastri, who also translated it. This book is on polity and discovers the various constitutions of state especially *Mandala* and *Saptanga* theories. The another name of Kautilya's is Vishnu Gupta.

The *Arthasastra* comprise the art of government. The list comprises the branches of internal and foreign administration, civil and criminal law as well as the art of warfare.

The *Arthasastra* comprise the art of government. The list comprises the branches of internal and foreign administration, civil and criminal law as well as the art of warfare. It been discovered from the oblivion of centuries by the fortunate discovery of a complete manuscript of the work and its publication by R. Shama Sastry in 1908. The discussions of *Arthasastra* centred in the first place upon a few basic concepts and categories. Such are the categories of the seven constituents of the state (saptang), the four traditional sciences *(vidyas)*, the four political expedients *(upayas)*, and the six types of foreign policy *(gunas)* as well as the concepts of the state system *(mandala)* and the king's coercive authority *(danda)*.

Kautilya mention that a king's provision of security and prosperity *(yoga-khsema)* for his own people by the technical term *tantra*, and his arrangement for keeping watch over the neighbouring rulers is expressed by another technical term *avapa*. The *tantra* portion comprising the first five Books *(adhikaranas)*, which are divided into ninety four subsection *(prakaranas)* and the *avapa* portion consisting of the next nine books, which are divided into eighty four subsections. The book consisting of a single *prakarana* may be regarded as somewhat outside the two divisions of *tantra* and *avapa*. The book one deals with the discipline and education of a king. He must be conversant with the knowledge of all the four *vidyas* (branches of learning), i.e. *anviksiki* (metaphysics), *trayi* (the three Vedas, of course, including the fourth or *Atharva-Veda*, and also the Itihasa Veda and the six Vedangas), *varta* (signifying pastoral pursuits, trade, industry and commerce, i.e. economics), and *dandaniti* (the science of polity or government).

Kautilya states that a king who is severe in repression becomes a terror to his people, and one who is mild in the award of punishment is treated by them with contempt, while he who awards punishment as deserved is respected. It must not be awarded wrongly nor allowed to remain in abeyance otherwise it will produce the condition of *matsya-nyaya* or anarchy. The king is trained to control the six internal enemies, viz. lust, anger, greed, vanity, arrogance and jealousy. Kautilya next discusses the institution of ministership, their appointment according to their requisite qualifications and the test of their honesty and loyalty by a method called *upadha* (allurement). The *buddhisacivas* or *matisacivas, i.e. mantrins* (counselors and policy-makers) are appointed after various tents.

In matters of grave importance, Kautilya continues all the *buddhisacivas* and *karmasacivas* should be convened together in a joint session and the king should do what the majority decides. Kautilya's statecraft is mainly based on an efficient system of espionage, the two main groups being the *samsthas* and the *sancharins,* the operation of the former being chiefly static and that of the latter mostly dynamic. The high state functionaries, including even the *mantrins,* were subject to their vigilance. The most interesting type of spies is the one called *ubhayavetana,* who was allowed by his own king to accept surreptitiously salary from his enemy, while engaged in collecting information about the latter's kingdom. Kautilya describe how a king should deal both with the groups of discontented, factious, ambitious, haughty, alarmed and provoked persons in his own and the enemy's kingdom. Kautilya advises the king to leave aside the wicked and untrained princes and to appoint instead of them a prince, whether or not the eldest, possessing the requisite princely virtues to the office of the commander-in-chief or of the heir-apparent.

The *Arthasastra* directs that the king must at once attend to all urgent calls of business and not put them off. Readiness for action is described as a religious vow for a king and the root of all royal business is his enterprise. The king is advised to arrange for storage of all kinds of oils, grains, sugar, salt, medicines, dry vegetables, fodder, dry fish, hay-stacks, firewood, metals, skins, charcoal, tendons, poison, horns,bamboo, barks of trees, strong timber, weapons, and armour which may last for many years. The Chief Treasury Officer *(sannidhata)* has charge of treasuries, warehouses, storehouses, godowns, arsenals and prisons. The Chief revenue Officer *(samaharta)* deals with the collection of revenue from the seven sources, viz. (1) forts and fortified towns (2) the countryside (3) mines (4) cultivated fields and flower and fruit gardens (5) forests (6) pens of domestic animals and (7) traffic-routes. The king is directed by Kautilya to examine constantly the character of all departmental heads *(adhyaksas)* and their subordinates, such as accountants *(samkhyayaka),* writers or clerks *(lekhaka)* and coin examiners *(rupa darsaka).* It is further laid down that no chief officer should be allowed to hold his office permanently. Kautilya prescribes measures against corruption. Trade in salt being a State monopoly, imported salt is highly taxed in Kautilya's system and adulteration of salt is punishable.

Dharmasthiya of the *Arthasastra* deals with the branch of civil law. The king is regarded as the final authority in judicial matters. He is assisted in arriving at legal decisions by a triad of judges *(dharmasthas),* who actually try lawsuits in the company of some specialists in legal sastras *(vyavahara).* The author describes the legal processes regarding statements of the plaintiffs and rejoinders of the respondents. The heads of law relate to marriage the question of proper and improper marital relations, widow remarriage, remarriage of males, dowry, divorce, etc. inheritance and partition of ancestral property. *Kantaka-sodhana* (removal of thorns or anti-social elements), deals with a number of miscellaneous topics. Those relate to public protection against deceitful and fraudulent artisans and merchants penalty for manufacturing counterfeit coins and for disturbing the currency fraud in respect of weights and measures remedies against providential calamities e.g. fire, flood, epidemics and famine protection from the acts of evil-doers living by secret and foul ways, seizure of criminals on suspicion, along with the stolen property or in the act of theft, *post mortem* examination in the case of sudden deaths, eliciting confession from suspects by questionings or physical tortures. The high functionaries who try criminal cases are called *pradestas.*

Reference is then made to the six political expedients *(gunas),* viz. peace *(sandhi),* war *(vigraha),* expedition *(yana),* neutrality or halt *(asana),* dubious attitude *(dvaidhibhava),* i.e. peacewith one and war with another and alliance *(samsraya).* According to Kautilya if a king deals carefully or doubtfully or carelessly with these expedients, he attains the condition of augmentation *(vrddhi),* stagnation *(sthana)* or deterioration *(ksaya)* of his dominion. He defines the twelve constitutents of the circle of states *(mandala),* viz. the *vijigisu* or the would be conqueror (in the centre), his immediate neighbor regarded as an enemy, he would be conqueror's friend, the enemy's friend, the friend's friend, and the enemy's friend's friend (the last five being in front), the rearward enemy, the rearward friend, the ally of rearward enemy, and the ally of rearward friend (the last four being in the rear), the mediatory king and the most powerful neutral king. Kautilya defines the three kinds of power *(sakti)* of a king, namely the power of deliberation, the power due to treasury and the army and the power of energy and their corresponding successes.

Proper utilization of the six political expedients in the field of diplomacy is discussed in Book Seven of *Arthasastra.* A king should always prefer peace to war in consideration of the immense disadvantages involved in waging war against an enemy for war leads to wastage of human life, enormous expenses of money, so journing in distant and strange lands, perpetration of cruel act. In case the *vijigisu* feels himself inferior to his enemy, he should try to enter into any one of the various *sandhis* described in this treatise. A king may march against an enemy in combination with his allies of superior, equal or inferior status by agreeing upon his share of the spoils of war. The destruction of an enemy must be undertaken in an open fight even at a heavy loss of men and money remove internal troubles caused by the *amatya* (minister), the king should keep the treasury and the army under his own control. Want of proper education and discipline is the cause of a king's vices due to anger and passion. The king is to guard against and provide for providential calamities, such as fire, flood, epidemics and pestilence. A king is advised by Kautilya to avert financial troubles in the interest of the prosperity of his people. The proper time for the enlistment of the six kinds of infantry: hereditary troops, mercenary troops.

Kautilya thinks that though the Kshatriya army is better than the Brahmana one, which can be won over by prostration, the Vaisya and Sudra armies consist of very virile men and they can be obtained in larger numbers. Kautilya is of opinion that success eludes the fool who consults the stars too much. The king should protect his own army by all possible means during its march through difficult and dangerous paths, the soldiers being required to be looked after when afflicted by disease and pestilence or in any other emergency. Economic guilds and political corporations in the shape of tribal republics, both being called by the generic title of *sangha.* The king is advised to acquire military aid from these *sanghas* since they are invincible on account of their corporate unity. Twelve describes the various Machiavellian contrivances which a weak *vijigisu should* use in fighting against a stronger one. The battle of intrigue is to be adopted by the weaker king against the stronger invader by producing internal disturbances through the agency of spies. Secret methods are to be applied against the high state functionaries, princes and chief army officers of the aggressor. Destruction of his stores and granaries is also recommended. The weak *vijigisu* may encompass the death of his enemy when entering the precincts of a temple for offering worship. How a *vijigisu* should sow seeds of dissension in the enemy's country before attempting to seize it, how in that act he should strive to enthuse his own men and frighten the men of his enemy by the proclamation of his own omniscience and his association with divinities.

The new conqueror should enjoy the fruits of his conquest by following the duties prescribed for a king and seeing that the proper division of castes *(varnas)* and stages of life *(asramas)* is strictly adhered to by the people. He should bestow favours, remit dues, distribute gifts and confer honours on the people conquered. A new conqueror should adopt the same mode of life, dress, language and customs as those of the conquered people. Kautilya deals with certain recipes for the destruction of a king's enemies and for causing in them blindness, insanity and various kinds of bodily diseases and deformities. Among these delusive devices are found certain medical formulas for making a man invisible to his enemies and providing him with the power of vision in night's darkness. Incantations are to be uttered for causing men and animals to fall. Remedies are to be used against the application of poisons and poisonous drugs by the enemy to the king's own troops. The *Arthasastra* is defined by the author as 'the science which treats of the means of acquiring and ruling the earth'. The word *kosa* denote the wealth of the state. From wealth *(kosa)* comes the power of the Government *(danda)*. With the treasury and the army *(kosadanda)* the earth is acquired with the treasury as the ornament. Kautilya cautions the king that he should always keep the army and treasury under his own control. The following are the means of increasing the wealth of the state:

- Ensuring the prosperity of state activities
- Continuing well tried policies
- Eliminating theft and other social evils
- Keeping strict control over government employees
- Increasing agricultural production
- Promoting trade and commerce
- Avoiding troubles and calamities
- Reducing (tax) exemptions and remissions
- Increasing cash income

Kautilya's Financial Measures

The *Arthasastra* gives a classified list of income sources, revenue from Crown enterprises, taxes and tolls, service charges and fines. Sometimes apart from the treasury where precious metals and jewellery were stored and coins minted, the wealth of the state

The *Arthasastra* gives a classified list of income sources, revenue from Crown enterprises, taxes and tolls, service charges and fines.

was kept in the commodity warehouses granaries, storehouses for liquids, salt and sugar and warehouses for forest produce. An important tax, *vyaji* or transaction tax is mentioned. The list is also dealing with the classification of revenue arising from mines, minerals, metal working, coinage and salt. The *pratikara,* denotes payment of taxes in kind – grains, cattle, gold or forest produce. *Pratikara* also includes *vishti* (labour), i.e. doing work for the state in lieu of paying taxes. Two terms *parihara* and *aakarada* used to describe authorized exemptions from payment of tax. *Ayudhiya* (supply of soldiers in lieu of is also found), payment of fines by the citizens for failure to obey rules or codes of conduct and for misdemeanours, crimes and other infractions of the law constituted a separate source.

The main aims of levying fines were to ensure the observance of the laws and regulations of the state and to protect the corpus of revenue. The state also levied a number of fees or charges for services rendered to the public-issuing passports, providing ferry services or escorts for caravans, making standard weights and measures. This leaves four major areas of state economic activity as the main sources of raising revenue-income from state property, state-controlled manufacturing and leisure activities, taxes paid in cash or in kind and trading. Kautilya devotes a chapter to methods of increasing the resources of a state when they are depleted after an expensive operation, such as a war. He suggests different sets of methods for collecting additional revenue. Levying special taxes on all groups within the population, cultivating an extra summer crop seeking voluntary contributions and selling honours expropriating temple property using a variety of methods to extract money from the gullible was to be used only against traitors and the wicked and consisted of methods which, appear to be of dubious morality.

The state raised revenue both by direct cultivation and by leasing out land to tenants. The crops grown on these lands (grains, beans and lentils, oilseeds, sugarcane, textile fibres) constituted a major part of the revenue and were accounted for separately. Water rate for taking water from water works built by the king: one fifth if lifted manually, one fourth if lifted by bullocks, one third if lifted mechanically, one fourth for taking water from natural reservoirs, or irrigated from rivers lakes and tanks. The wealth of the state has its source in the mining and (metallurgical) industry, the power of the state comes out of these resources. Wealth and a (powerful) army and more territory can be further increasing the wealth of the state. Mines which were neither too expensive nor too difficult to exploit were worked directly by the Crown and the rest were leased out. Smelting was state owned and trade in metals centralized. Fish, ducks and green vegetables, produced in or near reservoirs was the property of the state, on the grounds that land on which the water storage stood was state property.

Revenue from sale of alcoholic beverages made in state undertakings and sold in drinking places under the control of the Chief Controller of Alcoholic Beverages, calculated by taking into account the transaction tax, the countervailing duty and the sticking allowance. Net income from courtesans' establishments, for which the courtesans had to provide detailed accounts of payments received, person making payment and net gain (payment less expenses). The complete lists of taxes mentioned in *Arthasastra* are:

1. Customs duty *(sulka)* which consists of:

   Import duty *(pravesya)*

   Export duty *(nishkramya)* and

   Octroi and other gate tolls *(dwarabahirikadeya)*
2. Transaction tax *(vyaji)* including *manavyaji* (transaction tax for Crown goods)
3. Share of production *(bhaga)* including 1/6th share *(shadbhaga)*
4. Tax *(kara)*, in cash
5. Taxes in kind *(pratikara)* including

   Labour (vishti)

   Supply of soldiers (ayudhiya)
6. Countervailing duties or taxes *(vaidharana)*
7. Road cess *(vartani)*
8. Monopoly tax *(parigha)*
9. Royalty *(prakriya)*
10. Taxes paid in kind by villages *(pindakara)*
11. Army maintenance tax *(senabhaktham)*
12. Surcharges *(parsvam)*

While *kara* is generally assumed to be a tax paid in cash, and *pratikara* that paid in kind, the text does not usually make a distinction between the two.

State Trading

The profit margins on the sale of monopoly goods were a significant source of revenue. This was under the control of the Chief Controller of State Trading who was responsible for orderly marketing, maintaining buffer stocks, avoiding excessive profits and collecting the transaction tax. He was also responsible for the export of Crown commodities, keeping in mind the advantages to the country and the people of importing goods in exchange. Merchants who were authorized to all Crown commodities, at prices fixed by the Chief Controller, had to compensate the government for the loss sustained in foregoing the profit that would have been made had the goods been sold through Crown outlets. If these do not produce enough grain, the officers working under the Chancellor (i.e. *sthanikas and gopas*) shall make farmers prepare the ground, in summer, for a summer crop (in addition to the normal rainy season crop). Seeds shall be distributed (free) to the farmers on condition that anyone who neglects to take proper care shall pay penalty of double the estimated loss. When the crops ripen, the officials shall prevent the farmers from taking green or ripe grain, however, handfuls of vegetables or grain plucked by hand may be taken, if they are intended for worship of God and ancestors, for charity or for feeding cows. The grain on the ground shall be left behind to be gleaned by mendicants and village employees. Anyone taking away grain cultivated by him shall pay a fine of eight times the amount taken. Anyone taking grain cultivated by someone else shall pay a fine of fifty times the quantity, if he belongs to the same village. If the thief is an outsider, he shall be put to death.

Adequate resources have not been raised by the above means; the Chancellor shall ask the people of the city and the countryside to make voluntary contributions. Secret agents shall then be the first to give large amounts. They shall be pointed out as examples and the people asked for contributions. Other secret agents shall be used to reproach those who give little. The king may also ask the rich to give as much gold as they can, either voluntarily or in expectation of favours. Honours and status symbols (umbrella, headgear, decorations) may be bestowed on them in return for gold. Agents appointed by the state shall first take away the property of temples. They shall then pretend that the property was lost because the person with whom it.

Budget, Accounts and Audit

The Chancellor shall first estimate the revenue (for the year) by determining the likely revenue from each place and each sphere of activity under the different Heads of Account, total them up by place or activity and then arrive at a grand total.

Actual revenue shall then be estimated by adding receipts into the Treasury for the current year and receipts on account of (delayed) payments due from the previous year and deducting from this the following: expenditure on the king, standard rations for others, exemptions granted (by the king) by decree or orally and authorized postponements of payments into the Treasury. Outstanding revenue shall be estimated by taking into account the following: works under construction from which revenue will accrue only on completion, unpaid fines and penalties, dues not yet recovered, dues defiantly withheld and advances to be repaid by officials, outstandings of little or no value shall be ignored.

Income, Expenditure and Balance

Actual income is to be calculated under the headings – (i) current income (ii) transferred income and (iii) miscellaneous revenue.

Current income consists of receipts due and paid in the same year.

Transferred income is income from outstandings of earlier year as well as income earned (by one department) transferred to another.

Miscellaneous income is (of three kinds):

(*i*) Recovery of debts and dues which were earlier written off, fines paid by government servants, additional income (from surcharges and unanticipated revenue), compensation collected for loss of damage, gifts, confiscated property, interstate property and treasure trove.

(*ii*) The following deductions from (anticipated) expenditure, savings due to demobilization of the army, works abandoned before completion and economics meant in investment as against original budget.

(*iii*) Income due to profit, on sales: increase in the price of a commodity at the time of sale, profit from the use of differential weights and measures and increased income due to competition from buyers.

Actual expenditure shall be shown under the headings:

(*i*) Budgeted day to day expenditure

(*ii*) Unbudgeted day to day expenditure

(*iii*) Foreseen periodic (fortnightly, monthly or annual) expenditure.

The (net) revenue is to be calculated after deducting expenditure from income, taking into account the actual as well as deferred amounts.

Accounts

Every entry shall have the date of the transaction. One the receipt side, the revenue shall be classified according to the major Head of Account: cost price, share *(bhaga)*, transaction tax *(vyaji)*, monopoly taxes, fixed taxes, manufacturing charges, fines and penalties. On the debit side, expenditure shall be classified according to the major Heads, as given below:

1. Worship (of God and ancestors) and charitable expenses
2. The Place (expenditure of the King, Queens, Princes etc.)
3. Administration
4. Foreign Affairs
5. Maintenance of granary, depots and warehouses for commodities and forest produce (under separate subheads)
6. Manufacturing expenses
7. Labour charges
8. Defence (with separate subheads)
9. Cattle (and pastures)
10. Forests and game sanctuaries
11. (Consumables like) firewood and fodder

Income Side

Place	Period of accounting	Date and time of receipt	Head of account	Classification current year or outstanding dues	Quantity received	Name of payer	By whose order	Received by	Recorded by
1	2	3	4	5	6	7	8	9	10

Expenditure Side

Place	Period of accounting	Date and time of payment	Head of expenditure	Counter value received	Occasion	What was paid	Amount paid	For what use	Authority ordering payment	Withdrawn from store	Delivered By	Received by
1	2	3	4	5	6	7	8	9	10	11	12	13

Balance Columns

Place	Date & Time	Head of account	Dues left outstanding	Form in which balance received into the treasury	Quality	Amount received	Details of container	Delivered to (name of treasury official)
1	2	3	4	5	6	7	8	9

(Ref. Rangrajan – Kautilya)

Proper Maintenance of Account Books

All accounts shall be maintained in the proper form and legibly written without correction. Failure to do so shall be a punishable offence.

Timely Submission of Accounts

Monthly accounts: Day to day accounts (to be submitted once a month) shall be presented before the end of the following month and late submission shall be penalized.

Accounts of specific transactions: The net balance to the remitted to the Treasury is small, a grace of five days shall be allowed for making the remittance. If the accounts are delayed (beyond five days), the net balance shall first be remitted to the Treasury and then thorough audit, done taking into account the rules of business, (relevant) precedents, the circumstances and the calculations; a physical verification of the work shall be carried out. Whether the smallness of the remittance was justified or not then shall be judged by inference (supplemented) by information from secret agents.

Audit

Responsibility of Account Officers

- Present themselves for audit at the appointed time bringing with them their account books and the income to be remitted to the Treasury
- Be ready for audit when the audit officer calls him
- Not lie about the accounts
- Not try to interpolate an entry as if it was forgotten

Failure to conform to any of the above regulations is a punishable offence and in case a discrepancy is discovered during audit:

- The official concerned shall pay penalty if the discrepancy has the effect of either showing a higher actual income of a lower actual expenditure.
- The official shall keep the difference for himself in the converse case.

An auditor shall be ready when an accounts officer presents himself for audit; otherwise, he shall be punished.

There general principles for running an efficient and disciplined civil service are given. The first is that, unless controlled, civil servants will make money in unauthorized or fraudulent ways. The second is that good civil servants shall be suitably rewarded. The third is the very important principle enjoining civil servants to collect the right amount of revenue, neither more nor less and to reduce expenditure in order to leave a net balance to the state.

This section brings together general principles of establishment, financial discipline, embezzlement, etc. Attention was paid to recruitment of proper personnel for the civil service. Spies, masquerading as ascetics, were required to be on the lookout for men of spirit, intelligence and eloquence and to predict for them, prosperity and close association with minister. Their names were then to be secretly recommended to a minister for appointing them to the suitable positions. The king shall forgive a trifling offence and be content even if the revenue is small. He shall honour with rewards officials who brings great benefit (to the state)

Heads of Departments shall not remain permanently in one job and shall be rotated frequently. Officials, who have the (necessary) qualifications for being appointed as ministers shall be appointed as Heads according to their ability. Heads of Departments shall carry out their duties with the assistance of accounts, clerks, coin examiners, store keepers and supervisors. Clever assistance of military supervisor shall watch over subordinate officials such as accountants and clerks. The King shall have the work of Heads of Departments inspected daily, for men, by nature, fickle and, like horses, change after being put to work. The king shall acquaint himself with all the details – officer responsible, the nature of the work, the place of work, the time taken to do it, the exact work to be done, the outlay and the profit. Officers shall carry out the work as ordered without either colluding with each other or quarrelling among themselves. Officer negligent or remiss in his work shall be fined double his wages and the expenses incurred. An officer who accomplishes a task as ordered and better shall be honoured with promotion and rewards. Every official who is authorized to execute a task or is appointed as a Head of Department shall communicate (to the King) the true facts about the nature of the work, the income and the expenditure, both in detail and the total.

Financial Discipline

The following are the causes of loss to the Treasury due to officials failing to collect the revenue required from them:

- **Ignorance** of the work to be done or of the rules, regulations and customs;

- **Laziness** and disinclination to work hard;
- **Neglect** of duty due to indulgence in sensual pleasures;
- **Timidity** due to fear of public discontent or uproar, (reactions from) evil persons or of untoward results.
- **Corruption** (particularly) showing favours to selfish persons with whom the official has dealings;
- **Short temper** and tendency to violence (alienating those from whom he has to collect the revenue);
- **Arrogance** about his learning, his wealth or the support, he gets from highly placed persons; or
- **Greed** which prompts him to use false balances, weights or measures, or to make false assessments and calculations.

Kautilya recommends that the penalty shall be commensurate with the (gravity of the) offence. (i.e. not follow a rigid pattern but to take into account the circumstances of each case).

MANU'S ARTHA-DHARMA

Manu Smiriti

Manu Smiriti or *Manav Dharmasastra* is written in the Sunga age in Second Century B.C. under patronage of Pushya Mitra Sunga. It is evolved from Dhama-sutra literature which explains the moral orders. The *Manu Smriti* describes the *Achar* (rules & regulations), Vyvahar (practices) and *Prayaschita* (repentance) for socio economic and political structure of India. The Vannna-ashrama, political theories, economic regulations etc are defined in it. The *Manu Smriti* with Yajnavakya Smriti are still basis of Hindu Law. It has twelve chapters and 2694 anustubh couplets.

The opening chapter *Manu Smriti* sets forth the origin of the world, creation of beings, the origin of Smriti through Bhrgu, the epochs of time *(yugas),* the difference in *dharmas* according to them, the four classes of man, differences in their respective *dharmas.* Second chapter, with which the main subject matter begins, speaks of the four sources and grounds or proofs of *dharma,* the person for whom this *dharma* holds good and the area where it prevails, describe the *dharmas* as applicable to each of the four classes, Brahmana, Kshatriya, Vaisya and Sudra. Twice born *(dvijas),* are considered first; and the sacraments *(samskaras)* are described for them in relation to the four stages of life *(asramas)* through the *samskaras* beginning with birth and going up to study the establishment of the teacher, up to the end of the first stage called *brahmacharya* (studentship). In Chapter third, the householder's life, which is the second stage, is taken up; marriage of eight different forms, married life, daily and periodical observances, of a householder, the vital character and the important social role of the house holder, his five daily *yajnas (Daivayajna, Pitrayajna, Manushyayajna, Brhmayajna, Bhutyajna),* or sacrifices (i.e. study and teaching of scripture, propitiation of the manes, adoration of the God, reception of guests and gratification of other living beings, and the periodic *sraddhas* are described. Chapter four continues the description of the house holder's life with many details, some relating to *dharmas* already mentioned and some enjoining further *dharmas,* others relating to the ways of earning one's livelihood and yet others relating to a number of personal habits and details of daily routine and principles of character and conduct. Chapter five opens with the subject of proper food; two other topics dealt here are, death together with obsequies and pollution and purificatory ceremonies. The last section of this chapter speaks of women (wives and widows) and their special *dharmas.* Chapter sixth is devoted to a description of the two further stages of man, the *vanaprastha and sannyasa,* denoting life of retirement in forests and complete renunciation respectively. Chapter seventh and eight together form a section about rulers and their duties *(raja-dharma),* which include not only their qualities and equipment, but also the art of statecraft in peace and war and counsel, diplomacy, messengers, army, fort, wars, conquest, treatment of the conquered, administration of villages, communities, merchants, collection of revenue, punishment and clearance of anti-social elements – these are spoken of in Chapter seven. The next chapter deals with administration of justice and describes legal procedure in respect of the eighteen titles of civil and criminal disputes, judges, evidence, offences and punishments. The Chapter ninth states details about women, particularly from the standpoint of law, their *dharmas,* duties expected of and towards them, and their importance regarding progeny and the family and also about property, inheritance and partition, which arise in the wake of the family. The chapter concludes with a brief description of the *dharmas* of the Vaisyas and the Sudras. In the chapter tenth the people outside the pale of this system of *dharma* and those born by promiscuous mingling of the four classes and a system by which they could be fitted into the scheme are set forth. *Dharmas* permissible under such emergencies *(apad-dharmas)* are therefore dealt with. The main subject of the chapter eleven is different kinds of sins, major and minor, and their expiations *(prayascittas)* falls into two sections. The former section speaks of the theory of *Karma*, the fruits and kinds of birth high and low, which result from different acts, good and bad and through which the soul has to pass. The latter speaks of those *dharmas* which help the spiritual goal-the seeking of self knowledge *(atma-jnana)* and the attainment of the everlasting good *(nihsreyasa).* Incidentally the matter of doubts on questions of *dharma* and the constitution of *parisads* (assemblies of the learned).

The conception of *dharma* in the *Manu Samhita* is all comprehensive. The word *dharma* is from the root *dhr,* meaning 'to support' or 'to sustain'. It includes, besides civil, religious and spiritual matters, counsels of general prudence, safety and even personal habits, like those of cleanliness, sanitation and civic consciousness, rational behavior, courteous and polite ways of conduct and even other subjects of common sense, making it a guide to conduct the things in big and small. It is a network of diversified but interrelated duties. It is a consolidating scheme within which practices which are not objectionable and are not opposed to the teachings of the Vedas are included. Manu gives a leading place to *achara* handed down from generation to generation by well disciplined members of a community. The doctrine of *yuga-dharma,* which introduces an element of adaptation and adjustment has a parallel in the concept of *apad-dharma.* Lastly, the most important feature of this *dharma* is the inclusion of the spiritual purpose within its scope; the final realization of the self is not only dealt with as the legitimate and culminating part of it, but the very activities of life here are oriented too, and harmonized with, the spiritual end.

Manu says that there is hardly any activity of man which is not prompted by kama or desire, but to act solely on the urge of desire, which is the outcome of tamas is not praise worthy and so to enable man to act properly dharma was promulgated. This dharma is governed by the four ends of life or aims of human endeavour, called the purusarthas. Dharma as the first of these purusarthas. Moksha was included under the first purusartha, which was classified into the dharma of activity (pravrtti-dharma) and that of retirement (nivrtti-dharma), and the ends were counted as three, the trivarga. Dharma is the controlling factor and artha and kama are to be subject to it. Manu sets that there should be a balanced pursuit of the trivarga. In the second stage of life as the householder, scope has been given to artha and kama as regulated by dharma. "Dharma is the *satya,* but for enforcing it one should not adopt any violent or severe methods."

"Satyam Bruyat priyam bruyat na bruyat satyam apriyam
Priyam ca nanrtam bruyat esa dharmah sanatanah."

The scheme of the classes, their respective *dharmas,* and the obligatory character of the discharge of these, being itself considered a perfection to be aimed. With this doctrine of duty went the principle of *adhikara* of qualification. The modern theory of rights, irrespective of *adhikara,* is something alien to Manu's attitude towards life. The *sista* as a person who has studied in the proper manner the whole Vedas together with their supplementary and supporting literature. The term *sista* signifies a person of irreproachable character, who is free from desires, and whose acts are not prompted by any worldly motive. A body of *sistas* would be a *parisad* or assembly fit to decide a question of doubt in matters of *dharma.* The region where Manu's *dharma* held good, where the *sistas, sata or sadhus* were able to keep up the *dharma,* an expanding belt which starts with *Brahmavarta,* between the Sarasvati and the Drsadvati, and embraces the whole of the land between the seas in the east and the west and is called *Aryavarta*; in between there is the *Brahmarsi-desa,* comprising the Kurukshetra, Matsyas, Panchalas and Surasenas and the Madhya-desa between the Himalayas and the Vindhyas, up to Prayaga in the east.

The *samskaras,* are common to the three classes, Brahmana, Kshatriya and Vaisya, all of whom are called, for this reason *dvijas.* The fourth is called *eka-jati,* meaning thereby that be has no sacramental rebirth, that the Sudras may, if they want to acquire merit, follow in the footsteps of the *dvijas,* and do certain rights, the five daily sacrifices etc. The treatment of *brahmacharya* and *upanayana* embodies the ancient ideals of education and of the discipline to be observed by the student and the conditions of life in a teacher's establishment *(guru-kula)* contains several seminal ideas which would be of profit to educationists of all ages. After the *brahmacaryai* stage, one may elect to enter the next stage of the householder *(grhasthasrama).* The glorification of the ideal of a disciplined *grhastha,* gives the lie direct to the criticism that Hinduism is negative, pessimistic and other worldly. In the *grhasthasrama,*

Manu deals also with marriage. This institution again has been conceived as an instrument of *dharma* and meant for the discharge of ordained duties. Hence one could marry only a woman of one's own *varna*, but of a different *gotra*. Manu recognizes eight kinds of marriage, *brahma, daiva, arsa, prajapatya, asura, gandharva, rakshasa,* and *paisacha*. It is in the first four that excellent and virtuous issues are born. During the household life, men are enabled to discharge the three debts with which they are born-the debt to the God, to be discharged by performing sacrifices; the debt to the *rsis* (sages), by maintaining the study and teaching of the Vedas and allied learning and the debt to the ancestors *(pitars),* by begetting children. Daily, the householder should also do five propitiations *(yajnas):* the first, *brahma-yajna,* relates to the maintenance of learning and its tradition; *pitr-yajna* is the offering of water *(tarpana)* for the gratification of one' sancestors; *deva-yajna* consists of the obligations in the fire for the God; *bhuta-yajna* is the offering made to living beings, animals, birds, etc. *nr-yajna (Manushyayajna)* is the reception and attention paid to guests *(atithi-pujana).* The ancestors are to be further propitiated by *sraddhas.* The householder should gather only so much as is necessary for sustenance, his accumulations being just for the morrow, or for three days only, or only so much as a jar or a granary could contain. The third and fourth *asramas, vanaprastha and sannyasa,* are dealt with the conception of the king's position and activity. Under inheritance, Manu's special view is recorded that there are twelve kinds of legal sons. The king is called *kantaka-sodhana,* which is clearing the state of anti-social elements. The king should be impartial and punish those dear to him as he would do others. There is no blind exercise of regal power; the Ksatra shall always be guided and guarded by Brahmana.

The organization of society into these functional classes, four or three or two is of common Indo-Germanic origin, and its parallel could be sought in all ancient communities. The organization according to *varna* has served as a steel frame that has preserved the Hindu community down the centuries. Its marriage selection and vocational specialization have contributed to the refinement of the species. The *varna* organization is not like classes of today formed on material aims and competitive basis. It forms a co-operative effort. Manu speak a number of classes of persons born of certain types of sexual relation of both *anuloma* (wife of a lower caste) and *pratiloma* (husband from an inferior caste) type, some of these issues are given names which are also the names of certain tribes outside the pale of the *caturvarnya* – Nisada, Candala, Abhira. The *varna* organization served in this respect to impose an order on the heterogenous population and consolidate it. Manu emphasizes a body of personal ethical virtues as of fundamental importance and universal application. Some of the daily rites included in the five daily *yajnas* have a social and humanitarian bearing; for example, the *nr-yajna,* which is the entertaining of guests, and *bhuta-yajna,* which is the gratification of other living beings, dogs, insects etc. The householder should see that the causes no harm to others nor displease others even by begging of them. Hatred, vanity, pride, anger and severity should be avoided. Two sets of virtues and observances, *yamas* and *niyamas* must be observed. The *yamas* are continence, compassion, contemplation, truth, non attachment, non violence, not taking what is anothers, sweetness of behavior and self control. One wins heaven by being soft and subdued, non violent and generous. These ten qualities or *dharmas* are: fortitude, forbearance, self-control, not taking others' possessions, purity, sense-control, learning, knowledge of self, truth, and absence of anger. Similarly virtues as constituting the common *dharmas* of all the four *varnas* non-violence, truth, non-thieving, purity and sense-control. Outside of the Veda-enjoyed sacrifices, the principle of *ahimsa* should be observed in all matters and Manu lays due emphasis on the two basic principles-*ahimsa and satya.*

No appreciation of Manu can be complete without drawing attention to its *subhasitas* or observations of profound wisdom. One does not become an elder by reasons of one's grey hairs, he who is well read, though young, him the God deem an elder. He who is insulted goes to sleep happily and happily does he get up and move about in the world; it is he who has insulted that perishes. Contentment is the root of happiness; its opposite is the root of misery. *Dharma* is the only friend that accompanies one even in death; all the rest perishes with the body. Manu says that it is legitimate to take the characterization of the teaching as *raja-vidya* and *raja-guhya* (kingly secret) as having a special significance to the *rajarsis* or saintly kings for whom this wisdom was preeminently intended, though, as applicable to others also engaged in activity, this came to be esteemed as the king of *vidyas* or philosophies and the most precious of esoteric wisdom. The name *raja-vidya* might be taken in a straight manner as meaning the philosophy of the Kshatriyas, is supported by the *yogavasistha.* The *Yogavasistha* says that humanity went about gathering things for its life and began to indulge in mutual fight, it became necessary to have rulers over them, and they could not discharge their duty without punishing people and themselves entering into wars; but wars demoralized them, and to remove their depression and provide them with right evaluation *(samyag-drsti),* the sages taught them this philosophy. Doctrine of non-attachment called *Anasakti-yoga* or *Asparsa-yoga* strikes the balance between *karma* and *sannyasa* and between *pravrtti* and *nivrtti.* Along with the sterilization of *karma* by *phala-tyaga,* the *karma-yogin* is also to develop equanimity in respect of the outcome of his endeavours. It requires no demonstration to show that these are the leading ideas which run all through the *Gita. Manu Smrti,* Manu sets forth the *dharmas* of the different *varnas.* Manu includes among those of the Kshatriyas non-attachment to sense-pleasures, *visayesu aprasaktih.* The freedom from *matra-sparsas* (sense contacts) and *dvandvas* (pairs of opposites) is insisted on: one should not be depressed by loss nor exhilarated by gain, and should be out of the contamination of *matra-sanga. Indriya-sanga* (sense-attachment), *sanga-tyaga* (renunciation of attachment), and freedom from all *dvandvas* find mention. Manu states expressly that not only is the path of abandoning *karmas* called *nivrtta* (detachment); but that the disinterested performance of *karma,* by a person of *jnana* is also as much *nivrtta.* Manu praises the *grhasthasrama* shows a *grhastha* could become a *Vedasannyasika* (one who gives up Veda-ordained rituals), and practice *Karmayoga.* Manu speaks of these *grhasthas* who observe the *jnana-yajna,* which commentators have explained as referring to the *grhastha* who is a *Vedasannyasika.* Manu sums all the acts, those conducive to the everlasting welfare *(nihsreyasa)* or spiritual salvation are the greatest; for, of all kinds of activities, the knowledge of the Soul *(atma-jnana)* is the highest and as that alone brings immortality. The *dharma* expounded in the Dharma-sastra of Manu comprehends al the aspirations of man, leading up to the highest, namely, the everlasting beatitude for the realization of which all the other aspirations and pursuits are adjusted and synthesized.

VIVEKANANDA'S SOCIO-ECONOMIC ETHICS

Vivekananda was born in 12th January 1863 in the house of Vishvanath Datt, resident of Calcutta in Bengal. The child was named Narendra Nath. The early education of Narendra Nath was given through Bengali and English. The child showed special interest in Ramayana and particularly in the character of Rama. Narendra Nath used to hear it with rapt attention forgetting all childhood plays. Once he meditated in a room of his house with so much attention that the door of the room had to be broken to awaken him. Thus Yogic consciousness was evident in Vivekananda from the very beginning. He was admitted to the educational institution of Ishwar Chandra Vidyasagar. After it he entered Presidency College. At the college stage he had achieved an intimate knowledge of English literature, European history, philosophy, science, art, music and medicine.

Ramakrishna identified the spiritual powers of Narendra Nath at the very first sight. One the other hand, Narendra Nath felt that Ramakrishna was a bit abnormal. However he asked the old question. "Sir, Have you seen God?" The reply which he received was never expected. Ramakrishna told him "Yes, I see him just as I see you here". Narendra Nath was deeply impressed but not completely satisfied. He continued to meet Ramakrishna more often and gradually came under his influence.

In 1884 the father of Narendra Nath passed away due to heart attack. At this time Narendra Nath was only a graduate and studying law. Under these hard circumstances Narendra Nath had crisis of faith. Narendra Nath received his initiation in Vedanta from Ramakrishna. Who had extraordinary yogic powers. In 1885 he gave Narendra Nath the experience of attributesless *Samadhi* by his mere touch and ordered him that his first duty is to fulfil the mission of Ramakrishna. Narendra Nath was the leader of the association of the young followers of Ramakrishna. As the leader of this association, called Ramakrishna Mission, Narendra Nath propagated the views of Ramakrishna everywhere. Beloor near Howrah was made the head office of Ramakrishna Mission and the centre of its activities.

In 1888 Vivekananda left Calcutta. He went to Varanasi, Ayodhya, Lucknow, Agra, Vrindavan and Hathras. At Hathras he was accompanied by his disciple Sadanand. Both of them now toured Himalayas. In Himalayas Vivekananda had a vision of the soul of India. In February 1891 he went to Rajasthan, Bombay and Rameshwaram. From Rameshwaram he went to Kanyakumari. There he sat on a rock in the sea and had his realization of the great unity of India. At present there is on this rock the world famous Vivekananda Memorial. In 1893 Vivekananda heard that a Parliament of Religions was being organized in Chigago in USA. Before going to USA he went to Khetri, the king of this state was his disciple. It was this princely disciple who suggested the name of Swami Vivekananda which was adopted by Narendra Nath.

On May 31, 1893 Swami Vivekananda left Bombay for USA. In the way be went to Ceylon, Penong, Singapore, Hong Kong, Canton and Nagasaki. Seeing the influence of Indian culture and Sanskrit language at all these places he realized the spiritual unity of Asia.

He reached Chicago in mid July. Seeing the spectacular progress of knowledge and science at USA, he was highly impressed. After twelve days he reached the information office of the proposed Parliament of Religions. He was told that the parliament will be held in the first week of September and his name cannot be included in the list of delegates until it is recommended by someone in USA. While travelling in the train at Boston Swami Vivekananda met a rich lady of Messachusetts. She called him at her residence and introduced him to Professor J.H. Wright of the department of Greek studies at the Harward University. Wright was very much impressed by Vivekananda and introduced him to Dr. Bros, the chairman of the selection committee of the delegates by writing. He insisted that Vivekananda should be admitted as the representative of Hinduism at the Parliament of religions. He also gave Vivekananda rail ticket to Chicago and a letter of recommendation of lodging and boarding. Unfortunately Vivekananda lost these papers during the journey. However, these were received by a lady G.W. Hale who contacted Vivekananda and took him to the Parliament, where he was respectfully admitted as a delegate and arrangements of his stay were made along with other representatives from the East.

The Parliament of religions was inaugurated on 11th September 1893 at Columbus Hall. Religious leaders of the world had gathered there to hear Swami Vivekananda in the evening of the first day. They welcomed by prolonged clapping the first words of Vivekananda, "American brothers and sisters." After it he delivered a dozen lectures in USA, which made him famous in the West. New York Herald proclaimed him the greatest person at the Parliament of Religions and wrote that after hearing him we feel that how much foolish it is to send religious missionaries to the nation of such a great scholar. On the invitation he visited several places in USA and delivered lectures which had wide influence over American intelligentsia. He was offered the headship of department of Eastern philosophy at Harward University and Sanskrit language at Columbia University which he declined saying that he was a Sanyasin.

On 7th August 1895 Swami Vivekananda left USA for England. He was welcomed by heads of various churches and he delivered several lecturers in England. It is here that Miss Margaret E. Nobel; the later sister Nivedita met his teacher Vivekananda for the first time. His lectures on *Jnanayoga* in London particularly became famous. On 6th December 1895 Swami Vivekananda reached New York from England. Here he delivered lectures on *Karmayoga* and *Bhaktiyoga* at the residence of Miss S.E. Waldo who later on became his disciple known as Hari Dasi. Vivekananda delivered lectures in a very informal but influential style. Gradually, the number of his American disciples increased. In February 1896 he laid the foundation of the famous Vedanta Society of New York. He also delivered lectures on Vedanta philosophy in the philosophy department of Harward University. His lecture here on 25th March 1896 was so impressive that he was offered the chair of Eastern philosophy.

In April 1896 Swami Vivekananda left America for England and in the month of May delivered five lectures per week on Vedanta. He delivered three lectures, at Royal Institute of Painters, Picaddelli. He also spoke at Princess Hall, Annie Besant lodge and other well known Clubs and Educational institutions. Max Muller invited him to his residence at Oxford and was very much influenced by him. From England Swami Vivekananda went to Switzerland on the persuation of some of his friends. In August 1896 he was invited by Professor Paul Deussen of Kiel University of Germany. Deussen was very much impressed by Vivekananda and accompanied him on his return journey to London.

When Vivekananda reached India he was given a tumultuous welcome. A meeting of the disciples of Ramakrishna was called on first May 1897 at Bagh Bazar in Calcutta at the residence of Mr. Balram Bose. Vivekananda explained the problems of the country before this gathering and pleaded for their remedies. The meeting accepted his proposals and Ramakrishna Mission was established on May 5, 1897 with the express mission of serving humanity through the service of followers of various religions. Swami Vivekananda was elected president of the mission and Swami Yoganand and Swami Brahmanand were elected Vice-President and President of Calcutta Branch of the mission respectively. As president of Ramakrishna Mission Swami Vivekananda toured the whole of the country. In 1898 reached Darjelling but left for Calcutta in April to serve the people suffering from plague epidemic. The service rendered by followers of Ramakrishna Mission to the suffering people of Calcutta was a rare example.

In order to provide a centre in the Himalayas for practicing Vedanta Philosophy by his disciples from East and West, Vivekananda established Advaita Ashram at Mayavati, 50 miles away from Almora on 19th March 1899. It was at the chief organ of Ramakrishna Mission came out under the title *Prabuddha Bharata.* On 20th June 1899 Swami Vivekananda gain left for West with his disciples Sister Nivedita and Swami Turiyanand. He established centres at San Fransisco, Aukland and Alamada. He returned to Beloor in India on 24th January 1909, and went to Mayavati Ashram. He also toured other centres of the country. He suffered from diabetes and lung diseases. He stayed at Beloor for seven months and transferred all his responsibilities to his disciples. He went to Bodh Gaya on the insistence of Japanese Artist Okakura. From there he went to Varanasi and established a centre of Ramakrishna Mission there. On 4th July 1902 Swami Vivekananda left for his heavenly abode at the early age of 39 years.

Vivekananda realized the economic and social difficulties of the poor classes in India, who were without sufficient nutrition and suffering from various types of diseases. Vivekananda asked, "Who constitutes society?" and remarked, "For the luxury of a handful of the rich, let millions of men and women remain submerged in the hell of want and abysmal depth of ignorance, for if they get wealth and education, society will be upset." Vivekananda, "Not one of them had heard of what is meant by a socialism and anarchism. But political awakening is not possible by hungry people. Food and cloth are the first needs of life." First make the people of the country stand on their legs, by rousing their inner power; first let them learn to have good food and clothes and plenty of enjoyment then tell them how to be free from this bounding of enjoyment.

Vivekananda says that Illiteracy was the main cause of the low status of women. His disciple sister Nivedita organized women's education in India. She established a Math for this purpose. This Math observed all the rules of missionaries and provided education for character. Vivekananda even prescribed physical training to women sine he pointed out. The education of women was considered a remedy for problems concerning marriage and family. Vivekananda pointed out the evil of senseless growth of population. Expressing his feeling in this connection, Vivekananda said, "I have a strong hatred for child marriage." The truth is that, in this country, parents and relatives can ruthlessly sacrifice the best interest of their children and others for their own selfish ends, to save themselves by compromise to society." Education of women was suggested as one of the remedies for this state of affairs.

The most important social problem according Vivekananda, however, was the utter poverty of Indian masses. He realized that no spiritual uplift is possible without first solving the problem of poverty. He asked, "In all India, there are say, a hundred thousand really spiritual men and women, who for the spiritualization of these three hundred millions be sunk in savagery and starvation?". Empty stomach and religion go ill together. It was mockery to offer religion to a starving man.

Vivekananda believed that the ancient Indian system of social stratification based upon Varna is still the most scientific system. Calling it a kind of social communism.

Vivekananda believed that the ancient Indian system of social stratification based upon Varna is still the most scientific system. Calling it a kind of social communism. Vivekananda condemned the doctrine of *Adhikarvad.* He was however, not against giving the highest place to the learned and the scholars called Brahmins. He was rather proud of the fact that Varna system assigns highest place to the Brahmins. Inspite of his immense praise for Varna system Vivekananda was well aware of the fact that the present degeneration of that ancient idea into a rigid caste system is the cause of the degeneration of the nation. He condemned the present case-system in very clear words. He said, "In spite of all the ravings of the priests, caste is simply a crystallized social institution which after doing its service is now only be removed by giving back to the people their lost special individuality." He rebuked those who considered following of the caste restrictions necessary for religion. Distinguishing between religion and caste-system he said, "In religion there is no caste. A man from the highest caste and man from the lowest may become a monk in India and the two castes become equal. Caste system is opposed to the religion of Vedanta. Vivekananda realized that this stratification cannot be uprooted unless some better substitute is available.

During his tour of the West Vivekananda had occasions to study intimately, socialism, communism and their practical application.

During his tour of the West Vivekananda had occasions to study intimately, socialism, communism and their practical application. He had also occasions to discuss these theories with renounced people. He prophesied about India that the future of socialism is bright in this country. He investigated the causes of social and political decline of India and lamented that the privileged class have everywhere tried to exploit the lower classes. Chiding the upper classes "You, the upper classes of India, do you think you are alive?" Those whom your ancestors despised as "walking carrion", that the little of vitality there is still in India is to be found; and it is you who are the real "walking corpses". You merge yourselves in the void and disappear, and let 'New India' arise in your place. The masses are the backbone of the country because they produce all wealth and food. Vivekananda insisted on giving all facilities to the poor masses of India. Brahmin has more aptitude for learning on the ground of heredity than the pariah, spend no more money on the Brahmin's education, but spend all on the pariah. Give to the weak, for there all the gift is needed. These downtrodden masses of India, therefore, require to hear and to know what they really are." Masses are important because they are toilers. They have suffered oppression for thousands of years without murmur. They are, however, capable of carrying out a revolution. Exploited masses to the exploiters Vivekananda declared, "Very soon they will get above you in position. You have so long oppressed these forbearing masses: now is the time for their retribution."

Vivekananda was convinced that the labour classes have the potentiality of creating a social, economic and political revolution in the country. The inner processes in this revolution have been however very differently explained by Vivekananda. As against the role of economic and material forces in future revolution to be possible only through the spiritual forces. His socialism is different from the materialist socialism of the West. Democracy is based upon the three fundamental values of liberty, equality and fraternity. While praising these three principles Vivekananda interpreted them in spiritual sense. Pointing out the value of liberty as a natural right he said, "Liberty does not certainly mean the absence of obstacles in the path of misappropriation of wealth, etc. Our natural right to be allowed to use our own body, intelligence or wealth according to our will, without doing any harms to others; and all the members of society ought to have the same opportunity for obtaining wealth, education or knowledge."

Besides liberty equality is also necessary to realize democratic society. Equality is the way to freedom while inequality is the way to bondage. Pointing out the value of equality for liberty Vivekananda said, "No man and no nation can attempt to gain physical freedom without physical equality, nor mental equality." Absolute equality is impossible. It is against the law of nature. Though all beings are equally manifestations of God, yet difference is the basis of manifestation. Explaining this spiritual equality as fundamental principle of Vedanta, Vivekananda said, that the idea that one man is born superior to another has no meaning in *Vedanta*; that between two nations one is superior and other inferior has no meaning whatsoever. Thus Vivekananda considered democracy as the best form of Government. He was against monarchy though it has been praised in ancient Indian literature. Though he was very much aware of the defects of democratic forms of Government. Explaining his idea of democracy in the tradition of ancient Indian thought he said, "The voice of the ruled in the government of their land which is the watchword of the modern Western world, and of which the last expression has been echoed with a thundering voice in the declaration of the American government.

GANDHI

Mohandas Karamchand Gandhi was born on 2nd October 1869 at Porbander in Gujrat. After becoming the Bar at Law England on 1891. Gandhi returned India and started practices initially at Rajkot and later on in Bombay. In 1893 he received an offer from Indian firm headed by Dada Abdulla to deal with his cases in South Africa. In South Africa Gandhi was pained by suffering of Indian and protested against the discriminating treatment meted out to them. He formed Natal Indian Congress and raised voice against British. In Africa he also protested against the Asiatic (Black) Act and the Transvall Immigration Act. In 1915 Gandhi returned to India. He participated against British in Champaran *Satyagrah*, Kheda Movement and Ahmedabad Mill strike. The Rowlatt Act (1919) and the Jallianwallah Bagh tragedy moblised him to involve in active Indian politics. Gandhi launched Non-Co-operation Movement (1920), Civil Derobedience Movement (1930) and Quit India Movement (1942) to get freedom.

Moral Laws of Gandhi

Gandhi says that the moral laws are static. Moral laws are not relative to individual circumstance and are universally comprehensible. These laws are divine. The result moral laws is ultimately good. The conscience is a divine spark. It is, also the preceptor of moral laws. Mechanical activities are not the object of moral judgement. Rationalist and purpossivist Gandhi too regards only voluntary actions as the objects of moral judgement. "No action which is not voluntary can be called moral." While contemplating upon morality it is to be attended to that the work is good and done with a good intention. Its result is not in our control, the only one who rewards is God.

Generally, Gandhi believes that the means does not become good merely upon the pretence that the end is good. Thus end cannot justify the means. But Gandhi has also conceded exceptions to this rule. For example, it was Gandhi himself who originated and implemented the campaign against the notorious salt law. The exception has two aspects, the first where both the means and the ends are related to the same individual and the second comes into action when all the superior means have failed. Under such circumstances the use of even bad means may be right. But it is essential that the aim be good under every circumstance. His thoughts lack any originality. Gandhiji starts from Hindu religion and the metaphysical solution of eternal problems from a Hindu angle of vision form the basis of his philosophy. He has not sought to answer or solve the problem from an independent perspective of experience or reason. He gave to the old moral laws a completely new form. Gandhiji was the first one to introduce non-violence into the political field and he also made successful use of it. He declared punishment immoral. Gandhiji was the precursor of non-violent revolution.

Excessive emphasis upon repression of senses has led to his ethics becoming permeated with stringency.

Excessive emphasis upon repression of senses has led to his ethics becoming permeated with stringency. Probably his assumption regarding celibacy may strike one as untalented and even harmful to happy matrimonial life but a balancing stress upon qualities like non-violence, love, equanimity etc., have prevented his sermons from becoming utterly heartless. Actually, Gandhiji himself was an experimenter and did not recognize any means as final. Many critics express grave doubts regarding the probabilities of experimentation in non-violence. Progress is imminent in the attempts of making practical Vinobaji's campaign of Gandhism. Gandhiji endeavoured to discover the fundamental solution of all problems. Another major reason why his solution of existing problems and his sketches of man's future seem impractical is that human society has not achieved that level and man also lacks the necessary moral strength to successfully use those means. But the only conclusion which can be drawn from this is that society will have to acquire moral strength to proceed upon his path. Non-violence is a means in moral behavior. The means contradicting it are violence and use of brutal strength. From the ethical viewpoint, right is that which is good and conversely, bad is wrong. Now, the result of any moral action can consist of two aspects – individual and social upon the object. If any activity favours the perpetrator of the object, or if the result of an action benefits the individual and harms society, or it is favourable immediately but detrimental in the long run, then the activity cannot be said to be good because in order to be so, the result of an activity must be good for the individual and society, at present and in future.

In a hierarchical society, there is of course general progress but in the absence of a state of independent thought the person's personality remains dwarfed. Besides only the more immediate results of violence can be good. The tendencies of a violent person become degenerate and his character devolves. One who pursues non-violence may even have to sacrifice his life and bear pain without being rewarded. But even this suffering produces a result calculated to aggrandize the spiritual pleasure of both himself and his opponent. The patience of man is dependent upon his character. A non-violent person is conscious of intrinsic happiness although he may be undergoing extrinsic pain infliction. Even though the opponent does ostensibly resist and such overtures, he internally becomes addicted to this and finally submits himself. Use of force is admissible under any circumstances or not. In some exceptions it is both necessary and possible. Violence or resorting to force is objected to only when it is used either indiscriminately or for the interests of this or that class or individual. If a particular individual class refuses to abandon, by any means; it's incorrect and deplorable path and does immense harm to others then use of force also becomes necessary. The *Gita* goes to the extent of saying that although apparently alive, he is in reality dead. In this way, if it becomes irrefutably clear that use of force is in the interests of the offending person or class and all others concerned and also that peaceful means are not going to yield any desirable result then the use of force is both unavoidable and moral.

One who pursues non-violence may even have to sacrifice his life and bear pain without being rewarded. But even this suffering produces a result calculated to aggrandize the spiritual pleasure of both himself and his opponent. Gandhiji too has licenced resort to use of force in exceptional cases. All other means should have proved ineffective and use of force should be in positive interests of both, the one using it and the one upon whom it is used. It is also worth-noting that this action was purely for the sake of duty and done without attachment.

Cult of Non-Violence

"Without *Ahimsa* it is not possible to seek and find Truth. *Ahimsa* and Truth are so inter-twined that it is practically impossible to disentangle and separate them."

Gandhi said, "Without *Ahimsa* it is not possible to seek and find Truth. *Ahimsa* and Truth are so inter-twined that it is practically impossible to disentangle and separate them." Gandhian cult of non-violence was based upon his interpretation of human nature. Non-violence is the first article of my faith. Violence is the law of brutes while non-violence is the rule of human beings. Non-violence according to him is not merely an ideal, it is a fact.

Gandhi called his techniques of social reconstruction by the name *Satyagraha* and urged everyone to be a Satyagrahi. He prescribed seven vows for a *Satyagrahi viz.*truth, non-violence, *brahmacharya,* control of palate fearlessness, non-stealing and non possession. Most of the vows have been accepted by ancient Indian scriptures. Truth is the highest ideal in Gandhian political philosophy. There should be truth in thought, truth in speech and truth in action. Thus truth should be practiced in all walks of life-social, economic, political etc. The basic principle of non-violence rests on that what holds good in respect of oneself equally applies to the whole universe. *Ahimsa* is not the way of the timid and cowardly. It is the way of brave ready to face death. He who perishes with sword in hand is no doubt brave but he who faces death without raising his little finger and without flinching is braver. Gandhi firmly believed that no real democracy can be established by violent means. Gandhi insisted on non-violence as the only means for the achievement of the same ideal. Gandhi did not accept any chasm between ends and means. He said, "True democracy or the Swaraj of the masses can never come through untruthful and violent means. Individual freedom can have the fullest play only under a regime of unadulterated *Ahimsa*.

Brahmacharya means conduct adapted to the search of *Brahma* i.e. Truth. It means primarily chastity and ultimately control of all the senses. Gandhi's emphasis on *Brahmacharya* has always been a subject of controversy, as it clearly condemns marriage as a necessary evil. He said, "Hence one who would obey the law of ahimsa cannot marry, not to speak of gratification outside and marital bond." Gandhi however, permitted marriage to those who cannot live without it. According to this ideal a person performing sexual intercourse only for getting progeny is a *Brahamchari* though married. This ideal has always been held in high esteem in India.

Techniques of Social Revolution

The difference between Gandhian technique of social revolution and that of the French or Russian pattern is clear by the symbol of spinning wheel which Gandhi considered to represent the new social order. He invented it since it gives an occasion of physical labour and abolishes the difference between rich and poor. It removes class distinctions and establishes dignity of labour. On the question of the antiethical relationship of the poor and the rich as presented by Karl Marx, Gandhi though in a different way. Explaining his standpoint on this question, he said, "Exploitation of the poor can be extinguished not by effecting the destruction of a few millionaires, but by removing the ignorance of the poor and teaching them to non-cooperate with their exploiters. That will convert the exploiters also."

Gandhi introduced the spiritual practice of self-purification as one of the methods in political action. This marks the synthesis of spiritualism with politics. Pointing out the importance of self purification as a method he said, "Because the rulers, if they are bad, are so not necessarily or wholly by reason of birth, but largely because of the environment, that I have hopes of altering their course. It is perfectly true that rulers cannot alter their course themselves. If they are dominated by their environment, they do not surely deserve to be killed, but should be changed by a change of environment. But the environments are we, the people who make the rulers what they are. They are thus an exaggerated edition of what we are in aggregate. If my argument is sound, any violence done to the rulers should be done to ourselves. And since I do not want to commit suicide, nor encourage my neighbours to do so, I become non-violent myself and invite my neighbours to do likewise."

Satyagraha, the chief weapon of Gandian political action has been defined as soul-force by him. He said, "Its (Satyagraha's) equivalent in the vernacular rendered into English, means truth force. I think Tolstoy called it also soul force or love force and so it is." *Satyagraha* is bound to be non-violent, otherwise it turns into *duragraha. Satyagraha* is different from passive resistance also, it is active resistance, acting on the path of truth. Distinguishing Satyagraha from passive resistance, Gandhi pointed out, "the *Satyagraha* differs from passive resistance, as the north pole from the south. The latter has been conceived as a weapon of the strongest and excludes the use of violence in any shape of form. Its root meaning is holding on the truth, hence truth-force. I have also called it soul-force or love-force. In the application of *Satyagraha* discovered in the earliest stages the pursuit of truth did not admit of violence being inflicted on one's opponent but that must be weaned from error by patience and sympathy. For what appears to be truth to the one may appear to be error to the other and patience means self-suffering. So the doctrine came to mean vindication of truth not by infliction of suffering on the opponent, but on one's self." The most important characteristic of *Satyagraha* is that it can be used most successfully even by one individual and that too in every sphere of life. It is an ideal weapon of war of righteousness. It is latent in every one of us, we have to make it active. It is a universal course. In essence it is the introduction of truth in political life.

Explaining the working of *Satyagraha* as a political weapon Gandhi has insisted that it is based on truth and non-violence. Besides, it includes such techniques as involve mutual dialogue such as arbitration, negotiation etc. Besides, it also includes non-violent pressure tactics such as agitation, demonstration, picketing, dharna, economic boycott, non-payment of taxes, emigration, non cooperation, ostracism, civil disobedience and formation of parallel government. These steps were taken in the national movement under the guidance of M.K. Gandhi.

The idea of civil disobedience is a protest against unjust law. Explaining the validity of civil disobedience as a political instrument, Gandhi said "When you have failed to bring the error home to the lawgiver by way of petition of the like, the only remedies open to you if you do not wish to submit to error, are to compel him to yield to you either by physical force or by suffering in your person, by inviting the penalty for the breach of his laws. Hence *Satyagraha* largely appears to the public as civil disobedience or civil resistance." Gandhi distinguished between forced and willful disobedience of the laws, the latter is involuntary and reluctant disobedience of the laws.

Another instrument in the armory of *Satyagraha* is non-cooperation. This technique was widely used by Gandhi in India's political struggle against the British. Explaining non-cooperation as a method of political action Gandhi said, "Non cooperation is the method whereby we cultivate the fresh public opinion and get it enforced. When there is complete freedom of opinion that of the majority must prevail." When non cooperation alone does not work, *Satyagraha* becomes assertive and takes recourse to direct action. This may be sometimes embarrassing to his standpoint. He said, "The *Satyagraha* movement is not started with the intention of embarrassing a government while ordinary political agitation is often started with that object. And yet, if a satyagrahi finds his activities resulting in embarrassing the government, he will not hesitate to face it."

In spite of gradual application of more and more pressure and even non-violence direct action, Gandhi was against any violent agitation or destruction of public property. He spoke against the sabotage and destruction of bridges, roads etc., in clear words. He was also against any secret movement or plan of action, since according to him secrecy is violence. In his own words, "Secrecy aims at building a wall of protection around you. Ahimsa disdains all such protection. It functions in the open and in the face of odds, the heaviest conceivable." He was also against seizure of power by force. He did not accept forced establishment of Jatiya Sarkar of Bengal.

Another significant and novel instrument of political action developed Gandhi is fast. This is a weapon which very much depends upon the soul-force of the person wielding it. Gandhi himself used this weapon in the political field very successfully.

Gandhi wanted to organize a whole army of revolutionaries on non-violent ground. He prescribed qualification for the soldiers of independence movement which he called satyagrahis. These qualifications were as follows:

1. Living faith in God.
2. Faith in truth and non-violence as their creed and therefore faith in the inherent goodness of human nature.
3. Chaste life and readiness for sacrifice.
4. Absolute abstinence of intoxicants.
5. Habitual wearing of Khadi.
6. Desire to follow discipline.
6. Following jail rules unless they are against self-respect.

Gandhi himself followed these principles and asked others to follow his example. Though amenable to discussion his method was very much based upon faith and discipline. It was based upon dedication and selfishness. It required a lot of sacrifice on the part of the individual. In order to create a revolution in the country Gandhi demanded seven lakhs workers so that each village may get at least one revolutionary as base for the programme of revolution. This, however, could never be achieved and therefore, his great vision could never be realized.

Thus as opposed to state government Gandhi was more in favour of self-government and self-revolution. In fact his *swaraja* meant self-government. This idea is based upon the spiritual thinking that anything genuine and real can come only from within. Morally speaking all good comes from within, nothing can be imposed from outside. Anything imposed from outside is foreign to human nature and cannot be called moral. Explaining his idea of self-government Gandhi said, "Self-government means continuous efforts to be independent of the government control whether it is foreign or whether it is national. Swaraj government will be a sorry affair if people look up for the regulation of every detail of life."

In fact his *swaraja* meant self-government. This idea is based upon the spiritual thinking that anything genuine and real can come only from within. Morally speaking all good comes from within, nothing can be imposed from outside.

Gandhi however knew that in practice it is not possible to abolish the state all together nor is it possible to eliminate all use of force. Therefore, he concedes that the State and the government may exist and yet their powers should be reduced to minimum. He said, "I admit that there are certain things which cannot be done without political power, but there are numerous other things which do not at all depend upon the political power. This means that when people come into possession of political power the interference with the freedom of the people is reduced to a minimum. In other words a nation that runs its affairs smoothly and effectively without much state interference is truly democratic. Where such condition is absent the form of Government is democratic in name."

CONCEPT OF DEMOCRACY & SOCIETY

The ideal government according to Gandhi, is democracy. Gandhi, however, wanted to emphasise the principle of non-violence in the actual working of the democracy. He wanted to decentralize the whole political structure. He emphasized equality between human beings and was against too much difference in economic or political field. He wanted to run the government by reducing violence to the minimum. He prescribed social reform of criminals and opposed retributive punishment. He wanted to turn policemen into social reformers. He was against having a large army or military organization. In nutshell his social organization gives maximum freedom to the individual. This, however, does not mean that he gives less importance to the society. Pointing out the importance of social obligations in a society Gandhi said, "I value the individual freedom but you must not forget that man is essentially a social being. He has risen to the present status by learning to adjust his individualism. Individualism is the law of the beast of the jungle. We have learnt to strike the mean between individual freedom and social restraint for the sake of the well being of the whole society of which one is a member."

Gandhiji's concept of the relation between the society and the individual is based upon the ancient Indian *Varna* system. In the Varna system different individuals were classified according to their innate tendencies and were given social roles corresponding to them. This, according to Gandhi created conditions both for the individual development and social welfare. Explaining the law of *Varna* in Indian social system Gandhi said, "The law of Varna means that every one shall follow, as a matter of dharma duty, the hereditary calling of his forefathers is so far as it is not inconsistent with fundamental ethics. He will earn his livelihood by following that good of the people." Gandhi's appreciation of *Varna* system was based on his faith in Bhagwadgita which he considered to be his guide in every field of life. He did not think that caste system is a necessary corollary of *Varna* system. He was also against fixing rigidly the occupations of different *Varnas*. His was an integral approach to life. This is very much clear from his insistence that every one, howsoever scholarly he may be, must earn his bread by physical labour. Pointing out his ideal in this connection he said, "Brahmin is not only a teacher, he is predominantly too. But a Brahmin who refuses to labour will be voted down as an idiot, because the rishis of the old who lived in forests cut and fetched wood, tended cattle and even fought, but their pursuit in life was predominantly search after truth. Similarly, a Rajput without learning was good for nothing no matter how well he wields the sword. And Vaishya without divine knowledge sufficient for his own growth will be a veritable monster eating into the vitals of society as many modern. Vaishyas whether of the East or the West have become. They are, according to the Gita, no change incarnations of sin who live only for themselves."

In spite of praising Varna system in very clear terms, Gandhi was against casteism and untouchability. As it has been already pointed out, he did not trace caste system to Varna system. In fact he joined in the controversy on this issue and defended *Varna* system against the onslaught of Dr. B.R. Ambedkar. Replying him he said, "*Varnas* and Ashramas are institutions which have nothing to do with castes. The law of *Varna* teaches us that we have each one of us to earn out bread by following the ancestral calling. It defines not our rights but our duties. It necessarily has reference to callings that are conducive to the welfare of humanity and to no other. It also follows that there is no calling too low and none too high."

Gandhi says that *Varna* system, far from being the source of untouchability. Equality demands that we should not distinguish among human beings on the basis of social occupations. Gandhi, throughout his life, waged a war against the evil of untouchability. Elimination of untouchability means love for, and service of, the whole world, and thus merges into ahinsa."

Economic Ideas

Gandhi was not an economist in the academic sense. He was however very much conversant with the economic problems of the country and he thought over them with his characteristic basic approach. He himself said, "I am not an economist, but India may become a self-sustained country, growing all the produce she needs. This may be an utterly ridiculous proposition and the perhaps best proof that it cannot be true is that England is one of the largest importers in the world." Thus Gandhian economic programme was based upon the ideal of self-sufficiently. He never compromised ethical principles with economic progress. The ideal of man, according to him, is spiritual progress first and last and no economic progress can violate this principle. He, however, did not sharply distinguish between economics and ethics any more than the distinction between religion and politics. Thus *Khaddar* economics was based upon ethics.

The basic ideas of Gandhi, in economics as well as in politics were drawn from ancient Indian philosophy of life. Traditional Indian thinking is against giving an important place to consumption in life. It lays emphasis on minimizing the wants rather than maximizing them. It is against too many desires and sanctions only the minimum desires. Thus it is against production of such things which are classed among luxuries. Indian philosophy has always preached that man's life is for spiritual evolution and not for physical satisfaction. Born and brought up in the tradition of Indian philosophy and spiritualism, Gandhi, an ardent follower of *Gita*, developed an economic theory which was in tune with Indian spiritualism. His ideas, besides being based on Indian philosophy of life, were also equally derived from his experience of Indian social life of his time. He was very much perturbed by the abject poverty of his countrymen. He was moved by it and he scratched his brain to the maximum to find out the solution. But he wanted a solution which may lead to spiritual progress and not an opposite retrogression. Thus he wanted economic progress but not at the cost of spiritual values. He was against mechanization though he permitted that small machines are necessary for everyday life. The production of these machines obviously should be in public sector.

The basic ideas of Gandhi, in economics as well as in politics were drawn from ancient Indian philosophy of life. Traditional Indian thinking is against giving an important place to consumption in life.

Gandhi pleaded for decentralization of industries and that of all the economic functions including production, consumption and distribution. As early as in 1928 he declared, "According to me the economic constitution of India and for the matter of that the world should be such that no one under it should suffer from wants of food and clothing. Everybody should be able to get sufficient work to enable him to make the two ends meet. And this ideal can be universally realized only if the means of production of the elementary necessaries of life remain in the control of the masses. These should be freely available to all as God's air and water are or ought to be, they should not be made a vehicle of traffic for the exploitation of others. This monopolization by any country, nation or group of persons would be unjust. The neglect of this simple principle is the cause of destitution that "we witness today not only in this unhappy land but other parts of the world too."

He said, "the political and economic organization of the state shall be based on principle of social justice and economic freedom. While this organization shall conduce to the satisfaction of the national requirements of every member of society, material satisfaction shall not be its sole objective. It shall aim at healthy living and the moral and intellectual development of the individual. To this end to secure social justice, the state shall endeavour to promote small scale production carried on by individual or cooperative effort for the equal benefit of all concerned. All large scale collective production shall be eventually brought under collective ownership and control and in this behalf the state shall begin by nationalizing heavy transport, shipping, mining and the heavy industries. The textile industry shall be progressively decentralized." About state industries Gandhi remarked, "In all state-owned and state-managed enterprises, the workers shall be represented in the management through their elected representatives and shall have an equal share in it with the representatives of the Government."

Trusteeship Theory

The most important and yet the most controversial point in the economic philosophy of Gandhi is the theory of trusteeship. He was against capitalism and yet he was not against capitalists. He warned to use their genius as managers of industries. He was against destruction of anything including the capitalist class. His non-violent means were all pervasive including the economic field. He said, "In reality the toiler is the owner of what he produced. If the toilers intelligently combine, they will become an irresistible power. That is how I do not see the necessity of class conflict. If I though it inevitable, I shall not hesitate to preach it and teach it."

Explaining the mechanism to bring about trusteeship Gandhi said in answer to a question at the Round Table Conference in England, "Not merely by verbally persuasion, I will concentrate on means. Some have called me the greatest revolutionary of my time. It may be false, but I believe myself to be a revolutionary a non-violent revolutionary. My means are non-cooperation. No person can amass wealth without the cooperation, willing or forced, of the people concerned." The socialist thinkers within the country and also outside doubted the possibility of trusteeship. Gandhi, however, wanted to give it a fair trial though in his life time none except Jamna Lal Bajaj came somewhere near his ideal. He was against accumulation of wealth by violence but he was also against mass production or large scale nationalisation. In fact, he was against all mad race after wealth. He was aware of the dangers of state capitalism and therefore prescribed decentralization of industries. His idea was equitable distribution if not equal distribution. Labour, according to him, is the master of the means of production and is never a slave of it. Capital is the servant of labour and not its master. He like Karl Marx advised, the labourers to get united, for a non-violent struggle. Like Karl Marx again, he aimed at a stateless society, but this stage has to be achieved through non-violent revolution as anything secured through violence, according to Gandhi, is bound to fail in the end.

Suggested Question

1. Define the important characteristics of Indian Ethics. How can it be utilized in Modern Business?
2. Kautilya set the standard for developed economy. How his recommendation for prosperous economy are relevant today?
3. The *'Nishkam Karma'* of Bhagvadgita relates work with social economic, political and religious life. Explain with suitable examples.
4. Buddhism and Jainism set the protestant ethics for capitalist from economy, Explain.
6. Manu's socio-economic ethics still relevant in era of Globalisation. Comment.

Short Notes

(*i*) Buddhism & Globalisation

(*ii*) Jain Anuvrata & Modern Trade

(*iii*) Indian Trade Pattern

(*iv*) Trade and Ethic

References

1. Bhattacharya, Haridas (Ed), *The Cultural Heritage of India* (6, vol), 2000, Calcutta
2. Dasgupta, Surendranath, *A History of Indian Philosophy,* (4. vol), Cambridge University Press
3. Hopkins, E W, *the Ethics of India,* Yale University Press
4. RadhaKrishnan S. *India Philosophy* (2,Vol), London
5. Keith, A.B. *Indian Logic and Atomism,* Oxord.
6. Radhakrishnan. S, *Bhagvadgita,* London
7. Sharma Chandradhar, *A Critical Survey of Indian Philosphy,* Delhi, 1991
8. Singh Anand, *Pracheen Bhartiya Dharma: Udbhav Evam Swaroop,* Delhi, 2010
9. Singh Anand, *Tourism in Ancient India,* Delhi, 2004
10. *Arthasastra,* Ed. Rangrajan, L.N., Penguin, Delhi. 1992
11. Shah C.J. *Jainism in North India,* Delhi 2007

4

CHAPTER

CORPORATE SOCIAL RESPONSIBILITY & CORPORATE GOVERNANCE

One of the most revolutionary changes in capitalism over the last 50 years is the development of 'conscience'. Private business which is the hard core of this economic system has realized, and has been made to realize by several social, economical and political forces that it has social obligation to fulfill besides ensuring its own existence through profitable activity. Today partly due to the interdependence of the many groups in our society the social inducement of business has increased. The question of social responsibility originally associated with businesses, is now being posed with increasing frequency in regard to governments, universities, non-profit organizations, charitable organizations etc. In a modern industrial society the concept of social responsibility has become very relevant for a business organization, it remain vague and uncertain in its definition and interpretation. Business organizations have a close relationship with society. They draw various resources or inputs from society. They process and convert them into goods and services. These goods and services are made available to various section of society for satisfying their needs and wants. Because of this relationship and interaction, both have certain expectation from each other. As business organization have some aspirations and expectations from society, in consideration of it, society also expects that these organizations should conduct their business operations in a socially responsible manner and discharge their obligations and commitments towards society. Society in the context refers to such groups as an organizations employees, customers and the environment in which they operate.

The concept of social responsibility is not new. Although the idea was already considered in the early part of the twentieth century the modern discussion of social responsibility got a major impetus with the book 'Social Responsibilities of the Businessman', by Howard R. Bowen. He suggested that businesses should consider the social implications of their decisions. In a survey of 439 executives, 68 percent of the responding managers agreed with the following definition: 'Corporate social responsibility is seriously considering the impact of the company's action on society'. We can understand social responsibility better if we compare it with two similar concepts: Social obligation and social responsiveness.

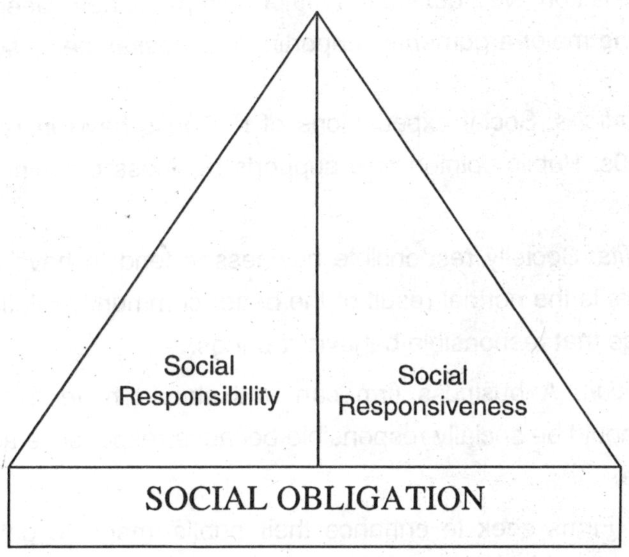

Levels of Social Involvement

Social obligation is the foundation of a business social inducement. A business has fulfilled its social obligation when it meets its economic and legal responsibilities and more. It does the minimum that the law requires. In contrast to social obligation, both social responsibility and social responsiveness go beyond merely meeting basic economic and legal standards. Social responsiveness adds a moral element to do those things that make society better and not to do those that could make it worse. Social responsiveness, then, requires business to determine what is right or wrong and thus seek fundamental truths. Societal norms guide this process. Let's look at this example to make it clear.

When a company meets pollution control standards established by the government, or doesn't discriminate against employees on the basis of their race in a promotion decision, the organization is fulfilling its social obligation and nothing more. Various laws say that employees may not pollute, or be biased against certain groups, and this company is abiding by those laws. However, when another company packages its products in recycled paper, or provides health care insurance for an employee's significant other, these firms are being socially responsive. How so? Although pressure may be coming from a number of societal groups, such businesses are providing something society desires, without having to be told to do so by law.

Social Responsibility versus Social Responsiveness

	Social Responsibility	**Social Responsiveness**
Major Consideration	Ethical	Pragmatic
Focus	Ends	Means
Emphasis	Obligation	Responses
Decision Framework	Long Term	Medium & Short Term

Arguments For & Against Social Responsibility

What are the specific arguments for and against business assuming social responsibilities? In this section, we'll outline the major points that have been presented.

Arguments For: The major arguments supporting businesses being socially responsible are

1. *Public expectations:* Social expectations of business have increased dramatically since the 1960s. Public opinion now supports business pursuing social as well as economic goals.
2. *Long run profits:* Socially responsible businesses tend to have more secure long run profits. This is the normal result of the better community relations and improved business image that responsible behaviour brings.
3. *Ethical obligation:* A business firm can and should have a social conscience. Businesses should be socially responsible because responsible actions are *right* for their own sake.
4. *Public image:* Firms seek to enhance their public image to get increased sales, better employees, access to financing and other benefits. Since the public considers social goals important, business can create a favorable public image by pursuing social goals.
5. *Better environment:* Business involvement can help solve difficult social problems, helping create a better quality of life and a more desirable community in which to attract and keep skilled employees.
6. *Discouragement of further government regulation:* Government regulation adds economic costs and restricts management's decision flexibility. By becoming socially responsible, business can expect less government regulation.
7. *Balance of responsibility and power:* Business holds a large amount of power in society. An equally large amount of responsibility is required to balance against it. When power is significantly greater than responsibility, the imbalance encourages irresponsible behavior that works against the public good.
8. *Stockholder interests:* Social responsibility will improve a business's stock price in the long run. The stock market will view the socially responsible company as less risky and open to public criticism. Therefore, it will award its stock a higher price earnings ratio.
9. *Possession of resources:* Business organizations have the financial resources, technical experts, and managerial talent to support public and charitable projects that need assistance.
10. *Superiority of prevention over cures:* Social problems must be addressed at some time. Business should act before these problems become more serious and costly to correct, taking management's energy away from accomplishing its goal of producing goods and services.

Arguments Against: The major arguments against business assuming social responsibility are:

1. *Violation of profit maximization:* This is the essence of the classical viewpoint. Business is being socially responsible when it attends strictly to its economic interests and leaves other activities to other institutions.
2. *Dilution of purpose:* the pursuit of social goals dilutes business's primary purpose, economic productivity. Society may suffer if both economic and social goals are poorly accomplished.
3. *Costs:* Many socially responsible activities don't cover their costs. Someone has to pay these costs. Business must absorb the costs or pass them on to consumers through higher prices.
4. *Too much power:* Business is already one of the most powerful sectors of our society. If it pursues social goals, it would have even more power. Society has given business enough power.
5. *Lack of skills:* the outlook and abilities of business leaders are oriented primarily toward economics. Business people are poorly qualified to address social issues.
6. *Lack of accountability:* Political representatives pursue social goals and are held accountable for their actions. Such is not the case with business leaders. There are no direct lines of social accountability from the business sector to the public.
7. *Lack of broad public support:* There is no broad mandate or outcry from society for business to become involved in social issues. The public is divided on the issue of business's social responsibility. In fact, it is a topic that typically generates heated debate. Actions taken under such divided support are likely to fail.

SOCIAL RESPONSIBILITIES OF BUSINESS TOWARDS DIFFERENT GROUPS

Responsibility towards the Customers

In a competitive market the customer is king and is the company's first priority because it exists for the customers. Earlier, the product selling approach was the basic approach of the managers who were considered capable when they were able to create demand. The Toyata management's customer, first philosophy has paid them rich dividends.

There are many Japanese corporations which strive towards customer satisfaction. On the contrary, developments in many Indian organizations indicate customer exploitation. Workers in the Japanese corporations fully cooperate with the management for improving production methods constantly with a view to maximizing customer satisfaction. In order to satisfy customers, a proper quality products needs to be designed and produced using proper quality materials, appropriate technology and well trained, motivated and committed human resources.

Social Responsibility to Prospects

Prospects are the possible or probable customers, that is, expected customers. It is always safer on the part of a company to identify its existing customers, and make forecast about the expected customers. Welfare programmes which benefit the prospective customers may convert potential customers to actual customers. When a company opts to take up a social welfare project, it may think in terms of priorities. Though the customers and prospects are in the mind of the project planner priorities must be taken into account. An organization may not be able to do all that it wants to do on account of various constraints and changing situations. On the contrary, it is always better to do one or a few most important things. Unless the priorities are proper, accomplishments cannot be proper and desired.

Social Responsibility to Community

A company is a part of the community or immediate society where it exists. Hence it has a great responsibility to be conscious and concerned with community welfare.

A company is a part of the community or immediate society where it exists. Hence it has a great responsibility to be conscious and concerned with community welfare. A community is a part of the society at large which provides the immediate social environment to the company. The company must, therefore, be committed to the welfare of the environment, since it has an important social role to play in the community. There are two important aspects of such a social role. One that the company should lend positive assistance to community objectives and secondly, it should not be instrumental to environment degradation. This calls for initiating pollution free and environmental friendly technology, conservation of the surrounding ecological environment, social afforesation, preventing emission of fumes and effluents, and so on not only to satisfy the government or legal provisions, but because of commitment to community welfare and environmental protection. Making extra efforts for industrial safety is another way of protecting the community. When the gas tragedy at the Union Carbide Plant in Bhopal resulted in loss of human lives and permanent invalidation of many people from around the factory, the importance of improving industrial safety and reducing occupational and industrial hazards came to attention. Protecting the community and preventing it from industrial hazards is the greatest responsibility of industrial establishments.

A good business enterprise can do its best to assist its community in solving various socio economic problems, it would be a useful step towards solving unemployment, poverty underdevelopment, social backwardness and so on by creating indirect employment opportunities for the people by putting up shops, townships, transport developments, markets etc. Business houses can set up educational institutions, social service institutions, technical education centres, hospitals and health centres in its community. They can also assist in natural calamities like earthquakes and floods in their communities, making social responsibility substantially conspicuous. Community development has been an important area where the corporate sector has made invaluable contributions in the past not only in India but all over the world. The contribution of the corporate sector has played a tremendous role in developing the communities of the economically developed nation.

Responsibility to Human Resources

An organisation's social responsibility is first visible in its approach to its internal environment. Responsibility to employees stems from a proper organizational philosophy and human resource policy. Fair wages, proper organizational climate, conducive working conditions, good career prospects, proper human resource development facilities, a proper environment for need satisfaction including self actualization needs are essential. All such aspects enable an organizations work force to gain a sense of belonging and confidence. Jamshedji Tata's vision of management as early as 1907 was almost identical. The Tata Iron and Steel Company (TISCO) which started its operation in 1911, is one of the largest single private sector enterprises in India and a leading producer of steel. It has fostered the philosophy of 'managing human resources with human considerations', as a prerequisite to managing business well from its inception. Companies like Cadbury's and Unilever are well known for their employee welfare policies among the global organisations operating in India.

An organisation's social responsibility is first visible in its approach to its internal environment.

Responsibility to Society and Ecological Environment

An organization owes social responsibility not only to the immediate social framework called community but to society at large and the ecological environment. In a global business environment the whole globe can be the society for an organization. The company's society would include people of all such places, cities or countries where the company operates or is expected to operate. It can also include its suppliers, dealers, wholesalers and retailers. The company has social responsibility to all such constituents of its society. It can be a good pay master to its suppliers, it can maintain a proper supply line and terms and conditions with its dealers, wholesalers and others. It can also help the society to tackle its social problems. Multi-national corporations which operate in India, make their contribution for socio-economic development of the economically weaker sections, participate in disaster management programmes arising due to natural calamities and even adopt villages for concentrated development activities.

Responsibility to Government

Social responsibility of a business may include a business firm's responsibility to the government also. It can pay its taxes, duties etc. to government honestly taking into consideration the organizations commitment to the government especially on social projects. Moreover, business firms constructively co-operates with the government in their social policies and progarmmes. For example, corporate contribution to the Prime Minister's Relief Fund is tremendous. Business organizations which are good tax payers and wholeheartedly participate in government social welfare projects gain better corporate image, indicating that this responsibility can be considered as a social responsibility of business law abiding corporate entities are bound to fulfill their responsibility to the government.

Social Responsibility to Global Business Environment

Globalisation of business has become an essential condition of business in the contemporary business environment. Global markets, global operation and technology, global corporate citizenship, global politics and strategies all make a global business environment. Every business organization has a responsibility to adhere to the conditions of such a global environment. The global customer needs globally approved quality, globally competitive pricing, globally approved technology and so on which may be related to global social responsibility. Due to globalization, a larger faster and greater growth of industrialization is expected in the future resulting in greater social responsibility being demanded from business enterprises. Companies with low social responsibility investment may even become unpopular in the eyes of the society in the years to come with the entry of large business houses and multinationals in the social arena, a number of innovative projects for social development are bound to be introduced in the future. As a result, there would emerge greater social awakening in the industrial circles towards social responsibility.

CORPORATE SOCIAL RESPONSIBILITY: INITIATIVES AND EXAMPLES

Aptech Limited

Aptech Limited, a leading education player with a global presence, has played an extensive and sustained role in encouraging and fostering education throughout the country since inception. As a global player with complete solutions, providing capability, Aptech has a long history of participating in community activities. It has, in association with leading NGO's, provided computers at schools, education to the underprivileged and conducted training and awareness-camps. Aptech students donated part of the proceeds from the sale of their art work to NGOs. To propagate education among all sections of the society throughout the country, especially the underprivileged, Aptech fosters tie-ups with leading NGOs throughout the country, including the Barrackpur-based NGO, Udayan, a residential school for children of leprosy patients in Barrackpur, established in 1970. The company strongly believes that education is an integral part of the country's social fabric and works towards supporting basic education and basic computer literacy amongst the underprivileged children in India.

CISCO System Inc.

Philanthropy at Cisco is about building strong and productive global communities, communities in which every individual has the means to live, the opportunity to learn, and the chance to give back. The company pursues a strong 'triple bottom line' which is described as profits, people and presence. The company promotes a culture of charitable giving and connects employees to non-profit organizations serving the communities where they live. Cisco invests its best-in-class networking equipment to those non-profit organizations that best put it to work for their communities, eventuating in positive global impact. It takes its responsibility seriously s a global citizen. Education is a top corporate priority for Cisco, as it is the key to prosperity and opportunity.

Infosys Technologies Limited

Infosys is actively involved in various community development programs. Infosys promoted, in 1996, the Infosys Foundation as a non-for-profit trust to which it contributes upto 1% PAT every year. Additionally, the Education and Research Department (E & R) at Infosys also works with employee volunteers on community development projects. Infosys leadership has set examples in the area of corporate citizenship and has involved itself actively in key national bodies. They have taken initiatives to work in the areas of Research and Education, Community Service, Rural Reach Programme, Employment, Welfare activities undertaken by the Infosys Foundation, Healthcare for the poor, Education and Arts & Culture.

ITC Limited

ITC partnered the Indian farmer for close to a century. ITC is now engaged in elevating this partnership to a new paradigm by leveraging information technology through its trailblazing 'e-Choupal' initiative. ITC is significantly widening its farmer partnerships to embrace a host of value adding activities: creating livelihoods. By helping poor tribals make their wastelands productive, investing in rainwater harvesting to bring much needed irrigation to parched dry lands, empowering rural women by helping them evolve into entrepreneurs, and providing infrastructural support to make schools exciting for village children. Through these rural partnerships, ITC touches the lives of nearly three million villagers across India.

Tata Consultancy Services

The Adult Literacy Program (ALP) was conceived and set up by Dr. F.C. Kohli along with Prof. P N Murthy and Prof. Kesav Nori of Tata Consultancy Services in May 2000 to address the problem of illiteracy. ALP believes illiteracy is a major social concern affecting one third of the Indian population comprising old and young adults. To accelerate the rate of learning, it uses a TCS-designed Computer-Based Functional Literacy Method (CBFL), an innovative teaching strategy that uses multimedia software to teach adults to read within about forty learning hours.

Goodearth Education Foundation (GEF)

Work of GEF was initiated in 1996 with a project in the Rai Bareilly district in Uttar Pradesh. The four-year project covered sixty three government schools and benefited15000 children. GEF is currently implementing projects in Thane district, Maharashtra (in 56 schools and balwadis), Alwar District, Rajasthan (this project is being implemented in partnership with the NGO Bodh Shiksha Samiti, covering 71 schools and balwadis) and Solan district, Himachal Pradesh (10 Balwadis) GEF Objectives include providing equal opportunities in pre-primary and primary education to all children, and quality of education by ensuring that it is relevant, effective and activity based.

Hindustan Construction Company (HCC)

HCC plays an active role in CSR initiatives in the fields of Health, Education, Disaster Management and Environment. Disaster Resource Network DRN is a worldwide initiative, promoted by the World Economic Forum (WEF). Trained volunteers and equipment resources from Engineering Construction and Logistics companies will complement the existing efforts of Government, NGO's and International Organisations in disaster management. It was during the WEF annual meet that the massive earthquake struck Gujarat in January 2001. The need for a trained and effective participation from industry was first felt there. The members of Engineering and Logistics segment of WEF came together to establish this network. The idea was further strengthened during the 9/11 incident where again the industry participated in the relief operations. DRN Worldwide was formally launched in New York in January 2002. And shortly thereafter, DRN-India initiative was launched.

Larsen and Toubro (L & T) Limited

Considering that construction industry is the second largest employer in India after agriculture, employing about 32 million strong workforce, L&T set out to regulate and promote Construction Vocational Training (CVT) in India by establishing a Construction Skills Training Institute (CSTI) on a 5.5 acre land, close to its Construction Division Headquartes at Manapakka, Chennai, CSTI imparts, totally free of cost, basic training in formwork, carpentry, masonry, bar-bending, plumbing and sanitary, scaffolder and electrical wireman trades to a wide spectrum of the rural poor. As a result of the good respone it received in Chennai, CSTI set up a branch at Panvel, Mumbai, initially offering training in formwork, carpentry and masonry trades. The Manapakkam and Panvel facilities together provide training to about 300 candidates annually who are inducted after a process of selection, the minimum qualification being tenth standard. Since inception, these two units have produced about 2000 skilled workmen in various trades, with about sixty percent of them being deployed to L&T's jobsites spread across the country. The success of this training initiative demonstrates that adoption of systematic training techniques are bound to yield efficient and skilled personnel in the shortest possible time and in the power to convert the potential of the Rural Youth in Construction and upgrading Rural Economy in a small way.

CSR Initiatives and Green Measures

India Inc has joined hands to fine-tune all its activities falling under CSR. For this, it has set up a global platform to showcase all the work done by Indian firms. Confederation of Indian Industry (CII) and the TVS Group collaborated to form the CII-TVS Centre of Excellence for Responsive Corporate Citizenship in 2007. It provides consultancy services and technical assistance on social development and CSR. According to a National Geographic survey which studied 17000 consumers in 17 countries, Indians are the most eco-friendly consumers in the world. India topped the Consumer Greendex, where consumers were asked about energy use and conservation, transportation choices, food sources, the relative use of green products versus traditional products, attitudes towards the environment and sustainability and knowledge of environmental issues.

Reliance Industries and two Tata Group firms, Tata Motors and Tata Steel, are the country's most admired companies for their corporate social responsibility initiatives, according to a Nielsen survey released in May 2009. As part of its Corporate Service Corps (CSC) programme, IBM has joined hands with the Tribal Development Department of Gujarat for a development project aimed at upliftment of tribals in the Sasan area of Gir forest. The financial services sector is going green in a steady manner. With an eye on preserving energy, companies have started easing the carbon foot print in their offices. The year 2009 witnessed initiatives including application of renewable energy technologies, moving to paperless operations and recognition of environmental standards. Efforts by companies such as HSBC India, Max New York Life and Standard Chartered Bank have ensured that the green movement has kept its momentum by asking their customers to shift to e-statements and e-receipts. State-owned Navratna Company, Coal India Ltd. (CIL) will invest US$ 67.5 million in 2010-11 on social and environmental causes. Public sector aluminium company NALCO has contributed US$ 3.23 million for development work in Orissa's Koraput district as part of its Corporate Social Responsibility (CSR) initiative.

CORPORATE GOVERNANCE

A system of checks and balances needs to be put in place among shareholders, directors, auditors, and management. There is now an increasing realization among modern and progressive companies that ethics and corporate social responsibility make good business sense. An ethical and socially responsible company generally conforms to the standards of good corporate governance. Good governance is essential for building goodwill and credibility, managing companies efficiently and transparently and preventing a variety of corporate crime like embezzlement, money laundering, kickbacks, expense account pending and price bid rigging. Corporate governance enables corporations to realize their corporate objectives, protect shareholders rights, meet legal requirements, and demonstrate to a wider public how they are conducting their business. Corporate governance, which broadly refers to the relationship between owners, directors and managers has received a lot of attention in recent years. A great deal of concern has been expressed all over the world about the shortcomings in the systems of corporate governance

Corporate governance is concerned with holding the balance between economic and social goals and between individual and community goals. The corporate governance framework is there to encourage the efficient use of resources and equally for accountability for the stewardship of those resources. The aim is to align as nearly as possible the interests of individuals, corporations and society. Corporate governance is the relationship among corporate managers, directors and providers of equity, people and institutions who save and invest their capital to earn a return. Best practices in the field of corporate governance may broadly be grouped under four categories: those relating to corporate boards and directors, those concerning operational management and control, those dealing with credibility and transparency of reporting, and those bearing upon shareholder democracy and minority protection. Given the fiduciary relationships that corporate director are subject to, there is an overwhelming need to ensure that they discharge their responsibilities to the best of their abilities to protect and promote the interests of all shareholders. At the same, time, there is also a pressing need to delineate the *directing and managing* aspects of governance. It is in this perspective that the role, responsibility and accountability, constitution, structure, independence, competence, remuneration, empowerment and evaluation of corporate boards and their directors needs to be considered. While a competent and independent board of directors is a prerequisite to ensure wealth is applied for the benefit of all shareholders, the board and the executive management of the company have to address in the first place, the all important task of creating and protecting such wealth and wealth creating assets and resources.

Corporate governance is concerned with holding the balance between economic and social goals.

Company law in India requires a company's board to provide an annual report to its shareholders. Disclosures have been prescribed, as have been the formats in which the company's financials are to be prepared, audited and submitted to the shareholders. Auditors reports is a significantly detailed document and is required to be actually read out at the annual general meetings of shareholders. Shareholders are required to decide on a number of matters and it is important that the company provides its shareholders adequate information to enable them to exercise their votes. Shareholders who subscribe to their equity capital on the basis of a public offer or a private placement, in either case relying upon the stated objectives of the company in the offer document. They exercise their rights in general meetings of shareholders of the company. Current company law requirements mandate a 75 percent majority in certain matters and a simple majority. There is, of course, a provision for poll in case of any doubts or when demanded by eligible shareholders. Reporting and disclosure requirements and best practices are developed to meet this need. More importance is also attached to protecting the interests of minority shareholders on the basis that by themselves, individually, they may not have the resources to do so when investing in risky instruments like company shares. SEBI requirements for highlighting risk factors in equity offers is an example of how potential investors should be made aware of the nature and extent of the risks involved in investing. Protection of shareholder interests should, therefore, be applicable of matters relating to transparency in accounting and reporting, majority oppression, biased management, non conforming to obligatory requirements and so on, but certainly not to issues arising from normal business risk that equity investments are subject to.

Disclosure and transparency are the partners of good governance, they demonstrate the quality and reliability of information, financial and non-financial provided by management to lenders, shareholders and public. Disclosure and transparency enable the investor to take informed decisions, it is essential that all the relevant information is made available to the shareholders. The US EDGAR (Electronic Data Gathering and Retrieval) systems allow the issuer companies to file all the relevant information in a secure manner electronically. A similar facility has been made available to Indian investors through the EDIFAR (Electronic Data Information Filing and Retrieval) system. Corporate governance has been articulated very eloquently by Michael Jensen, Jonathan Charkham and others. Let us look at corporate governance in various countries and analiyse suggestions for improving it. This is divided into three parts: (1) Corporate governance in industrially developed countries (2) Corporate governance in India (3) Reforming corporate governance.

Corporate Governance in Industrially Developed Countries

1. Anglo-American Model : The distinctive features of the Anglo-American model of corporate governance are as follows: (1) The ownership of companies is more or less equally divided between individual shareholders and institutional shareholders. Though the combined holding of institutional shareholders is often more than 50 percent, rarely does a single institutional investor have more than 10 percent stake in a company (This may be because of various restrictions applicable to institutional investment). (2) Companies are typically run by professional managers. There is a fairly clear separation of ownership and management. Managers enjoy substantial freedom in running the companies and the typical chief executive officer considers himself as John Wayne, wielding complete control. (3) Though, in theory the management is supposed to be chosen by the directors, in practice it is often the other way. Hence, directors are rarely independent of management. (4) Most institutional investors are reluctant activists. They view themselves as portfolio investors. The high churning ratio of these investors suggests that they have a short term orientation. If they are not satisfied with a company's performance, they simply sell its securities in the market. (5) The disclosure norms are comprehensive, the rules against insider trading tight and the penalties for price manipulation stiff. These measures provide adequate protection to the small investor and promote general market liquidity. Incidentally, they also discourage large investors from taking an active role in corporate governance.

In a nutshell, Jonathan Charkham characterizes the Angle-American model as the high-tension model because of the important role of the chief executive officer, active capital markets, short-term and credible takeover threats.

German – Japanese Model

The German and the Japanese models of corporate governance, despite some differences among them, share certain important commonalities to justify being bracketed together, their distinctive features are described below:

1. Banks and financial institutions have substantial stakes in the equity capital of companies. In addition, cross holdings (referred to as *keiretsu* in Japan) among groups of firms is common in Japan.
2. Institutional investors in Germany and Japan view themselves as long term investors. They play a fairly active role in management. In general, the long term commitment of institutions and the close monitoring provided by them seem to have helped companies immensely.
3. In Germany and Japan, the disclosure norms are not very stringent, checks on insider trading are not very comprehensive and effective and the emphasis on liquidity is not high. All this tends to impair the efficiency of the capital market.
4. There is hardly any market for corporate control in Germany and Japan. Takeovers, let alone hostile takeovers are very rare.

Corporate Governance in India

The discussion on corporate governance in India may be divided into two parts. We first will look at corporate governance in the private sector and the second at corporate governance the public sector.

Corporate Governance in the Private Sector

The distinctive features of corporate governance the private sector are as follows:

1. There are three broad categories of shareholders, promoters (or foreign parent companies in the case of multinationals), financial institutions (including mutual funds) and individual investors. On the average, the three categories of shareholders are more or less equally important though there are wide variations across companies.

2. For electing the directors, the *majority rule voting* system is typically followed. The *proportionate rule voting* system (also referred to as the cumulative voting system) is rarely ever, followed.
3. Company broads generally comprise of three types of directors: promoter directors (functional directors in the case of professionally managed companies), professional directors and institutionally nominated directors. Institutionally nominated directors are either senior executives of the institutions or persons of repute. These tendencies are further strengthened by the dynamics of small groups wherein the promote directors pay special attention to cultivate others.
4. In general, institutional investors have been supportive of promoters. They interfere only when a crisis develops or when there is a clear evidence of malafide behavior on the part of the management or when there is a directive to them from the government. Institutional nominees on company boards hardly have any incentive to monitor the behavior and performance of the management seriously.
5. Scattered and ill organized individual shareholders are not in a position to play a meaningful role in electing directors. Further, the majority rule voting system prevents even a well-organised substantial minority to have any say in the election of board of directors.
6. In general, the family managed companies seem to display greater entrepreneurial vigor act more proactively and exercise stricter control. The degree to which these aberrations may occur depends on the level of integrity of the controlling family.
7. Professionally managed companies, in general, react somewhat slowly to new opportunities and challenges, put greater emphasis on systems, favour the interest of incumbent management over that of shareholders and set relatively easy performance standards. In the nutshell, the corporate governance system in the private sector may be characterized as the entrenched system, given the firm hold of the promoters over the companies managed by them and the disinclination and/or inability of others to challenge them.

Corporate Governance in the Public Sector

The salient features of corporate governance in the public sector are as follows:

1. The equity shares are owned wholly or substantially (meaning 51 percent or more) by the government. (Technically, of course, the shares of the central public sector undertakings are held in the name of the President of India)
2. The boards of public sector undertakings, appointed for all practical purposes by the controlling administrative ministry, comprise of three categories of directors: (i) functional directors, who are full time employees of the concerned public sector undertaking (ii) government directors who are bureaucrats from the controlling administrative ministry, and (iii) outside directors.

3. There is, in general, a good deal of political and bureaucratic influence over the management of public sector undertakings. As a result, the autonomy of the management is often substantially eroded.
4. Public sector undertakings are constrained by various regulations and administrative guidelines. Further, they are subject to the CAG audit and are accountable to the parliament. This leads to an excessive emphasis on observing rules, regulations and guidelines. Efficiency and performance are often sacrificed at the alter of propriety.
5. Chief executives of public sector undertakings have short tenures, often one to five years. It is uncommon to find a chief executive (typically designated as Chairman and Managing Director) who has been at the helm of affairs for more than five years. Such a short tenure, coupled with limited freedom, leads to a myopic outlook. It is rare to find a visionary leader guiding the destiny of a public sector undertaking with a long planning horizon. Most of the chief executives seem to be concerned with fulfilling short-term targets emanating from the Memorandums of Understanding (MOUs). Incidentally, the MOUs appear to be the outcome of an elaborate budgetary game between the management and the government.
6. In general, performance standards are soft, compensation levels low, incentives for performance poor and real accountability weak.

In summary, the corporate governance system in the public sector may be characterized as the 'transient system' with the key players, viz. politicians, bureaucrats, and managers taking a myopic view of things.

Code of Conduct for Corporate Governance

SEBI prescribes that there should be a conduct for board of director. It shall be obligatory for the board of a company to lay down the code of conduct for all board members and senior management of a company. This code is conduct shall be posted on the website. All board members and senior management personnel shall affirm compliance with the code of conduct. The annual report of the company shall contain a declaration to this effect signed by the CEO and COO. While drafting the code of conduct for corporate governance for the entire corporate sector, the following aspects can be kept in view:

- Prescribing of ethical values which are universally acceptable
- Providing for highest standards of functioning as board of directors in an impartial and objective manner
- Ensuring transparency in functioning
- How requisite care and diligence has to be ensured in functioning
- Encouraging discipline
- Avoiding conflict of interest
- Ensuring confidentiality

- Providing of requisite incentives for efficient and effective functioning
- Respecting one another
- Loyalty to the organization
- Providing motivation

In this context, a reference can be made to the Organisation for Economic Co-operation and Development (OECD) which has prepared guidelines for multinational enterprises. These provide principles and standards for good practice consistent with applicable laws. The general policies of the OECD lay down that enterprises should contribute to economic, social and environmental progress with the view to achieving sustainable development, respect for human rights of those affected by their activities consistent with the host government's international obligations and commitments. Something on these lines can be thought of for the corporate governance code. In short, the code of conduct must enthuse the board of directors and executives of the company to set goals to arrive at the most right decisions in the interest of the company and ultimately of the country.

Measures to Improve Corporate Conduct

The paradigm shift in the approach to corporate governance is quite evident in the recommendations by committees on the issue in the context of four different countries. The measures that were suggested for improving corporate conduct include:

1. Improving financial disclosure norms
2. Making relevant non financial disclosures mandatory
3. Making the management more accountable towards fulfilling its responsibility to society at large
4. Changing the composition and functioning of company boards with greater proportion of competent non-executive directors
5. Formation of audit committees consisting exclusively of non-executive independent director
6. Suggesting ways of effective involvement of institutional investors in the management and conduct of the affair of a company
7. Facilitating free play of market forces in securing a change of management.

The over-riding objective of corporate governance is to maximize the market value of shareholders wealth. To facilitate the realization of this objective:

Freedom, Accountability, Alignment of interests, Contestability, Introduce the cumulative voting system, Adhere to one share one vote principle, Limit the size of the board, Remove restrictions on institutional investors, Encourage employees to own stock, grant real autonomy and raise accountability, Enhance contestability.

Suggested Question

1. Emmunerate the principal factors which have led to the recognition of the social responsibilities of business.
2. Why is the social responsibility of business receiving so much attention these days?
3. Conrast social responsibility and social responsiveness. How are they related to social responsibility and why?
4. What does social responsibility mean to you? Do you think business firms show be socially responsible? Why?
5. What is corporate governance? Discuss the importance of corporate governance in the current business world.
6. Discuss the main features of corporate governance in the Indian private sector.
7. What are the measures to promote better corporate governance practice in the public sector.
8. Discuss the basic features of Anglo American model of corporate governance.

References

1. Michael C. Jensen, '*The Modern Industrial Revolution Exit, and the failure of Internal Control System*, Journal of Finance, July 1993.
2. Jonathan Charkham, *Keeping Good Company: A Study of Corporate Governance in Five Countries*, Clarendon Press, 1994.
3. Prasanna Chandra *Financial Management, Theory & Practice,* (TMH Publication), 2005.
4. David & Decenzo, *Human Relations Personal & Professional Development*, Prentice Hall, USA, 1997
5. Harold Koontz, Heinz Weihrich, *Essentials of Management*, Mcgraw Hill, Publishing Co. Los Angeles
6. Michael & Hill, J. Stewart Black, Lyman W Porter *Management*, Pearson Education, Delhi. *Organisation Theory & Behaviour: Text and Cases*, B.S. Moshal, Axe Boks Pvt Ltd., New Delhi 2008.
7. Stephen P. Robbins, Mary Coutter, *Management*, Prentice Hall of India, New Delhi.
   http://www.karmayog.org/newspaperarticles9994.htm
   http://timesfoundation.indiatimes.com/articlesho/4662536.cms
   http://www.idef.org/india/CSR/aspx
   http://www.karmayog.org/CSR.2008sectors/index.htm

5 CHAPTER

ETHICAL MANAGERIAL PRACTICES

Ethics in Marketing

Marketing is a key functional area in the business organization that provides a visible interface with not only customers, but other stakeholders such as the media, investors, regulatory agencies.

Marketing is a key functional area in the business organization that provides a visible interface with not only customers, but other stakeholders such as the media, investors, regulatory agencies, channel members, trade associations, as well as others. Marketing practitioners must recognize that they not only serve their enterprises but also act as stewards of society in creating, facilitating, and executing the efficient and effective transactions that are part of the greater economy. In this role, marketers should embrace the highest ethical norms of practicing professionals and the ethical values implied by their responsibility toward stakeholders. Thus it is important that marketing ethics should be examined from an individual, organizational, and societal perspective. The purpose of this chapter is to define, examine the nature and scope, identify issues, provide an ethical marketing framework from a practical and academic perspective.

Definition of marketing ethics

Ethics are a collection of principles of right conduct that shape the decisions people or organizations make. Ethics is the philosophy of human conduct that helps people differentiate between good or bad, and right or wrong. Practicing ethics in marketing means deliberately applying standards of fairness, or moral rights and wrongs, to marketing practice in the organization. For marketers, ethics in the workplace refers to rules, standards and principles that govern the conduct of organizational members. Therefore, ethical marketing can be defined as "practices that emphasize transparent, trustworthy, and responsible personal and organizational marketing policies and actions that exhibit integrity as well as fairness to consumers and other stakeholders (Murphy, Laczniak, Bowie and Klein, 2005). The new definition of marketing developed by the American Marketing Association (2004) states that, "marketing is an organizational function and a set of processes for creating, communicating, and delivering value to customers and for managing customer relationships in ways that benefit the organization and its stakeholders". This definition emphasizes the importance of delivering value and the responsibility of marketers to be able to create meaningful relationships that provide benefits to all relevant stakeholders. This is the first definition of marketing to include concern for stakeholders beyond the organization and customers.

Thus marketing ethics focuses on principles and standards that determine acceptable marketing conduct, as established by various stakeholders and the organization responsible for marketing activities. Many of the basic principles have been codified as laws and regulations to help marketers conform to society's expectations of conduct. But marketing ethics goes beyond legal and regulatory issues. Ethical marketing practices and principles are core building blocks in establishing trust, which help build long-term marketing relationships.

Importance of Marketing Ethics

The relationship between a customer and an organization exists because of mutual expectations built on trust, good faith, and fair dealing in their interaction. Reputation of an organization is one of its greatest intangible assets. Reputation is not a trait or state in possession of organization, rather it exists in the collective minds of various stakeholders. It is tied to the perceptions of the corporate image, brand, and mental associations in the minds of key stakeholders. The value of positive reputation is difficult to quantify but its importance cannot be overlooked. A single negative incident can influence the perception of corporate image instantly and for years afterwards, affecting sales and customer relationships. Thus protecting a firm's reputation is a critical priority. Adhering to ethical standards and practices is one of the ways in which organizations can avoid ethical lapses and misconducts.

Moreover, when an organization behaves ethically, customers develop more positive attitudes about the firm, its products, and its services. When marketing practices depart from standards that society considers acceptable, the market process becomes less efficient—sometimes it is even interrupted. Not employing ethical marketing practices may lead to dissatisfied customers, bad publicity, a lack of trust, lost business, or, sometimes, legal action. Thus, most organizations are very sensitive to the needs and opinions of their customers and look for ways to protect their long-term interests.

All organizations face significant threats from ethical misconduct and illegal behavior from employees and managers on a daily basis. Marketers often devise schemes that appear legal but are so ethically flawed that they result in scandals and legal hassels. Overbilling clients, deceptive sales methods, fraud, antitrust and price fixing are some of the marketing ethics risks. Instead of ignoring, covering up, and assuming that no one will ever learn of the ethical lapses, organizations need to resolve these issues as soon as possible. Organizations need to devise mechanisms and establish suitable infrastructure to discover, disclose, expose and deal with such events as they occur. If these issues remain unresolved or reach the level of civil litigation, it attracts a lot of negative publicity, which not only tarnishes the image of the company, but also draws intense scrutiny to the company.

Scope of Marketing Ethics

Marketing ethics not only requires an attempt to make ethical decisions, but also to avoid the unintended consequences of marketing activities.

Marketing ethics not only requires an attempt to make ethical decisions, but also to avoid the unintended consequences of marketing activities. This requires consideration of key stakeholders and their relevant interests (Fry and Polonsky, 2004). Market orientation has been found as the key variable in the successful implementation of marketing strategies (Homburg, Krohmer, and Workman, 2004). But a successful marketing strategy has not always been associated with meeting the needs and demands of all stakeholders (Miller and Lewis, 1991). There is evolving concern that organizations must focus on not just their customers, but also the important communities and groups that hold the firm accountable for its actions. A new emerging logic of marketing is that it exists to provide both social and economic processes, including a network of relationships to provide skills and knowledge to all stakeholders (Vargo and Lusch, 2004).

Stakeholders designate the individuals, groups and communities that can directly or indirectly affect, or be affected by, a firm's activities (Freeman, 1984). Marketing stakeholders can be viewed as both internal and external. Internal stakeholders include various departments, the board of directors, employees, and other interested internal parties. External stakeholders include competitors, advertising agencies, suppliers, regulators and others such as special interest groups (Miller and Lewis, 1991). The various relationships should be identified and interests understood. The complexity surrounding a determination of the effects of marketing transactions on all relevant stakeholders requires the identification of stakeholders in the exchange process (Fry and Polonsky, 2004). Based on these developments, there is a need for marketing to develop more of a stakeholder orientation rather than a narrow customer orientation. Stakeholder orientation in marketing goes beyond markets, competitors, and channel members to understanding and addressing all stakeholder demands. As a result, organizations are now under pressure to demonstrate initiatives that take a balanced perspective on stakeholder interests (Maignan, Ferrell, and Ferrell, 2005).

Key Ethical Issues in Marketing:

Marketing practices are deceptive if customers believe they will get more value from a product or service than they actually receive. Deception, which can take the form of a misrepresentation, omission, or misleading practice, can occur when working with any element of the marketing mix. Because consumers are exposed to great quantities of information about products and firms, they often become skeptical of marketing claims and selling messages and act to protect themselves from being deceived. Thus, when a product or service does not provide expected value, customers will often seek a different source.

Product Related Issues: Product-related issues most often concern with the quality of products and services provided. Among the most frequently voiced complaints are ones about products that are unsafe, that are of poor quality in construction or content, that do not contain what is promoted, or that go out of style or become obsolete before they actually need replacing. An organization that markets poor-quality or unsafe products is taking the chance that it will develop a reputation for poor products or service. In addition, it may be putting itself in jeopardy for product claims or legal action. Sometimes, however, frequent changes in product features or performance, such as those that often occur in the computer industry, make previous models of products obsolete. Such changes can be misinterpreted as planned obsolescence.

Pricing Related Issues: Pricing practices cause customers to believe that the price they pay for some unit of value in a product or service is lower than it really is. The deception might take the form of making false price comparisons, providing misleading suggested selling prices, omitting important conditions of the sale, or making very low price offers available only when other items are purchased as well.

Promotion Related Issues: Promotion practices are deceptive when the seller intentionally misstates how a product is constructed or performs, fails to disclose information regarding pyramid sales (a sales technique in which a person is recruited into a plan and then expects to make money by recruiting other people), or employs bait-and-switch selling techniques (a technique in which a business offers to sell a product or service, often at a lower price, in order to attract customers who are then encouraged to purchase a more expensive item). False or greatly exaggerated product or service claims are also deceptive. When packages are intentionally mislabeled as to contents, size, weight, or use information, that constitutes deceptive packaging. Selling hazardous or defective products without disclosing the dangers, failing to perform promised services, and not honoring warranty obligations are also considered deception.

Distribution Related Issues: Ethical questions may also arise in the distribution process. Because sales performance is the most common way in which marketing representatives and sales personnel are evaluated, performance pressures exist that may lead to ethical dilemmas. For example, pressurizing vendors to buy more than they need and pushing items that will result in higher commissions as temptations. Exerting influence to cause vendors to reduce display space for competitors' products, promising shipment when knowing delivery is not possible by the promised date, or paying vendors to carry a firm's product rather than one of its competitors are also unethical.

Marketing Research Related Issues: Information gathered from research can be important to the successful marketing of products or services. Consumers, however, may view organizations' efforts to gather data from them as invading their privacy. They are resistant to give out personal information that might cause them to become a marketing target or to receive product or sales information. When data about products or consumers are exaggerated to make a selling point, or research questions are written to obtain a specific result, consumers are misled. Without self-imposed ethical standards in the research process, management will likely make decisions based on inaccurate information.

Direct Marketing Issues: Objectionable direct marketing practices range from minor irritants, such as the timing and frequency of sales letters or commercials, to those that are offensive or even illegal. Among examples of practices that may raise ethical questions are persistent and high-pressure selling, annoying telemarketing calls, and television commercials that are too long or run too frequently. Marketing appeals created to take advantage of young or inexperienced consumers or senior citizens— including advertisements, sales appeals disguised as contests, junk mail (including electronic mail), and the use and exchange of mailing lists—may also pose ethical questions.

Consumers develop an identity in the market place that is shaped both by who they are and by what they see themselves as becoming.

Overfocus on Materialism: Consumers develop an identity in the market place that is shaped both by who they are and by what they see themselves as becoming. There is evidence that the way consumers view themselves influences their purchasing behavior. This identity is often reflected in the brands or products they consume or the way in which they lead their lives. The proliferation of information about products and services complicates decision making. Sometimes consumer desires to achieve or maintain a certain lifestyle or image results in their purchasing more than they need or can afford. Does marketing create these wants? Clearly, appeals exist that are designed to cause people to purchase more than they need or can afford. Unsolicited offers of credit cards with high limits or high interest rates, advertising appeals touting the psychological benefits of conspicuous consumption, and promotions that seek to stimulate unrecognized needs are often cited as examples of these excesses.

Issues Related to Marketing to Children: Children are an important marketing target for certain products. Because their knowledge about products, the media, and selling strategies is usually not as well developed as that of adults, children are likely to be more vulnerable to psychological appeals and strong images. Thus, ethical questions sometimes arise when they are exposed to questionable marketing tactics and messages. The proliferation of direct marketing and use of the Internet to market to children also raises ethical issues. Sometimes a few unscrupulous marketers design sites so that children are able to bypass adult supervision or control; sometimes they present objectionable materials to underage consumers or pressure them to buy items or provide credit card numbers. When this happens, it is likely that social pressure and subsequent regulation will result. Likewise, programming for children and youth in the mass media has been under scrutiny for many years.

Issues Related to Portrayal of Women In Marketing Efforts: As society changes, so do the images of and roles assumed by people, regardless of race, sex, or occupation. Women have been portrayed in a variety of ways over the years. When marketers present those images as overly conventional, formulaic, or oversimplified, people may view them as stereotypical and offensive. Examples of demeaning stereotypes include those in which women are presented as less intelligent, submissive to or obsessed with men, unable to assume leadership roles or make decisions, or skimpily dressed in order to appeal to the sexual interests of males. Harmful stereotypes include those portraying women as obsessed with their appearance or conforming to some ideal of size, weight, or beauty. When images are considered demeaning or harmful, they will work to the detriment of the organization.

Advertisements, in particular, should be evaluated to be sure that the images projected are not offensive.

Recent Trends in Ethical Marketing:

Relationship Marketing and Ethics: Relationship Marketing has come to be recognized as a reasonable practice leading to positive relationships between buyers and sellers. It allows buyers and sellers to work together. However, there are disadvantages to this approach- relationship marketing requires time to develop a list of expected conduct or "rules of behavior." According to a recently published book on this subject, a shift in emphasis in marketing ethics – towards buyers interests and away from seller's interests – characterizes the new country. If this is true, new challenges are presented for marketing ethics and professionals in the field of marketing who want to conduct business in an ethical way.

Green Marketing and Ethics: Rising concern about certain environmental issues like conservation of natural resources, reducing pollution, protecting endangered species, and control of land use has left marketers scrambling for ways to present themselves as being environment conscious. It is imperative for them to know about the relevance of Green Marketing in order to protect the environment and to improve the quality of life. The three Rs of environmentalism are Reduce, Reuse, and Recycle. Many companies are finding that consumers are willing to pay more for a green product. Toyota has become quite successful with their hybrid cars.

Green marketing refers to the development and distribution of ecologically-safe products.

Green marketing refers to the development and distribution of ecologically-safe products.

It refers to products and packages that have one or more of the following characteristics: (1) are less toxic, (2) are more durable, (3) contain reusable materials, or (4) are made of recyclable material. In short, these are products considered "environmentally responsible". To sight an example, in West Germany and Canada, Procter & Gamble has found high consumer acceptance of pouches of liquid detergents and fabric softeners so consumers can refill rather than discard large plastic bottles.

Cause – Related Marketing and Ethics: Cause-related marketing emerged as one of the ways to help a particular company improve its image or to increase market share. The technique involves associating a business with a cause. If flawed Cause-related marketing can hurt a company by creating an impression of exploiting a charity. It is important for the firm to be transparent and honest about what it is doing. There should also be a fit between the company and the cause. A good fit would be, for example, might be a bottled water company and a cause, it deals with providing clean water for poor people in Asia and Africa.

Social Marketing and Ethics: Social marketing is a tactic used solely to help society by dealing with a social problem. Social Marketing is defined as the use of marketing principles and techniques to influence a target audience to voluntarily accept, reject, modify, or abandon a behaviour for the benefit of individuals, groups or society as a whole. Social marketing is usually done by a non-profit organization, government, or quasi-government agency. The goal is either to steer the public away from products that are harmful to them and /or society (e.g., illegal drugs, tobacco, alcohol, etc.) or to direct them towards behaviors or products that are helpful to them and / or society (e.g., having family meals, praying together, etc.).

Ethical Norms and Values for Marketers

Professional associations and accrediting bodies have identified guidelines for ethics in marketing. The American Marketing Association commits itself to promoting the highest standard of professional ethical norms and values for its members. Norms are established standards of conduct that are expected and maintained by society and / or professional organizations. Values represent the collective conception of what people find desirable, important and morally proper. Values serve as the criteria for evaluating the actions of others. Marketing practitioners must recognize that they not only serve their enterprises but also act as stewards of society in creating, facilitating and executing the efficient and effective transactions that are part of the greater economy. In this role Marketers should embrace the highest ethical norms of practicing professionals and the ethical values implied by their responsibility toward stakeholders (e.g., customers, employees, investors, channel members, regulators and the host community).

1. Marketers must accept responsibility for the consequences of their activities and make every effort to ensure that their decisions, recommendations, and actions function to identify, serve, and satisfy all relevant publics: customers, organizations and society
2. Honesty, Integrity and Quality are far more important than quick profits (Shel Horowitz)
3. Rights and duties in the marketing exchange process: - Participants should be able to expect that products and services are safe and fit for intended uses; that communications about offered products and services are not **deceptive;** that all parties intend to discharge their obligations, financial and otherwise, in **good faith;** and that appropriate internal methods exist for equitable adjustment and / or redress of grievances concerning purchases.
4. Organizational relationships: - Marketers should be aware of how their behavior influences the behavior of others in organizational relationships. They should not demand, encourage, or apply coercion to encourage unethical behavior in their relationships with others.
5. Conduct your business so as to build long term loyalty. When you get a customer, you want to keep that customer and build a sales relationship that can not only last years, but also create a stream of referral business. (Shel Horowitz)
6. Marketers must do no harm. This means doing work for which they are appropriately trained or experienced so that they can actively add value to their organizations and customers. It also means adhering to all applicable laws and regulations and embodying high ethical standards in the choices they make.

7. Marketers must foster trust in the marketing system. This means that products are appropriate for their intended and promoted uses. It requires that marketing communications about goods and services are not intentionally deceptive or misleading. It suggests building relationships that provide for the equitable adjustment and / or redress of customer grievances. It implies striving for good faith and fair dealing so as to contribute toward the efficacy of the exchange process.
8. Marketers must embrace, communicate and practice the fundamental ethical values that will improve consumer confidence in the integrity of the marketing exchange system. These basic values are intentionally aspiration and include honesty, responsibility, fairness, respect, openness and citizenship

References:

1. American Marketing Association. "*What Are The Definitions of Marketing and Marketing Research*?," available at http://www.marketingpower.com/content4620.php, accessed December 8, 2004.
2. Ferrell, O.C. 2004. "Business Ethics and Customer Stakeholders." Academy of Management Executive, Vol. 18, No. 2, 126-129.
3. Ferrell, O.C. and L. Ferrell. 2005. "Ethics and Marketing Education." Marketing Education Review.
4. Freeman, R.E. 1984. Strategic Management: A Stakeholder Approach. Boston: Pitman.
5. Fry, M. and M.J. Polonsky. 2004. "Examining the Unintended Consequences of Marketing," *Journal of Business Research*, Vol. 57, 1303-1306.
6. Homburg, C., H. Krohmer, and J.P. Workman. 2004. "*A Strategy Implementation Perspective of Market Orientation,*" *Journal of Business Research*, Vol. 57, 1331-1340.
7. Maignan, I., O.C. Ferrell, and L. Ferrell. 2005. "A Stakeholder Model for Implementing Social Responsibility in Marketing." *European Journal of Marketing*, forthcoming.
8. Maignan, I., O.C. Ferrell, and L. Ferrell. 2004. "Corporate Social Responsibility and Marketing: An Integrative Framework." *Journal of the Academy of Marketing Science*, 32 (1): 3-19.
9. Miller, R.L. and W.F. Lewis. 1991. "A Stakeholder Approach to Marketing Management Using the Value Exchange Models," *European Journal of Marketing*, Vol. 25, No. 8, 55-68.
10. M Mohamed Labbai. "Social Responsibility and Ethics in Marketing." International Marketing Conference on Marketing & Society, 8-10 April, 2007, IIMK
11. Murphy, P.E., G.R. Laczniak, N.E. Bowie, and T.A. Klein. 2005. *Ethical Marketing*, Upper Saddle River, N.J: Pearson Prentice-Hall.
12. Vargo, S.L. and R.F. Lusch. 2004. "*Evolving to a New Dominant Logic for Marketing.*" *Journal of Marketing*, Vol. 68 (January 2004): 1-17.

ETHICS IN FINANCE

There is a general assumption that ethics and finance are poles apart. At the fundamental level finance is all about making money, the means of achieving which does not really matter. Status and recognition depend on how much profit is made regardless of how it is made. It is believed that people in the financial sector are inherently less ethical than those elsewhere. "Within this finance paradigm," Dobson observes, "a rational agent is simply one who pursues personal material advantage ad infinitum. In essence, to be rational in finance is to be individualistic, materialistic, and competitive. Business is a game played by individuals, as with all games the object is to win, and winning is measured in terms solely of material wealth. Within the discipline this rationality concept is never questioned, and has indeed become the theory-of-the-firm's sine qua non". But this assumption does not stand the test of empirical tests. Yes, there may be larger temptations here given the money that can be made, and perhaps even bigger opportunities. But once again, it is the power of context that is relevant. It is not that professionals in the financial sector are inherently less ethical, but given the environment of the financial sector, there may be larger incidence of unethical behaviour.

The financial system, at its heart, is all about trust. The word credit is derived from the Latin word 'credere,' which means 'to believe.' Billions and trillions of financial transactions taking place everyday are all based on trust. People who work in finance are placed in a fiduciary position of trust; first, by their employers, if they're not self-employed, but more importantly, by members of the general public, over whose assets they are given control. Their daily business involves working with other people's money, or doing other things that affect the public's investment decisions, and if they are unethical people, their clients, and the public, are at high risk for being cheated. Ethics of finance is narrowly reduced to the mathematical function of shareholder wealth maximization. Ethics seen from the stakeholder perspective is the privilege of the immediate and remote stakeholders as much as it is the obligation of the firms towards them.

Conventionally economics is seen as a moral science and philosophy directed at a shared 'good life'. Adam Smith characterized it in terms of a set of external material goods and internal intellectual and moral excellences of character. For Dobson (1993), the true role of ethics in finance is to be found in the acceptance of 'internal good' ('good' in the sense of 'right' rather than in the sense of 'physical product'), which, he adds, is what classical philosophers describe as 'virtue'—that is, the internal good toward which all human endeavor should strive. He contends: "If the attainment of internal goods were to become generally accepted as the ultimate objective of all human endeavor, both personal and professional, then financial markets would become truly ethical."

Theoretical assumptions

Ethical dilemmas and ethical violations in finance can be attributed to an inconsistency in various ethical assumptions that have tried to shape the field of economics. Adam Smith in his book 'Wealth of the Nations' commented, "'All for ourselves, and nothing for other people, seems, in every age of the world, to have been the vile maxim of the masters of mankind." However, a section of economists influenced by the ideology of **neoliberalism**, interpreted the objective of economics to be maximization of financial growth through accelerated consumption and production of goods and services. Proponents of the ideology hold that liberation of financial systems would ensure economic growth through competitive capital market system ensuring promotion of high levels of savings, investment, employment, productivity, foreign capital in flows and thereby welfare along with containing corruption. In other words, it was recommended that governments of the impoverished nations should open up their financial systems to global market with the least regulation over the flow of capital. The recommendations however met with serious criticisms from various schools of ethical philosophy. The pragmatically oriented ethicists believed that blind submission to the a priori claims which are merely ideological, could be ethically counterproductive. The welfare claim of the Laissez-faire finance is disputed because, welfare would be overridden given a conflict with liberty. Further, history of finance does not suggest that firms always maintain principles of honesty and fairness under unregulated environments. The prudence and ethics of recommendations to the countries which were impoverished by the ravages of centuries of colonial exploitation, subsequent cold wars and subjection to imperial hegemony to unconditionally open up their economies to transnational finance corporations is fiercely contested by ethicists from various quarters. Further, the claim that deregulation and the opening up economies bringing down corruption too is contested.

There is also a conflict between two other schools of thought, financial economic theory that characterizes the modern capitalist system and the agency theory. The modern financial-economic theory is based on the **rational-maximizer** paradigm, which holds that individuals are self-seeking (egoistic) and that they behave rationally when they seek to maximize their own interests. The behavioral assumption of the modern financial-economic theory runs counter to the ideas of trustworthiness, loyalty, fidelity, stewardship, and concern for others that underlie the traditional principal-agent relationship.

The modern financial-economic theory is based on the rational-maximizer **paradigm, which holds that individuals are self-seeking (egoistic) and that they behave rationally when they seek to maximize their own interests.**

The traditional concept of agency is based on moral values. The **principal-agent** model of relationships refers to an arrangement whereby one party, acting as an agent for another, carries out certain functions on behalf of that other. But if human beings are rational maximizers, then agency on behalf of others in the traditional sense is impossible. The agency theory assumes that both the agent and the principal are self-interested and aim to maximize their gain in their relationship. This theory is value-free because it does not pass judgment on whether the maximization behavior is good or bad. "The job of agency theory is to help devise techniques for describing the conflict inherent in the principal-agent relationship and controlling the situations so that the agent, acting from self-interest, does as little harm as possible to the principal's interest." (DeGeorge, 1992).

The ethical dilemma presented by the problem of conflicting interests has been addressed in some areas of finance, such as corporate governance, by converting the agency relationship into a purely contractual relationship that uses a carrot-and-stick approach to ensure ethical behavior by agents. In corporate governance, the problem of conflict between management (agent) and stockholders (principal) is described as an agency problem. The agency theory turns the traditional concept of agency relationship into a structured (contractual) relationship in which the principal can influence the actions of agents through incentives, motivations, and punishment schemes. The principal essentially uses monetary rewards, punishments, and the agency laws to command loyalty from the agent.

Importance of Ethics in Finance

Ethics are important because finances make people do some strange things. The spreadsheet does not have a conscience, and the goal of working with spreadsheets is to make numbers add up in a way that is pleasing to the organizations and it's constituents. Unfortunately, people can move around numbers in all sorts of ways to make them add up 'correctly'. The famous 'Enron' case is a textbook example of why financial ethics are important. The trouble with Enron was that everyone was happy as long as the numbers kept looking good. However, much mischief was afoot at Enron and the company was running fast and loose with ethical principles. Because of this, companies adopt financial management ethics in order to have an outside source of guidance. People are afraid (and rightly so) that without a moral barometer, anything is possible on that spreadsheet.

Given the many scandals of recent years, many companies have done their best to publicize their codes of ethics, and to acknowledge their responsibility to the public. These firms know that public confidence in their finance people matters a great deal, and unethical behavior (or even the perception of such behavior) on the part of a firm means that people will stay away from that firm, and they may stay away from all the others as well.

Ethical Issues in Finance

This global financial crisis has been the deepest, broadest and most hurting financial crisis since 1929. This crisis has caused a massive break down of trust: trust in the financial system, trust in bankers, trust in business, trust in business leaders, trust in investment advisers, trust in credit rating agencies, in politicians, in the media and in the process of globalization. If look at the complex gamut of the causes of the crisis, almost all of these relate to how the financial system operated.

If we look at the loaning schemes in market we would observe that sub-prime borrowers are being given loans at teaser rates. And these borrowers are led to believe that they would never lose as the price of the house they were buying will only keep going up. The loans are sliced and diced, built into complex products and rated by rating agencies. Dazzled by these ratings, gullible investors lap up the mortgage based assets (MBA) not realizing the risk they are taking. Meanwhile investment banks take the MBAs off their balance sheets so that they could leverage once more and repeat the cycle of sub-prime lending. In such cases the behaviour of actors across the chain of the financial sector turn out to be unfair, unethical and immoral. Such behaviours are swayed by the opportunity of making quick profit afforded by information asymmetries. The borrowers are never adequately warned that there is a good chance that asset prices could even fall.

Another ethical issue exposed by the crisis is that of moral hazard in the banking system – something that has come to be called privatization of profit and socialization of costs. Banks enjoy an implicit guarantee of government bailout. This is true regardless of whether a large segment of the banking sector is owned by the government as in our country, or whether the banks are privately owned as is the case in most countries. Governments, regardless of their political affiliations, can hardly afford to have large institutions fail. This "too big to fail" syndrome enables financial institutions to take risks that, say a soap manufacturer, cannot take. If as a result banks make huge profits, they can reward themselves with generous pay packets and bonuses. And if loans sour and the balance sheets crash, no worry since the bank will be bailed out at tax payers expense.

Insider trading is another grave ethical issue observed in financial markets. It refers to trading in the securities of a company to take advantage of material 'inside' information about the company that is not available to the public. Such a trade is motivated by the possibility of generating extraordinary gain with the help of information that is not yet made public. It gives the trader an unfair advantage over other traders in the same security. Insider trading was legal in some European countries until recently. In the United States, the 1984 Trading Sanctions Act made it illegal to trade in a security while in the possession of material nonpublic information. The law applies to both the insiders, who have access to nonpublic information, and the people with whom they share such information.

Some of the most frequently occurring ethical violations in finance relate to insider trading, stakeholder interest versus stockholder interest, investment management, and campaign financing. Business in general and financial markets in particular are replete with examples of violations of trust and loyalty in both public and private dealings. Fraudulent financial dealings, influence peddling and corruption in governments, brokers not maintaining proper records of customer trading, cheating customers of their trading profits, unauthorized transactions, insider trading, misuse of customer funds for personal gain, mispricing customer trades, and corruption and larceny in banking have become common occurrences.

Some of the most frequently occurring ethical violations in finance relate to insider trading, stakeholder interest versus stockholder interest, investment management, and campaign financing.

Conclusion

In an effort to address the ethical problems in business and finance the conceptual foundation of the modern capitalist system has been reexamined and changed to one that is consistent with the traditional model of agency relationship. The rational-maximizer assumption that underlies the modern financial-economic theory is being questioned and the idea that all human actions are motivated by self-interest is rejected. The proponents of this view embrace an alternative assumption—that human beings are to some degree ethical and altruistic—and emphasize the role of the traditional principal-agent relationship based on honesty, loyalty, and trust. Duska (1992) argues: "Clearly, there is an extent to which [Adam] Smith and the economists are right. Human beings are self-interested and will not always look out for the interest of others. But there are times they will set aside their interests to act on behalf of others. Agency situations were presumably set up to guarantee those times."

The idea that human beings can be honest and altruistic is an empirically valid assumption. This idea should be embraced and nurtured. As Bowie (1991) points out: "Looking out for oneself is a natural, powerful motive that needs little, if any, social reinforcement. . . . Altruistic motives, even if they too are natural, are not as powerful: they need to be socially reinforced and nurtured."

John Stuart Mill said that if we make men honest, good and decent, then they will make themselves honest, good and decent engineers, doctors and teachers, and to add to it, financial sector professionals too. The financial sector is, after all, a reflection of the society in which it operates. So, the approach to bring ethical values into finance has to begin not by special efforts to enforce or regulate ethical standards in finance, but by fostering a value system in society at large.

References:

1. Bowie, Norman E. (1991). "Challenging the Egoistic Paradigm." Business Ethics Quarterly.
   1. 1-4.
2. Bowie, Norman E., and Freeman, Edward R., eds. (1992). *Ethics and Agency Theory: An Introduction*. New York: Oxford University Press.
3. DeGeorge, Richard T. (1992) "*Agency Theory and the Ethics of Agency.*" In Norman E. Bowie and Edward R. Freeman, eds. *Ethics and Agency Theory: An Introduction*. New York: Oxford University Press.
4. Dempsey, Mike. (1999). "*An Agenda for Window-Dressing or for Radical Change?*" http://panopticon.csustan.edu/cpa99/html/dempsy.html.
5. Dobson, John. (1993). "*The Role of Ethics in Finance.*" *Financial Analysis Journal.* November-December: 57-61.
6. Duska, Ronald R. (1992). "*Why Be a Loyal Agent*? A Systematic Ethical Analysis." In *Ethics and Agency Theory: An Introduction*. Norman E. Bowie and Edward R. Freeman, eds,, New York: Oxford University Press.
7. Dr Duvvuri Subbarao, (Governor of the Reserve Bank of India), Keynote address at the Conference on "*Ethics and the World of Finance*", organised by Sri Sathya Sai University, Prasanthi Nilayam, Andhra Pradesh, 28 August 2009.
8. Nadler, Paul S. (1989). "*Ethics and the Financial Community.*" *Secured Lender.* January-February.

   http://www.helium.com/items/1387999-the-importance-of-financial-management-ethics

ETHICS IN HUMAN RESOURCE MANAGEMENT

Human Resource Management is at the heart of many of the issues that affect the individual's capacity to work thereby contributing to overall organizational profitability. Human resource managers are responsible for recruitment, selection, orientation, performance evaluation, training and development, IR and health, and safety issues. They not only ensure better manpower utilization in the organization but are also responsible for creating a healthy culture of work. Ethics as a system of moral principles is also one of the considerable concerns to human resource executives.

Scholars in the field of business ethics have given high priority to employees and the employment relationship. They focus on the rights of employees and the procedural justice of employment practices. The nature of relationships between employees and employers can vary greatly. At one extreme, the relationships can be casual, short-term, and probably involve strictly instrumental exchanges of small amounts of time and labour for limited rewards At another extreme is the employment relationship that consumes the majority of an employee's time and emotional energy, with the expectation of a lifelong career within one organization, determining not only financial rewards and immediate lifestyle, but a person's lifetime opportunities for personal development.

Traditionally, many companies viewed employees as a cost centre in relation to the business and attempted to minimise costs through tight labour contracts and provision of the bare minimum of health and safety standards. Ethical human resource management takes the view that employees are far from cost but are in fact a unique value adding component of business operations. They need to be valued and treated with a lot of care and concern. Organizations need to make themselves into 'employers of choice'. This is where sound human resource (HR) development and systems become important so that HR leaders can strategically support the organization for the good of the organization itself.

As human resources influence many of the key systems and business processes underpinning effective delivery, it is well positioned to foster an ethical and high performance culture. HR can be the key organizational partner to ensure that what the organization is saying publicly aligns with how people are treated within the organization. HR is in the enviable position of being able to provide the tools and framework for the executive team and CEO to embed ethics and morality into the brand and the strategic framework of the organization. It is the only function that influences across the entire enterprise for the entire 'lifecycle' of the employees who work there – thus it has considerable influence if handled correctly. HR is poised for this lead role as it is adept at working horizontally and vertically across and within the organization, so important for creating an ethically sound organization.

Ethical issues are complex. It is difficult to determine whose interest are involved and what consequences your actions, or lack thereof, might have on them—the shareholders, employees, customers, guests, and public. Ethical decisions concern conformity to moral standards or to the standards of conduct. Defining acceptable behavior is not easy. The difficulty lies in maintaining a proper balance between the common good and personal freedom, between the legitimate business needs of an organization and a worker's feeling of dignity and worth. As an HR professional, you might think that your decisions and actions are appropriate if nothing is done, as many at Arthur Andersen and Enron did, and presumably still do, but the final call isn't any individuals to make. Ethics is both a corporate and societal issue, easily becoming a legal and criminal one as well.

Stakeholder Theory and Ethical HRM

Stakeholder theory is based on two principles that balance the rights of the claimants on the corporation with the consequences of the corporate form.

Stakeholder theory is based on two principles that balance the rights of the claimants on the corporation with the consequences of the corporate form. The first, the principle of corporate effects, states that the corporation and its managers are responsible for the effects of their actions on others. This principle is drawn from the theory of utilitarianism which holds that moral worth of actions or practices is determined solely by their consequences. A corporation is thus seen as responsible for its impact in all areas that would necessarily include its social impact.

The second principle of corporate rights, states that the corporation and its managers may not violate the legitimate rights of others to determine their own future. This principle is drawn from the deontological ethical theory of Kant (1724–1804) based on the respect-for-persons principle that persons should be treated as ends and never only as means. This implies that the corporation must treat its stakeholders as rational beings with a right to pursue their own interests without undue interference.

Employees are identified as key stakeholders in the organization. They are closely integrated with the firm and contribute to the firm in fundamental ways. Employees actually 'constitute' the firm and are the most important factor or 'resource' of the corporation. They represent the company towards other stakeholders, and act in the name of the corporation. They are greatly affected by the success or failure of the firm. Thus according to the stakeholder theory the organization is required to treat its employees as an end in their own right and to bear the consequences of its behaviour towards employees. This stance is consistent with pluralist assumptions of the employment relationship. The parties have entered into a contract with consent and voluntary action. The organization has positive obligations by virtue of its acceptance of the benefits of employees' contribution and vice versa. Employees have the fundamental rights to liberty and safety within the workplace including: freedom of association, the right to organize, collective bargaining, abolition of forced labour, equality of opportunity and treatment, and other standards regulating conditions across the entire spectrum of work-related issues. Some authors also suggest that employees have the right to meaningful work. In addition, employees have the right to 'respect', which includes the rights to freedom, well-being, and equality. This view of ethical HRM implies that the organization will not only act in the interests of its employees and do so with the intent of furthering those interests, but also involve employees in decisions regarding those interests. In the light of these claims it is clear that demands on the organization of ethical HRM are very high.

Significance of Ethics in HRM

The benefits of undertaking ethical human resource management include greater engagement of employees which may lead to decreased staff turnover, opportunities for greater innovation as employees feel valued and potential to be considered an employer of choice. An engaged workforce leads to increased production, innovation and good word of mouth advertising for the company as an employer.

Any kind of ethical lapse or violation on the part of organization's HR team can lead to enormous loss for the organization. Energy levels at work drop, gossip and rumors abound, attendance floats, turnover excels, clients lose trust, and profits decrease to the point of extinction. Due to the nature of the position, the HR department is usually right in the middle. HR people need to make quick decisions regarding whether they will support "what is right" or "turn their head." Within the process of decision making someone usually gets hurt economically, but we can't overlook the physical and psychological impacts. Morale can be destroyed overnight and productivity becomes nonexistent when a manager is known to have violated the company Code of Ethics or values for the sake of selfish and personal gain. Enron's bankruptcy has had enormous adverse affect upon its employees and its many investors. What is interesting is how the ethical violation injures, one way or another, every person that has contact with the situation.

The final loser in the ethical mess of today's 21st century age is no doubt society. We can think of it as social pollution. Corporate transgressors cause enormous loss for future generations. Some issues are small and cause ripples in society, others shout greatly and bring tidal waves of repercussions. Economic systems work best when they are supported by the rule of law and customs and practices based upon reciprocity. We cannot do business as a culture if trust is lost, values have no meaning, and everything has to be solved through litigation. Good reputations and solid ethical decisions in business create value. It is the HR people who have resting on their shoulders the role of ethics guardian and monitor for today's enterprise. They are the ones who are most passionate about supporting and developing the employees.

Key Ethical Issues in HRM

Ethics sometimes fall by the wayside when organizations do not have a solid value-based culture starting from the top and working its way down. When this occurs, it is typically HR that is called to get involved. The discussions on ethical issues that may arise in the employment relationship include the ethics of discrimination, and employees' rights and duties. While some argue that there are certain inalienable rights of workplace such as a right to work, a right to privacy, a right to be paid in accordance with comparable worth, a right not to be the victim of discrimination, others claim that these rights are negotiable.

Issues such as sexual harassment toleration, knowingly hiring illegal immigrants, violation of privacy, biased performance reviews, wage and hour violations for the sake of saving overtime pay, terminating whistle-blowers for reasons totally unrelated to performance are some examples of unethical HR practices.

In 1991 a survey of 1,078 respondents- mostly Human Resources Vice Presidents or Directors- reported that the most serious ethical problems faced by today's HR professionals have to do with managers making personnel decisions based on factors other than performance. Ten most serious ethical situations reported by these HR managers are as follows:

- Hiring, training or promotion based on favoritism
- Allowing differences in pay, discipline, promotion etc, due to friendships with top management.
- Sexual harassment
- Sexual discrimination in promotion
- Using discipline for managerial and non-managerial personnel inconsistently
- Not maintaining confidentiality
- Sexual discrimination in compensation
- Non performance factors used in appraisals
- Arrangements with vendors or consulting agencies leading to personal gain
- Sexual discrimination in recruitment or hiring.

Some other key ethical issues related to organizations' HR practices as highlighted by Wikipedia are as follows:

- Discrimination issues include discrimination on the bases of age, gender, race, religion, disabilities, weight and attractiveness.
- Issues arising from the traditional view of relationships between employers and employees, also known as 'At-will employment.'
- Issues surrounding the representation of employees and the democratization of the workplace like union busting, strike breaking.
- Issues affecting the privacy of the employee like workplace surveillance, drug testing etc.
- Issues affecting the privacy of the employer that is whistle-blowing.
- Issues relating to the fairness of the employment contract and the balance of power between employer and employee like slavery, indentured servitude, employment law.
- Occupational safety and health related lapses.

All of the above are also related to the hiring and firing of employees. An employee or future employee cannot be hired or fired based on race, age, gender, religion, or any other discriminatory act.

Ethical HR Practices

Ethics is not something that could be achieved through establishment of procedures, drawing codes of ethics, or enactment of law or any other heteronymous means. It needs to be ingrained into the culture of organizations. Ethics should become the way of working in the organizations. Though market need not be the cause of moral or ethical hazards it may serve an occasion for such hazards. The moral hazards of HRM would keep on increasing as far as human relations and the resources embedded within humans are treated merely as commodities. Ethical practices in human resource management include valuing human capital, providing safe and healthy workplaces and a work/life balance; embracing diversity in human resources and continual skills development for all employees.

HR professionals can ensure ethical working by following the given steps:

It is the responsibility of HR professionals to ensure the maintenance of highest standards of professional and personal conduct.

They need to encourage their employers to make the fair and equitable treatment of all employees a primary concern.

HR professionals strive to make their employers profitable in terms of monetary profits as well as promote effective employment practices that will further encourage effective individual performance.

They should instill in the employees and the public a sense of confidence about the conduct and intentions of their employers.

They have to maintain loyalty to their employers and pursue their objectives in ways that are consistent with the public interest.

They should maintain the confidentiality of privileged information.

All in all HR professionals need to create a safe and healthy work environment. In most jurisdictions there are minimum standards which must be met in relation to employee health and safety. It is also possible to go further than the bare minimum and create a workplace health promotion program. Implementing a workplace health promotion program is also an opportunity to improve employee engagement and value human capital.

Suggested Question

1. Define the term 'Marketing Ethics' Discuss same ethical issues in marketing with the help of suitable examples.
2. Enumerate various norms and values that are must follow in order to behave like an ethical marketer.
3. In right of Principal – Agent Theory discuss the importance of ethics in financial management.

4. Discuss the importance of ethics in Human Resource Management in the right of state holds Theory.
5. Discuss some ethical issues in financial management.
6. What can H.R. Professionals do to ensure ethical working in the organisation?

References

1. Commerce Clearing House, "1991 SHRM/CCH survey," CCH *Human Resource Management* services, June 26, 1991.
2. Coro Strandberg, '*The Role of Human Resource Management in Corporate Social Responsibility: Issue Brief & Roadmap*' Strandberg Consulting, May 2009.
3. David Ardagh, '*The ethical basis for HRM professionalism and codes of conduct. Chapter 9 of 'Human Resource Management: Ethics and Employment'* (2007), Edited by
4. Ashly H. Pinnington, Rob Macklin & Tom Campbell, pg 152
5. Michelle Greenwood and Helen De Cieri, '*Stakeholder theory and the ethics of HRM.*' Chapter 7 of '*Human Resource Management: Ethics and Employment*' (2007), Edited by
6. Ashly H. Pinnington, Rob Macklin & Tom Campbell, Pg 119
7. Tracey Lloyd, '*Ethical Human Resource Management: Use Corporate Social Responsibility Practices to Value Human Capital*'. http://ethical-business-management.suite101.com/article. cfm/ethical_human_resources_management
8. Wendell French, '*Looking Ahead in Human Resource Management*,' Chapter 23 of 'Human Resource Management' 1997.

http://en.wikipedia.org/wiki/Business_ethics#Ethics_of_human_resource_management

STRESS

No one's life is free of stress. Regardless of how sensible, intelligent or privileged we are, we will be challenged at times by frustration, losses and conflict. Stress comes from negative events, such as failing a college course, but stress is part of many positive events too, such as starting a new job or having a baby. Stress is inescapable as death and taxes.

A certain amount of stress is probably healthy it energies us and challenges us to grow. But stress is generally experienced as an uncomfortable, unhealthy force that many of us would be happier without. If one has experienced the death of a loved one or a divorce, one would have first hand knowledge of the emotions that such stress can bring. But we should not forget that the psychological part of us exists in our biological part and that what affects our mind also affects our body.

If stress is inevitable and too much then it is a threat to our psychological and physiological well being, then coping well with stress is of paramount importance. A healthy and happy person is someone, who can enjoy the good times and cope with the bad. Sometimes we can cope with stress by removing it – by changing jobs or trying to tackle the factors or causes causing stress. But we cannot remove all the stress from our lives and will have to cope with some of it. Generally, we are better able to cope with the kinds of stress that we have had previous experience with and that we can control somewhat. Good social support also improves our ability to cope with stress. Simply disclosing our feelings to friends (or a psychotherapist) has been shown to improve immune system functioning and reduce need for medical care. But there will be times when we cope ineffectively with stress. The trick, of course, is to cope as effectively as possible and not to worry too much about the stress.

What is Stress?

Modern life is full of stress. As organizations become more complex, the potential for and amount of stress increases. Urbanisation, industrialization and the increase in scales of operations are causes of increasing stresses. These are the inevitable consequences of socio-economic complexity. People feel stressed as they can no longer have complete control over what happens in their life. The telephone goes out of order, the power is shut off, the water supply is disrupted, an expected promotion is denied, son or a daughter does not do well in college, prices of essential commodities increase disproportionately to the income, and so on and so forth and we feel frustrated and then stressed out.

Stress refers to the body's physiological, emotional & psychological response to an individuals well being. When the response is in the form of a deviation from healthy functioning, the state is called *DISTRESS*.

Stress refers to the body's physiological, emotional & psychological response to an individuals well being. When the response is in the form of a deviation from healthy functioning, the state is called *DISTRESS*. The reaction that activates and motivates people to achieve their goals, change their environment & face life's challenges is called *EUSTRESS*. In other words, this is the stress that is required for survival. A stressor is an environmental stimulus that affects an organism in physically or psychologically injurious ways, usually producing anxiety, tension and physiological arousal. ANXIETY is a generalized feeling of fear and apprehension that may be related to a particular event or object and is often accompanied by increased physiological arousal. Physiological arousal, often the first change that appears when a person reacts/responds to a stressor, includes changes in autonomic nervous system that brings about increased heart rate, faster breathing, higher blood pressure, sweating palms and dilation of the pupils. Whenever something negatively affects someone, physically or psychologically, the person may experience the effects of stress. STRESS is a non-specific, often global, response by an organism to real or imagined demands made on it; it is an emotional response. The key is that not all people view a stimulus or a situation in the same way; a person, must appraise s situation as stressful for it to be stressful. This broad definition recognizes that everyone experiences stress at some time, but that stress is also an interpreted state; stress is a response on the part of an individual.

Types of Stress

The degree of stress experienced depends on many factors. First, the demand must be perceived (people must be aware that it exists) as threatening (having the potential to hurt them if they do not react appropriately), second, the threat must be something that is important to people (has the potential to substantially affect their well being). Finally people experiencing the threatening demand must be uncertain about the outcome (not sure if they can deal with it effectively). Based on the stress experienced, it has been classified into various types.

Constructive and Destructive Stress

The word stress often has a negative connotation. It generally refers to aggravated feelings because of unpleasant experiences. The impact of distress includes ulcers, heart attacks, depression and suicides. Distress is the destructive form of stress. On the other hand, sometimes stress also has a positive impact, resulting in a feeling of excitement and enthusiasm. This is also known as enstress or constructive stress. Some degree of emotional or psychological arousal is necessary to motivate us for most of our daily activities. This constructive stress gives us the energy to excel in our work and to be creative.

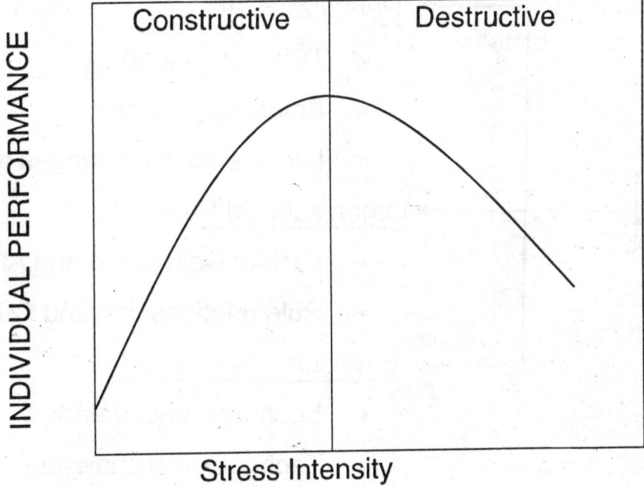

Episodic and Chronic Stress

Throughout a normal day, week, month or year, we are likely to experience a wide range of stress levels, from crisis to relaxation, as we react to deadlines, emergencies and vacations.

"The pattern of high degree of stress followed by an interval of relief is referred to as episodic stress." We endure anxiety, cope with the challenges and then relax. An elevated level of stress is necessary during crisis situations as it creates a sense of readiness to fight or flee followed by a period of relaxation and renewal. Unfortunately, the patterns of stress, people face because of job insecurity, cost of living, deadlines and poor relationships are continuous. These types of situations produce what is known as chronic stress, in which a person can neither fight nor flee. This stress is constant and addictive. The after effects of such stress may vary from aggression and irritability to just bearing the pressure calmly. The cost of maintaining continuously high levels of chronic stress is often a serious health breakdown.

Sources of Stress

Stress is a reality of our everyday life. The work and non work domains of one's life are closely inter twined. The stresses and strain experienced in one domain are carried over to the other. Thus, if one experienced much distress at work, that stress will be carried over to the home, which will heighten the sense of awareness of even small distresses experienced in the family sphere. Likewise stresses experienced at home or with friends or from other non work facets can be carried over to the work place which might heighten and compound the stresses experienced at work. There appears little doubt that one of the major adverse influences on job satisfaction, work performance, productivity, absenteeism and turnover is the incidence of stress at work. Stress is a complex and dynamic concept. It is a source of tension and frustration and can arise through a number of interrelated influences on behavior, including the individual, group, organizational and environmental factors.

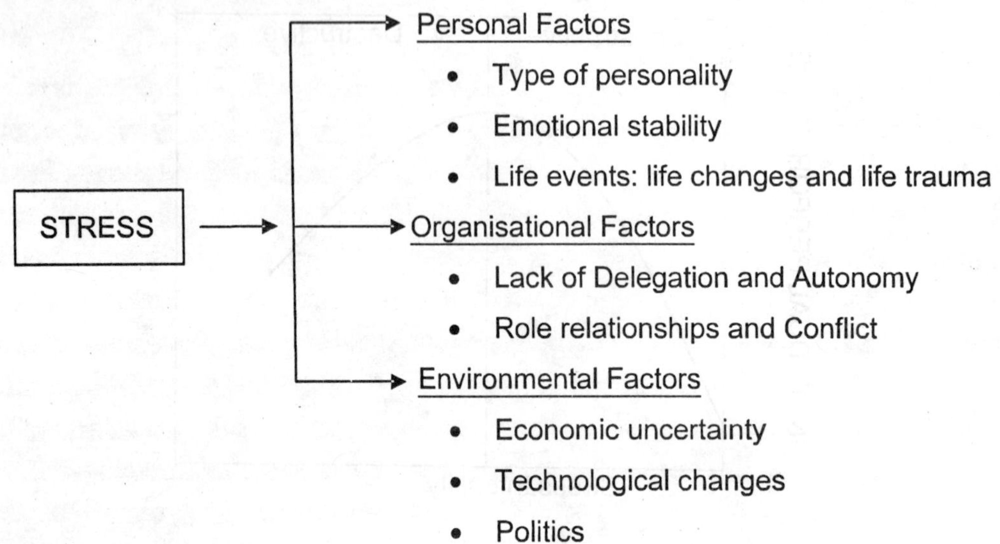

Personal Factors

Personality and Stress

Personality plays a significant role in how we perceive stress. An experience that is stressful for one person may be part of normal days for another. Our personality types play a critical role in determining our reaction to stress.

Type A Personality

The main characteristics of people with Type A personality are that they are impatient, competitive, aggressive, restless and under intense perceived time pressure, always attempting to accomplish several things at one time. The type B personalities do not feel rushed even under pressure and they take things in a more relaxed manner and enjoy a variety of non work oriented activities. As type A personalities tend to work under tight deadlines and devote long hours accomplishing their duties and responsibilities, they achieve promotions at a very rapid speed. Initially they report a high level of job satisfaction and do not encounter a high incidence of health problems. However, they seldom manage to retain good health for a long time and therefore it becomes detrimental for them to reach top level positions in the organization.

Emotional Stability

Hardiness is a person's ability to cope with stress. People with stable and strong personalities have an internal locus of control are strongly committed to activities in their lives and view change as an opportunity for advancement and growth such people are seen as relatively unlikely to suffer illness if they experience high levels of pressure and stress. On the other hand people with low hardiness may have more difficulties in coping with pressure and stress. Optimism is the extent to which a person sees life in positive or negative terms. Optimistic people tend to handle stress better. They will be able to see the positive characteristics of the situation and recognize that things may eventually improve. In contrast, less optimistic people may focus more on the negative characteristics of the situation and expect things to get worse and not better.

Life Events

Life stressors generally are categorized in terms of life change and life trauma. In recent years, a great deal of research has focused on the stressful nature of important life events. Major events and changes in our lives require adjustment and coping whether they are negative changes such as divorce, death of a spouse, improvement etc or positive changes such as marriage, change of job, residence etc. Negative life events are clearly a source of stress: Death of a family member learning that one has a life threatening illness, being assaulted and loss of a job are potent source of stress. Natural disasters also can potently stressful negative life events. Other studies have documented the stressful impact of witnessing violence, being physically or sexually assaulted and other stresses of modern life. It is probable that daily hassles are an important source of stress, we must be cautions in estimating how potent they are. If we are not happy or not feeling well, it may be that we would remember to write down more of the hassles of the day or indeed, would be more likely to experience events like slow drive home through traffic as a hassle. That is, hassles may be both a cause and a result of stress.

Importantly, there is also reason to believe that positive life events may be stressful under some circumstances. Marriage, birth of a child, job promotion and buying a house are examples of events that most people think of as positive, but they may also require stressful adjustments in patterns of living. Hence, positive life changes can be another source of stress of which we are typically unaware. The relationship between stressful life events and physical illness has been the subject of a great deal of research.

Organisational Factors

Stress at the organizational level can emanate from different factors:

Lack of Delegation and Autonomy

Research into managers in various types of organizations showed that delegation of responsibility to middle managers require great skill, which is too seldom present. There is clear correlation between lack of autonomy and stress at work. Stress is often caused by the hierarchical structure of the organization not permitting sufficient autonomy. As a result, projects are frequently delayed and also manager's authorities within their own departments are undermined.

Role Relationships and Conflict

One potential major source of work stress arises from role incongruence and role conflict. Role stress can lead to difficulties in communication and interpersonal relationships and can have an adverse affect on morale, performance and effectiveness at work and health. There are number of sources which are responsible for role stress at work.

ROLE AMBIGUITY

When the individual is not clear about the various expectations people have from his or her role, he or she faces conflict which may be called role ambiguity. Role ambiguity may be due to lack of understanding of the cues available. Role ambiguity may be in relation to activities, responsibilities, priorities, norms or general expectation. Generally, role ambiguity is experienced by people occupying roles newly created in the organization, roles in organizations undergoing change, or process roles (with less clear and concrete activities).

Role Stagnation

As the individual grows physically, he or she also grows in the role the individual occupies in an organization. He or she expects to learn new things, take up challenging tasks, prepare for higher responsibilities etc. When the role does not provide such opportunities, the individual experiences role stagnation. This becomes an acute problem especially when an individual has occupied a role for a long time and keeps performing the same routine functions.

Role Expectation Conflict

When there are conflicting expectations or demands from different role senders (people having expectation from the role), the role occupant may experience this stress. They may be conflicting expectations from the boss, subordinates, peers or clients.

Role Overload

When the role occupant feels that there are too many expectations from the significant role senders in the role set, he or she experiences work load. When there is an expectation from the organization to accomplish more than the ability of the person, it results in work overload. It has been found that for top and middle level managers, unreasonable deadlines and constant pressure are the frequent stressors in their jobs.

Role Underload

Most people wish to remain occupied and face optimum challenges while performing their jobs. Work underload occurs when people have insufficient work to fill their time or are not allowed to use enough of their skills and abilities. Employees who are underloaded often feel bored, weary, are prone to injury and frequently absent from work.

Career Development

One of the major sources of stress in organization today is the aspiration level of employees. The issues related to career planning and development such as job security, promotion, transfers and other developmental processes like under promotion (failure to grow in the job as the aspiration levels or over promotion (promotion to a job that exceeds the competency levels of employees) or personal inadequacy can create high anxiety and stress among the persons concerned.

Demands for improved business competitiveness & lower operating costs have frequently led to restructuring of organizations and reductions in staffing levels. This has placed greater pressures on remaining staff and result in growing number of work related health problems, work stress and less efficient work force. There are broadly five organizational situations that are likely to create role problems and therefore stress for the individual:

1. **Responsibility for the Work of Others -** Reconciling, overlapping or conflicting objectives of groups and organization of groups and individuals of self and superiors.
2. **Innovative Functions –** Conflicting priorities and different psychological demands between the routine and administrative aspects of the job and the creative side.
3. **Integrative or Boundary Functions –** The particularly stressful role of the coordinator, link person or outside contact, perhaps due to the lack of control over their demands or resources.
4. **Relationship Problems –** Difficulties with a boss, subordinates or colleagues. For some people, particularly those with a technical orientation, the need to work with other people is a worrying complication
5. **Career Uncertainty –** If future career prospects become doubtful the uncertainty may quickly become stressful and spread to affect the whole of person's work.

A summary of sources of Role Stress at work is given below:

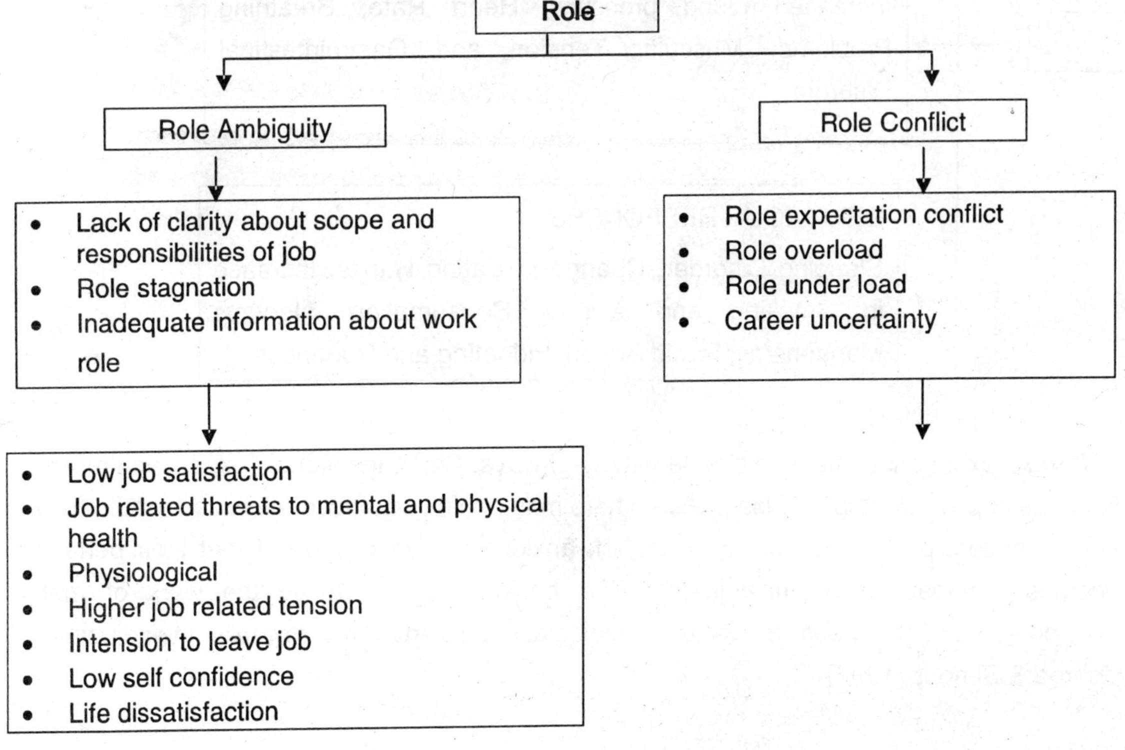

- Low motivation to work
- Depression
- Greater futility
- Lower self esteem

- Physiological strain
- Low job satisfaction
- Job related tension

- Greater Futility
- Lower Self-Esteem

Environmental Factors

The environment in which the organization operate has a profound impact on their working. The economic, political and technological events happening in the external environment causes stress in varying degrees as they have many uncertainties associated with them. The anxiety around by uncertain environmental factors is carried over into the work place and then to our personal lives.

Responses to Stress

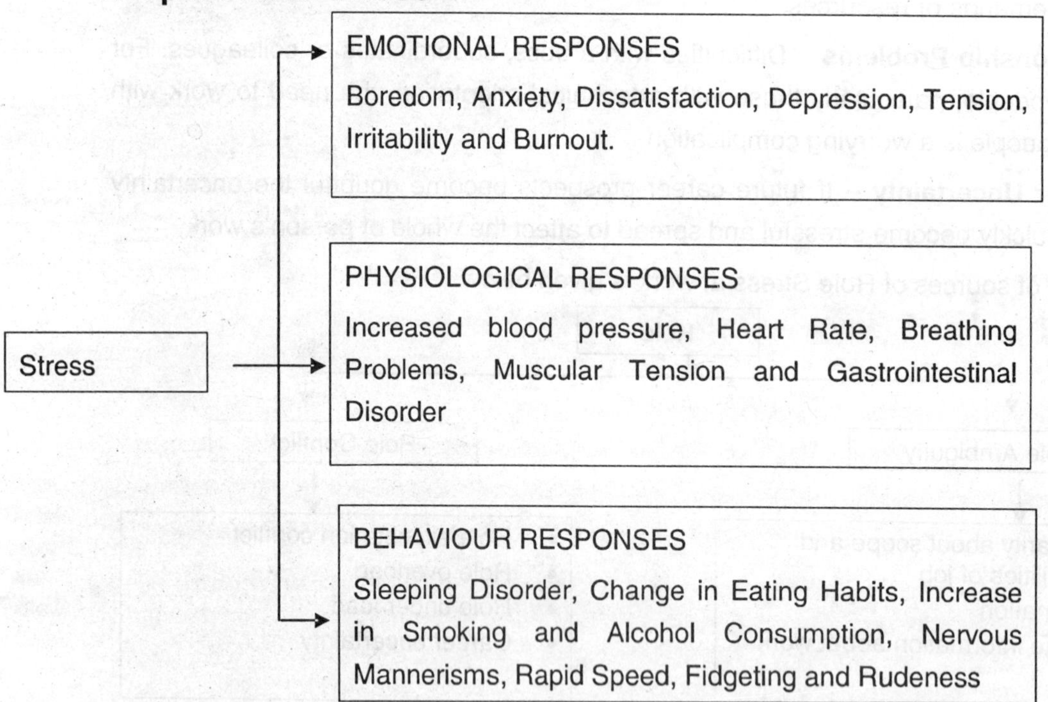

People experience stress in a wide variety of ways. Some individuals experience modest increases in physiological arousal, while others may exhibit significant physical symptoms. In extreme cases, people become so aroused, anxious and disorganized that their behavior becomes maladaptive or maladjusted. The basic idea underlying the work of many researchers is that stress activates a biological predisposition towards maladjustment (Monroe & Simons, 1991)

Emotional, Physiological and Behavioural

Psychologists who study stress typically divide the stress reaction into emotional, physiological and behavioural components.

Psychologists who study stress typically divide the stress reaction into emotional, physiological and behavioural components.

Emotionally, people's reactions often depend on their frustration, their work related pressures, and their day to day conflict when frustrated, people become angry or annoyed; when pressured, they become aroused and anxious; when placed in situations of conflict, they may vacillate or become irritable and hostile.

Physiologically, the stress response is characterized by arousal i.e. changes in the autonomic nervous system that causes increased heart rate, higher blood pressure, faster breathing, sweating palms and dilation of pupils. Arousal is often the first change that occurs when a person feel stressed.

Behaviourally, stress and its arousal response is related. The reaction leads to sleep disorders, changes in eating habits, increase in smoking and alcohol consumption, nervous mannerisms such as rapid speech, fidgeting and rude behavior.

Burnout

A stress reaction especially common in people with high standards is burnout. Burnout is a state of emotional and physical exhaustion, lowered productivity and feelings of isolation, often caused by work related pressures. Although burnout is most often work related, pressures caused by family, financial or social situations can create the same feelings. Burnout victims develop negative self concepts because they are unable to maintain the high standards they have set for themselves.

Studying Stress: Focus on Physiology

Psychologists want to know how today's increasingly complex lifestyles affect the physical and psychological well being of individuals. For example, does intense competition make business people more susceptible to heart attacks? How can psychologists help people cope with life stressors, such as having a baby? How can therapists help veterans who are trumatised by war? These questions have helped researchers develop theories of stressors. One of the best known theories is Hans Selyes "General Adaptation Syndrome" or GAS.

Selye's General Adaptation Syndrome

In the year 1930, Hans Selys (1907-1982) began a systematic study of stressors and stress. Selye conceptualized people's responses to stress in terms of General Adaptation Syndrome (A syndrome is a set of responses; in the case of stress, it is a set of behaviourally defined physical symptoms)

According to Selye people's response to a stressor occurs in three stages.

1. An initial short term stage of *alarm*
2. A longer period of *resistance,* and
3. A final stage of *exhaustion*

During the alarm stage, people experience increased physiological arousal. They become excited, anxious or frightened. Bodily resources are mobiised. Metabolism speeds up dramatically and blood is diverted from the skin to the brain, resulting in pale appearance.

Later on in the stress response, people may also experience loss of appetite, sleeplessness, headaches, ulcers or hormonal imbalances; their normal level of ability to cope with stressors decreases.

Because people cannot stay highly aroused for very long, the initial alarm response usually leads to resistance. During this stage, physiological and behavioural responses become more moderate and sustained. People in the resistance stage often are irritable, impatient, and angry, and they may be constantly tired. This stage can persist for a few hours, several days or even years although eventually resistance begins to decline. Couples who suffer traumatic divorces sometimes exhibit anger and emotional fatigue years after the conflict has been resolved in the court.

The final stage is exhaustion, stress saps psychological energy; adaptability is depleted. If people don't reduce their level of stress, they can become too exhausted to adapt. At that point, they again become extremely alarmed and finally give up. The air traffic controller who takes no vacations, works long shifts, and is being expected to do more with less help may show the symptoms of maladjustment or withdrawal. In extreme cases of constant stress, as in war, serious illness or death may occur. Of course, not everyone shows the same behaviour.

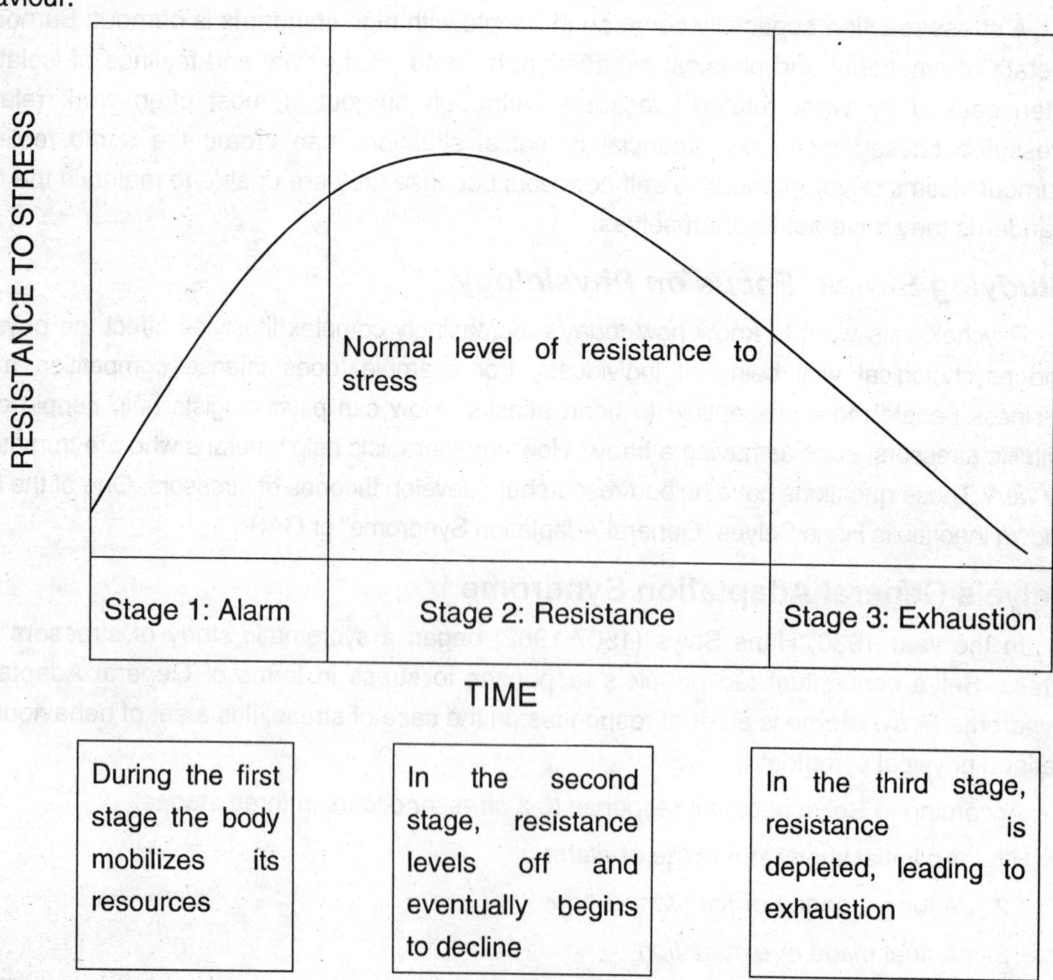

GAS FIGURE

Coping

Most people need a way to cope with anxiety and with the physical ailment produced by stress. Some people seek medical and psychological help; while others turn to alcohol and other drugs.

What is Coping

In general, coping means dealing with a situation. However, for a psychologist, coping is the process by which a person takes some action to manage environmental and internal demands that cause or might cause stress and that will tax the individual's inner resources. This definition of coping involves five important components. *First,* coping is constantly changing and being evaluated and is therefore a process or a strategy. *Second,* coping involves managing situations, not necessarily bringing them under complete control. *Third,* coping is effortful. It does not happen automatically. *Fourth,* coping aims to manage cognitive as well as behavioural events. *Finally,* coping is a learned process.

Coping means dealing with a situation. However, for a psychologist, coping is the process by which a person takes some action to manage environmental and internal demands that cause or might cause stress and that will tax the individual's inner resources.

Effective coping methods and ineffective coping methods are two broad methods/ strategies to deal with stress.

Effective Coping

Effective methods of coping either remove the source of stress or control our reactions to it.

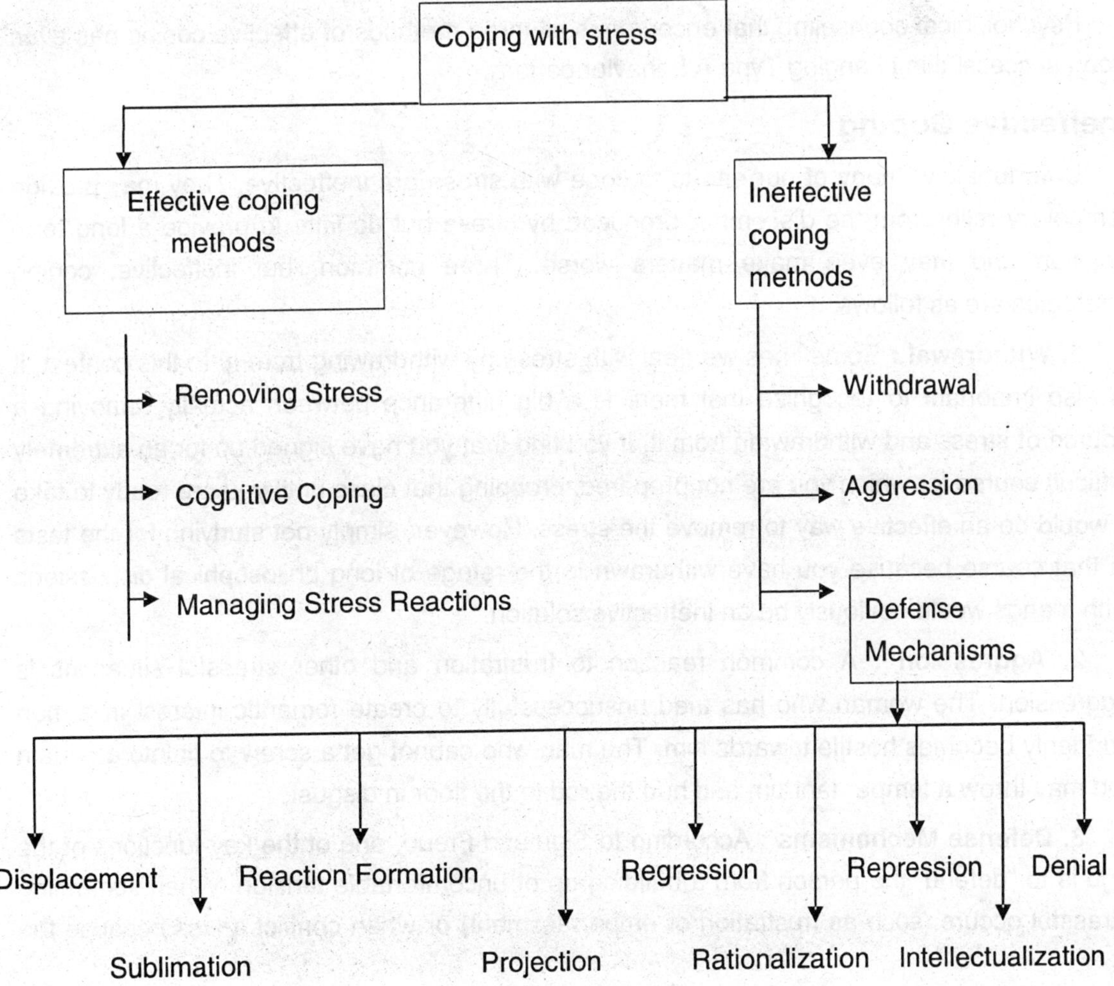

1. Removing Stress : One effective way of dealing with stress is to remove the source of stress from our lives. If an employee holds a job that is stressful, discussions could be held with the employer that might lead to a reduction in the pressures of the job, or the employee could simply resign. In a variety of ways, coping with stress can take the form of locating its sources and eliminating it. Unfortunately, this is not always possible. It is not always feasible or appropriate to quit a job, and some sources of stress, such as death of a spouse, just cannot be removed.

2. Cognitive Coping : Our cognitions are intimately linked to our reactions to stressful events. One effective method of coping then, can be changing how we think about or interpret the events that push and shove our lives. Finding an interpretation that is realistic and minimizes the stress of the events of our lives is a key part of coping with stress.

3. Managing Stress Reaction : When the source of stress cannot realistically be removed or changed, another effective option is to manage the reaction to the stress. For example, an individual may decide to start a new business knowing fully well that the first year or two will be hectic he would be unwilling, then to remove the source of the stress. One strategy might be to schedule as much time as possible for relaxing activities, such as aerobic exercises, hobbies or time with friends. Another would be to seek special training from a psychologist in controlling the bodily reactions to stress by learning to deeply relax the body muscles.

Psychological counseling that encourages all three methods of effective coping has even been successful in changing Type A behavior pattern.

Ineffective Coping

Unfortunately, many of our efforts to cope with stress are ineffective. They may provide temporary relief from the discomfort produced by stress but do little to provide a long term solution and may even make matters worse. Three common, but ineffective, coping strategies are as follows:

1. Withdrawal : Sometimes we deal with stress by withdrawing from it. In this context, it is also important to recognize that there is a big difference between actually removing a source of stress and withdrawing from it. If you find that you have signed up for an extremely difficult course for which you are not prepared, dropping that class until you are ready to take it would be an effective way to remove the stress. However, simply not studying for the tests in that course because you have withdrawn to the refuge of long philosophical discussions with friends would obviously be an ineffective solution.

2. Aggression : A common reaction to frustration and other stressful situations is aggression. The woman who has tried unsuccessfully to create romantic interest in a man suddenly becomes hostile towards him. The man who cannot get a screw to fit into a curtain rod may throw a temper tantrum and hurl the rod to the floor in disgust.

3. Defense Mechanisms : According to Sigmund Freud, one of the key functions of the ego is to "defend" the person from a building up of uncomfortable tension. When something stressful occurs (such as frustration or embarrassment) or when conflict arises because the superego blocks an id desire, tension is created that must be discharged somehow. Freud believed that the ego possesses a small arsenal of defense mechanisms that are unconsciously used to discharge tension. When they are not overused, defense mechanisms can be relatively harmless crutch to a healthy personality – all of us use them to some extent. The major defense mechanisms are as follows:

(*a*) **Displacement :** When it's unsafe or inappropriate to express aggressive or sexual feelings toward the person who is creating such (such as a boss who pressures you), that feeling can be directed toward someone safe (such as getting at your friend when you are actually angry with your boss)

(*b*) **Sublimation :** Stressful conflicts over dangerous feelings or motives are reduced by converting the impulses into socially approved activities, such as school work, literature, sports and so on.

(*c*) **Projection :** One's own dangerous or unacceptable desire or emotions are not seen as one's own but as the desires or feelings of others. A person who has stressful conflicts about lying might perceive himself as having little lying habit but views other people as being compulsive liars.

(*d*) **Reaction Formation :** Conflicts over dangerous motives or feelings are avoided by unconsciously transforming them into the opposite desire. A woman who wishes her hateful mother would die might devote herself to finding ways to protect her mother's health.

(*e*) **Regression :** Stress may be reduced by returning to an earlier pattern of behavior, such as a business executive who has a stomping, screaming, temper, tantrum when his company suffers or major setback.

(*f*) **Rationalisation :** Stress is reduced by "*explaining it away*", in ways that sound logical and socially acceptable. A man who is rejected by his lover may decide that he is glad because she has so many faults or because he really did not want to give up the single life.

(*g*) **Repression :** Potentially stressful, unacceptable desires are kept out of consciousness without the person being consciously aware that the repression is occurring.

(*h*) **Denial :** Uplifting or threatening thoughts and emotions related to stressful events are not allowed into conscious awareness. For example, a person who finds that she has blood pressure during a routine medical checkup may never again think about the upsetting fact, even though her physician has urged her to change her habits of diet and exercise.

(*i*) **Intellectualisation :** The emotional nature of stressful events is lessened at times by reducing it to cold, intellectual logic. For example, the person who learns that he has lost a large sum of money in an overly risky investment may think about it in a detached way as a temporary debit in a successful lifelong programme of investment, rather than as a painful financial mistake that should be avoided in the future through careful planning.

Defense, mechanisms can be effective in the short run in helping us feel better, but they inhibit long term solutions to stress if they distort reality to a great extent. For example, suppose a student copes reasonably well with the stress of failing a course in college by deciding that her teacher graded his test paper unfairly because he use to ask many questions in class. If his teacher is actually fair and competent, he would be distorting reality by using the defense mechanism of rationalization. A simple change in study habits or test taking strategies might make a big difference in his grades, but he will never see the need for change if he distorts reality through rationalization. The other defense mechanisms can be harmful in similar reality distorting ways.

Taking responsibility for preventive behaviors can be an important step toward better physical and mental health. There are a number of steps one can take to cope, manage stress, and stay healthy:

- *Increase Exercise* – People are able to cope better when they improve their physical fitness, usually by exercising. In addition, increased exercise will lower blood pressure and reduce the risk of heart disease.
- *Eat Well* – People feel better and cope better when they eat well and have a balanced diet. This also means not being overweight.
- *Sleep Well* – People react better to life when they have had a good night's sleep; reaction time improves, as does judgment.
- *Be Flexible* – Life is unpredictable; accept that fact, and day to day changes and surprises will be easier to handle.
- *Keep Stress at School or the Office* – Work related stressors should be kept in the work environment. Bringing stressors home will only make stress worse. People are more likely to be involved in substance abuse and domestic violence when they bring stressors home with them.
- *Communicate* – Share your ideas, feelings and thoughts with the significant people in your life. This will decrease misunderstanding, mistrust, and stress.
- *Learn to Relax* – In this fast-paced society, seldom people take the time to relax and let uncomfortable ideas and feelings leave them. Learn meditation, yoga, or deep breathing. Schedule sometime each day for yourself.
- *Seek Support* – Social support from family, friends and self help groups helps you appraise situations differently. Remember, you have to appraise a situation as stressful for it to be stressful. Social support helps you keep stressful situations in perspective.

Yoga advocates control over the body, the senses and the mind. It recommends perfection.

Astanga Yoga

Yoga advocates control over the body, the senses and the mind. It recommends perfection. A sound mind needs a sound body. Sensual attachment and passions distract the body as well as the mind. They must be conquered. To overcome them, *Yoga* gives us the Eightfold Path of Discipline (*Astanga Yoga*):

1. *Yama* – It means abstention and includes the five vows. It is abstention from injury through thought, word or deed (*ahimsa*), from falsehood *(satya)*, from stealing (*asteya),* from passions and lust (*brahmacharya)* and from avarice i.e. non-possession (*aparigraha*).
2. *Niyama* – It is self-culture and includes external and internal purification (*shaucha*), contentment (*santosa*), austerity (tapas), study (*svadhyaya*) and devotion to God (*ishvara pranidhana*).
3. *Asana* – it means steady and comfortable posture. There are various kinds of postures which are a physical help to meditation. This is the discipline of the body.
4. *Pranayama* – It means control of breath and deals with regulation of inhalation, retention and exhalation of breath. It is beneficial to health and is highly conducive to the concentration of the mind. But it must be performed under expert guidance otherwise it may have bad after-effects.
5. *Pratyahara* – It is control of the senses and consists in with drawing the senses from their objects. Our senses have a natural tendency to go to outward objects. They must be checked and directed towards the internal goal. It is the process of introversion.

   These five are called external aids to Yoga (*bahiranga sadhana*), while the remaining three which follow are called internal aids (*antaranga sadhana*). These five disciplines are very important for the business world. The various disciplines regarding food habit, regular exercise and control of senses keep workers happy and satisfied. It enhances the productivity and cohesiveness in the organization.
6. *Dharana* – It is fixing the mind on the object of meditation like the tip of the nose or the mid-point of the eyebrows or the lotus of the heart or the image of the deity. The mind must be steadfast like the unflickering flame of the lamp.
7. *Dhyana* – It means meditation and consists in the undisturbed flow of thought round the object of meditation (*pratyayaikatanata*). It is the steadfast contemplation without any break.
8. *Samadhi* – It means concentration. This is the final step in Yoga. Here the mind is completely absorbed in the object of meditation. In *dhyana* the act of meditation and the object of meditation remain separate. But here they become one. It is the highest means to realize the cessation of mental modifications which is the end. It is the ecstatic state in which the connection with the external world is broken and through which one has to pass before obtaining liberation.

Samadhi is of two kinds: Conscious or *samprajnata* and supraconscious or *asamprajnata*. In the former consciousness of the object of meditation persists, in the latter it is transcended. The former is *Ekagra*, the latter is *Niruddha*. In the former the mind remains concentrated on the object of meditation. The meditator and the object of meditation are fused together, yet the consciousness of the object of meditation persists. This state is said to be of four kinds:

(a) *Savitarka* – When the *Chitta* is concentrated on a gross object of meditation like the tip of the nose or the mid-point of the eyebrows or the image of the deity.

(b) *Savichara* – When the *Chitta* is concentrated on a subtler object of meditation like the dhyana.

(c) *Sananda* – When the *Chitta* is concentrated on a still subtler object of meditation which produces joy, like the senses.

(d) *Sasmita* – When the *Chitta* is concentrated on the ego substance with which the self is generally identified. Here we have conscious ecstasy where individuality persists.

Asamprajnata Samadhi is that supra-conscious concentration where the meditator and the object of meditation are completely fused together and there is not even consciousness of the object of meditation. Here no new mental modifications arise. They are checked (*niruddha),* though the latent impressions may continue. If fire is restricted to a particular fuel, it burns that fuel alone; but when that fuel has been completely burnt, the fire also dies down. Similarly in conscious concentration, the mind is fixed on the object of meditation alone and modification arises only in respect of this object of meditation; but in supra-conscious concentration, even this modification ceases. It is the highest form of *Yoga* which is divine madness, perfect mystic ecstasy difficult to describe and more difficult to attain. Even those who attain it cannot retain it longer. Immediately or after very short time, the body breaks and they obtain complete liberation.

Yoga generates certain supra-normal powers. But they should be avoided and attention should be fixed only on liberation which is the end of human life. The ideal is *Kaivalya*, the absolute independence and eternal and free life of the *Purusa* free from *Prakrti.*

Suggested Question

1. Define stress. What are its important constituents? Explain it with suitable examples.
2. What are the important coping strategies/techniques to manage stress? How it can be helpful for organizational stress?
3. What are the various causes of stress? Explain the physiological process of stress given by Seyle's General Adaptation Syndrome.
4. Define the various stages of *Astanga Yoga*. How it can be instrumental in removing stress?

References

1. Pareek Udai, *Understanding Organisational Behaviour*, Oxord University Press, New Delhi,2004.
2. Mullins J Laurice, *Management and Organisational Behaviour,* Pearson Education Ltd – Harlow, 2002.
3. Bennelt Roger, *Organistional Behaviour*, Pitman Publishing, Great Britain, 1997
4. Atkinson L. Rita, Atkinson C. Richard, Smith E. Edward, Ben J. Daryl, Hocksema Nolen Susan, Hilgard's, *Introduction to Psychology*, 12th Edition, Harcourt Brace College Publishers, Brace & Company, USA, 1996.
5. Lahey. B. Bengamin, *Psychology An Introduction*, Mcgraw Hill, USA, 1998.
6. George, M. Jennifer, Jones. R Gareth, *Understanding and Managing Organisational Behaviour,* Addison – Wesley Publishing Company, Inc. USA.

7 CHAPTER

GLOBALIZATION AND ITS IMPACT

Globalization

Refers to the integration of national economies into the international economy through trade, foreign direct investment, capital flows, migration and the spread of technology.

Globalization (*or globalisation*) refers to the integration of national economies into the international economy through trade, foreign direct investment, capital flows, migration and the spread of technology. However, globalization usually driven by a combination of economic, technological, socio cultural, political and biological factors can also refer to the transnational circulation of ideas, languages or popular culture through acculturation. An early description of globalization was penned by the American entrepreneur-turned-minister Charles Taze Russell who coined the term corporate giants in 1897. It was the 1960s that the term began to be widely used by economists and other social scientists. Globalization as the elimination of state enforced restrictions on exchanges across borders and the increasingly integrated and complex global system of production and exchange that emerged as a result. Sometimes the terms internationalization and globalization are used interchangeably but there is the term 'internationalization' refers to the importance of international trade, relations, treaties etc. owing to the immobility of labor and capital between or among nations. Globalization is the result of systematic trends manifesting the market economy's grow-or-die dynamics, following the rapid expansion of transnational corporations. This is a multi faceted and irreversible phenomenon within the system of the market economy and it is expressed as: economic globalization, namely, the opening and deregulation of commodity, capital and labour markets which led to the present form of neoliberal globalization, political globalistion, i.e., the emergence of a transnational elite and the phasing out of the all powerful nation state of the statist. A deep historical origin of a form of globalization has been in existence since the rise of trade links between Sumer and the Indus Valley Civilization in the third millennium B.C. Early form of globalized economics and culture existed during the Hellenistic Age, when commercialized urban centres were focused around the axis of Greek culture over a wide range that stretched from India to Spain, with such cities as Alexandria, Athens and Antioch at its center. Others have perceived an early form of globalization in the trade links between the Roman Empire, the Parthian Empire, and the Han Dynasty and the Indian Empire. The increasing articulation of commercial links between these powers inspired the development of the Silk Road, which started in western China, reached the boundaries of the Parthian empire and continued towards Indian subcontinent. With 300 Greek ships a year sailing between the Greco Roman world and India, the annual trade may have reached 300000 tons.

An early form of globalization in the trade links between the Roman Empire, the Parthian Empire, and the Han Dynasty and the Indian Empire.

The Islamic Age may be an important phase of early stage of globalization, when Jewish and Muslim traders and explorers established a sustained economy across the Old World resulting in a globalization of crops, trade, knowledge and technology. Globally significant crops such as sugar and cotton became widely cultivated across the world in this period. Pax Mongolica of the thirteenth century had globalizing effects. It witnessed the creation of the first international postal service, as well as the rapid transmission of epidemic diseases such as bubonic plague across the newly unified regions of Central Asia. These pre-modern phases of global or hemispheric exchange are sometimes known as archaic globalization. Largest systems of international exchange were limited to the Old World. The Age of Discovery brought a broad change in globalization, being the first period in which Eurasia and Africa engaged in substantial cultural, material and biological exchange with the New World. It began in the late fifteenth century, when Portgual sent the first exploratory voyages around the Horn of Africa and to the America which was discovered in 1492 by Christopher Columbus. In the sixteenth century, Portuguese started establishing trading posts (factories) from Africa to Asia and Brazil, to deal with the trade of local products like gold, spices and timber, introducing an international business center under a royal monopoly.

Global integration continued with the European colonization of the America initiating the Columbian Exchange, the enormous widespread exchange of plants, animals, foods, human populations, communicable diseases, and culture between the Eastern and Western hemispheres. It was one of the most significant global events concerning ecology, agriculture and culture in history. New crops that had come from the America via the European seafarers in the sixteenth century significantly contributed to the world's population growth. This phase is sometimes known as proto-globalization. It was characterized by the rise of maritime European empires, in the sixteenth and seventeenth centuries, first the Portguese and Spanish Empires and later the Dutch and British Empires. In the seventeenth century, globalization became a private business phenomenon when chartered companies like British East India Company (founded in 1600), often described as the first Multinational Corporation, as well as the Dutch East India Company (founded in 1602) were established. British East India Company became the first company in the world to share risk and enable joint ownership of companies' through the issuance of shares of stock. The nineteenth century witnessed the advent of globalization approaching its modern form. Globalization in this period was decisively shaped by nineteenth century imperialism. The first phase of 'modern globalization' began to break down at the beginning of the twentieth century. In the middle decades of the twentieth century globalization was largely driven by the global expansion of multinational corporations based in the United States and Europe.

Globalization, since World War II, is largely the result of planning by politicians to break down borders hampering trade to increase prosperity and interdependence thereby decreasing the chance of future war. Their work led to the Bretton Woods conference, an agreement by the world's leading politicians to lay down the framework for international commerce and finance, and the founding of several international institutions intended to oversee the processes of globalization. These institutions include the International Bank for Reconstruction and Development (the World Bank) and the International Monetary Fund. Globalization has been facilitated by advances in technology which have reduced the costs of trade, and trade negotiation rounds, regionally under the auspices of the General Agreement on Tariffs and Trade (GATT), which led to a series of agreements to remove restrictions on free trade. After the World War II, barriers to international trade have been considerably lowered through international agreements. The important features of Global trade practices are:

- Promotion of free trade
- Elimination of tariffs, creation of free trade zones with small or no tariffs
- Reduced transportation costs
- Reduction or elimination of capital controls
- Creation of subsidies for global corporations
- Harmonization of intellectual property laws across the majority of states
- Supranational recognition of intellectual property

Cultural globalization, driven by communication technology was understood at first as a process of homogenization. A contrasting trend soon became evident in the emergence of movements protesting against globalization and giving new momentum to the defense of local uniqueness, individuality, and identity. The Uruguay Round (1986 to 1994) led to a treaty to create the WTO to mediate trade disputes and set up a uniform platform of trading. Other bilateral and multilateral trade agreements, including sections of Europe's Maastricht Treaty and the North American Free Trade Agreement (NAFTA) have also been signed in pursuit of the goal of reducing tariffs and barriers to trade.

Features

Economic globalization demonstrates that it can be measured in different ways. These centers around the four main economic flows that characterize globalization:

1. Goods and services, exports plus imports as a proportion of national income or per capita of population.
2. Labour/people , net migration rates, inward or outward migration flows, weighted by population

3. Capital, inward or outward direct investment as a proportion of national income or per head of population
4. Technology, international research and development flows, proportion of populations using particular inventions such as the telephone, motorcar, broadband.

Globalization is a multivariate approach to measuring the world's most globalized country Belgium is the most globalized, followed by Austria, Sweden, the United Kingdom and the Netherlands. The least globalized countries according to the Haiti, Myanmar, the Central African Republic and Burundi.

Effects

Globalization has various aspects:

1. **Industrial** – emergence of worldwide production markets and broader access to a range of foreign products for consumers and companies. International trade in manufactured goods increased more than 100 times (from $95 billion to $12 trillion) in the 50 years since 1955.
2. **Financial** – emergence of worldwide financial markets and better access to external financing for borrowers. By the early part of the 21st century more than $1.5 trillion International currencies were traded daily to support the expanded levels of trade and investment.
3. **Economic** – realization of a global common market, based on the freedom of exchange of goods and capital. Interconnections of these markets, however, meant that an economic collapse in any one given country could not be contained as happening in recent US economic crises.
4. **Health Policy** – On the global scale, health becomes a commodity. In developing nations under the demands of Structural Adjustment Programs, health systems are fragmented and privatized. The result influenced by global trade and global economy, health policy is directed by technological advances and innovative medical trade. Global priorities, in this situation, are sometimes at odds with national priorities where increased health infrastructure and basic primary care are of more value to the public than privatized care for the wealthy.
5. **Political** – some use globalization to mean the creation of a world government which regulates the relationships among governments and guarantees the rights arising from social and economic globalization. With the influence of globalization and with the help of The United States own economy, the People's Republic of China has experienced some tremendous growth within the past decade.
6. **Information** – increase in information flows between geographically remote locations. Arguably this is a technological change with the advent of fibre optic communications, satellites, and increased availability of telephone and internet.

7. **Language** – the most popular first language is Mandarin (845 million speakers) followed by Spanish (329 million speakers) and English (328 million speakers).
8. **Competition** – Survival in the new global business market calls for improved productivity and increased competition. Due to the market becoming worldwide, companies in various industries have to upgrade their products and use technology skillfully in order to face increased competition.
9. **Ecological** – the advent of global environmental challenges that might be solved with international cooperation, such as climate change, cross boundary water and air pollution, over fishing of the ocean and the spread of invasive species. Economic development historically required a dirty industrial stage and it is argued that developing countries should not, via regulation, be prohibited from increasing their standard of living.
10. **Cultural** – growth of cross cultural contacts, advent of new categories of consciousness and identities which embodies cultural diffusion, the desire to increase one's standard of living and enjoy foreign products and ideas, adopt new technology and practices and participate in a world culture. Spreading of multiculturalism and better individual access to cultural diversity. Others consider multiculturalism to promote peace and understanding between people. Greater international travel and tourism. WHO estimate that up to 500000 people are on planes at any one time. Worldwide fads and pop culture such as Pokemon, Sudoku, Idol series, You Tube, Orkut, Face book and MySpace, accessible to those who have Internet or Television, leaving out a substantial segment of the Earth's population.
11. **Social** – development of the system of non-governmental organizations as main agents of global public policy, including humanitarian aid and developmental efforts. Development of a Global Information System, global telecommunications infrastructure and greater transborder data flow, using such technologies as the Internet, communication satellites, submarine fiber optic cable and wireless telephones. The creation of the international criminal court and international justice movements. Crime importation and raising awareness of global crime fighting efforts and cooperation. The spread and increased interrelations of various religious groups, ideas and practices.

Globalisation of Markets

Globalisation of markets refers to the process of integrating and merging of the distinct world markets into a single market. This process involves the identification of some common norm, value, taste, preference and convenience and slowly enable the cultural shift towards the use of a common product or service. A number of consumer products have global acceptance. For example, Coca-Cola, Pepsi, Chinese Food, Indian Curry, Yoga Culture,

McDonald's burgers, Levis Jeans, Indian masala dosa, Indian Hyderabadi biryani, Citicorp credit cards etc.

The globalization of markets may have following features:

- The size of the company need not be too large to create a global market. Even small companies can also create a global market. *For example,* Harry Ramsden, a small British company with an annual sales of US $ 16 million is trying to sell its product of fish 'n' chips in Japan based on the Japanese culture. Small companies who cut and polished diamonds based in Surat of Gujarat (India) and monopolisez the world trade of diamonds.
- The distinctions of national markets are still prevailing even after the globalization of markets. These distinctions require the companies to formulate different strategies for each market. *For example,* Coca-Cola, Pepsico and McDonald employ separate strategies for each country.
- Most of the foreign markets are the markets for non-consumer goods like industrial products, machinery, equipment, raw materials, computers, software, financial products etc.
- The global business firms compete with each other frequently in different national markets including their home markets. *For example,* Coca-cola is the global rival of Pepsi. Similarly Ford and Toyota, Boeing and Airbus etc. Though these companies compete with each other they create a global market.

Globalisation of Production

Factors influencing the location of manufacturing facilities vary from country to country. They may be more favourable in foreign countries rather than in the home country. *For example,* cheap labour in developing countries, availability of high quality and cheap raw material in other countries etc., enable the companies to produce the products of high quality and low cost in various foreign countries.

Companies globalize the production facilities due to the following reasons:

- Imposition of restrictions of imports by the foreign countries forces the MNCs to establish the manufacturing facilities in other countries. Toyota of Japan established its plants in USA and UK due to the import restrictions.
- Availability of high quality raw materials and components in other countries.
- Availability of inputs at low cost in foreign countries. Nokia established its firm in China.
- Availability of skilled human resources at low cost
- Liberal labour laws in the foreign countries
- To reduce the cost of transportation and easy logistics management
- Facility of exporting to other neighbouring foreign countries
- To design and produce the products as per the varying tastes of customers in foreign countries.

Therefore, the companies tend to produce in different locations of the world in order to enhance the quality, reduce the cost of production, cost of transportation and delivery time to the various markets. Thus, the globalization of production is locating the manufacturing facilities in a number of locations around the globe to take the advantages of national differences in cost, quality and availability of inputs and of reaching various markets at the shortest possible span of time. The process of globalization of production helps the companies to design the following strategies:

- Low cost leadership, Superior quality and Superior speed

For example, Jet airlines, Boeing 777 has 132500 major components. These components are produced in 545 different locations of the globe. A small optical company in USA, i.e., Swan Optical, manufactures its eyewear in low cost factories in Hongkong, China, Japan, France and Italy. In addition to the globalization of markets and production, a number of factors enable the process of globalization at the fast rate.

Globalisation of Investment

Globalisation of investment refers to investment of capital by a global company in any part of the world.

The creation of General Agreement on Tariffs and Trade (GATT) reduced the trade restrictions significantly. Further, the establishment of World Trade Organization has contributed for the elimination of investment barriers phenomenally. Many countries reduced investment barriers. Government of India reduced the barriers on investment allowing more than 51 percent of foreign investment in Indian companies. Globalisation of investment refers to investment of capital by a global company in any part of the world. Global company conducts the financial feasibility of the new projects in different countries of the world and invest the capital in that country where it is relatively more profitable. Globalisation of investment is also known as Foreign Direct Investment. Foreign Direct Investment (FDI) occurs when a firm invests directly in new facilities to produce or market a product or service in a foreign country. Coca-Cola acquired a number of bottling companies especially from Parle throughout India by investing the capital directly. It directly invests the capital in a number of countries.

The reasons for the increase in the global investment include:

- There has been a rapid increase in the volume of global trade
- Many countries provided more congenial environment for attracting direct investment. *For example,* Government of India provided for automatic approval for FDI up to 51% of capital of a company. It extended this up to 100% for the cigarette industry.
- Significant amount of FDI is directed to the developing countries in Asia and Eastern Europe.
- Small and medium size companies have started investing in various countries.
- In addition to increase in the volume of FDI, its composition has also been changing. Initially FDI was directed mostly towards USA. FDI, recently has been directed towards other countries like UK, Japan, France, China etc.

- With the recent globalization process, FDI has been directed even towards the developing countries.
- Limitations of exporting and licensing force the domestic companies to enter foreign markets through FDI.
- Global companies in order to have the control over manufacturing and marketing activities, invest in the foreign countries.
- Liberalising the measures of flow of foreign capital across the borders by various countries. Indian Government allowed foreign Institutional Investors (FIIs) to invest in Indian capital markets after registration with the SEBI.
- International firms go for FDI in order to avoid the restrictions imposed by the host country on exports. Toyota, a Japanese automobile company increased its investment in USA, UK and other countries consequent upon the imposition of restrictions on exports of automobiles by the host countries.

The other factor which contributes for the increase in global investment is the sourcing of funds globally. In other words, procuring investment internationally. Most of the MNCs procure funds from any source in the globe, wherever the cost of capital is low with feasible terms and conditions. The liberalizations announced by the Indian Government allowed the Indian companies to procure capital from other countries by issuing equity, debentures, bonds, euro issues, global deposit receipts (GDRs) etc. Reliance, Dr. Reddy's Laboratories, Satyam Computers etc., procured investment from USA and European countries.

Important sources of capital from the globe include:

- International Bank for Reconstruction and Development, IBRD provides capital to public and private sector companies of member countries.
- International Finance Corporation (IFC) provides loans at very low rate of interest and at liberalized terms and conditions even to the private sector companies. Hence, it is also known as soft loan window.
- International Development Association provides loans at liberalized conditions to the private sector companies of their developing countries.
- Asian Development Bank, African Development Banks etc., also provide loans to the private sector companies of their respective member countries.
- Mutual Funds of various countries also invest in companies based in foreign countries.
- Investors have also started investing in shares of foreign companies.

The Modes of globalistion of investment include:

- Acquisition of foreign companies
- Joint Ventures
- Long-term loans
- Issuing Equity Shares, Debentures, Bonds
- Global Deposit Receipts etc.

Globalisation of Technology

The globalization of technology include:

- Companies with latest technology acquire distinctive competencies and gain the advantages of producing high quality products at low cost. With these advantages, these companies enter the foreign markets and introduce their latest technology in foreign countries also.
- Companies may have technological collaboration with the foreign companies through which technology spreads from country to country.
- The foreign companies allow the companies of various other countries adopt their technologies on royalty payment basis or on outright purchase basis.
- Companies also globalise the technology through the modes of joint ventures and mergers.

Companies spread latest technology throughout the globe and technology itself makes the global company possible and fasten the process of globalization. Technology makes a company to acquire distinctive competencies over other foreign companies and paves the way for entering foreign markets. In addition, the latest development in information technology has enabled the global company to develop into a virtual global company.

The development of microprocessors paved the way for the growth of high power, superior speed low cost computing and handling vast amount of information. These have been revolutionary changes in global telecommunications consequent upon the developments in microprocessors. According to Moore's Law, the power of microprocessor technology doubles output and its cost of production reduces by half every 18 months. The development in microprocessors and telecommunications improved the speed and efficiency of coordinating the operations of global business firms.

The internet and World Wide Web are the backbone of future global business. The activities of the global companies across the globe are coordinated, monitored and controlled with the help of internet. The various facilities of the internet and world wide web like e-mail, voice mail, data, real time video communications such as video conferencing enable the global business companies to operate efficiently. The executives of a new automobile company in India can visit the home page of the Japanese and US automobile companies by using www search engine and download information on product designs, specifications, models, price, service to the customers, market information etc. This new Indian automobile company can make use of the information in designing its cars and pricing them.

When cultures receive outside influences, they ignore some and adopt some. One classic cultural aspect is food. Someone in America can be eating Japanese noodles for lunch while someone in Sydney, Australia is eating classic Italian meatballs. India is known for its curry and exotic spices. France is known for its cheeses. North America is known for its burgers and fries. Mcdonald's is a North American company which is now a global enterprise with 31000 locations worldwide. Usage of Chinese and Indians characters in tattoos are ever growing. These tattoos are popular with today's youth despite the lack of social acceptance of tattoos in China. The internet breaks down cultural boundaries across the world by enabling easy, near-instantaneous communication between people anywhere in a variety of digital forms and media.

Globalisation and Global Institution

Globalisation results in increased business activity so institution which can manage, regulate and police the global market, become necessary. Important global institutions which are performing these are General Agreement on Tariffs and Trade (GATT), replaced in 1995 by World Trade Organisation (WTO), International Monetary Fund (IMF), World Bank and United Nations. The World Trade Organisation is known police man for international trade. It ensures that all member countries follow the rules and regulation regarding international trade. All members are required to honour the trade theatre. In May 2005, there were 148 members of WTO collectively they account for 97% of world trade. WTO facilitates free trade by requiring members to reduce tariffs and also giving MFN status to members. A dispute settlement mechanism has been desired to resolve trade related dispute among member countries. It has proved instrumental in reducing investment barriers and in opening up markets of different member countries. It can be raised that without WTO it would have not been possible to globalize the market, production, investment *to the extent are now home.*

International Monetary Fund and World Bank both were established in 1944 following Bretton Wood Summit. The functions of IMF are to promote free trade among nations and also ensure smooth order in international monetary system. IMF provide loans to countries which suffer chronic balance of payment problem and whose currencies loose value in international market. It has helped many countres like Mexico, Argentina, Russia, Thailand and even India. But IMF loans are given with certain condition attached to them. By these conditions IMF prescribes specific economic policies to be followed by the concerned country, so that stability can be ensured to the country's economy. These conditions have generated controversies. The critics charge that IMFs policies promote interest of developed countries. Sometimes it is also said that policy prescriptions of IMF are an attack on national sovereignity. World Bank aims at promoting economic development. It provides loans at low rate of interest to developing countries for undertaking development projects in infrastructure, education etc. However it is not as much controversial as IMF. United Nations was established by *nation* in 1945 to preserve peace through international cooperation and collective security. Membership of UN is more than 200. A nation which becomes member of UN agrees to accept the obligations of the UN charter. UN charter is an international treaty that establishes basic principles of international relation. The charter outlines four objectives:

(*i*) To maintain international peace and security

(*ii*) To develop friendly relation among nations

(*iii*) To cooperate in solving international problems and in promoting respect for human right.

(*iv*) To be a centre for harmonizing the actions of nations.

UN is known for its peacekeeping role, however its goals also include promotion of higher standard of living, full employment and condition of economic and social progress and development. All these are necessary for a vibrant global economy to achieve the UN works in close association with other international institutions. Basic thinking behind this thought is that poverty anywhere is a threat to prosperity and peace.

Declining Trade Barriers and Globalisation

Many countries of the world erected favourable trade barriers during 1930. These barriers were in the form of high tariff on import of manufactured goods. These aimed at protecting domestic industries against foreign competition. But after World War II it was realized that economies could be taken back on track only through free trade of goods and services and capital. It was this realization which led to establishment of GATT rounds of negotiations, under GATT led to reduction of tariffs and to increase international flow of goods and services. Uruguay round, which started in 1986 and completed in 1993, led to establishment of trade policeman, WTO. Trade barriers were further reduced by this round of talks and services were also brought under negotiation. Uruguay round provided protection to patents, copyrights and trademarks.

Average tariff rate on manufactured products

		1913	1950	1990	2003
1	France	21%	18%	5.9%	4%
2	Germany	20%	26%	5.9%	4%
3	USA	44%	14%	4.8%	4%
4	Japan	30%	-	5.3%	4%
5	Italy	18%	25%	5.9%	4%

New round of talks were launched in 2001 known as Doha round. Agenda of negotiations include cutting tariff on industrial goods, services and agricultural goods, phasing out subsidies on agricultural products, reducing barriers to cross border investment and limiting the use of antidumping laws. But negotiations are yet to conclude. However, many countries have been progressively reducing restrictions on foreign direct investment. According to UN almost 1885 changes were made in direct investment and this created a favourable environment for FDI. There has been dramatic increase in the number of bilatered investment treaties designed to protect and promote investment countries. In 2003, 2265 such treaties in the world involved more than 160 countries.

Globalisation and National Sovereignty

It is often said that globalization shifts power away from national government and towards supranational organization such as the World Trade Organisation. Policies in these organizations are formulated by bureaucrats. These policies are composed on democratically elected governments of nation states e.g. patent laws, subsidy to agriculture, tariff rate etc.

this limits nations ability to control its own destiny. WTO is policeman of international trading system. It adjudicate on disputes among member nations and also issues to member states to change their trade policies that violate GATT regulations. If violation does not comply, the WTO permits other states to impose appropriate trade sanctions on the violation. Under new system many decisions that affect billions of people are no longer made by local or national governments but instead if challenged by many WTO member nation, would be deferred to a group of unelected bureaucrats sitting behind closed doors in Geneva. The bureaucrats can decide whether or not people in California can present the destruction of the last virgin forests or determine if carcinogenic pesticides can be banned from their foods or whether European countries have right to ban dangerous biotech harmones in meat. Against this some politician and economists say that power of organization such as WTO, UN comes from agreement among member nations. These organizations came into being only to some of the interest of nations and not to submit. Further membership of these organizations has increased not by possible submission but by voluntary association. If these organizations fail to serve the interest of members, they are free to dissociate themselves under such condition these supranational organizational will loose their existence. So real power is still with nation states.

Advantages and Disadvantages of Globalisation

Advantages	Disadvantages
➢ Free flow of capital & its growth ➢ Capital employment ➢ Free flow of technology ➢ Increase in industralisation ➢ Spread of production facilities ➢ Balanced development of world economy ➢ Increase in production & consumption ➢ High quality product at low price ➢ Exchange and demand for a variety of products ➢ Increase in job and income ➢ High standard of living ➢ Balanced human development ➢ Increase in welfare and prosperity	➢ Domestic business adversely affected ➢ Human resource exploitation ➢ Decline in demand for domestic product ➢ Increase in inequality ➢ National sovereignty at stake ➢ Danger of commercial & political colonialism

Globalisation ensures free flow of capital from one country to another. This helps narrow down differences in rate of interest across countries. Further rate of return on investment also becomes attractive. Technological flow also improves due to globalization. Obvious industralisation process among different countries, particularly among developing countries accelerates due to globalization. The capital constraint has been a great limitation in industralisation process of developing countries. As a result of industralisation of UDCs, world development takes place in balanced manner. Resources of world are more efficiently used and consumers get variety of product at fair price. This increase income, employment, standard of living of people living on this earth. But there are certain disadvantages as well, companies in developing countries may not be able to compete with multinationals as they have superior technology. Trends in recent globalization show that inequality among nations has increased over the years. Some fear that globalization may bring neo-colonialism.

Globalisation in India

India adopted new economic policy in July 1991. New policy is combination of liberalization, privatization and globalization. This was a radical shift from earlier policy of license, quota, and permit (LQP). New policy aimed at making Indian economy strong enough so that in future conditions like those prevailing in 1990 would not arise. This can be achieved only by increasing growth rate of the economy and increasing level of exploitation of domestic resources. Globalisation means integrating a national economy with world economy. After 1991 Government of India took a number of measures in this direction. These are:

- Indian companies have been permitted to collaborate with foreign companies
- Restrictive laws like FERA, MRTP were scrapped and replaced by FEMA and competition Law
- Import tariffs were reduced
- Almost all sectors of the economy were opened up for FDI. In many sectors 100% FDI has been permitted
- Import quota was abolished
- General reduction in tariffs
- Foreign institutional investors have been permitted to operate in Indian capital market
- Incentives and facilities have been given to NRIs
- Indian companies have been allowed to issue ADR and GDR to mobilize capital from foreign countries.
- Exchange rate policy has been liberalized in August 1994 Indian currency was made convertible on current amount. Although rupee is not full convertible, there are transactions on capital amount for which rupee is convertible. Tarapore committee has recommended full convertibility to be implemented in phased manner.
- At present India is following policy of managed floating rate in exchange rate. Impact of globalization can be seen by following table.

Principal Exports of India (US$ Million)

		90-91	2006
1	Major traditional items	3521	10549
2	Major non-traditional items	13229	74199
3	Minerals, fuels, lubricants	834	5361
4	Others	31	12982

Anti-Globalisation

Globalization has been one of the most hotly debated topic in international economics over the past few years. Globalization has also generated significant international opposition over concerns that it has increased inequality and environmental degradation. When a country has little material or physical product harvested or mined from its own soil, large corporations see an opportunity to take advantage of the 'export poverty' of such a nation. Where the majority of the earliest occurrences of economic globalization are recorded as being the expansion of businesses and corporate growth, in many poorer nations globalization is actually the result of the foreign businesses investing in the country to take advantage of the lower wage rate. Sweat Shops are widely used by sports shoe manufacturers. There are factories set up in the poor countries where employees agree to work for low wages. Then if labour laws alter in those countries and stricter rules govern the manufacturing process the factories are closed down and relocated to other nations with more conservative, laissez-faire economic policies designed to focus on anti-sweatshop campaigns and education of such. In the USA, the National Labor Committee has proposed a number of bills as part of Decent Working Conditions and Fair Competition Act, which have so far failed in Congress.

The world today is so interconnected that the collapse of the subprime mortgage market in the US has led to a global financial crisis and recession on a scale not seen since the Great Depression. Government deregulation and failed regulation of Wall Street's investment banks are important contributors to the subprime mortgage crisis. A flood of consumer goods such as televisions, radios, bicycles and textiles into the United States, Europe and Japan has helped to fuel the economic expansion of Asian tiger economies in recent decades. In South Africa, some 300000 textile workers have lost their jobs due to the influx of Chinese goods. Opportunities in richer countries drives talent away from poorer countries, leading to brain drains. Brain drain has cost the African continent over \$4.1 billion in the employment of 150000 expatriate professionals annually. Indian students going abroad for their higher studies costs India a foreign exchange outflow of \$10 billion annually. The booming economies of China and India are planetary powers that are shaping the global biosphere. In 2007, China overtook the United States as the world's biggest producer of CO_2. At present rates, tropical rainforests in Indonesia would be logged out in ten years and in Papua New Guinea in 13 to 16 years. A major source of deforestation is the logging industry, driven spectacularly by China and Japan. Thriving economies such as China and India are quickly becoming large oil consumers. The *State of the World 2006* report said the two countries Indian & China high economic growth lead to extreme level of pollution. The world's ecological capacity is simply insufficient to satisfy the ambitions of China, India, Japan, Europe and the United States as well as the aspirations of the rest of the world in a sustainable way.

Globalization, the flow of information, goods, capital and people across political and geographic boundaries, has also helped to spread some of the deadliest infectious diseases known to humans. Starting in Asia, the Black Death killed at least one third of Europe's population in the fourteenth century. Even worse devastation was inflicted on the American supercontinent by Europe. Modern modes of transportation allow more people and products to travel around the world at a faster pace, they also open the airways to the transcontinental movement of infectious disease vectors. One example of this occurring is AIDS/HIV. Approximately 1.1 million persons are living with HIV/AIDS in the United States. In 2006, the tuberculosis among foreign born persons in the United States was 9.5 times that of US born persons. The United Nations Office on Durgs and Crime (UNODC) issued a report that the global drug trade generates more than $320 billion a year in revenues. Worldwide, the UN estimates there are more than 50 million regular users of heroin, cocaine and synthetic drugs. Endangered species is second only to drug trafficking. Traditional Chinese medicine often incorporates ingredients from all parts of plants, the leaf, stem, flower, root and also ingredients from animals and minerals. The use of parts of endangered species (such as seahorses, rhinoceros horns, saiga antelope horns and tiger bones and claws) has created controversy and resulted in a black market of poachers who hunt restricted animals.

The anti-globalization movement is a term used to describe the political group who oppose the neoliberal version of globalization, while criticisms of globalization are some of the reasons used to justify this group's stance.

The anti-globalization movement is a term used to describe the political group who oppose the neoliberal version of globalization, while criticisms of globalization are some of the reasons used to justify this group's stance. Anti-globalization may also involve the process or actions taken by a state or its people in order to demonstrate its sovereignty and practice democratic decision making. Anti-globalization may occur in order to maintain barriers to the international transfer of people, goods and beliefs, particularly free market deregulation. The anti-globalization movement developed in opposition to the perceived negative aspects of globalization. While it is true that globalization encourages free trade among countries, there are also negative consequences because some countries try to save their national markets. The main export of poorer countries is usually agricultural goods. Larger countries often subsidise their farmers (like the EU Common Agricultural Policy), which lowers the market price for the poor farmer's crops compared to what it would be under free trade. The deterioration of protections for weaker nations by stronger industrialized powers has resulted in the exploitation of the people in those nations to become cheap labour. Due to the lack of protections, companies from powerful industrialized nations are able to offer workers enough salary to entice them to endure extremely long hours and unsafe working conditions, though economists question if consenting workers in a competitive employers market can be decried as exploited. It is true that the workers are free to leave their jobs, but in many poorer countries, this would mean starvation for the worker and possible even his/her family if their previous jobs were unavailable. The low cost of offshore workers have enticed corporations to buy goods and services from foreign countries. The laid off manufacturing sector workers are forced into the service sector where wages and benefits are low, but turnover is high. This has contributed to the deterioration of the middle class which is a major factor in the increasing economic inequality in the United States. Families that were once part of the middle class are forced into lower positions by massive layoffs and outsourcing to another country. This also means that people in the lower class have a much harder time climbing out of poverty because of the absence of the middle class as a stepping stone. The surplus in cheap labor coupled with an ever growing number of companies in transition has caused a weakening of labour unions in the member countries. Unions lose their effectiveness when their membership begins to decline. As a result union's hold less power over corporation's that are able to easily replace workers, often for lower wages and have the option to not offer unionized jobs anymore.

For example, a country that experiencing increases in labour demand because of globalization and an increase the demand for goods produced by children, will experience greater a demand for child labor. This can be hazardous or exploitive, e.g., quarrying, salvage, cash cropping but also includes the trafficking of children, children in bondage or forced labor, prostitution, pornography and other illicit activities.

WORLD TRADE ORGANISATION

GATT was changed into WTO on 1st January, 1995 to pursue and oversee the implementation as well as further liberalization of trade in services, agriculture and intellectual property rights.

After the end of Second World War, which had destroyed the global economy, the Bretton Woods conference was held in the year 1944, to restore the global economy. The three international institutions were set up: the World Bank, IMF and GATT with the object of promoting world trade and investments by minimizing trade barriers between countries. GATT started working in Geneva in 1948 and after eighth round of negotiations in 1986 in Uruguary, an agreement was signed. Subsequently, GATT was changed into WTO on 1st January, 1995 to pursue and oversee the implementation as well as further liberalization of trade in services, agriculture and intellectual property rights. An important achievement of WTO was signing of TRIPS (Trade Related Aspects of Intellectual Property Rights) and TRIMS (Trade Related Investment Measures) and GATS (General Agreement on Trade in Services).

Regulation of International Trade

WTO, which replaced GATT in 1995, regulates the conduct of trade among its member states. The principles and rules agreed by member countries and imposed by WTO are as under :

- *Non-discrimination:* the Most Favoured Nation (MFN) principle. Any advantage, favour, privilege or immunity affecting tariffs or other trade regulation instruments granted to one contracting party (CP), must immediately be extended to all other CPs.
- *Quotas are Prohibited with the Following Exceptions:* Balance of payments difficulties and infant industries in developing countries.
- *Fixing of Tariff Levels:* Most tariffs are fixed (bound) but if they are to be raised by WTO members which adversely affect other WTO members, they must be compensated.
- *Multilateral Negotiation to Reduce Protection:* Negotiation among members in a series of rounds to reduce tariffs and other forms of protection has been spectacularly successful. Average tariffs have been reduced from around 40% in 1947 to about 3% today.
- Regional economic integration is permitted under certain conditions despite being discriminatory in nature.
- *Protection Against Dumping and Sudden Influxes of Imports:* Countries are permitted to raise protection (through anti-dumping duties), where dumping or sudden influxes of imports occur. Dumping is charging an export price below the normal value, usually the domestic price. Safeguard measures are permitted where a surge of imports threaten a particular industry.

- *Dispute Settlement:* If one (country partner) CP, believes that another is in breach of these rules, a complaint can be lodged and a dispute settlement procedure implemented.

The Most Favoured Nation principle is essential, because without it there would be strong temptation for the more important trading nations to negotiate bilateral deals. Such deals would undermine the whole idea of a fair trading system operating under WTOs applicable rules. Tarrifs are favoured over non tariff barriers because they are relatively transparent. This means that their level is clear. They also permit more efficient producers to expand their market share, if their efficiency advantage more than offsets the tariff. The level of protection afforded by a quota is more difficult to assess. With the level of imports fixed due to quota there can be no expansion of imports whatever the difference in efficiency between the importer and domestic producers. It is also easier to carry out negotiations over the level of tariffs. There are several advantages of negotiating tariff reductions in multilateral rounds:

- With a large number of countries involved there are important advantages to be gained for each country's exporters in terms of market access. These gains provide a political counterweight to those arguing for the retention of protection.
- Negotiating reductions in protection across the whole range of goods means that the advantages to be gained from increased exports can discourage the desire of protected industries to retain their protection.
- Political pressure can be brought to bear on the more recalcitrant countries to reduce the level of their protection.
- Over time the emphasis of the WTO negotiations has shifted towards tariff reductions
- *Reduction of non-tariff barriers:* When countries cannot raise tariffs, they increase (non-tariff barriers) NTBs. This is called new protectionism and WTO is trying to reduce them.
- Unregulated areas like agriculture, services and textiles, intellectual and trade-related investment.

General Agreement on Tariffs and Trade (GATT) came out of 'ashes of the Havana Charter'. During the period of great depression and World War II different countries adopted protectionist policy by introducing numerous trade barriers. After the war, allied powers felt the need for liberal trading pattern to revive the war torn economics. In this respect, an international conference on trade and employment was held in 1947-48. It was ratified by the US congress. Almost same time some countries (23) agreed to continue extensive tariff negotiation for trade concessions at Geneva. This came to be known as General Agreement on Tariffs and Trade. It was signed on 30 October 1947 and became operative on 1st January 1948. GATT was a multinational treaty, it was not an organization. Its function was to call international conferences to decide on trade liberatiration on multilateral basis.

Conferences of GATT are known as 'round' since 1947, seven rounds of talks took place under GATT, eighth round, known as Uruguay round, started in 1986 and concluded on 15th April 1994 at Marakesh, Morocco. As result of agreement among nations under Uruguay round, WTO come into being on 1st January 1995 and GATT lost existence. Final agreement of Uruguay round of talks can be divided in two parts.

(a) Agreement on WTO which requires establishment of WTO

(b) Agreement containing ministerial decisions and declarations regarding trade in goods, services, intellectual property and multilateral trade.

The agreement also contains dispute settlement rules and trade policy mechanism. Agreement contains 16 Articles Now WTO has 151 members, India is one of the founder members. Thus the World Trade Organisation (WTO) provides the basic framework for conduct of international trade and sets up the norms for the conduct of such trade.

Structure of WTO

Ministerial conference consisting of representatives of all member nations is the highest decision making body of WTO. It has to meet at least once every two years. It can take decision on all matters under any of the multilateral trade agreements. So the ministerial conference is the highest authority of WTO. Then there is a general council which also consists of representatives of all members. It looks after the operation of the WTO agreement and ministerial decision on regular basis. The council also acts as Dispute Settlement Body and as a Trade Policy Review Body under different terms of references and under different chairmen. The general council sits in Geneva, generally once in a month.

At the third level of hierarchy, there are three councils (1) council for trade in goods or goods council (2) council for trade in services (3) council for trade related aspects of intellectual property. First council oversees the functioning of the multitrade agreements, second council oversees the functioning of general agreement on trade in services and third council oversees matters regarding (TRIPS). Thus, these three councils are responsible for overseeing the working of agreements in WTO. These councils also consist of all members of WTO. These councils can establish their subsidiary bodies as required.

Further, the ministerial conference can establish committees on trade and development, on balance of payment restrictions and on budget, finance and administration. These committees are to carry out such function as are assigned to them by the agreement or by the general council. The secretariat of the WTO is headed by the Director General. Ministerial conference appoints the Director General and defines his powers, function, duties, condition of service and terms of office. The Director General is appointed for a period of four years and is assisted by four deputes. Day to day affairs of WTO are supervised by the Director General. As far as possible decision in WTO are taken by councils. When consensus is not arrived at any matter, then it is decided by 2/3rd majority voting on the basis of one country and one vote. But in case of interpretation of the provision of the agreement and various a member's obligations required majority is 3/4th and amendments relating to general principles like MFN status, must be approved by all members.

Objectives of WTO

Objectives of WTO have laid down the preamble of the agreement establishing WTO.

1. It aimes at raising standard of living, ensuring full employment increasing income, production and trade in goods and services.
2. To ensure that world's resources are optimally utilized and also to make development sustainable by protecting and preserving the environment and by increasing the means required for this development.
3. To make positive efforts so that developing countries, particularly least developed countries compare a share in the international growth process in accordance with the needs of their economic development.
4. These objectives are to be achieved by entering into improved and mutually advantageous management directed towards substantial reduction of tariffs and other barriers of trade and elimination of discriminatory treatment in international trade relations.
5. To develop an integrated, viable and more durable multilateral trading system and to link trade policies and environmental policies.

Functions of WTO

Functions of WTO are mentioned in Article III of the agreement. Main purpose of WTO is to provide a framework for implementation, administration, operation and further the objectives of this agreement and of the multilateral trade agreements. It is to provide a forum for negotiations among its members. It is to provide a framework for the implementation of the results of such negotiation as may be decided by the ministerial conference. Administering the understanding of settlement of disputes and the trade policy review mechanism are also function of WTO. WTO is to cooperate with IMF and World Bank so that greater coherence can be achieved in global economic policy.

WTO Agreements

Uruguay Rounds of negotiations, which led to establishment of WTO, contain following agreements:

1. Multilateral Agreements on Trade in Goods or GATT rules 1994
2. General Agreements on Trade in Services (GATS)
3. Agreement on Trade Related Aspects of International Property Rights (TRIPS)
4. Understanding on rules and procedures governing the settlement of disputes
5. Multilateral Trade Agreements
6. Trade Policy Review Mechanism

1. Multilateral Agreements on Trade in Goods : This is the general agreement defining GATT 1994 and includes agreements related to trade in goods GATT 1994 includes GATT 1947 as amended up to January 1, 1995 and the provisions of specified legal instruments and understandings among members regarding legal rights and obligations, state trading activities, balance of payment conditions, customs unions and free trade area.

Agreement on agriculture deals with domestic subsidies, export subsidies, minimum market access commitment, domestic support, sanitary and food aid operations. Domestic subsidy should not be more than 10% of total agricultural production in a particular year. Developing countries are required to reduce tariffs on agricultural product by 24% over a period of 10 years (from January 1995). Least developed countries are not required to reduce their tariff.

Agreement on textile and clothing is to integrate textile and clothing sector into GATT 1994. All restrictions under multilateral agreement (1974) were to be phased out by 2005. Thus quantitative restrictions (Q.Rs.) were to be abolished by 2005. All members are required to take steps to improve market access and avoid discrimination against import. Technical negotiations, standards, testing and certification procedures should not create unnecessary obstacle to trade. However countries have right to protect human, animal or plant life or health or environment. Agreement on TRIMS finds that certain investment measures restrict and distort trade e.g. quantitative restrictions, export obligations, local content rule, national treatment, investment in identified areas etc. The agreement requires removal of such measures within two years for developed countries, five years for developing countries and seven years for least developed countries.

Agreement on dumping authorizes importing country to take anti dumping measures if dumped imports cause injury to domestic industry. But anti dumping investigation will be terminated if margin of dumping is less than 2% of export price, less than 3% of total imports of that product subject to a ceiling of 7% of all such dumped imports. Agreement on subsidies and countervailing measures is applicable to non agricultural products. Subsidies are classified as red, green and amber. Red are prohibitive, amber actionable and green unactionable subsidies.

2. Agreement on Trade in Services : This agreement applies to all internationally traded services. Foreign services and service supplies and domestic services and service providers are to be treated on equal footing. However, governments may indicate specific most favoured nations exemptions, to be reviewed after five years. Governments have agreed to set up working parties on (1) trade in services and environment to examine and report on the relationship between services trade and environment (2) professional services to examine and report on discipline necessary to ensure that measures relating to service standards, licensing requirements etc. do not constitute unnecessary barriers to trade.

3. Agreement on Trade Related Intellectual Property Rights (TRIPS) : This agreement extends to seven categories on intellectual property (1) copyright and related rights (2) trade marks (3) geographical indications (4) industrial design (5) patents including micro-organism and plant varieties (6) integrated circuits (7) trade secrets.

Protection period available is as under – 50 years for copyright and related rights, 20 years for broad casting organization, 10 years for industrial design, 20 yeas patent protection for any invention, 10 years for long out design of integrated circuit. All members are required to provide product patent. To bring legislation conforming to the provisions of the agreement. transition period has been given to developed countries, east European countries and developing countries for one year, five years and ten years respectively. Least developed countries have been given eleven years.

4. Dispute Settlement System : Disputes among members regarding rights and obligation under the provisions of the agreement are to be resolved by a Dispute Settlement Board in 30 days (DSB). If consultation and good offices of the Director General fail to resolve the dispute, the complainant member can ask the DSB to appoint a panel of three experts within 30 days. There is also a provision of the appellate review by a standing appellate body of seven members to be established by the DSB who will report to the DSB between 60-90 days. DSB will adopt the report within 30 days which will be unconditionally accepted by the parties to the dispute.

1. **Plurilateral Trade Agreement (PTA) :** This agreement include agreement on trade in civil aircraft, agreement on government prominent, international dairy agreement and international bovine meat agreement. First of these agreements was made in Geneva in April 1979, subsequently modified, rectified and amended. Last three were concluded at Marakesh on 15th April 1994.
2. **Trade Policy Review Mechanism** : This aims at ensuring smooth functioning of multilateral trading system. To achieve this, the agreement encourages the establishment of the Trade Policy Review Body (TPRB). Each member is required to report to the TPRB about the trade policies and practices pursued by it. TPRB undertakes an annual overview of developments in the international trading system affecting multilateral trading system. The overview shall be assisted by an annual report by the Director General setting out major activities of the WTO and highlighting significant policy issues affecting the multilateral trading system.

Free Trade versus Protection

Free trade is amply supported by earlier 'trade theories'. These theories claim that free trade enables firms and countries to specialize in the activities they perform best leading to greater efficiency, more production and higher standards of living throughout the world. More jobs are created, consumers enjoy a wider choice of goods, firms have wider markets and there is increased communication between people in different nations leading to world peace and increase in global business. Yet many nations continue to use restrictive measures, in order to improve their balance of payments. Other reasons include the following:

- Saving domestic jobs particularly when foreign competitors are paying their work force extremely low wages. The difficulty with this argument is that, there are several determinants of unit labour costs: productivity differences can be more than offset the effects of low wages, thus goods made in high wage nations may actually be cheaper than in low wage regions.

- Protecting 'infant industries'. The justification for protecting infant industries is that certain types of business require economies of scale in production, marketing, research and development, finance and general management, in order to be able to compete on the world stage. Foreign competition would prevent this from happening. Although local consumers may suffer in short term but should be better off in the long term. Objections against this infant industry argument are that:
  1. If the industry concerned really does have a bright future than local and international capital markets should be willing to finance short run losses in anticipation of expected long term gains. Hence, there should not be any need for government support.
  2. To the extent that economies of scale exist, they can soon be realized through mergers of domestic firms or by joint ventures with foreign firms.
  3. Government officials and politicians have to decide which industry is infant and needs protection. These officials do not possess business experience to make such decisions fairly.
  4. Infant industries might never grow up in the absence of foreign competition, which generally helps in improving efficiency.
- Protecting old and inefficient industries while they are modernizing. The counter argument is that unprofitable industry should be allowed to close and any business with reasonable future prospects ought to be able to attract private investment for its modernization.
- Diversifying the domestic economy, especially if the country depends only on few items for its foreign earnings.
- Defending strategic industries like defence, space and nuclear energy. The counter argument against this is that, foreign industries can always be taken over during war. Further, direct subsidies by government are better than imposing trade barriers.
- Some countries also protect basic industries such as agriculture or certain types of manufacturing on the ground of national security though security is more assured in a cooperating world.
- Stimulating production in industrial sectors, which supply goods that compete with imports. Retaliation by other countries is the obvious problem with this approach.
- Retaliation against unfair trade practices by foreign suppliers e.g., dumping. The WTO defines dumping, as any sale in an export market at a price below the price charged in the supplying firms own country in addition to transport and foreign distribution cost.

Whatever the motivation disposal of surplus stock or penetration of markets, dumping is an unfair trading practice under the WTO regulations (under article 6 of the GATT agreement), hence the governments of affected countries are permitted to impose special import taxes on offending products. Under EU rules, the price considered is that which the exporting firm charges to non related local distributor, not the price charged to end consumers. If all distributors are related to exporter, then price charged to end consumes is considered. Problems arise in determining transport costs and if the company has several subsidiaries where different prices are charged and none in home country. Trade restrictions may benefit some parts of a country's economy, but will damage others because potential importers are denied access to foreign products and the overall pattern of domestic activity is distorted, apart from inviting retaliation.

Trade Barriers

Protection can take barriers and subsidies. A tariff is a tax levied when good is imported. It is an instrument of trade policy used as a source of government income and raises the price of imported goods to protect domestic producers. To an exporter it represents an extra cost. Tariffs are discriminatory taxes on imports, they are imposed on imported but not on domestic products. Tariffs may be:

- *Ad-valorem:* A percentage of the value of the goods imported, for example, a 25 percent US tariff on imported trucks value.
- *Specific:* A fixed amount per unit, per litre or whatever, for example, 3$ per barrel of imported oil. As a rule, the level of tariffs is generally lower on raw material and semi-finished goods as opposed to finished products.

Non-tariff Barriers (NTBs)

NTBs can be defined as any governmental measure other than a tariff that affects the volume or direction of trade. The main types of NTBs are as under:

The main types of NTBs are as under:
1. Quotas are direct limits on the volume of imports.
2. Indirect taxation to discriminate against imports

1. Quotas are direct limits on the volume of imports.
2. Indirect taxation to discriminate against imports.
3. *Regulations/Standards:* There are adequate rules relating to product safety, the environment, consumer protection, etc.
4. Government procurement policy.
5. *Exchange controls:* By restricting supply of foreign exchange, imports can be restricted.
6. Voluntary export restraints (VER) is a quota on trade imposed from the exporting country's side instead of the importer's country as a part of mutual adjustment between two countries.
7. Border formalities – administrative regulations that delay transit and entail expenses

International Monetary System

The international monetary system is the set of arrangements to facilitate the exchange of one currency for another in an orderly manner, establishing rules for exchange of currencies, providing liquidity in the international financial system and prudential supervision of the same. Since these areas are the primary responsibility of national governments, the system works on the basis of agreements and institutions established by agreements. The most prominent of these are the International Monetary Fund (IMF), World Bank, Organisation for Economic Cooperation and Development (OECD), Bank for International Settlement, G7 and G22.

WTO – Current Issues

The current issues before WTO are as follows:

1. The USA wants to include labour standards in the agenda and exclude anti-dumping and peak tariffs from it but retain the existing IPR regime.
2. EU on the other hand opposes the phasing out of subsidies in agriculture.
3. Developing countries want flexibility in implementation of 'patent protection' apart from issues of providing food security and development issues.
4. There are differences on further liberalizing agreement on upgrading services, agricultural subsidies, and market access.
5. Making rules for common investment and competition law.
6. Agricultural subsidies by developed countries and not opening their markets to developing countries.

The Gold Standard: This system operated from 1870 to 1914. Under this sytem, currencies were convertible into gold at a fixed rate and this automatically fixed their exchange rate. US was first country to leave it. India also does not follow it. Her currency is based on US dollar and Euro.

The Bretton Woods System: In July 1944, representatives of 44 countries met in Bretton Woods, Hampshire drafted and signed an agreement to set up IMF (International Monetary Fund). USA, being at that time a most powerful and rich country, influenced the system. The characteristics of this system were:

1. The dollar was the centre of system with a fixed exchange rate into gold ($35 an ounce).
2. Other IMF members had a rate of exchange with the dollar, which was allowed to vary within 1% plus or minus.
3. IMF members contributed gold and foreign exchange to the IMF and borrowings were available to support a currency.
4. Exchange rates had to be freely convertible for current transactions.
5. Exchange rates could be changed as a result of a fundamental disequilibrium in the balance of payments.
6. Member countries could sell dollars to the Federal Reserve of US for gold at the official price.

Floating Exchange Rates

In 1973, bretton Woods's system broke down and was replaced by a system of floating exchange rates. Under this system governments no longer set an exchange rate for their currency and its value was allowed to fluctuate to achieve equilibrium in a country's balance of payments. Floating exchange rate system has continued to this day. Companies could also try to hedge, covering the risk of exchange rate fluctuations by buying and selling in the forward exchange market. Alternatively the companies could borrow in the foreign currency, convert the borrowings into its domestic currency and use the flow of funds from overseas to pay off the loan. Two following features of the IMF helped promote the global currency exchange flexibility in respective country's external adjustment:

1. *IMF Lending Facilities:* The IMF is ready to lend foreign currencies to members to help ride them out for periods during which their current accounts were in deficit but a tightening of monetary or fiscal plicy would have an adverse effect on domestic employment. A pool of gold and currencies contributed by members, provided the IMF with the resources to be used in these lending operations. Further gold or foreign currencies only up to a limit, could be borrowed from the fund, but only under increasingly stringenet fund supervision of the borrower's macro-economic policies. IMF Conditionality is the name for this surveillance.
2. *Adjustable Parities:* Although each country's exchange rate was fixed, it could be changed devalued or revalued against the dollar, if the IMF agreed that the country's balance of payment was in a situation of fundamental disequilibrium. It was meant to cover countries that suffered permanent adverse international shifts in the demand for their products. Without devaluation, such a country would experience higher unemployment and a higher current account deficit until the domestic price level fell enough to restore internal and external balance.

International Capital Movement

One fundamental change that has occurred is the removal of barriers to the movement of capital and the increasing size of these movements. This is seen most spectacularly in the case of middle income economies where the net private capital flow in real terms has increased four times from 1980 to 1996 and Foreign Direct Investment by multinationals has increased more than three times. This has resulted in following developments:

- Capital Market Efficiency: capital can flow to, where the returns on its use are highest, benefiting the provider and user.
- Freedom of establishment and trade in services.
- Financial institutions find it hard to assess the riskiness of their asset base.
- Asset prices are influenced by speculation and the markets are subject to herd like behavior.
- The growth in the volume of international capital transactions is such that official reserves are insufficient to be able to act as a lender of last resort.
- There is now an excessive level of indebtendness among developing and some developed countries.
- The IMF and World Bank currently can only react to crisis rather than anticipate them.
- Liberalisation has extended to national banking environments as well as international management of currencies. The fundamental problem that bank loans are large superstructures of debt built on relatively small foundation of liquid assets. So, if some debts fail the whole bank is likely to be at risk.

UNO & Its Ethics

The name United Nations was suggested by United States President Frankling D Roosevelt and was first used in Declaration by the United Nation of Jan 1, 1942 during the second world war. When representatives of 26 nations pledged their government continued fighting together against the Axis powers. The charter was signed on 26 June 1945 by the representatives of 50 countries. The United Nations came into existence on 24 October 1945 with the deposit of requisite number of ratification of the charter with the US Department of State, United Nations day 15 celebrated on 24 October each year. The official languages of the UN are Chinese, English, French, Russian and Spanish. The UN has six principal organs established by the founding charter. All have their headquarters in New York except the international Court of Justice which has set in the Hague. The six principal UN organs are as follows:

1. The General Assembly: It is composed of all members, is the main deliberative body. Each member has to vote. It means once a year, commencing on the First Tuesday following September, the general debate is organized over period of two weeks, beginning from the third week of September. At the start of each session, the assembly elects a new President and 21 Vice Presidents and Chairmen of its main committees. Every year sessions may be called within twenty four hours at the request of the Security Council on the vote of any country or a majority of United Nations member. Decisions on important questions, such as peace and security, new membership and budgetary matters require a two third majority. Other questions require a simple majority of members present and voting. The General Assembly has right to discuss any matter within the scope of the Charter with the exception of any selection or dispute on the Agenda. The Security Council may take recommendations on any such questions or matters, while it has no power to compel action by any Government. Its recommendation is seen to carry the weight of world opinion.

2. The Security Council : It has many responsibilities, under the Charter for the maintenance of international peace and security. It is so organized as to be able to function continuously. A representative of each of its member must be present at all times at UN headquarters but it may meet elsewhere as best facilitates to its work. The Presidency of the Council rotates monthly according to English Alphabetical order and members names. The council consists of 15 members, 5 permanent members and 10 non-permanent elected for two years by a two third majority of a general assembly. Each member has one vote. Retiring members are not eligible for re-election. Any other member of the United Nations may participate without a vote in the discussion of questions affecting its interest. Permanent members of security councils are China, France, Russia, UK and USA.

3. The Economic and Social Council : It is responsible under the General Assembly for co-ordinating the functions of the UN with regard to international economic, social, cultural, educational, health and related matters. It consists of 54 member states elected by a two-third majority of the General Assembly for 3 year term. One third of the members retire each year. Retiring members are eligible for elections each member has a vote. Decisions are made by a majority of the members present and voting. The Council holds one week substantiative session, alternating between New York and Geneva and one organizational session, in New York. Special session may be held if required. The President is elected for one year and is eligible for immediate re-election. The UN has 6300 dollar a year to spend for economic and social development.

4. Trusteeship Council : It was established to ensure that the government responsible for administering Trust territories. They take adequate steps to prepare them for self government or independence.

5. The International Court of Justice : It is the principal judicial organ of the UN. It has a dual role to settle in accordance with international law, the legal disputes submitted to it by states and to give advisory opinion on legal questions referred to it by duly authorized internal organs and agencies. The number of judges in the International Court of Justice is fifteen.

The Secretariat Services – These are five organs of the UN which administer their programmes and carry out the organizations day to day work with its increasing staff of some 8900 at the UN headquarters in New York and all over the world. Apart from these important organs there are also many non-political, specialized agencies affiliated to the UNO. They are: The World Health Organisation (WHO), UNESCO and IMF. The UNO has successfully tried to prevent the outbreaks of war on many occasions. It prevented a war between England and Egypt on the question of Suez Canal. Before this it checked the Korean war from turning into World War. It has so far succeeded in preventing Arab-Israel conflict from developing into world war.

Besides doing much valuable political work, the UNO has also tried to remove poverty and disease. This work is done through its various specialized agencies. IMF has been giving monetary help to the underdeveloped countries, ILO has done much to improve the condition of labourers all over the world. Similarly UNESCO is trying to spread education. Apart from political work the UNO is doing much useful work in social and economic fields. There are many countries who are not satisfied with the working of the UNO. They point out that it is dominated by the American block. Infact the vote power given to big five is making its working ineffective in times of crisis. It could not restrain Israel from invading Lebnon and massacring thousands of unarmed and innocent Palestinians. Inspite of all these shortcomings and weakness. The UNO remains the only hope for the world. It is the only body which can bring about world peace. Recently its efforts for cease fire could be achieved between Iraq and Iran and in this way decade old war was ended. But in case of America's attack on Iraq the UN looked helpless.

Preamble

We The Peoples of the United Nations Determined

- To save succeeding generations from the scourge of war, which twice in our lifetime has brought untold sorrow to mankind, and
- To reaffirm faith in fundamental human rights, in the dignity and worth of the human person, in the equal rights of men and women and of nations large and small, and
- To establish conditions under which justice and respect for the obligations arising from treaties and other sources of international law can be maintained, and
- To promote social progress and better standards of life in larger freedom

And For These Ends

- To practice tolerance and live together in peace with one another as good neighbours, and
- To unite our strength to maintain international peace and security, and
- To ensure, by the acceptance of principles and the institution of methods, that armed force shall not be used, save in the common interest, and
- To employ international machinery for the promotion of the economic and social advancement of all peoples

Have Resolved to Combine our Efforts to Accomplish These Aims

Accordingly, our respective Governments, through representatives assembled in the city of San Francisco, who have exhibited their full powers found to be in good and due form, have agreed to the present Charter of the United Nations and do hereby establish an international organization to be known as the United Nations.

The important articles of United Nations charter are:

Article – 1

All human beings are born free and equal in dignity and rights. They are endowed with reason and conscience and should act towards one another in a spirit of brotherhood.

Article – 2

Everyone is entitled to all the rights and freedoms set forth in this declaration, without distinction of any kind, such as race, colour, sex, language, religion, political or other opinion, national or social origin, property, birth or other status. Furthermore, no distinction shall be made on the basis of the political, jurisdictional or international status of the country or territory to which a person belongs, whether it be independent, trust, non-self-governing or under any other limitation of sovereignty.

Article – 10

The General Assembly may discuss any questions or any matters within the scope of the present Charter or relating to the powers and functions of any organs provided for in the present Charter, and, except as provided in Article 12, may make recommendations to the Members of the United Nations or to the Security Council or to both on any such questions or matters.

Article – 11

1. The General Assembly may consider the general principles of co-operation in the maintenance of international peace and security, including the principles governing disarmament and the regulation of armaments, and may make recommendations with regard to such principles to the Members or to the Security Council or to both.
2. The General Assembly may discuss any questions relating to the maintenance of international peace and security brought before it by any Member of the United Nations, or by the Security Council, or by a state which is not a Member of the United Nations in accordance with Article 35, paragraph 2, and except as provided in Article 12, may make recommendations with regard to any such questions on which action is necessary shall be referred to the Security council by the General Assembly either before or after discussion.
3. The General Assembly may call the attention of the Security Council to situations which are likely to endanger international peace and security.
4. The powers of the General Assembly set forth in this Article shall not limit the general scope.

Article – 12

1. While the Security Council is exercising in respect of any dispute or situation the functions assigned to it in the present Charter, the General Assembly shall not make any recommendation with regard to that dispute or situation unless the Security Council so requests.
2. The Secretary General, with the consent of the Security Council, shall notify the General Assembly at each session of any matters relative to the maintenance of international peace and security which are being dealt with by the Security Council and shall similarly notify the General Assembly, or the Members of the United Nations if the General Assembly is not in session, immediately the Security Council ceases to deal with such matters.

Article – 13

1. The General Assembly shall initiate studies and make recommendations for the purpose of: (a) promoting international co-operation in the political field and encouraging the progressive development of international law and its codification, (b) promoting international co-operation in the economic, social, cultural, educational and health fields and assisting in the realization of human rights and fundamental freedom for all without distinction as to race, sex, language or religion.
2. The further responsibilities, functions and powers of the General Assembly with respect to matters mentioned in paragraph 1 (b).

Article – 23

1. The Security Counsil shall consist of fifteen Members of the United Nations. The Republic of China, France, the Union of Soviet Socialist Republics, the United Kingdom of Great Britain and Northern Ireland, and the United States of America shall be permanent members of the Security Council. The General Assembly shall elect ten other Members of the United Nations to be non-permanent members of the Security Council, due regard being especially paid, in the first instance to the contribution of Members of the United Nations to the maintenance of international peace and security and to the other purposes of the organization and also to equitable geographical distribution.
2. The non-permanent members of the Security Council shall be elected for a term of two years. In the first election of the non-permanent members after the increase of the membership of the Security Council from eleven to fifteen, two for the four additional members shall be chosen for a term of one year. A retiring member shall not be eligible for immediate re-election.
3. Each member of the Security Council shall have one representative.

Article – 24

1. In order to ensure prompt and effective action by the United Nations, its members confer on the Security Council primary responsibility for the maintenance of

international peace and security and agree that in carrying out its duties under this responsibility the Security Council acts on their behalf.

2. In discharging these duties the Security Council shall act in accordance with the Purposes and Principles of the United Nations. The specific powers granted to the Security Council for the discharge of these duties are laid down.

3. The Security Council shall submit annual and, when necessary, special reports to the General Assembly for its consideration.

Article – 26

In order to promote the establishment and maintenance of international peace and security with the least diversion for armaments of the world's human and economic resources, the Security Council shall be responsible for formulating, with the assistance of the Military Staff Committee, plans to be submitted to the Members of the United Nations for the establishment of a system for the regulation of armaments.

Article – 28

1. The Security Council shall be so organized as to be able to function continuously. Each member of the Security Council shall for this purpose be represented at all times at the seat of the Organization.
2. The Security Council shall hold periodic meetings at which each of its members may, if it so desires be represented by a member of the government or by some other specially designated representative.
3. The Security Council may hold meetings at such places other than the seat of the organization as in its judgment will best facilitate its work.

Article – 32

Any member of the United Nations which is not a member of the Security Council or any state which is not a member of the United Nations, if it is a party to a dispute under consideration by the Security Council, shall be invited to participate, without vote, in the discussion relating to the dispute. The Security Council shall lay down such conditions as it deems just for the participation of a state which is not a member of the United Nations.

Article – 39

The Security Council shall determine the existence of any threat to the peace, breach of the peace, or act of aggression and shall make recommendations, or decide what measures shall be taken to maintain or restore international peace and security.

Article – 40

In order to prevent an aggravation of the situation, the Security Council may before making the recommendations of deciding upon the measures provided for, call upon the parties concerned to comply with such provisional measures as it deems necessary or desirable. Such provisional measures shall be without prejudice to the rights, claims, or position of the parties concerned. The Security Council shall duly take account of failure to comply with such provisional measures.

Article – 41

The Security Council may decide what measures not involving the use of armed force are to be employed to give effect to its decisions, and it may call upon the members of the United Nations to apply such measures. These may include complete or partial interruption of economic relations and of rail, sea, air, postal, telegraphic, radio and other means of communication and the severance of diplomatic relations.

Article – 42

Should the Security Council that measures provided would be inadequate or have proved to be inadequate, it may take such action by air, sea, or land forces as may be necessary to maintain or restore international peace and security. Such action may include demonstrations, blockade and other operations by air, sea or land forces or members of the United Nations.

Article – 43

1. All members of the United Nations, in order to contribute to the maintenance of international peace and security, undertake to make available to the Security Council, on its call and in accordance with a special agreement or agreements, armed forces, assistance and facilities, including rights of passage, necessary for the purpose of maintaining international peace and security.
2. Such agreement or agreements shall govern the numbers and types of forces, their degree of readiness and general location and the nature of the facilities and assistance to be provided.
3. The agreement or agreements shall be negotiated as soon as possible on the initiative of the Security Council. They shall be concluded between the Security Council and members or between the Security Çouncil and groups of members and shall be subject to ratification by the signatory states in accordance with their respective constitutional processes.

Article – 48

1. The action required to carry out the decisions of the Security Council for the maintenance of international peace and security shall be taken by all the members of the United Nations or by some of them, as the Security Council may determine.
3. Such decisions shall be carried out by the members of the United Nations directly and through their action in the appropriate international agencies of which they are members.

Article – 57

1. The various specialized agencies, established by intergovernmental agreement and having wide international responsibilities as defined in their basic instruments, in

economic, social, cultural, educational, health and related fields shall be brought into relationship with the United Nations.

2. Such agencies thus brought into relationship with the United Nations are hereinafter referred to as specialized agencies.

Article – 62

1. The Economic and Social Council may make or initiate studies and reports with respect to international economic, social, cultural, educational, health and related matters and may make recommendations with respect to any such matters to the General Assembly to the members of the United Nations and to the specialized agencies concerned.
2. It may make recommendations for the purpose of promoting respect for and observance of human rights and fundamental freedoms for all.
3. It may prepare draft conventions for submission to the General Assembly with respect to matters falling within its competence.
4. It may call, in accordance with the rules prescribed by the United Nations, international conferences on matters falling within its competence.

Article – 63

1. The Economic and Social Council may enter into agreements with any of the agencies defining the terms on which the agency concerned shall be brought into relationship with the United Nations. Such agreements shall be subject to approval by the General Assembly.
2. It may co-ordinate the activities of the specialized agencies through consultation with and recommendations to such agencies and through recommendations to the General Assembly and to the Members of the United Nations.

Article – 64

1. The Economic and Social Council may take appropriate steps to obtain regular reports from the specialized agencies. It may make arrangements with the members of the United Nations and with the specialized agencies to obtain reports on the steps taken to give effect to its own recommendations and to recommendations on matters falling within its competence made by the General Assembly.
2. It may communicate its observations on these reports to the General Assembly.

Indian Constitution as a Source of Ethics

Indian Constitution provides socio-economic security and freedom to its citizens through its fundamental rights, fundamental duties and directive principles of state policy. The fundamental duties are defined as the moral obligations of all citizens to help promote a spirit of patriotism and to uphold the unity of India. These duties – set out in part IV-A of the

Constitution – concern individuals and the nation. Like the Directive Principles, they are not legally enforceable.

Right to Equality

Right to equality is an important right provided for in Articles 14, 15, 16, 17 and 18 of the constitution. It is the principal foundation of all other rights and liberties and guarantees the following:

Equality before law: Article 14 of the constitution guarantees that all citizens shall be equally protected by the laws of the country. It means that the state cannot discriminate against a citizen on the basis of caste, creed, colour, sex, religion or place of birth

Social equality and equal access to public areas: Article 15 of the constitution states that no person shall be discriminated on the basis of caste, colour, language etc. Every person shall have equal access to public places like public parks, museums, wells, bathing ghats and temples etc. However, the state may make any special provision for women and children. Special provisions may be made for the advancements of any socially or educationally backward class or scheduled castes or scheduled tribes.

Equality in matters of public employment: Article 16 of the constitution lays down that the state cannot discriminate against anyone in the matters of employment. All citizens can apply for government jobs. There are some exceptions. The Parliament may enact a law stating that certain jobs can only be filled by applicants who are domiciled in the area. This may be meant for posts that require knowledge of the locality and language of the area. The state may also reserve posts for members of backward classes, scheduled castes or scheduled tribes which are not adequately represented in the services under the state to bring up the weaker sections of the society. Also, there a law may be passed which requires that the holder of an office of any religious institution shall also be a person professing that particular religion.

Abolition of untouchability: Article 17 of the constitution abolishes the practice of untouchability. Practice of untouchability is an offense and anyone doing so is punishable by law. The Untouchability Offences Act of 1955 (renamed to Protection of Civil Rights Act in 1976) provided penalties for preventing a person from entering a place of worship or from taking water from a tank or well.

Abolition of titles: Articles 18 of the constitution prohibits the state from conferring any titles. Citizens of India cannot accept titles from a foreign state. However, Military and academic distinctions can be conferred on the citizens of India. The awards of Bharat Ratna and Padma Vibhushan cannot be used by the recipient as a title.

The right to equality works for promoting dignity of the individual along with a sense of belonging to the country and security of being the citizen of India without discrimination of any sort. It restores the faith of individual in the rule of democracy and promotes a spirit of sharing and brotherhood among the people living in the country. At the same time the act also recognizes that there are still sections that need special protection/chances to develop to their fullest potential. Hence, provides for opportunities for such sections so that they may also become equal to the other citizens of the country.

Right to Freedom

The Constitution of India contains the right to freedom, given in articles 19, 20, 21 and 22, with the view of guaranteeing individual rights that were considered vital by the framers of the constitution. The right to freedom in Article 19 guarantees the following six freedoms:

1. Freedom of speech and expression, which enable an individual to participate in public activities. The phrase, freedom of press has not been used in Article 19, but freedom of expression includes freedom of press. Reasonable restrictions can be imposed in the interest of public order, security of state, decency or morality.
2. Freedom to assemble peacefully without arms, on which the state can impose reasonable restrictions in the interest of public order and the sovereignty and integrity of India.
3. Freedom to form associations or unions on which the state can impose reasonable restrictions on this freedom in the interest of public order, morality and the sovereignty and integrity of India.
4. Freedom to move freely throughout the territory of India though reasonable restrictions can be imposed on this right in the interest of the general public, for example, restrictions may be imposed on movement and travelling, so as to control epidemics.
5. Freedom to reside and settle in any part of the territory of India which is also subject to reasonable restrictions by the state in the interest of the general public or for the protection of the scheduled tribes because certain safeguards as are envisaged here seem to be justified to protect indigenous and tribal peoples from exploitation and coercion. Article 370 restricts citizens from other Indian states and Kashmiri women who marry men from other states from purchasing land or property in Jammu & Kashmir.
6. Freedom to practice any profession or to carry on any occupation, trade or business on which the state may impose reasonable restrictions in the interest of the general public. Thus, there is no right to carry on a business which is dangerous or immoral. Also, professional or technical qualifications may be prescribed for practicing any profession or carrying on any trade.

The constitution also guarantees the right to life and personal liberty, which in turn cites specific provisions in which these rights are applied and enforced:

Protection with respect to conviction for offences is guaranteed in the right to life and personal liberty. According to Article 20, no one can be awarded punishment which is more than what the law of the land prescribes at that time. This legal axiom is based on the principle that no criminal law can be made retrospective, that is, for an act to become an offence, the essential condition is that it should have been an offence legally at the time of committing it. Moreover, no person accused of any offence shall be compelled to be a witness against himself. Compulsion in this article refers to what in law is called Duress (injury, beating or unlawful imprisonment to make a person do something that he does not want to do). This article is known as a safeguard against self incrimination. The other principle enshrined in this article is known as the principle of double jeopardy, that is, no person can be convicted twice for the same offence.

Protection of life and personal liberty is also stated under right to life and personal liberty. Article 21 declares that no citizen can be denied his life and liberty except by law. This means that a person's life and personal liberty can only be disputed if that person has committed a crime.

Rights of a person arrested under ordinary circumstances is laid down in the right to life and personal liberty. No one can be arrested without being told the grounds for his arrest. If arrested the person has the right to defend himself by a lawyer of his choice. Also an arrested citizen has to be brought before the nearest magistrate within 24 hours. The rights of a person arrested under ordinary circumstances are not available to an enemy alien. They are also not available to persons detained under the Preventive Detention Act. Under preventive detention, the government can imprison a person for a maximum of three months. It means that if the government feels that a person being at liberty can be a threat to the law and order or to the unity and integrity of the nation, it can detain or arrest that person to prevent him from doing this possible harm. After three months such a case is brought before an advisory board for review.

Child labour and beggary is prohibited under right against exploitation. The right against exploitation, given in Articles 23 and 24, provides for two provisions, namely the abolition of trafficking in human beings and beggar (forced labour) and abolition of employment of children below the age of 14 years in dangerous jobs like factories and mines. Child labour is considered a gross violation of the spirit and provisions of the constitution.

Right to freedom of religion, covered in Articles 25, 26, 27 and 28, provides religious freedom to all citizens of India. The objective of this right is to sutain the principle of secularism in India. According to the constitution, all religions are equal before the state and no religion shall be given preference over the other. Citizens are free to preach, practice and propagate any religion of their choice.

All minorities, religious or linguistic, can set up their own educational institutions in order to preserve and develop their own culture. In granting aid to institutions, the state cannot discriminate against any institutions on the basis of the fact that it is administered by a minority institution.

Right to constitutional remedies empowers the citizens to move a court of law in case of any denial of the fundamental rights. For instance, in case of imprisonment, the citizen can ask the court to see if it is according to the provisions of the law of the country. If the court finds that it is not, the person will have to be freed. This procedure of asking the courts to preserve or safeguard the citizens' fundamental rights can be done in various ways. The court can issue various kinds of writs. These writs are habeas corpus, mandamus, prohibition, quo warrant and certiorari. When a national or state emergency is declared, this right is suspended by the central government.

Directive Principles of State Policy

Article – 38 State secure a social order for the promotion of welfare of the people

1. The state shall strive to promote the welfare of the people by securing and protecting as effectively as it may a social order in which justice, social, economic and political, she inform all the institutions of the national life.
2. The state shall, in particular, strive to minimize the inequalities in income and endeavour to eliminate inequalities in status, facilities and opportunities not only amongst individuals but also amongst groups of people residing in different areas or engaged in different vocations.

Originally Article 38 was what is contained in clause (1). It incorporates part of the preamble within it concerning justice, social, economic and political. This clause has often been relied upon to sustain and demand social welfare measures and to remind the state about the kind of society the constitution expects it to create. Clause (2) which was added by the constitution (forty-four amendment) Act, 1978, recognises group equality. It recognizes that grave inequalities of income and status exist amongst different groups of people which need to be minimized.

Article - 39. Certain principles of policy to be followed by the state

The state shall, in particular, direct its policy towards securing:

(*a*) That the citizens, men and women equally, have the right to an adequate means of livelihood

(*b*) That the ownership and control of the material resources of the community are so distributed as best to subserve the common good

(*c*) That the operation of the economic system does not result in the concentration of wealth and means of production to the common detriment

(*d*) That there is equal pay for equal work for both men and women

(*e*) That the health and strength of workers, men and women and the tender age of children are not abused and that citizens are not forced by economic necessity to enter avocations unsuited to their age or strength.

Article - 39-A. Equal justice and free legal aid

The state shall secure that the operation of the legal system promotes justice, on the basis of equal opportunity and shall in particular, provide free legal aid, by suitable legislation or schemes or in any other way, to ensure that opportunities for securing justice are not denied to any citizen by reason of economic or other disabilities.

Article - 40. Organisation of village panchayats

The state shall take steps to organize village panchayats and endow them with such powers and authority as may be necessary to enable them to function as units of self government.

Article - 41. Right to work, to education and to public assistance in certain cases

The state shall, within the limits of its economic capacity and development, make effective provision for securing the right to work, to education and to public assistance in cases of unemployment, old age, sickness and disablement and in other cases of unserved want.

Article - 42. Provision for just and humane conditions of work and maternity relief

The state shall make provision for securing just and humane conditions of work and for maternity relief. These directives, like those contained in Article 38, relate to economic rights. The state is required to make provision for just and humane conditions of work and for maternity relief. Upholding the claim of non-regularised female works for maternity relief, the court has stated.

Article - 43. Living wage, etc., for workers

The state shall endeavour to secure, by suitable legislation or economic organization or in any other way, to all works, agricultural, industrial or otherwise, a living wage, conditions of work ensuring a decent standard of life and full enjoyment of leisure and social and cultural opportunities and, in particular, the state shall endeavour to promote cottage industries on an individual or co-operative basis in rural areas.

Article - 44. Uniform civil code for the citizens

The state shall endeavour to secure for the citizens a uniform civil code throughout the territory of India. This article requires on the state to take steps for establishing a uniform civil code throughout the territory of India. Two objections were put forward in the constituent assembly against the making of a uniform civil code applying throughout India: firstly, it would infringe the fundamental right to freedom of religion mentioned in Article 25 and secondly, it would be a tyranny to the minority.

Article - 45. Provision for early childhood care and education to children below the age of six years

The state shall endeavour to provide early childhood care and education for all children until they complete the age of six years.

Article - 46. Promotion of educational and economic interests of scheduled castes, scheduled tribes and other weaker section

The state shall promote with special care the educational and economic interests of the weaker sections of the people and in particular of the scheduled castes and the scheduled tribes and shall protect them from social injustice and all forms of exploitation.

Article - 47. Duty of the state to raise the level of nutrition and the standard of living and to improve public health

The state shall regard the raising of the level of nutrition and the standard of living of its people and the improvement of public health as among its primary duties and in particular, the state shall endeavour to bring about prohibition of the consumption except for medicinal purposes of intoxicating drinks and of drugs which are injurious to health.

Article - 48. Organisation of agriculture and animal husbandry

The state shall endeavour to organize agriculture and animal husbandry on modern and scientific lines and shall, in particular, take steps for preserving and improving the breeds and prohibiting the slaughter of cows and calves and other milch and draught cattle.

Article - 48-A. Protection and improvement of environment and safeguarding of forests and wild life

The state shall endeavour to protect and improve the environment and to safeguard the forests and wild life of the country. The environment (protection) act 1986 and various other laws providing for the protection of environment, forest and wild life are among the steps taken under this article.

Article - 49. Protection of monuments and places and objects of national importance

It shall be the obligation of the state to protect every monument or place or object of artistic or historic interest, (declared by or under law made by parliament) to be of national importance, from spoliation, disfigurement, destruction, removal, disposal or export, as the case may be.

Article - 50. Separation of judiciary from executive

The state shall take steps to separate the judiciary from the executive in the public services of the state.

Article - 51. Promotion of international peace and security

The state shall endeavour to:

(*a*) Promote international peace and security

(*b*) Maintain just and honourable relations between nations

(*c*) Foster respect for international law and treaty obligations in the dealings of organized peoples with one another, and

(*d*) Encourage settlement of international disputes by arbitration.

Fundamental Duties

Article - 51-A. Fundamental duties

It shall be the duty of every citizen of India:

(*a*) To abide by the constitution and respect its ideals and institutions, the National Flag and the National Anthem

(*b*) To cherish and follow the noble ideals which inspired our national struggle for freedom (*c*) To uphold and protect the sovereignty, unity and integrity of India

(*d*) To defend the country and render national service when called upon to do so

(*e*) To promote harmony and the spirit of common brotherhood amongst all the people of India transcending religious, linguistic and regional or sectional diversities to renounce practices derogatory to the dignity of women

(*f*) To value and preserve the rich heritage of our composite culture

(*g*) To protect and improve the natural environment including forests, lakes, rivers and wildlife and to have compassion for living creatures

(*h*) To develop the scientific temper, humanism and the spirit of inquiry and reform

(*i*) To safeguard public property and to abjure violence

(*j*) To strive towards excellence in all spheres of individual and collective activity so that the nation constantly rises to higher levels of endeavour and achievement

Suggested Question

1. What is globalization? Give arguments in favour of globalization.
2. Globalisation is undermining national sovereigny. In the light of above statement discuss advantages and disadvantages of globalization.
3. What measures have been taken to globalise Indian economy?
4. How is WTO instrumental in regulation of various aspects of trade?
5. Indian constitution is a protector and facilitator of Indian economy & society. Explain.
6. The motive behind foundation of UNO is to establish peace & order in global world. Verify the statement with suitable examples.

References

1. P. Subha Rao – *International Business*, Delhi, 2000
2. Charles Hill – *International Business,* Delhi, 1991
3. N V Badi – *International Business,* Delhi, 2006
4. Misra & Puri – *Indian Economy,* Delhi, 2008
5. M L Jhingan – *International Economics,* Delhi, 2005
6. Datta & Sunderam – *Indian Economy,* Delhi, 2009
7. United Nations Charter, *Wikipedia*

8

CHAPTER

INDIAN SOCIAL SYSTEM–AS A SOURCE OF ETHICS

The culture of the Aryans and the Indus settlers have been largely responsible for shaping the social stratification that finally led to the emergence of the four-fold Varna system.

India's culture and social structure have undergone tremendous change in the course of several thousand years of its history, but its continuity has not been broken. The existence of the Indus valley civilization is shown by the ruins discovered at various parts of India. The culture of the Aryans and the Indus settlers have been largely responsible for shaping the social stratification that finally led to the emergence of the four-fold Varna system. The hierarchy based on birth was further rationalized by the doctrine of *Karma* which propagated that birth in higher or lower caste is the inexorable consequence of one's own deeds in earlier lives. This belief was so inculcated that the people of the lower castes were convinced that their low status in society and exploitation by the higher castes was entirely justified. In the development of doctrine of *Karma*, the notion of *Purusartha,* the *Ashrama* system and even the traditional pattern of economy, the contribution of the non-Aryans elements seems to have been much greater than that of the Aryans.

Indian culture and institutions have maintained their continuity over several millennia, despite changes that they had to undergo in the course of their long history. The culture of Indus civilization was vastly different from the culture and world view of the Vedic Aryans but the strands of continuity can hardly be missed. The rise of Buddhism posed a mighty challenge to the way of life, beliefs and rituals based on the Vedas. But Brahmanical revival combated Buddhism strongly and asserted again the divine authority of the Vedas. Though the Vedic age could not be revived, links with the Vedic heritage were brought out prominently. The continuity of Indian tradition can be easily seen in institutions, rituals and languages of Modern India. For instance, the Grihya Sutras which were composed around the sixth century B.C., is about two thousand five hundred years old, lay down that the following rituals are essential for the marriage ceremony: *Kanyadana, Agni Sthapana* and *Homa, Panigrahana, Laja Homa, Agni Parinayana* and *Saptapadi* etc. These rituals form an integeral part of the traditional marriage ceremony even today. In Hindu society, the emphasis on rituals seems to be exceptionally high. There are numerous rituals connected with *rites de passage,* calendaric fasts, festivals, and pilgrimages besides the daily worship of Gods and Goddesses. Millions of people from all corners of India congregate on specific occasions such as the Kumbha, without any invitation or announcement. The study of the dynamics of Indian society and culture suggests that the chief sociological function of this excessive emphasis on rituals in Hindu society has been to justify the supreme position of the dvijas, particularly the Brahmanas. In the Rigvedic times the Aryans justified their supremacy primarily on the basis of their special physical features based on race. But, in course of time, due to the compulsion of absorbtion of local tradition, the racial features of the Aryans were inevitably compromised. However, these elites would not have liked to give up their position of supremacy. The criteria based on racial features were, substituted by those of the observance of rituals. The dominant elites claimed superiority on the basis that they alone were sanctified through sacraments.

Karma has been the characteristi c of Indian society and culture.

Karma has been the characteristic of Indian society and culture. All theistic schools of philosophy, which accept the Vedas as the ultimate divine authority, subscribe to this doctrine. But even prominent *Nastika* atheist schools of thought which do not believe in the divine authority of Vedas, like Buddhism and Jainism, nevertheless accept the essentials of this doctrine. The belief that one's good and bad deeds are bound to be rewarded or punished, tends to strengthen adherence to norms and is thus a strong support to processes of social control. Belief in the doctrine of *Karma* also performs the latent function of providing support to the caste system. The firm belief that one's birth in a particular caste is determined by his own deeds of earlier lives was shared by the people of the lower as well as the higher castes. The people belonging to the lower castes too believed that their low status in society and the privileges of the supper castes were fully justified.

Though stratification based on birth is common to most pre-modern societies, the intricate norms of marriage and sharing of food and water (commesality) which were imposed severely by the Indian caste system which formed its integral part are surely unique. Such complex rules governing various aspects of life are found in no other society. The caste system thus is a unique feature of Indian society. The norms of marriage enforced by the caste system were indeed complex. These included the rules of endogamy, exogamy and hypergamy. A caste was typically endogamous. No one was allowed to marry outside the caste. But, while marrying within the caste, one could not get married to a person belonging to his own exogamous sub-caste, *Gotra* or *Pravara.* Any violation of the caste norms of marriage was severely punished in traditional Indian society. The entire family was liable to be ex-communicated. The caste restrictions on the sharing of food and water were quite complicated and these too were strictly imposed. There was an intricate classification of food. The uncooked foodstuffs could be freely accepted. Food made entirely of milk and milk products by persons of other castes was generally considered acceptable even by the Brahmanas. But, the Brahmana could not eat food made of cereals, even if it was fried. People of other castes would however take food made of cereals if it was fried (*Pakka*) but not if it was only boiled (Kachha). Even water could not be taken from the hands of people belonging to very low castes and by Hindus from the hands of Muslims and Christians. It was commonly held that by any deviation from the caste rules of sharing food and water one surely loses his *Dharma*.

India is marked by many differences pertaining to geographical features, racial elements, language, customs, modes of dress and eating etc. Its identity as a socio-cultural whole is clearly perceived both by Indians and outsiders. The traditional Indian perform pilgrimage to all the four *Dhamas* which are located in the extreme east, west, north and south of India. People from all parts of India congregate in their millions at specific times for events such as the *Kumbha.* Indian culture is a product of interaction between innumerable diverse people and cultures. The *Aryans* looked upon the pre-Aryans and their Gods and modes of worship with contempt. For instance, they referred to them with disdain as '*Sisnadevah*' or the worshipers of *phallus.* But in later times the worship of *phallus* as *Siva Linga* has become acceptable throughout the country. The devout Hindus consider the Vedas as embodiment of divine truth, and at the same time worship the *phallus* (*Shiva Linga)* with extreme devotion. This is only one example of the grand process of cultural synthesis that has been going on in India for several millennia. For instance, hardly any one is conscious that the holiest of holy rivers the Ganga, derives its name not from any Aryan source but from the Mongol word '*Kyang*', which means river.

It is widely recognized that the traditional social culture, is pan-Indic. The great epic *Mahabharata* brings together diverse cultural patterns spread over this vast country in one common framework. The induction of non-Aryan cultural elements was greatly facilitated by the second Brahmanical revival during which the Smrtis, Epics and Puranas were composed. The rise of Buddhism had given a big jolt to the supremacy of the Brahmanas and many aspects of Vedic precepts. To combat the influence of Buddhism among the people at large and to re-establish the acceptance of their supreme position the Brahmana elites had to give up those Aryan practice which were repugnant to the bulk of the common people. They had also to take over and integrate with the tradition of elite culture, the customs, deities and modes of worship prevalent among the non-Aryan common folk. Many tribal and village gods have thus become an integral part of the higher or great tradition of Hinduism. Certain structural and cultural factors seem to have contributed greatly to the unique pattern of unity in diversity of India. Through the ages, the caste system has provided a mechanism for the integration of diverse peoples and cultures in a broad framework. The spirit of accommodating diversities has permeated Indian culture. The readiness to accept new or different elements without giving up those that have been in existence has been greatly responsible for its rich diversity.

The roots of the *Varna* system has been found in the *Rigveda* where earliest social stratification was based on colours i.e. Aryans and non-Aryans.

Varna System

The roots of the *Varna* system has been found in the *Rigveda* where earliest social stratification was based on colours i.e. Aryans and non-Aryans. Slowly fourfold system of *Varna* classification was evolved. The *Purushsukta* of tenth mandal of *Rigveda* mentions that the supreme being created Brahmana from his mouth, Kshatriya from his arms, Vaisya from his thigh and Sudras from his feet. The R*igvedc Varna* was based on *Karma* or profession. In the later vedic age the idea of *Karma* or profession was lost and in place of it birth as criteria was introduced. This important function of the *Varna* that role of rituals in establishing and sustaining the social order perhaps explains the unique and excessive elaboration and importance of ritual in India. The metaphysical doctrine of '*Karma*' has provided a powerful rationalization for inequality based on birth and has made it acceptable to the wide masses. According to the *Karma* doctrine, this life is one link in the infinite chain of births and rebirths, and each being is born in a specific position according to his own deeds in past lives.

In *Rigveda,* the word *'Varna'* clearly refers to the colour of skin of the people of two different races. The *Purusasuka,* where the origin of the four classes is described, the word *Varna* does not occur. The poet Visvamitra prays to Indra to destroy the blacks through his brilliance. At one place a poet says that Indra has destroyed black armies. Due to different racial features the disdain of the Aryans towards the Dasas was as so great that they were called *Amanusya* or non-human. In the course of time, the Aryans settled down on the land and developed cordial relations with the *Panis (non-Aryans).* A poet prays to the god Pushan: 'O Pusha, one who does not want to give, make him liberal and soften the heart of the Pani'. And we find some hymns of Brbu, a leader of Panis:

'Among Panis, Brbu is the greatest;
His heart is as large as the plains of Ganga;
He who is ready to give immediately;
His thousand noble gifts of cows are running like wind,
Therefore all our poets praise the noble prince, the giver of thousands.'

The commercial terminology in Sanskrit owes a great deal to the Panis. Among such terms are *apana* or market, *panama* or to sell, *panya* or commodity, *pana* or coin, and *vanik* or the trader. In the word *vanik* the sound of *pa* has changed to *va,* which is not uncommon in the evolution of languages. It is common to add the letter *ka* for making diminutives in the Avesta as well as in the Sanskrit language. The word *vanijya* or trade is derived from the word *vanik.* In the *Purusasukta,* this class is called Vaisya or 'the sons of Vis'. In the *Rigveda,* the word Vis is used for people. In *Zend-Avesta,* the word Vis means many families or a village. In *Rigveda* every individual had the right to choose his profession according to his ability and achievements. He could become a priest or a warrior, or an ordinary man. The word *Brahma* means hymn and also the power inherent in the hymn. Brahmana is one who is the repository of hymns. In *Rigvedic* age priesthood was considered the highest profession. But becoming a successful priest was not easy. The priest was expected to compose such hymns which would lull wealthy enemies to sleep and swollen rivers to lower their level so that armies would cross them without difficulty. A poet vividly describes that everybody has to do some work or the other to earn his livelihood:

'I am a poet, my father is a physician,
My mother grinds corn with stone;

Striving for wealth,

We follow different occupations.'

Since the professions of priest and warrior were considered nobler it is not surprising that many people aspired to these. A person who could neither compose hymns nor become a warrior, the only profession left for him was that of the economy. This profession is considered lower than that of priest and warrior. *Vis* was the third rank in the social stratification. The *Rigveda* the word *Sudra* is not mentioned except in the *Purusasukta,* which is considered to be of a later origin. The *purusasukta* contains a myth about the origin of the four fold social structure. All the four ranks are mentioned together. It is asserted that all the four ranks originated from the great sacrificed Purusa. The occupations of the four ranks are related symbolically to the parts of the body of the Purusa. Obviously, this is an organismic analogy between man and society, legitimizing the varyng ranks and functions of different groups.

'The Brahmana was his mouth,

The Rajanya was made of his two arms;

His thighs became the Vaisya,

From his feet was produced the Sudra.'

The Brahamana has been called the mouth of the *Purusa* and is placed highest in society. His special function pertains to speech. Being a priest, invoking Gods is his privilege. *Rajanya (Kshatriya)* is born of the arms of *Purusa* and has the privilege of wielding arms. The thighs of the *Purusa* became Vaisya. The occupation of Vaisya is domestication. From feet was produced the Sudra. Just as the feet are the lowest in the body, Sudras are the lowest in society. The composition of the *Purusasukta* and its inclusion in the *Rigveda* was probably the first attempt to systematize, justify and legitimize the exploitation of the non-Aryan masses by Aryans. The easiest way was to find some supernatural basis. This tendency of imputing divine sanction is a characteristic of the period of later Samhitas and Brahmanas.

***Rigveda* was probably the first attempt to systematize, justify and legitimize the exploitation of the non-Aryan masses by Aryans.**

In the *Avesta,* the land of seven rivers is mentioned as one of the settlements of Aryans. In this land, the leader of Aryan migration, Yim, married a demoness and gave his sister, Yimuk, to a demon. The issues born of these unions have been referred to as abnormal in the *Avesta*, and monkeys and beats in the Pahlavi texts. These descriptions allude to the racial admixture which took place in that early era. It is also said that to avoid deformity, Yim married his sister Yimuk and thus preserved racial purity. From this myth it is quite clear that during the earliest era of settlement the Aryans married indigenous women, but when the children born of such unions had dark complexions, snub noses and other non-Aryan features, such marriages were avoided. But, in the course of time, such relations crystallized into endogamous as well as hereditary groups. In the later Samhitas hypergamy is permissible. Thus, the Aryans or men of the upper Varnas could have Sudra wives.The *Aitareya Brahmana* puts forth another mythical justification: 'The God created the Brahmana with Gayatri, the Rajanya with Tristubh and the Vaisya with Jagati, but he did not create the Sudra with any metre.'

The priest was neither a military strategist nor a poet, his sole job was to preserve the hymns and employ them in various complicated sacrifices which were to be performed for the fulfillment of different wishes. The Aryans had by now settled down in the Indo-Gangetic plains. For the settled agricultural way of life such Gods were no more needed. The Gods now were expected to fulfil their mundane wishes and solve their day-to-day problems. The centre of civilization shifted further east. The land of seven rivers finds the land of Kuru and Pancala became the seat of the Aryan culture. The river Sarasvati in the west and the river Drasadvati in the east formed its boundary. The priestly elites preserved the highest position for themselves. There are many assertions in the later Samhitas that are meant to establish their supreme position. The sacrament of initiation, *Yajnopavita (Upanayana-Samskar),* played an important part in rationalizing and strengthening the system of Varna. The first three Varnas acquired a privileged position themselves. In the *Atharvaveda*, for the first time, we get the description of initiation. The poet conceives the sun as the child who is to initiated into studentship by his teacher. Gradually, the sacrament of initiation became much more elaborate. The *Taittiriya Aranyaka* prescribes that a Brahmana should wear a *Yajnopavita* of antilope skin or of cloth. It asserts that the sacrifice which is performed while wearing a *Yajnopavita* is spread out, or becomes successful, whereas the sacrifices of him who does not wear a *Yajnopavita* would not spread. *Yajnopavita* became the most essential part of intiation.

In *Satapatha Brahmana*, the Brahmana and Kshatriya Varnas are identified with the twin Gods Mitra and Varuna: 'Mitra is priesthood and Varuna is nobility and the priesthood is the conceiver and then nobility is the doer.' It is asserted that Mitra or the priest could stand without Varuna, the nobility, but not Varuna the nobility without Mitra, the priest. It is concluded, 'therefore a Kshatriya who wants to do something should seek guidance from a Brahmana, for he verily succeeds only when he is guided by Brahmana'. Gradually, the three Varnas other than the Brahmana developed a kind of apathy for the ritualistic way of life, and a new school of thought appeared in Aranyakas and Upanisads. In these texts it is asserted that expensive, cumbersome and prolonged sacrifices do not lead to real knowledge. It was a challenge against the supremacy of the Brahmanas, and signified loss of faith in sacerdotal science inherent in it. People began to doubt the efficacy of these sacrifices. Another interesting feature of the Upanisads is that its major contributions are primarily from Kshatriyas, lower Varnas and women. The teachings of the Upanisads are in a simple language, therefore they earned great popularity among the people. The supremacy of the Brahmanas was challenged in various overt and covert ways. Many established teachers (Brahmanas) approached kings (Kshatriyas) to acquire the ultimate knowledge. Pravahana Jaibali, king of Panchala, instructed Gautma and claimed that Brahmanas do not Bramha this knowledge, only the Kshatriyas possess it. The glorification of Kshatriyas are mentioned in the *Brhadanyaka Upanisad* : 'the Brahmana being not strong enough, the most excellent power or Kshatriya was created. Therefore (at the Rajasuya sacrifice the) Brahmana sits down below the Kshatriya. He confers that glory on the Kshatriya alone' The theologians approached king Asvapati of Kekaya carrying fuel in their hands like students to get the knowledge of self'. Even the kings sometimes approached persons of lower classes to get knowledge of self. Jansruti Pautrayana approached a cartman named Raikva for instruction. In the Upanisadic literature dark complexion is not considered necessarily bad. The *Brhadaranyaka Upanisad* mentions rituals for having a dark complexioned son. Ritual even for the birth of a daughter, which is very uncommon in the Indian elite tradition, is also found. The Upanisads mark a new epoch in the history of Indian thought. The idea found in the Upanisads are in marked contrast to the traditional way of thinking which always looks back to the golden past. The Upanisads are refreshingly forward looking. They expect the new generation to be better than the older ones. In the *Brhadaranyaka Upanisad*, the father blesses his new born son to be more learned than his father and his grandfather. The concept of rebirth is introduced. In the *Rigveda,* as well as the Avesta, the dead go to live with their forefathers in heaven. The idea of souls taking another birth is found in a rudimentary form in Austric cultures. This idea of transmigration of the soul was developed in the classical Indian systems of metaphysics specially in *Samkhya, Yoga* and *Vedanta.* It crystallized into the theory of *Karma,* which rationalized and provided the rock bed to the system of Varna hierarchy for thousands of years.

During the Upanisadic era, the Varna hierarchy and the strong patriarchal order that constituted the foundation of the ancient Indian social structure were badly undermined. The *Grihya Sutras* seem to mark a systematic and concerted effort on the part of the priestly elites to re-establish their supremacy and resuscitate the social order in which they would have an unrivalled position. The hierarchy could no more be established on the basis of race. Because of this, criteria of ritual purity were introduced by the *Grihya Sutras* to take the place of racial purity. In the *Grihya Sutras,* for the first time, a number of *Samskaras* or sacraments were explicitly codified. These *Samskaras* are to begin before the birth of a child and this process lasts for many years even after the death of an individual.

The *Dharma Sutras* introduced many new rules about not taking food from the house of persons of lower Varnas. The *Baudhayana Dharma Sutra,* because of its archaic language seems to be the earliest among the *Dharma Sutras.* Gautama allows a Brahmana student to take food from the house of all the three higher Varnas but after completing his studentship he should not take food from the house of Kshatriya and Vaisya Varnas. He was expected to take food only at the house of a Brahmana householder. Apastamba further propounds that even among Brahmana householders, he should eat only in the house of a true Brahmana. In times of distress a Brahmana could eat the food prepared in the house of a Sudra who was under his protection for the sake of spiritual merit. In the *Dharma Sutras,* the priestly elites made it a point to assign a lower position to Kshatriyas. It is provided that even a king should make way for a Brahmana on the road. The gap between the two higher *Varnas* definitely widened. A Brahmana of ten years and a Kshatriya of a hundred years stand to each other in the relation of father and son. The Sudras constituted the fourth *Varna.* Apastamba and Vasistha refer to the Sudras and outcaste as burial grounds. Apastamba, Gautama and Vasistha provide that serving the three higher Varnas is their sole occupation. Gautama provided that for serving the three higher Varnas he would get remnants of their food, cast-off shoes, umbrellas, garments and mats. When a Sudra servant is unable to serve his Aryan employer due to old age or illness, the Aryan employer was expected to support him.

During the Upanisadic era, Sudras too participated in metaphysical discussions. In the revivalist era, the priestly elites scrupulously forbade even the listening to recitation of Vedas for Sudra. Apastamba and Gautama provide that if a Sudra tries to converse with an Aryan on an equal footing, walks on the road side-by-side with him or sits on the same couch, he should be given corporal punishment.

Among the prominent ethno-cultural strains are the Aryan, the civilized Mediterranean, the Australoid, and the Mongoloid. In the early Rigvedic times, though there existed the notion of superiority based on race, the division of society was not as rigid and elaborate as found in the post-Rgvedic treatises. In the Buddhist literature, the people described are highly commercial, liberal, affluent and happy. It appears that in the north-eastern parts of India which became the seat of Upanisads and Buddhism, trade and commerce flourished extensively, and liberal ideas developed among the elite of that region. Though the Upanisads picture many respectable teachers as belonging to the lower Varnas, they do not directly criticize the Varna hierarchy. On the other hand, Buddha openly declared the Varna system unreasonable and reprehensible, as all human beings belong to a common human species, whatever be the colour of their skin. He refuted the Vedic myth of the origin of the Varna hierarchy and declared it to be false. The Buddhist texts praise kings and warriors, Brahmanas who were well versed in the three Vedas and Vaisyas or rich *Sresthis* who liberally made gifts to the new religion, and skilful craftsmen. In the Buddhist text, the supremacy of the Brahmanas was openly challenged. The Buddha declared that one cannot be considered superior just because of birth or lineage. He declares:

'By mere birth no one becomes a Brahmana,

By mere birth no one becomes an outcaste.

By deeds one becomes a Brahmana,

By deeds one becomes an outcaste.'

During a discussion with a young Brahmana, Buddha systematically argued that all Varnas, white or black, belong to one human race. It is remarkable that in the Buddhist texts show norms and values of the rising puritanical middle class. These values promoted trading activities and the formation of capital. The advice given to traders in *Digha Nikaya* brings out the commercial spirit of the Buddhist era:

'Making money like the bee,

Who does not hurt the flower;

Such a man makes his pile,
As an ant-hill gradually;
The man grown wealthy,
Thus, can help his family,
And firmly binds his friends to himself
He should divide his money into four parts
On one part he should live,
With two expand his trade
And the fourth he should save
Against a rainy day.'

Buddhism was the greatest challenge to the priestly elites for it gained great popularity among the masses.

Buddhism was the greatest challenge to the priestly elites for it gained great popularity among the masses. Many kings, *Sresthis* found Buddhism more suitable and they contributed to spread it in India and abroad. The religion of the pre-Aryans, reasserted itself among the people. The priestly elites were quite conscious of all these forces. It was clear to them that the ancient Vedic religion could not be revived in its earlier form. Many old Aryan practices had therefore to be rejected and non-Aryan customs found entry into the revived religion. For restoring the Varna hierarchy, the backbone of the traditional Indian social structure, the Smrtis came into existence. In the revival of the Sutra period many ancient Indo-European rituals and customs were consolidated into aphorisms or Sutras. The *samskaras* were introduced in an effective manner primarily by the Sutras. Since the Smrtis belong to the revivalist era, all the authors of Smrtis adopted the names of Vedic seers to get authority for what they said. The Manu Smrti is the first attempt of the priestly elites in this direction. Manu armed with the ancient myth of creation and various sacraments, together with the doctrine of *Karma,* tried to revive the bygone golden age by re-establishing the ancient system of Varna hierarchy. In this process women and Sudras were the greatest losers.

The Manu Smrti reflects the strong resentment of the Brahmanical elites against the Buddhist leveling influence.

The Manu Smrti reflects the strong resentment of the Brahmanical elites against the Buddhist leveling influence. It has been categorically asserted that the dominance of priestly elites and the hierarchy based on Varna must be re-established not only through religious prescriptions but by the full might of the king and the state. The use of arms to restore their supremacy is openly commended. Manu calls punishment, the sons of the creator. The king is enjoined to establish Varna hierarchy through the power of punishment. Other twice-born people, too, are exhorted to resort to arms if they are in any way hindered in carrying out the duties prescribed for their particular Varnas. In the Smrti era, once again the Brahmanas ensured unquestionably the supreme position for themselves. Manu declares that the Brahmana from the very birth is an eternal incarnation of the sacred law. Manu calls the Brahmana a great God just like fire, be he ignorant or learned, just as the fire does not get contaminated, so also a Brahmana, although he may follow even a low occupation. He should always be honoured and should be considered great. This is in marked contrast to the theory of equality proclaimed by the Buddha. Birth in a particular Varna was considered enough for securing all sorts of privileges. It appears that by the time Manu Smrti was composed, norms of ritual purity had substituted those of racial purity. Manu declared that the Brahmana is the lord of all Varnas because of his superiority of birth and observances of rituals and sacraments. He says that a non-Aryan may have Aryan appearance, therefore one must judge a person by his acts, not by his physical appearance.

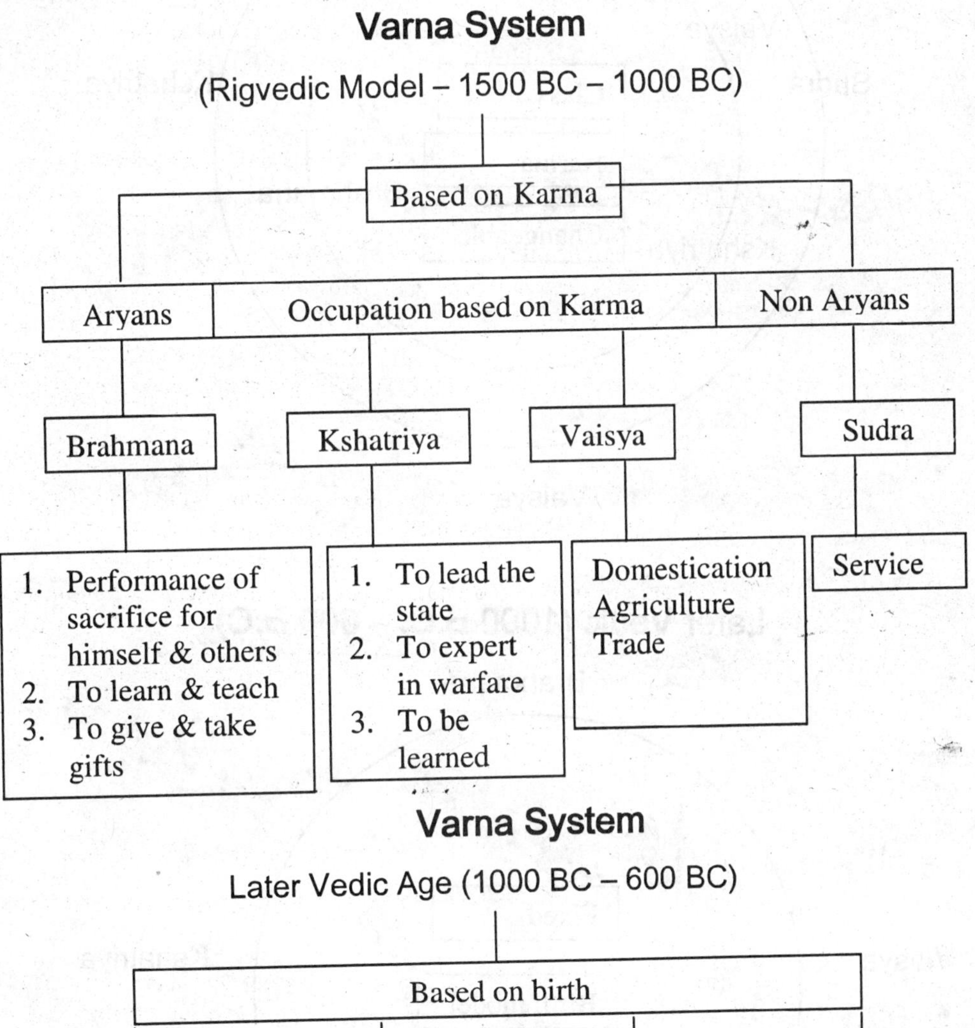

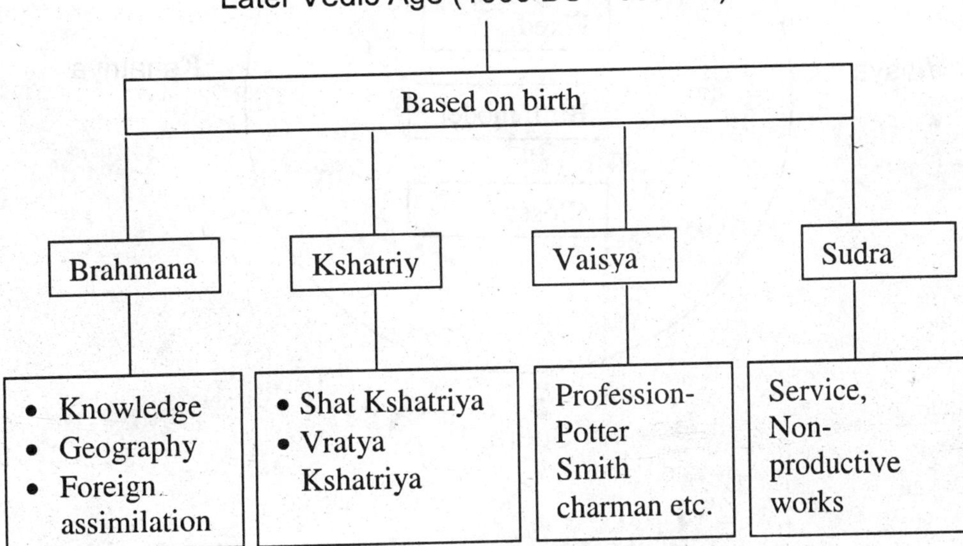

Rigvedic (1500 BC – 1000 BC)

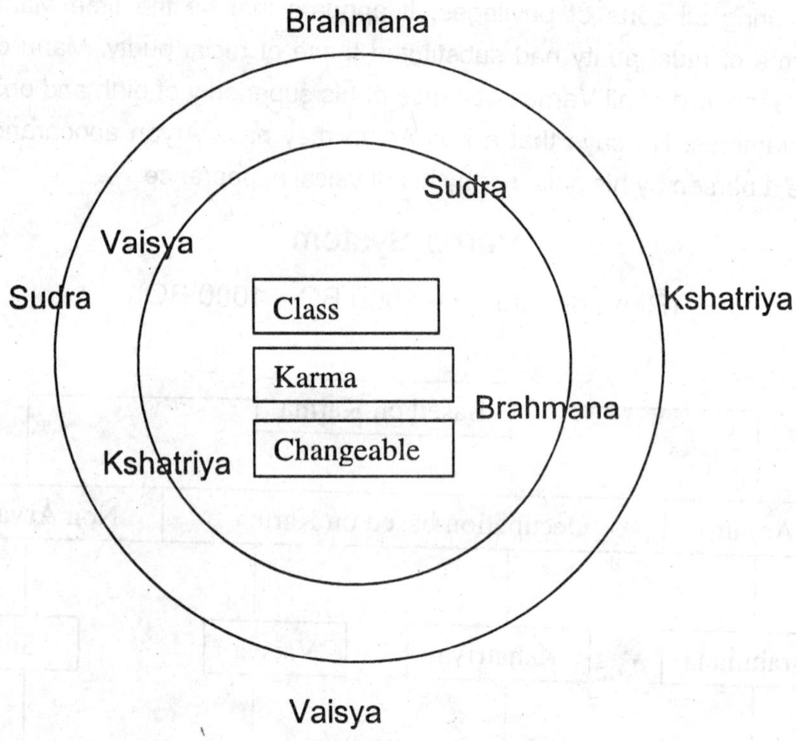

Later Vedic (1000 B.C. – 600 B.C)

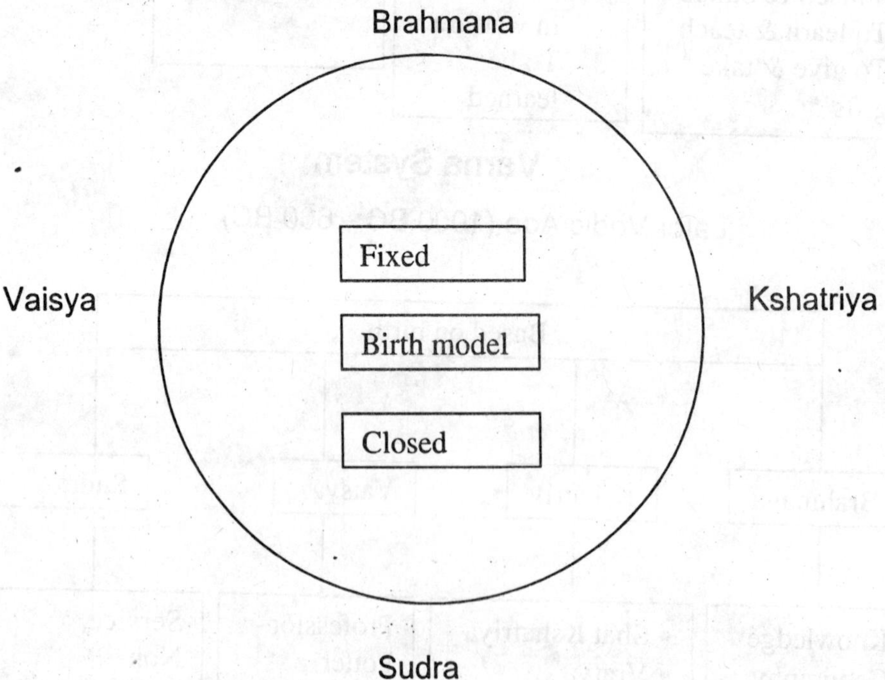

(Anatomical Theory)

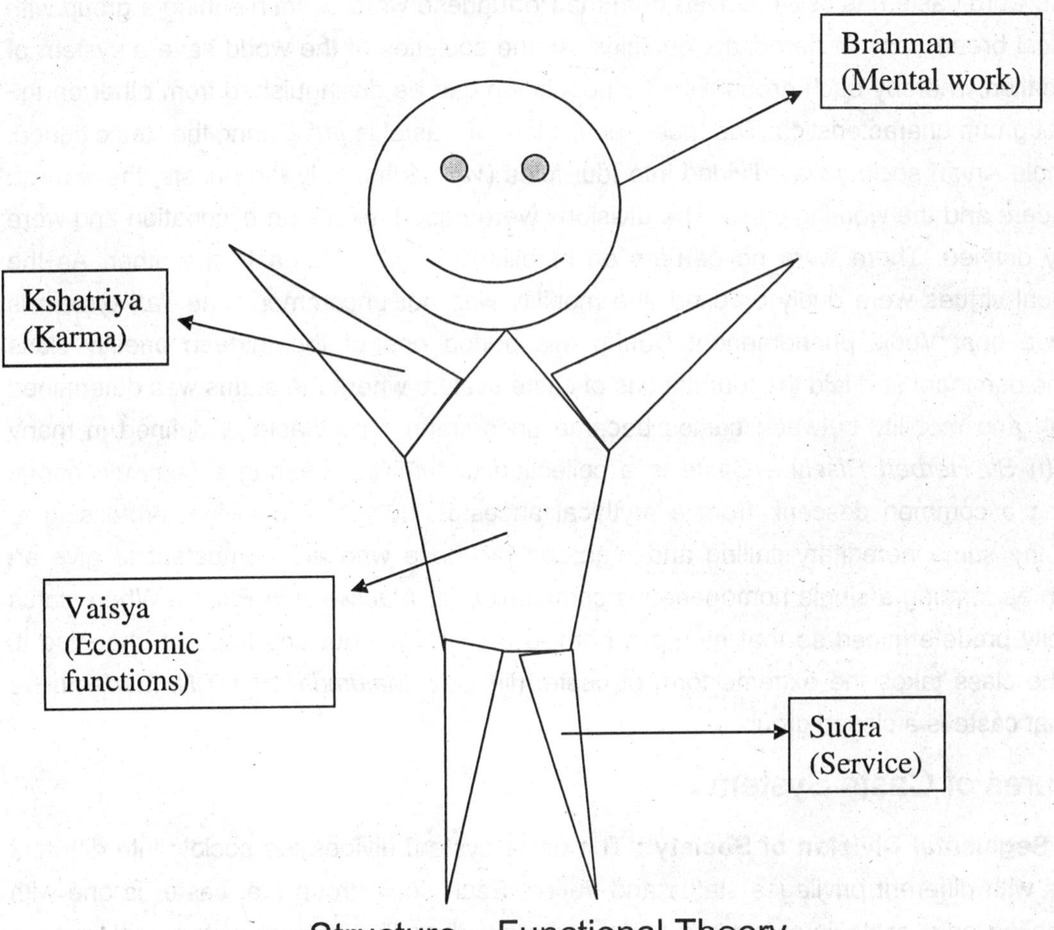

Structure – Functional Theory

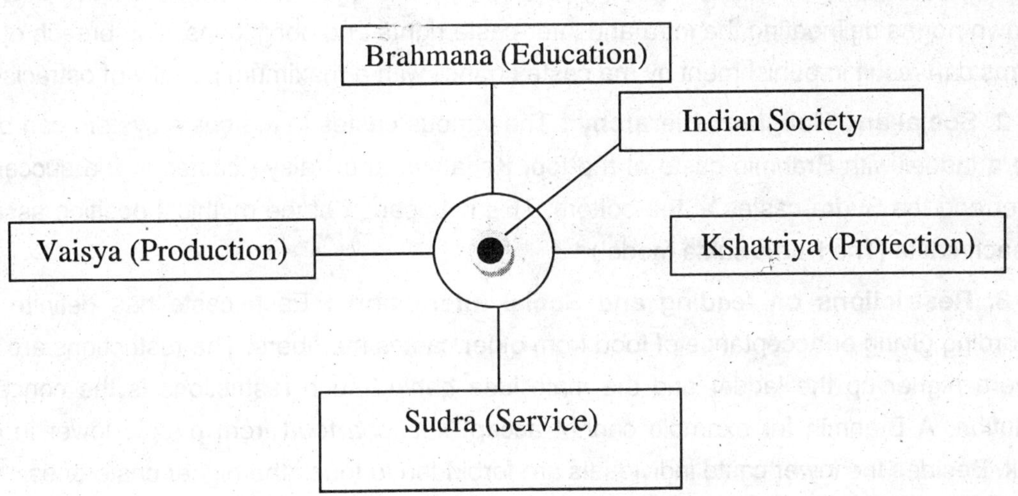

Caste

The word caste has been derived from the Portuguese word *casta* meaning a group with its typical breed, race or hereditary qualities. All the societies of the world have a system of stratification whereby each group within a population can be distinguished from other on the basis of group characteristics. The Indian equivalent of 'caste' is *jati.* During the Vedic period, the whole Aryan society was divided into four folds (*varnas)* namely the priests, the warrior, the traders and the working class. The divisions were based mainly on occupation and were loosely defined. There were no barriers on mobility from one Varna to the other. As the individual virtues were duely credited, the mobility was not uncommon. The *Jati* system is mainly a post Vedic phenomenon. During this period one of the thirteen priestly class became dominant and laid the foundations of caste system where the status was determined by birth and mobility between castes became uncommon. The Caste is defined in many ways (i) *Sir Herbert Risely* – Caste is a collection of families, bearing a common name, claiming a common descent, from a mythical ancestor, human and divine, professing to follow the same hereditary calling and regarded by those who are competent to give an opinion as forming a single homogeneous community. (ii) *Maclver and Page* – When status is wholly predetermined so that men are born to their lot without any hope of changing it, then the class takes the extreme form of caste. (iii) *D.N. Majumdar* and *T.N. Madan* have said that caste is a closed group.

The Indian equivalent of 'caste' is *jati.*

Caste is a collection of families, bearing a common name, claiming a common descent, from a mythical ancestor, human and divine, professing to follow the same hereditary calling and regarded by those who are competent to give an opinion as forming a single homogeneous community.

Features of Caste System

1. Segmental Division of Society : The caste system divides the society into different groups with different privileges status and duties. Each such group (i.e. caste) is one with 'we' feeling and, caste interests are more important than the interest of the society as a whole. The status of a person is determined not by his virtues but by the caste he is born in. The membership of a caste can be acquired only by birth (ascribed status) it. Each caste has its own norms delineating the intra and inter-caste rights and obligations. The breach of such norms can result in punishment by the caste council with a maximum penalty of ostracism.

2. Social and Religious Hierarchy : The various castes in the caste system can be put into a ladder with Brahmin caste at the top, Kshatriya and Vaisya castes in the succeeding order and the Sudra castes at the bottom. This is because of the mythical position assigned to each caste (The Purus sukta model)

3. Restrictions on feeding and Social Interaction : Each caste has definite rules regarding giving or acceptance of food from other castes members. The restrictions are more severe higher up the ladder and the main idea behind such restrictions is the concept of pollution. A Brahmin for example cannot accept *kuchcha* food from people lower in caste rank. Besides the lower caste individuals are forbidden to touch the higher caste ones.

4. Endogamy : Each caste is divided into subcastes which have their respective *gotras. Gotra* exogamy and caste endogamy are an important feature of caste system. No one can marry outside one's caste but a few castes originated because of marriage between such ostracized individuals and their respective families.

5. Fixed Occupation : Each caste has a traditional occupation and deters its members from opting any other. Even the attempts of members from other castes to follow its occupation are not welcome. This however is not an essential element of a caste today because today such restrictions have lost all ground.

6. Civil and Religious Disabilities : Each caste enjoys certain privileges while the lower castes face many disabilities. They are not allowed to mix-up with higher caste subjects. Their houses are located on the outskirts of villages or towns. Brahamin are the most privileges ones followed by kshatriya and vaisya castes.

Merit of Caste System

1. In a caste it is the responsibility of one's caste members to take care of individual. Caste is responsible for the welfare of its members, their actions, marriage and their participation in caste matters. Care for the orphans is a caste matter. Caste provides protection to them as also helps them to use higher within the caste. All this is made possible by the overwhelming support of the caste members.
2. Each caste has its traditional occupation and everyone, right from his childhood, knows about his profession to be. He can thus be well trained over the years. The wonders of craftsmanship of ancient and medieval India are a testimony of the development of crafts and the credit for this mainly goes to the caste system. The fixed occupation also removed the uncertainty about the future and career settlement in life.
3. As one could marry only within his caste, it ensured purity of the genome. It also enhanced the ritual purity.
4. All possible functions within the society are distributed among the castes so that there be not any discord. Even the norms for interaction between members of different castes are well laid reducing the chances of conflict resulting in greater stability of society.
5. Definite norms for all have a strong bearing on the intellectual make-up of members of each caste. They think in terms of equality with other members of the caste. It also develops feeling for one's caste members.

Demerits of Caste System

Everyone in the society thinks in terms of caste and not society. Caste interests dominate at the cost of rest of the society resulting in hate and mutual disrespect between different caste groups. Within a caste there are always persons who can perform better than in the traditional occupation but as there is lack of occupational mobility their talent goes waste. This waste has proved costly for the development of society. Each caste has rules regarding mobility of its members. At times too many people are not required but members. At times too many people are not required but members cannot go out for fear of ostracism. Obviously each family has to be content with what every work they get, even at the cost of standard of living. Caste system is highly undemocratic whereby higher castes enjoy at the cost of lower ones down the hierarch. Sudra castes and the untouchables are the most miserable lot living in utter poverty in thatched huts and hunger. All soio-economic disabilities of lower castes are the direct result of caste system.

Changes in the Caste System

The British introduced throughout India uniform legal, legislative and judicial systems. The British transferred the judicial powers of the caste councils to the civil and criminal courts which affected the authority which the Panchayats had held over the members. Questions of assault, adultery, rape and the like were taken before the British Courts for decision. In civil matters such as marriage, divorce, caste-based occupational disputes, disputes between husband and wife decision are now in purview of court. Some of the social reform movements launched by social reformers during the British rule also attacked the caste system and its inequalities. These reform movements 'did not succeed in removing the rigidity of the caste system in this period' but the popular western ideas and values such as Liberty, equality and fraternity, democracy, rationalism, individualism, women's liberation, secularism, humanitarianism etc. made their inroads into India. These ideas had deeply influenced the western educated Indians. People who had hitherto been the targets of atrocities, deprivation, exploitation and humiliation could now voice their protest by asserting their rights.

The religious basis of the caste has been attacked. Caste is no more believed to be divinely ordained. It is being given mere a social and secular meaning than a religious interpretation. Restrictions on food habits have been relaxed. Distinction between *pakka* food and *kachcha* food has almost vanished. Caste is not very much associated with hereditary occupations. Caste no longer determines the occupational career of an individual. Occupations are becoming more and more caste-free. Endogamy, which is often called the very essence of the caste system, still prevails. Inter caste marriages though legally permitted, have not become the order of the day. Most of the legal, political, educational, economic and other disabilities from which the lowest caste people had suffered have been removed by the constitutional provisions. They are given special protection also. Adult franchise and reservation have given them a strong weapon to protect their interests. Caste continues to be a segmental division of Hindu society. Caste with its hierarchical system continues to ascribe status to the individuals. Caste panchayats, which used to control the behavior of caste-members, have either come very weak or disappeared. Restrictions imposed by the caste on social intercourse are very much relaxed. Distinction between *touchable* and *untouchable* is not much felt especially in the community of literate people.

Education makes people liberal, broad-minded, rationale and democratic. Educated people are believed to be less conservative and superstitious. On the contrary, caste-consciousness of the members has been increasing. Every caste wants to safeguard its interest. For fulfilling this purpose castes are getting themselves organsied on the model of labour unions. Caste and politics have come to affect each other now. Caste has become an inseparable aspect of our politics. Elections are fought more often on the basis of caste. Selection of candidates, voting analysis, selection of legislative party leaders, distribution of ministerial portfolios etc., are very much based on caste. M.N. Srinivas says, is virtually the politics confrontation of dominant castes. The political confrontation between the dominant castes such as Lingayat and Vokkaligas in Karnataka and Reddys and Kammas in Andhra Pradesh are well known. Mutual interdependence of castes which existed for centuries and was reinforced by the institutional system of *jajmani is* not found today. The *vertical solidarity* of castes has been replaced by *horizontal solidarity. 'Live and* let live' policy which was once associated with the caste makes no sense today. Caste looks at the other with suspicision, contempt and jelousy and finds in it a challenger, a competitor. Excessive *caste mindedness* and *caste-patriotism* have added to this competition. The economic base of a caste and its hold over the political power virtually determine the intensity of this competitiveness. Though caste panchayats are dwindling, caste organizations are on the increase. Some of these organizations have their own written constitutions and managing committees through which they try to preserve some of the caste rules and practices. Caste organizations run their own papers, bulletins, periodicals etc., through which they regularly feed information to the members regarding the activities of caste organization and achievements of caste members.

Due to the process of industralisation number of non-agricultural job opportunities were created. This new economic opportunity weakened the hold of the upper castes people who owned vast lands. People of different castes, classes and religions started working together in factories, offices, workshops etc. This was unthinkable two centuries ago. The growth of cities has drawn people of all castes together and made them to stay together ignoring many of their caste restrictions. The upper caste people started looking to modifying their life-style on the model of the west. Thus they became more and more westernize without bothering much about caste inhibitions. The modern means of transport such as train, bus, ship, aeroplane, trucks etc. have been of great help for the movement of men and materials. Caste rules relating to the practice of purity and pollution and untouchability could no longer be observed. The modern means of communication such as newspapers, post, telegraph, telephone, radio, television etc., have helped people to come out of the narrow world of caste.

SAMSKARAS

Whole integrated scheme of thought and practice is divided into: (1) *jnana-kanda* (2) *upasana-kanda* (3) *karma-kanda.*

Hinduism provides a comprehensive scheme for the enlightenment, elevation and purification of man. Whole integrated scheme of thought and practice is divided into: (1) *jnana-kanda* (2) *upasana-kanda* (3) *karma-kanda. Jnana, upasana* and *karma* denote respectively knowledge, meditation and action as taught by the scriptures. The word *karma,* covers all the activities of a person, including the practice of universal ethical virtues, general and particular social duties, symbolic and mystic rituals. *Karma* purifies the mind and when it is in the form of a sacrament, it brings about the complete sanctification of the personality. The Sanskrit word *samskara* is derived from the root *kr* with the prefix *sam* and suffix *ghan* is added to it. It is used in different senses. *Samskara* has the sense of education, cultivation, training, refinement, perfection and grammatical purity, polishing, embellishment, decoration and ornament, impression, operation and influence, a purificatory rite, sacred rite or ceremony, consecration, sanctification and hallowing, merit of action etc. Hindu sacraments aimed at not only the formal purification of the body but also at sanctifying, impressing, refining and perfecting the entire individuality of the recipient.

The first systematic attempt at describing the *samskaras* is found *Grihya-Sutras.*

The first systematic attempt at describing the *samskaras* is found *Grihya-Sutras.* It is in the *Vaikhanasa-smarta-Sutras* that a clear distinction between the *samskaras* relating to the body *(astadasa samskarah sarirah)* and sacrifices in general is met. The *Grihya-Sutras* generally deal with the bodily *samskaras* beginning with *viviha* (marriage) and ending in *samavartana* (graduation). The number of *samskaras* in the *Grihya-Sutras* fluctuate between twelve to eighteen. The Hindus of early times believed that they were surrounded by superhuman influences, good or evil and they sought to remove the evil influences by the various means they devised for the purpose and they invoked the beneficial ones for timely help. The means adopted for the removal of evil influences, the first was propitiation. The second means was deception. The evil influences were diverted either by hiding the person exposed to them or by offering his substitute. The third means was to resort to threat and direct attack, when the above two methods failed either by the person himself or by any one officiating or administering authority. The Gods were also invoked to prevent the evil influences reaching the recipient of the *samskara.* Water, fire, noise, a staff, or other materials were also employed for driving away the troublesome influences. As hostile influences were shunned by people, favourable influences were attracted and invited for their benefit. It was believed that every period of a man's life was presided over by a deity and therefore, whenever occasion arose, that deity was invoked to confer boons and blessings on the person concerned. Touching, breathing, feeding, anointment, dramatic utterances etc. were frequently used for this purpose.

Samskaras have a cultural purpose governing the evolution of the society, because they comprehend sacrifices and rites that have for their aim domestic felicity resulting from the gain of cattle, progeny, long life, wealth, prosperity, strength and intellectual vigour. The cultural purpose sought to be served by the ancient rites and ceremonies chiefly related to the formation and development of personality. This moulding of character was not mere patternizing aimed at affording the subject timely orientation and help. The performance of the *samskaras* served the purpose of self expression. One performed the *samskaras* for expressing his own joys, felicitations and even sorrows at the various events of life. They helped also in imparting to life a higher religious sanctity. Impurity associated with the material body real or imaginary is removed by the performance of the *samskaras*. The whole body is consecrated and made a fit dwelling place for the soul. The *samskaras* serve as a mean between the ascetic and the materialistic conception of life. The advocates of the ascetic ideal try to worship the Spirit ignoring the urge and significance of the body. The upholders of materialism do not go beyond the body and deny the spiritual aspect of life, they are deprived of the peace and joy of the Spirit. It is the aim of the *samskaras* to make the body a valuable possession, a thing not to be discarded, but made holy and sanctified, so that it might become a fitting instrument of the intelligent Spirit residing in it.

The *samskaras* embrace various elements and express the beliefs, sentiments and knowledge the Hindus had about the nature of the universe of human life and man's relation to the superhuman powers believed to guide or control his destiny. The first and most important requirement of the sacrament is the sacred fire invariably kindled in the beginning of every rite. The family hearth is the first and holy of holies. The sacred fire that is kept burning in every house becomes and perpetual sign of all the influences that binds men to the family and enter into his social relations. Prayers, appeals and blessings are also constituents of the *samskaras*. Prayers are also offered for the attainment of intellectual stimulation, purity and communion with the deity. Blessings in the form of wishers and appeals are expressed, when a person undergoes the *samskaras*, by those interested in him and it is also believed that they will benefit the person who prays. Another important constituent of the *samskaras* is sacrifice. The belief is that the Gods also, like men are propitiated by praise and prayer, man naturally thinks that the Gods accept presents and gifts like men. Bath, sipping of water, lustration and baptismal sprinkling with water are used as purificatory media in the performance of the *samskaras*. Bath is regarded as the complete washing off of physical, moral and spiritual impurities. Sipping of water and lustration are partial or symbolic baths. Ceremonial purification is a universal feature in almost all the *samskaras*. The eastern direction is associated with light, warmth, life, happiness and glory. The western direction is associated with darkness, chill, death and decay. The northern direction is associated with Soma (Moon) symbolizing peace, gentleness and agreeableness and the southern direction with Yama, the God of death. The recipient of a *samskara* has to face the direction appropriate the occasion. At various stages of the *samskaras* many taboos are observed taboos connected with articles of food, with lucky and unlucky days, months and years. Magical elements are also found mixed with the *samskaras*. The Hindus accept the existence of supernatural powers associated with the dangers and problems of life, confronted them frequently and demanded vigilance, investigation and prompt action. The supernatural powers had to be controlled or made use of by directive or coercive procedure. The term *magic* is applied to this tendency of man to control those powers. By divination people seek to discover the will of supernatural powers, desire to know the causes of their past and present misfortunes and what will happen in the future, so that they may determine at any moment what will be the best way to follow. It is believed that natural phenomena indicate the purpose of the superhuman forces.

Symbolism is another constituent of the *samskaras*. A symbol is a material object or an apparent action adopted to convey a mental or spiritual significance.

Symbolism is another constituent of the *samskaras.* A symbol is a material object or an apparent action adopted to convey a mental or spiritual significance. Psychologically, a symbol stimulates the human mind in the right direction for the achievement of an object in view, or an ideal to be approximated or realized. The *samskaras* are full of apt symbols, which present concrete and idyllic pictures of ideas to be understood and the ideal to be reached. The influence of the *samskaras* covered the whole life of an individual, his physical, mental and spiritual training was combined to create for the Hindu a sacramental atmosphere fragrant with spiritual significance.

1. Garbhadhana : The first sacrament is known as *garbhadhana,* which means placing the seed in the womb. Procreation is not to be looked upon as a biological phenomenon but it should be seen in a socio-ethical context. Procreation of children was regarded as necessary for paying off the debts to the forefathers and failure to comply with the injunction of the scripture in this regard was considered a sin. Fulfillment of this sacred duty entailed physical fitness and psychological willingness of the couple, selection of a suitable time, proper regard to the eligibility of the parents and the sense of their duty to the race.

2. Pumsavana : After the conception is ascertained, the child in the womb is consecrated by the second *samskara* called *pumsavana* through the treatment of the pregnant mother the child in the womb should be influenced and so medical and mental treatment of the mother was prescribed. *Pumsavana* is performed in the third or fourth month of pregnancy or even later on a day when the moon is in a male constellation, particularly the *tisya-nakshatra.* The mother is required to fast on the day and in the night the sprouts of the banyan tree are pounded and the juice is dropped into her right nostril with the verses beginning with, *Hiranyagarbhah* etc. The conjunction of the moon with a male constellation is symbolic of a male child, hence the term literally means male procreation through the stimulation of the foetus. The giving of the juice of the banyan is a device or a symbolic treatment to nourish the child properly.

3. Simantonnayana : The third sacrament is called *simantonnayana* in which the hair of a pregnant woman are ceremoniously parted. When a woman is in her pregnancy, it is believed, she is attacked by evil spirits and for her protection proper rites should be performed. The religious intention behind the performance of the *samskara* is to bring prosperity to the mother and long life to the unborn child. In order to keep her in good cheer, she is addressed as *raka* (fullmoon) and *supesa* (of beautiful limbs). With caressing attention the husband himself parts the hairs of the pregnant wife and after that he ties the *unumbara* (fig tree) branch round her neck with the words of blessings are uttered, 'Be the mother of heroic sons, be the mother of living sons.' After the sixth month of pregnancy, the husband should avoid tonsure and the performance of *sraddha.*

4. Jatakarman : The *jatakarman* ceremony is made up before the severing of the navel string. The first item is *medhajanana* (the generation of talent), which is performed repeating the formula, '*Bhus tvayi dadhami, bhuvas tvayi dadhami, bhur bhuvah svas tvayi dadhami' (bhuh* (the earth) I place in thee, *bhuvah* (the sky) I place in thee, *svah* (heaven) I place in thee). The child is fed with ghee and honey with a thin gold strip. These substances are symbolic of strength and intelligence. All possible instance of long life, such as *risis* (seers), *pitrs* (the manes), Agni (fire) and soma (Moon) are cited before the child. The third item relates to *sakti* (strength). The father dramatically tells the babe, 'Be a stone, be an axe, be an imperishable God. Next the umbical cord is severed and the child is washed and given an opportunity of sucking the breast of the mother. The birth of a child is regarded as the fruition of a conjugal life.

5. Namakarana : The choice of a name for the child is often connected with religious ideas. The child is frequently named after a God who is regarded as its protector. It is named after a saint whose blessings are sought for it. The adoption of the father's name is prevalent. *Namakarana* is ordinarily performed on the tenth or twelfth day after the birth of the child.

6. Niskramana : *Niskramana* is taking of the child for the first time out of the house. In the beginning the child is confined to the lying-in chamber and then to the house in which it is born. On the day of the *niskramana,* a square area in the courtyard from where sun can be seen is plastered with cow dung and clay, the sign of a *svastika* is marked on it and over it grains of rice are scattered by the mother. The child is brought out by a nurse and the ceremony ends when the father makes the child look at the sun with the sound of conch-shell and the chanting of Vedic hymns. It recognizes a vital need of the growing child brought face to face with the sublime splendor of the universe.

7. Annaprasana : *Annaprasana* is the first feeding of the child with solid food. On the day of the feeding ceremony, the sacramental food is prepared out of cleaned materials, while muttering appropriate Vedic hymns. Honey and butter in a golden pot are suggested by some authorities. One oblation is offered to Speech (Vac), another to Vigour (Orja or Ojas). The significance of this sacrament is that it marks the weaning of the child from the mother at the proper time.

8. Cudakarana (Churakarma) : The purpose of which is the achievement of long life and beauty for its recipient. Life is prolonged by tonsure and shortened without it. Susruta, states that shaving and cutting the hair and nails remove impurities and gives delight, lightness, prosperity, courage and happiness. The Grihya-Sutras says that the *cudakarana* ceremony should take place at the end of the first year or before the expiry of the third year, though later authorities extend the age to the seventh year. The arrangement of the hair tuft *(sikka* or *cuda)* as the very name of the *samskara.* Connection between *sikha* and life is thus explained by Susruta that 'Inside the head, near the top, is the joint of a *sira* (artery) and a *sandhi* (critical juncture). There in the eddy of hairs is the vital spot called *adhipati* (overlord). Any injury to this part causes sudden death.

9. Karnavedha : *Karnavedha* is the sacrament connected with the piercing of the ear, performed between the first and the fourth year of the child. The piercing of the ears is a custom undoubtedly ornamental in its origin. Susruta says that the ears of a child are to be piercing for protection and decoration. The same authority explicitly prescribes the piercing of the ears for preventing hydrocele and hernia. The type of needle is gold for Kshatriya, silver for Brahmana and Vaisya.

10. Vidyarambha : *Vidyarambha* marks the beginning of study or the learning of the alphabet. The alphabet is regarded as the route to all knowledge, just as rivers lead to the ocean. This sacrament is also known as *vidyarambha, aksararambha and aksaralekhana.* This *samskara* is performed in the fifth year of the child but according to Visvamitra, it may be extended up to the seventh. When the sun is in the northern hemisphere an auspicious day is to be fixed for its performance. It is prohibited during the rainy season when Visnu who gives light is supposed to be asleep.

11. Upanayana : *Upanayana* or the sacrament of initiation marks the beginning of secondary education. The Hindu ideal of *upanayana* has made universal education the indispensable test and insignia of the race. The most striking feature of the *upanayana* lies in the belief that by its performance the initiation is given a cultural and spiritual rebirth. The physical birth of a child is crude, as it is associated with animality, but rebirth through discipline and learning is considered exalted and holy. A Brahmana is to be initiated at the age of eight, a Kshatriya at eleven and a Vaisya at twelve. The last permitted limit of age for the performance of the *upanayana* of a Brahmana is sixteen, of a Kshatriya twenty two and of a Vaisya twenty four. A Brahmana is initiated in the spring, a Rajanya (Kshatriya) in summer, a Vaisya in autumn and a Rathakara (chariot maker) during the rainy season. This choice of a season according to the *varna* has reference to temperament, the three seasons and the three *varnas* are respectively calm, hot and pliable.

The next item to be observed is the last meal with the mother, which marks the end of childhood and the beginning of a career outside the home. A *kaupina* (loin cloth) is offered to him to cover his privy parts. Social consciousness has already dawned upon the boy, so from now onward he is particularly instructed to observe social decorum and to maintain his own dignity and self control. *Mekhala* (girdle) is another equipment given to the initiate and it is tied repeating a verse which has this meaning, 'A daughter of faith, a sister of the sages, possessed of austerity, beneficent to all creatures.' The constant wearing of the *yajnopavita* suggests that the life of the twice born is a continuous sacrifice necessitated by the socio-religious duties. Similarly, *ajina* (deer skin) and *danda* (staff) are also presented to the student, who has to lead a strict life of discipline almost like an ascetic. *Surya darsana* (looking at the sun) indicates the need of constant exertion and watchfulness on the part of the celibate student, who turns to the sun as to a perpetual witness, *hrydaya sparsa* (touching the heart) symbolizes the mental and emotional communion between the teacher and the taught, *asmarohana* (climbing the stone) suggests the need for steadfastness in studies and character, *hasta grahana* (taking by the hand) as the teacher's charge is quite significant. The sacrament of *upanayana* performed at the beginning of study marks the dawn of a new life. The student is now an *upanita* one who is introduced to a life of perfect discipline. If a student acts in the manner suggested by the symbolism of this sacrament, he is bound to be a successful scholar and a full fledged citizen fit to share the responsibility of the world.

12. Vedarambha : *Vedarambha* is not mentioned in the earliest lists of the *samskaras* preserved in the Dharma Sutras. Every student has to master his own branch of the Vedas settled by his parentage and in consequence this sacrament is performed differently in the case of different types of students. It still emphasizes the predominance of the Vedas in the curriculum of studies.

13. Kesanta : The *kesanta* is a sacrament connected with the first shaving of the student's beard, when his age is about sixteen years. He is required to exercise greater watchfulness over his youthful impulses, and so by this sacrament he is once more reminded of his vows of *brahmacarya. Kesanta* was also called *godana* (the gift of a cow), the reason being that at the end of the ceremony the student offered a cow to the teacher.

14. Samavartana : *Samavartana* is also called *snana* (bath). An *avabhrtha snana* or ritual bath is taken, as it is customary on the completion of all sacrifices. An erudite scholar is called a *nisnata or snata* because he is considered to have crossed the ocean of learning and discipline. There were three types of *snatakas* or graduates, *vidya snataka* (versed in learning), *vrata snataka* (proficient in discipline), and *ubhaya sanataka* (distinguished in both). Completion of learning and return home is a very momentous event in a student's life, because he is either prepared to marry and plunge into the busy life of the world, he has acquired the Vedic knowledge that may give him the power to keep off from the turmoil of the world. Those students who choose the first path are called *upakurvana,* that is, who honour the preceptor by gifts on their leaving his residence to enter the married life and those pupils who choose the second path are known as *naisthika,* that is, who dedicate themselves to lifelong studentship. In every case the permission *(anujna)* of the teacher is regarded as necessary. The student does not pay anything to the *acarya* except service till the study is complete, but when he leaves, it is expected that he should honour him with an acceptable fee according to his means. Even though a student is not able to pay the teacher anything material, he should at least go to him for his permission. The ceremonies, connected with *samavartana* mainly consist of two items (1) shutting the *snataka* in a room in the morning and (2) his undergoing the formal bath. The first is symbolic of the *snataka's* splendor. The formal bath symbolizes washing away the divinity or superhuman influence, lest it be defiled by worldly, cooling down the heat of the ascetic celibate student life, crossing the ocean of learning. The *snataka* after taking his bath puts off the meager ascetic insignia of a student and accepts the comforts of life which were denied to him previously. Dressed in his new attire, he proceeds in a chariot or on an elephant to the nearest assembly of the learned to which he is introduced as a competent scholar by his teacher.

15. Vivaha : *Vivaha,* marriage is the source of all domestic sacrifices and ceremonies. The sacrament of marriage impresses upon a person that earthly life is not to be despised, rather, it should be consciously accepted and elevated to the level of a spiritual experience. The eight forms of marriage mentioned are *paisada, rakshasa, gandharva, asura, prajapatya, arsha, daiva and brahma.* The last four are approved religiously *(prasasta)* but the first four are not *(aprasasta).* In the case of the approved marriages, the sacrament is a condition precedent, while in the case of the unapproved ones, it may be performed after the marriage on the basis of non religious considerations. Normally, a person should marry in the same *varna* but outside the same *gotra* (clan), and *pinda* (consanguinity). *Anuloma* marriage (in which the wife is of an inferior caste) was permitted but not encouraged, *pratiloma* marriage (in which the husband is of an inferior caste), though tolerated early, was later on discouraged and banned. Restrictions regarding *sagotra* and *sapinda* marriages have been invariably observed their breach is regarded as incest and is legally forbidden. A marriage sacrament consists of items pertaining to the pre marital, marital and post marital stages. These are *vagdana* (betrothal), *vara varana* (formal acceptance of the bridegroom), *kanya dana* (gift of the bride to the bridegroom by the legitimate guardian), *vivaha homa* (marriage offerings), *panigrahana* (clasping the hand), *hrdaya sparsa* (touching the heart), *saptapadi* (seven steps symbolic of prosperity and felicity), *asmarohana* (mounting the stone, symbolic of stability), *suryavalokana* (looking at the sun, as a witness to the sacrament), *dhruva darsana* (looking at the Pole star a symbol of constancy), *triratra vrata* (three nights continence), *caturthikarma* (fourth day ceremony or the formal unification of the couple). The marital union is effected not by the wife and the husband alone, but by society, the guardians and the supernatural powers, the symbols of spirituality. Such a marriage is therefore regarded as indissoluble. The marriage is a permanent union and not a temporary contract is symbolized by the five items beginning with *asmarohana.* Marriage is not a licence for indulgence but a human institution aiming at moderation in conjugal life is symbolized by the *triratra vrata* (three nights continence) observed at the end of the nuptials.

16. Antyesti : The last sacrament is the *antyesti.* Baudhayan says, Death is inevitable in the case of a man who is born. Therefore one should not be happy at birth nor bemoan death. People give their dues to their mother, father, preceptor, wife, son, disciple, cousin, maternal uncle, agnates and cognates and consecrate their cremation with proper sacrament. The disposal of the dead by cremation was treated as a sacrifice and became the prevalent mode, though in special cases burial and water burial also were allowed. Death and the disposal of the dead fall under the following heads:

- Approach of death: The person whose death is near bids farewell to his assembled relatives and the world. The alms and gifts are distributed for his future happiness.
- Pre-disposal ceremony: Oblations are offered into the sacrificial fire maintained by him. It has become customary now to drop Ganga water and *tulasi* leaves into the mouth of the dying.

- The bier: A special oblong frame is prepared to remove the dead body to the place of cremation and the body is formally laid on it with the chanting of religious hymns.
- Removal of the corpse: Bier was put on a bullock cart with the verse, 'I harness these two bullocks to the cart for the conveyance of your life so that you may repair to the region of Yama. Now the bier is carried by men, the nearest relatives and friends of the deceased, as an act of honour to him.
- The funeral procession: The chief mourner, usually the eldest son of the dead person, is followed by relatives and friends, as he proceeds to the place of cremation.
- *Anustarani* (the accompany cow): She is believed to be helpful in crossing the ocean of mortality. She is given away as gift and let off.
- The cremation-burning of the corpse: The preliminaries to it include *abhiseka* (washing the corpse) and the piling of the pyre. Next, fire is applied to the pyre with the Vedic hymns.
- *Udakakarma* (offering of water): It is supposed that it cools the dead after the body undergoes cremation.
- Consoling the mourners: the disconsolate survivors are soothed in their distress by an expert quoting a number of stories showing the transitory nature of life.
- *Asauta* (impurity): Social segregation
- *Asthisanhayana* (collecting the bones)
- *Santi-karma* (pacificatory rite)
- *Smaraka* (raising a mound over the remains of the dead)
- *Sraddha* (offerings to the dead)
- *Sapindikarana* (affiliation of the dead with the manes)

This last sacrament takes into account the sentiments and requirements of the dead and the surviving, who are faced with the inevitable event of life, namely, death.

In rituals, life is regarded as a cycle. It starts from where it ends. From birth to death it is a continuous series of incidents moving round one pivot, the desire to live, to enjoy, to think and ultimately to retire. All the *samskaras* and allied ceremonies emanate from this. In the beginning of civilization, life was much simpler than it is at present and it was not divided into compartments. Social institutions, beliefs, sentiments, arts and science were all closely inter woven. The *samskaras* covered all these fields of life. Religion was then an all embracing factor in life and it afforded sanctity and stability to all possible aspects of existence for which end they also utilized all the moral and material resources they could command.

THE ASHRAMAS

The term Ashrama is not mentioned in Vedas or the Brahmana literature. In *Taittiriya Brahmana* human life is described as having four parts. The first reference of Ashramas are found in *Chandogya Upanishad.* In it only three ashramas are mentioned. The first reference of all four ashramas are mentioned in *Jabala Upanisad.* Apastamba speaks of four Ashramas. But their names and sequence are not the same as became prevalent later. These are Grahasthya or the stage of householder, Aharyakula or staying in teacher's house, Mauna or stage of being a Muni and Vanaprasthya or stage of living in forests. The *Gautama Dharmasutra* speaks of four Ashramas in the same sequence which came to be traditionally established. Brahmachari or student, Grihastha or householder, Bhisksu or ascetic and Vaikhanasa or hermit. The *Baudhayana Dharma Sutra* also enumerates four Ashramas. These refer to Brahmachari, Grhastha, Vanaprastha and Parivrajaka. Baudhayana says that an Asura, Kapila the son of Prahlada made these divisions.

These are Brahmacharya, Grhastha, Vanaprastha and Sannyasa. Human life is conceived to be of one hundred years. It is divided into four equal parts for four stages of life.

It appears that the system of Ashramas has a non-Aryan origin. The Rigveda mentions a hymn in which the priest exhorts the newly married couple to live in the house happily with sons and grandsons. Thus, *Rigveda* does not mention Vanaprastha or Sannyasa. Manu speaks of four Ashramas. These are Brahmacharya, Grhastha, Vanaprastha and Sannyasa. Human life is conceived to be of one hundred years. It is divided into four equal parts for four stages of life.

Brahmacharya Ashrama

In the Atharvaveda Upanayan or initiation is mentioned for the first time, nearly with all its main features. From the initiation starts the Brahmacharya Ashrama. The ceremony of initiation seems to be very ancient. It may have already been practiced by the Aryans when they had not entered the Indian sub-continent. In *Rigveda*, the word Brahmachari occurs for Brhaspati when he wanders without his wife. Thus, it indicates that during studentship the student had to live the life of celibacy. In *Atharvaveda*, the sun is described as a Brahmachari. It describes that he wears a girdle, offers fuel sticks on the fire, wears the skin of black antelope and it is said that he takes birth again by initiation. In *Taittiriya Samhita* of black *Yajurveda* the story of Nabhanedistha, the son of Manu is found who was student and was deprived of the property by his father.

In the Brahmana literature the stage of Brahmacharya is indicated. In *Taittiriya Brahmana* the story of Bharadvaja who remained a Brahmacari for three parts of his life is mentioned. But Indra commented that despite the long period spent in the Brahmacharya stage, what he had mastered out of the Vedas was as insignificant as three handfuls out of three mountains. The Vedas are endless. In this story, though the four Ashramas are not mentioned, human life is described as having four parts.

The *Satapatha Brahmana* describes the ceremony of Upanayana or initiation in a elaborate way. The various duties are prescribed for a Brahmacari or a student. These are teaching Savitri *Mantra,* serving in teacher's house, begging for alms, putting fuel-sticks on the fire, not sleeping during day and not taking honey. A student is called *Antevasi* or one who lives near a teacher in *Satapatha Brahmana.*

The various duties are prescribed for a Brahmacari or a student. These are teaching Savitri *Mantra*, serving in teacher's house, begging for alms, putting fuel-sticks on the fire, not sleeping during day and not taking honey. A student is called *Antevasi* or one who lives near a teacher in *Satapatha Brahmana*.

The proper age for entering the *Brahmacarya Ashrama* differs according to the Varna of the boy. According to *Asvalayana Grihya Sutra* a Brahmana should be initiated in the eighth year after the conception. The maximum age limit for performing initiation of a Brahmana is sixteen years. He should wear an antelope skin or a reddish yellow garment. He should wear the girdle of Munja grass and take the staff of Palasa wood.

A Kshatriya boy should be initiated in the eleventh year after the conception. The maximum limit for performing initiation of a Kshatriya boy is the twenty second year. He should wear the skin of a spotted deer or a light red garment. His girdle should be made of bow string. His staff should be made of Udumbara wood.

A Vaisya boy should be initiated in the twelfth year. The maximum limit for performing initiation of a Vaisya boy is twenty four. He should wear a goat skin or a yellow garment. His girdle should be made of wool. His staff should be of Bilva wood.

Manu follows the Sutras. He provides even lesser age for all the three higher Varnas. He says that in case a Brahmana desires proficiency in sacred learning his initiation should be performed in the fifth year after conception, that of a Kshatriya who wishes to become powerful in the sixth and that *Yajnopavita* of a Vaisya who longs for success in his business in the eighth.

The Yajnopavita is an essential feature of initiation since ancient times. The *Taittiriya Brahmana* and *Satapatha Brahmana* mention it. The Grihyasutras of Gobhila and Khadira prescribe that an initiated student should take as his *Yajnopavita* a cord or a garment or simply a rope of Kusa grass. When the cord is suspended over his left shoulder, so that it hangs down on his right side he becomes *Yajnopavitin.* When the cord is suspended over his right shoulder, so that it hangs down on his left side, be becomes *Prachinavitin.* Being *Prachinavitin* he offers sacrifices to the Manes. The *Apastamba DharmaSutra* provides that a householder must always wear a garment over his left shoulder and under his right arm, or he may use a cord instead of a garment. Baudhayana provides that the sacred cord should be made of *Kusa* grass or cotton and should consist of thrice three strings.

Manu prescribes different types of sacred cords for the persons of different Varnas. The sacred cord of a Brahmana should be made of cotton, should be twisted to the right and consist of three threads that of a Kshatriya of hempen threads and that of Vaisya of woolen threads. Teaching of Savitri is also an essential feature of initiation. The *Satapatha Brahmana* mentions it. All the teachers of Dharma Sutras follow this.

The initiated student should wear two garments. The Parasara, Asvalayana and Baudhayana Grihyasutras prescribe that the upper garment of a Brahmana should be the skin of black deer for Kshatriya the skin of Ruru deer and for a Vaisya the skin of a cow or a goat. Baudhayana and Asvalayana prescribe only the skin of goat for a Vaisya. According to Parasara Grihyasutra if a suitable skin cannot be secured the cow skin should be employed by students of all Varnas. The student should avoid certain things, some for short time, others during the whole period of studentship. The Asvalayana Grihyasutra prescribes that for three nights or twelve nights or a year after initiation the student should not eat *Ksara* and *Lavana* and should sleep on the ground. Baudhayana, Bhardwaja, Parskara and Khadira Grihyasutras also provide similarly.

The period of studentship may last for forty eight years, or twenty four years or twelve years or until the student has learnt the Vedas according to Hiranakesin Grihyasutra. Manu provides that a student should study thirty years or eighteen years or nine years or until he has perfectly learnt the Vedas. According to the *Sankhayana Grihyasutra*, the daily putting on of fuel, going for alms, sleeping on the ground and obedience to the teacher are the standing duties of a student. Other Sutras make a similar provision. Manu follows them. He provides that a student should offer fuel in sacred fire, beg for food, sleep on the ground, offer libations of water to the gods, sages and manes. The student should recite Samdhya prayer in the morning and evening according to the *Asvalayana Grihyasutra*. Manu prescribes that a student should perform prayer standing during morning and sitting in the evening. He should keep all his organs and mind, under control. Later Smrti writers follow Manu.

Grhastha Ashrama

Gautama calls householder's life as the source of all Ashramas because only in this order off springs are produced.

Gautama calls householder's life as the source of all Ashramas because only in this order off springs are produced, in other people do not procreate. Baudhayana makes a similar provision and quotes passages from Vedas for support. In the Rigveda we find: 'May we, O Agni attain immortality through progency.' In the Taittiriya Samhita it is said: 'A Brahmana when born owes three debts, he owes Brahmacarya to the sages, sacrifice to the gods and progeny to his ancestors.'

Manu follows the Dharmasutras. He provides: 'As all living creatures subsist by receiving support from air, similarly people of all orders subsist by receiving support from the house holder.' Manu declares the order of householder the most exalted. He says: 'Because men of the three orders are daily supported by the householder with gifts of sacred knowledge and food therefore the order of householder is the most excellent order.' Gautama provides that the householder should worship gods, manes, men, beings and Risis. It is obligatory on him to recite a portion of the Vedas daily and to offer libation of water to the manes. Other rites than these he may perform according to his ability. The sacred fire must be kindled on his marriage or on the division of the family estate. The domestic rituals are to be performed in that fire.

Apastamba provides that food of a householder for Vaisvadeva should be prepared by the persons of the first three Varnas. But in a following verse he provides that even a Sudra may prepare food under the superintendence of men of the first three Varnas. The nails and hair of Sudra cooks should be cut daily or on eighth day or on the days of the full and new moon. In case the Sudra cook prepares without supervision the food should be kept on fire and should be spinkled with water.

Manu also provides that with the sacred fire kindled at the wedding a householder should perform domestic ceremonies and five great sacrifices and should cook his food. He also gives an explanation for the daily performance of the five great sacrifices. He says that the householder has five slaughter houses: the hearth, the grinding stone, the broom, the pestle and mortar, the water-vessel, by using these he is bound by the fetters of sin. In order to successfully expiciate the sin committed by means of all these five slaughter houses the great sages have prescribed for householders the daily performance of the five great sacrifices. It appears that Manu was influenced by Buddhist and Jain religions, because in the earlier texts such incident is not found. Gautama provides that the householder should make gifts to the persons of the Brahmana Varna begging for their teachers or in order to defray the expenses of their wedding or for medicine for the sick, to those who are without means of subsistence, to those who are going to offer a sacrifice, to those engaged in study, to travelers and to those who have performed the Visvajit sacrifice. But he should not give anything for unlawful purposes even though he may have made such a promise. Apastamba also provides similarly.

A householder is expected to feed his dependents before he takes his meal. Gautama and Apastamba provide that the householder should feed his guests, the infants, the sick people, the pregnant women, the females under his protection, the very aged men and those of low condition. But when especial guests like teacher, parents, friends visit his house, he should ask for orders before the preparation of the dinner. According to Gautama and Apastamba, when an officiating priests, his teacher, his father-in-law, paternal or maternal uncles visit him Madhuparka or honey mixture must be offered to them. If they have been once honoured in this manner, the ceremony need by repeated only after a year. Manu adds a king, Snataka and son-in-law to the list. It appears that honouring son-in-law is a later development.

Vanaprastha

Vanaprastha is the third stage of life. Manu says that when a householder sees his skin wrinkled, and his hair white and the sons of his sons, then he may resort to the forest. He should abandon all food raised by cultivation and all his belongings. His wife may either accompany him or she may live with her sons. He should take with him the sacred fire and the implements required for domestic sacrifices. He should live in the forest duly controlling his senses.

While living in the forest the Vanaprasthi should subsist on roots and fruits and should practice austerities.

Gautama provides that while living in the forest the Vanaprasthi should subsist on roots and fruits and should practice austerities. He should eat wild growing vegetables only and he should worship Gods, manes, men, beings and Risis, according to Gautama Dhrmasutra. Manu follows him. Gautama Dharmasutra also provides that a Vanaprasthi may even use the flesh of animals killed by carnivorous beasts.

Gautama prescribes that he should wear a skin or a tattered garment. He should take bath in the evening or in the morning. He should always wear his hair in braids, the hair on his body, his beard and his nails being unclipped. Manu follows Gautama. At another place

Manu provides that he should take bath thrice daily in the morning, at noon and in the evening. Yajnavalkaya also makes a similar provision.

The Vanaprasthi should not eat anything grown on ploughed land, though it may have been thrown away by some body, nor roots and fruits grown in a village though he may be tormented by hunger. The Vanaprasthi may store sufficient food for a month or for a year. According to Apastamba Dharmasutra, he should throw away his old grain in the month of Asvin. Manu and Yajnavlkya Smrtis follow this.

Manu says that a Vanaprasthi may live according to the rules of the Chandrayana Vrata or lumar penance, daily diminishing the quantity of his food in the bright half of the month and increasing it in dark half or he may eat on the last days of each fortnight, once a day only and that too boiled barley gruel. The *Apastamba Dharmasutra* provides that the Vanaprasthi may live on water and then on air. Manu follows this. According to Manu he should continue this practice until his body sinks to death. It is a kind of suicide, the reason for making such provision could be the asceticism propagated by the Buddhists and the Jains. In order to combat the influence on these heterodox sects the Brahmana elites took over many of their ideas pertaining to non-violence and ascetism which made them venerable among the people, thus taking out the wind from their sails.

Sannyasa

Sannyasa is the fourth stage of human life. According to *Apastamba Dharmasutra,* in this stage the Sannyasi should live without a fire, without a house, without pleasures, without protection. Remaining silent and uttering speech only on the occasion of the daily recitation of the Vedas, begging so much food only the village as will sustain his life, he should wander about neither caring for this world nor for the heaven.

An ascetic shall not possess any store. He must be chaste. He must not change his residence during the rainy season.

Gautama says that an ascetic shall not possess any store. He must be chaste. He must not change his residence during the rainy season. He should enter a village only in order to beg. He should beg late after people have finished their meal, without returning twice, abandoning all desires for sweet food. He should wear a cloth to cover his nakedness. Some declare that he should wear an old rag after having washed it. Apastamba and Baudhayana make a similar provision. Apastamba adds that abandoning truth and falsehood, pleasure and pain, the Vedas, this world and the next, he should seek the *Ataman*. But Apastamba asserts that this opinion is opposed to the *Sastras*. Because if salvation were obtained by the knowledge of the *Ataman* alone then he ought not feel any pain even in this world.

Baudhayana disapproves the last two orders. He says that only studentship and the order of householder are to be followed by people. One who praises other orders becomes dust and perishes. Manu says that a twice born person should enter the order of Sannyasa only after studying Vedas having begotten sons and having offered sacrifices. He should offer Prajapatya sacrifice, give all his property as the sacrificial fee and then he should become a Sannyasi.

Manu follows the Dharma Sutras and lays down the proper conduct of a Sannyasi. He prescribes that a Sannyasi should neither possess a fire nor a dwelling, he may go to a village for his food, he should be indifferent to everything, firm of purpose, meditating and concentrating his mind on Brahman: 'A potsherd instead of an alms-bowl, the roots of trees for a dwelling, coarse worn-out garments, life in solitude and indifference towards everything are the marks of one who has attained liberation.'

It seems that the Manu Smrti was also influenced by the Jain doctrine. It is provided in the Manu Smrti that a Sannyasi should drink water after straining it with a cloth. His hair, nails and beard being unclipped, carrying an alms bowl, a staff, and a water pot, let him continually wander about controlling himself and not injuring any creatures.

Following *Gautama Dharmasutra,* Manu prescribes that a Sannyasi should always go to beg when no smoke ascends from the kitchen, when the pestle lies motionless, when the embers have been extinguished, when the people have finished their meal, when the remanants in the dishes have been removed. Manu says that a Sannyasi should not desire to die, let him not desire to live, let him wait for his appointed time, as a servants for a payment of his wages.

A Sannyasi is expected to remain always alone.

A Sannyasi is expected to remain always alone. It is prescribed that a Sannyasi should remain lone because if they are two, they would form a pair, if they are three, they are like a village and if more than three live together, they become like a town. A Sannyasi should not form a pair or village or a town, by doing so he swerves from his Dharma, because then a Sannyasi would talk about the ruler, about the alms obtained and due to closeness, sentiments of affection, jealousy would arise among them. Bad ascetics undertake many activities interpreting texts for gaining money or honour and gathering pupils around them. There are four actions for a Sannyasi: meditation, purity, begging and remaining alone. Vyasa forbids Sannyasa on the ground of its having become a Kali-Varjya or forbiddened in the Kali age. These last two orders appear to be of non-Aryan origin. The first inkling of the Vanaprastha Ashrama is found in the Chandogya Upanisad as Yajnavalkya wants to distributes his property among his wives. It is well known that the Upanisads represent a revolt against the Brahmanical supremacy and orthodoxy.

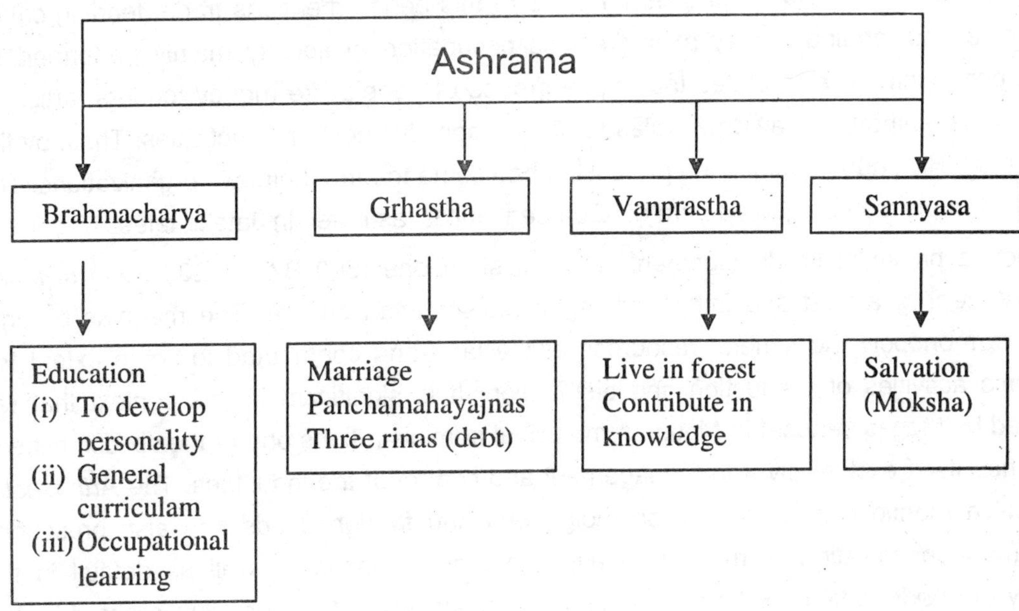

GUILD (SHRENI) ORGANISATION

Origin & Development

Guilds may be defined as union of workers, labourer, craftsman, merchants and traders.

Guilds may be defined as union of workers, labourer, craftsman, merchants and traders. Some scholars equate the guilds even with the modern day of 'Chamber of Commerce'. Different terms in ancient Indian texts, like *Shreni, Nigama, Gana, Puga, Vrata and Sangha* have been used to denote corporate organisations.

The origin of craftsmen & traders guilds in India is traced in sixteenth century B.C. whether, guilds existed in Vedic age or in Harappan phase is still a matter of debate among the scholars. But Brihadaranyaka Upanishad is one context mentions about guilds. R.C. Majumdar is of the opinion that possibility of guild system even in Vedic era cannot be ruled out altogether arbitrararily. For our easy understanding of knowledge to trace out its development, guilds may be divided into four phases where literary evidences are available:

(*i*) First Phase (600 B.C. – 300 B.C.)

(*ii*) Second Phase (300 B.C. – 200 B.C.)

(*iii*) Third Phase (200 B.C. – 300 A.D.)

(*iv*) Fourth Phase (300 A.D. – 600 A.D.)

Sixth century B.C. in Indian history is important and unique that witnessed emergence of Mahajanpadas (formation of territorial states). It also witnessed two towering personalities of Buddha and Mahavira who introduced new socio-ethical tenets for society. Formation of Mahajanpadas and new ideological bent of mind led to the shifting of loyalty from tribal organisation to geo-political cum territorial identifications. The use of writing helped in the codification of some rules, regulations, ethical norms and above all chartered accountancy in trading business. The *Gautama Dharma Sutra* of this period mentions trade, tending cattle, agriculture and lending money at interest as occupation of society mainly performed by vaisya community. It also states that these groups of people like money lenders, artisans, traders have authority to lay down rules for their respective economic activities. Thus, by the fifth century B.C. above mentioned profession had come to form their own organizations. The glaring example may be quoted here of 'Eighteen Guilds' as noted in Jataka tales.

Second phase of its development, albeit a short one (300 B.C. – 200 B.C.) saw the establishment of a vast and fairly well organized mauryan empire. The mauryas brought under its monopoly the mineral resources of the land and contributed to some extent the economic activities of production and distribution. It is significant in this context that (as recorded by Megasthenese) in Mauryan municipal administrations one of the six committees concerned itself exclusively with management and control of the industries. The *Arthasastra* of Kautilya mentions rate of profit on indigenous and foreign goods and also prescribes punishment for violation of rules, specially economic offenses as well as default in the delivery of goods in time. Side by side, some concessions & facilities were granted by the state to these bodies. Port Mauryan phase (200 B.C. – 300 A.C.) is again marked by intense activities in the field of trade & commerce. The Mauryan disintegrated into a number of kingdom that led to the slackening of state control over economy and administration, hence guilds again assumed more power and influence. Literary and epigraphic evidence of the period refer to a number of guilds and their number being much greater than eighteen as noted earlier in Buddhist text. Two dozen guilds of artisans are mentioned in *Mahavastu.* Epigraphs from Sanchi, Bharhut, Mathura, Bodhgaya and other sites refer to a number of donations made by different types of flourishing guilds. The fourth phase (300 A.D. – 600 A.D.) better known as Gupta Era was more conducive and fruitful to the development of trade and commerce. Trade with Roman empire was an important source of earning bullion declined in this age when Romans were invaded and shattered by barbarian tribes. However, there was an increase in trading business, particularly with the countries of South-East Asia. Hence arts and crafts prospered considerably. Detailed rules are laid down in law books like Narada, Brihaspati etc. for efficient functioning of guilds and business partnership. The chief of artisans and traders guilds acted as member of advisory board of district administration. The type of work a guild was expected to perform were to be incorporated into a documents (*samvidapatra)* and all the intending members were required to be acquainted with it. There are various evidences note from epigraph that prove and indicate longevity and credibility of guilds.

Scholars also believe that social pathology of human psychology forced people for cooperative effort in various field of activity mainly economic activities. The advantage of pooling of resource of skill must have been obvious reason for the development of guild in ancient times. Some other important factors responsible for this cooperative ventures were of varied nature and interest. Historians views based on sources, mainly emphasize safety and security reasons coupled with localizations of crafts and growing trend of urbanization from sixth century B.C. onwards were the factors for such development. Introduction of iron played a significant role in the development of economy. Money economy provided a great impetus to urbanistion which accelerated the growth of industries, trade and commerce. Introduction of writing technique helped in keeping accounts and record have also contributed towards the growth of chartered accountancy and guilds.

Structure

A guild was well knit and efficiently managed organization. It was a three tier body comprising the general assembly, executive officers and the oldermen. Each of them were designated definite sphere of power and authority. For the successful working of an organization engaged in economic activities, the pre-requisites are availability of raw material, skilled workforce, infrastructure like means of transport and efficient managerial organization. It may be observed here that ancient Indian Guilds generally had all these essential factors in a good measure. Guilds usually functioned on democratic line, none of these bodies was so placed as to become dominant over the other two. The democratic norms were strictly enforced and in case of secure breaches of guild rules, the royal authority influenced to enforce compliance.

Guilds members representing diverse people, hence maintenance of confidence among its members was most essential. This was sought to be achieved by various means like *Madhayastha*. There was no limit either minimum or maximum number of members for a guild. Sutra stories invariably maintain the number in round figure, hundred, five hundred or one thousand. Rights, duties and privileges of the member of guilds have been laid down clearly in Smriti texts. After admission into guilds a member shared equally with the other members of the assets and liabilities of the guilds. This concept of equality sharing of liabilities and assets would have provided a deterant to wrangling. On being authorized by majority of members, a member could execute a contract on behalf of the guild and that was deemed as done by all. Guild was always headed by a chief known as *Parmukha Jeystha.* Craftsmen guild in Buddhist sources is often designated as *Jatthaka*. There are references in Jataka stories to *Sarthvahas*, the head of Carvan merchants. He was an experienced and intelligent man possessings knowledge of the routes through which carvans passed. The head of a merchant guild was generally known as *Sethi (Sresthi)* who was a merchant cum bankers and was a rich man of the locality. In Pali literature *Sethis* often find mention as business magnates in the cities and as belonging to the landed aristocracy in the village. They controlled to a great extent both the rural and urban agencies of production and distribution often a head of the guild was designated after the trade and calling of particular guild he represented like *Vaddhaki jethaka* (head of carpenters), *Satthvaha jethaka* (head of carvans merchant), *Kammara Jethaka* (head of smith) etc.

The head of the guild was mostly pre occupied with looking after the interact of the guild with the government at various levels and in attending to inter guild matters. He could not thus have enough time to attend the deliberation of guild assembly on every business issue. Therefore to look after the day to day affairs of the guild as also to land a helping hand to the head in the discharge of disciplines, executive officers came to be appointed. Their number was three to five and they were known as *Karya Chintak.* The guild had a democratic set up. The most important thing to note in this context is that though the older man and executive officers exercised considerable authority, their powers were not arbitrary, as they were required to work within the framework of guild rules and not violate guild laws and wage and were ultimately answerable to the general assembly. In case of any internal organizational dispute or when the assembly found it difficult to remove a powerful, defiant chief, the matter was to be referred to the king who intervened and settled the matter amicably. It means guilds were functioning on democratic line and it was three tier body structure, meant for performing different type of activities in their authorized capacity.

Guilds performed different functions and provided congenial atmosphere for craftsmen, allowing them sufficient time and opportunities for encourageme nt toward creativity and originality in the arts they were engaged.

Functions

Guilds performed different functions and provided congenial atmosphere for craftsmen, allowing them sufficient time and opportunities for encouragement toward creativity and originality in the arts they were engaged. In early times, in India as a protective measure against theft, people buried their ornaments and the precious article under house floor. But, emergence of guild solved this problem to some extent by way of accepting people's deposit in their organization. References are noted about banking function of guilds. Guild not only accepted deposit but also lend out money to the people at 9-12% interest rate annually. In the mauryan period, Kautilya devised a exploit the guild to the advantage of the state. The details regarding it is given in *Arth sastra* indicate that by that time guilds had interred into the sphere of credit and money lending. Guilds also performed judicial functions. They exercised judicial authority in relation to the members and officers of the guild. Guilds investigated and decided the cases (other than criminal one) of their members in accordance with their own laws and punished the erring member accordingly. They could punish who showed hostility to the executive officer or Alderman or obstructed a member from making a relevant speech or created dissertation in the guild or betrayed guild secrets. The guilds could take up only civil cases for disposal. Cases involving heinous crimes were beyond the scope of their jurisdiction and were dealt with by the king's court alone. Besides managing their own affairs and banking functions, guilds also played some part in state administration. The state being predominantly occupied with matters relating to defence and conquest of new territories and central administrations, the participation of local bodies including guilds in the state administration would have been welcome, as it lessened the administrative burden of the state, and also helped in maintaining such conditions as were conducive to the general welfare of individual. Like village Panchayat, economic guilds were saving as institutions of self government. In village, inhabited people following are profession or craft, the head of the guild also acted as village head. Epigraphic evidences of Gupta period also show that the administration at the district headquarters was carried out by its head with the active cooperations, consultation and assistance of a board which had *Nagar Sresthi, Pratamakulka, Sarthavatva* etc. It means guilds also performed to some extent, some administrative functions as well. Scholars also believe that they issued coins in some region because some seats have been found, indicating this aspect of guild in ancient time. On the basis of close scrutiny of available record and references, it may be conducted that guilds functions were of varied nature, mainly performing trading and commercial business and providing apprenticeship to its members. Apart from this, guilds performed some administrative judicial, philanthropic and banking function, thereby assisting the state and people.

Special Feature

It is also worthwhile to mention some features of guild system that controlled and organized the economic aspect of society in ancient times. The pursuit of trade or occupation for the most part came to be hereditary and became an important basis of the organization of guilds in India. Second important feature of guilds is found in its localization of crafts and trade. Certain localities or cities became famous for certain crafts. Varanasi was well known for its cloth *Kaushaya, Dantapura,* a city in Kalinga as the name indicates, would have been famous for Ivory Craft. *Sataka,* a kind of cloth become very popular in Mathura region. It means Mathura was centre of *sataka* production, a variety cloth, popular among the people. Third important and unique characteristic is noted in the form of their peculiar banner and

Insignia. Some guilds had guild insignia as a device. The sealing of the joint corporation of merchant cum bankers, the carvan merchants and artisans (Srestta-Sartthavaha-Kalka-Nigama) from Vaisali belonging to the Gupta period, show the device which has been identified as money chest. Some of the guilds were assigned insignia by royal charter and this was considered a matter of rare distinction and prestige for them.

They carried their banners in procession during festive occasions, giving an identification mark to a guild. Fourth important feature of guild was that they had their own exclusive rules and laws which were based on customs and tradition. The laws were related to various aspects of guild activity, organization, production, pricing, quality control etc. The guilds had the right to manage their own affairs according to their customs show that they enjoyed considerable degree of autonomy. Fifth special feature as noted by scholars in general is found in apprenticeship. Skilled craftsmen were considered a valued asset, hence importance was attached to the apprentice training. Young trainees were attached to the master craftsmen, who stayed with him during the training period. The system of apprenticeship, as in European guild system, was a sort of contract which was binding on the master and pupil, and the sphere of their activity and obligation were clearly defined. If an apprentice deserted a teacher who was not wicked he was to be compelled by force to stay with him and was also liable to corporal punishment and confinement. Some epigraphs of the period refer to these types of activities of guilds giving a strong impression of industrial apprenticeship. The system of apprenticeship, though not free from draw-backs, generally worked well. The credit of successful training of artisans and craftsmen by the system of apprenticeship to a great extent goes to the guilds which were main agencies of manufacturing, banking and mercantile activities. The system of apprenticeship ensured the availability of trained men at all times, which contributed to the progress in arts and crafts, turning out products of high quality and design.

Guild and State

In certain ancient works like Amarkosha, guilds have been mentioned as one of the constituents of state. They had a distinct and well defined structure and sphere of authority. They enjoyed considerable autonomy and commanded a status and influence which were not based on delegation of power by the state but flowed from their own inherent rights. They had developed their own laws based on usages and tradition to regulate their works and activities, with very little interference from the state.

The guilds enjoyed such great importance and privileges in the society that even kautilya, a votary of strong centralized government with its control over various spheres of activity, recommends certain privileges and concession to the corporate bodies. In contrast to individual artisans, a guild was granted grace of seven days for the fulfillment of its obligation beyond the date agreed in the deal. He prescribed reservation of accommodation for various guilds in the city plan. The state showed due regard for the protection of rights of the artisans, working as member of a guild. Megasthenese mentions that in the city administration of Mauryas these was a separate committee to take care of matters relating to industries and commercial business. It is also gleaned, as noted from a charter of sixth century, that trading committees submitted to the ruler a letter of demand with a view to safeguarding their interest and were able to secure several immunities and concession such as all trust were to be administered by the guilds and not by the state. Guilds were even exempted from customary taxes and other levies as a mark of concession to corporate bodies. The state earned sizable income by levying taxes on the articles, manufactured and sold by guilds. It was therefore in the interest of the state to secure and maintain conditions conclusive to the development of guilds. The state constructed and maintained roads which facilitated the development of trade and commerce in which guilds played an important role and the state, in turn earned more revenue. Guilds were also entitled to subsides and loans from the state which helped them in developing different arts and crafts and line of production in which they were engaged. This increased prosperity of the guilds and led to the rise of government revenue by way of taxes levied on their profits. The rulers in some cases, made permanent endowments with the guilds with instructions to do needful, generally a charitable work with the interest accruing from the endowment made with them (Akshaynivi). For such purpose, the kings seem to have reposed greater faith in the guilds known for their honesty, credibility, efficiency and stability. It was generally considered prudent on the part of the king to keep the chiefs of the guilds in good humour and ancient law givers enjoin that the king should honour award and gift to the representative of guilds.

The elements of state control in the post mauryan period were loosened and guilds enjoyed considerable freedom in their own sphere whenever they were at fault, royal intervention became necessary and law givers have justified its legitimacy. Famous ancient law giver Birhispati states that the king is the highest authority to pass a judgement. If a guild cheated the king of his share of profit earned in trade, it was to pay eight time as such and was punished, if it moved to another place without information. The king had the authority to enforce the maintenance of law, contracts and agreements between individual members and guilds. Manu mentions that a member of corporation who after duly entering into an agreement breaks it through avarice, was to be banished by the king from his realm, and could also be given the punishment of fine and even imprisonment. These references clearly indicate that state upholded its legal authority in case of confrontation and justified its authority by way of exercising the power and prerogative of the king. It was king's privilege to decide the question of compatibility between rules of guilds and sacred laws (the latter having precedence over the former), and his authority in this matter was final. Hence, there was scope for royal intervention in guild affairs which a king, so inclined could resort to for selfish ends. Such a situation, as and when it arose, would naturally have led to tension in guild-state relations. But state intervention in guild affairs sometime had advantage for guilds as a whole. It would have provided check against stalemate in the conduct of guild affairs and dictatorial attitude of the guild authority. The appointment of an officer (bhandigarika) to act as a bridge among the different guilds, mentioned in a Jatak stories, may be indicative of the state asserting its right of supervision over guilds. Ryz Davids believes that this official dealt not only with king's exchequer but also supervised the commodities produced and goods marketed by the guilds.

Liability and Relevance

No other institutions in ancient times, except guilds, drew much attention of economic historians who are impressed with its viability and efficient functioning. Currency system had great advantages in trade and commerce and coins were first introduced by traders and merchants. Cunningham believe that punch marked coins were issued with prior permission of state by the guilds. The Arthasastra of Kautilya says that state gold smith shall employ artisans to manufacture gold and silver coins (rupya suvarna) from bullion of citizen and country people.

The social, economic and cultural life in ancient India was very much affected by the guild system. Social mobility and cultural intermixing brought a cohesive atmosphere in the existing society. The mercantile community by employing and encouraging the artisans and workers considerably improved the social and economic condition. The vaisya has been defined as one who would provide food for others and pay taxes. It suggests that mercantile group (vaisyas) of people, because of their association with industries and trading business, led the society based on production relation. In this way, these people gave a push to the political economy of the state. The vaisyas worked in close association with Sudras. The upper two classes, because of economic prosperity of the trading community, felt insecure and consequently prayed for the protection of two upper Varna people. U N Ghosal is of the view that Brahmanas and Kshatriyas were two dominant forces in the society with their close political alliance and thought to be united against the economic prosperity of the mercantile group. Here an important point to be noted is that of a major contribution in the field of economy by the Vaisyas and Sudras. They took workers and artisan within their fold of economic activities in the form of guild as an economic institution. The economic prosperity of these people are incentive and encouragement to others. Manu states that one may adopt the profession of others in odd circumstances, defined as *Apad dharma*. This concept of *Apad dharma* affected the rigid rules of existing caste system. The use of iron technology on large scale led to a significant transformation of the means of production thereby influenced the production relation. Consequently increasing prosperity of lower order, especially vaisyas, tempted the upper two classes to adopt their profession.

During post mauryan phase, flourishing industrial and commercial progress on account of Indo-Roman trade, the whole economic situation underwent a considerable change and prescribed that traditional profession could not be maintained strictly on Varna line. The *Gautama Dharma Sutra* mentions that all the members of upper Varna's could not earn their livelihood by their traditional means of profession, therefore they got themselves engaged in other non-traditional works. Such changes in society, though limited, in form of profession, brought occupational mobility and created an atmosphere of social homogenity. The guild also contributed to the Sudra's sense of participation in different activities of production. It was essential for big commercial magnets to encourage skilled Sudra workers and artisans so that these could be sufficient production of commodities in economic field. The necessity of employing such artisans in the production activity largely contributed to their importance in the society. A Smith quotes from *Digha Nikaya* gives impressions that Sudras as artisans and workers were employed by Chanda, a business tycoon or industrialist.

The technique of locating necessity and desire of people in general by the crafts guilds led to the promotion of market. The process encouraged different type of commodities and their use in the society. The inhabitants of the cities and towns, on account of their higher individual income and an atmosphere of liberalism, lived a better life than some royal people. Therefore, we have different kinds of dresses and garments very much in practice within the city life which are mentioned in texts and noted in archaeological findings. The production oriented attitude led to the emergence of production centre suitable to the trades for the same purpose. Gradually, these trading and producing centres developed and specialized in their respective field. Some important cities that emerged as centre of industry, trade and commerce were Champa, Vaisali, Saravasti, Kausambhi, Mathura, Ujjain, Avantika, Bharucha, Pushkalwati etc. These cities flourished as centre of trade and industry where traders, artisans, some craftsmen and skilled labourers began to live in large numbers. Definitely it encouraged people's industrial sense of culture and boosted state economy. With the commercial progress, by way of specialisation in different industrial arts and crafts, several trade routes were built which became operational during the ancient period. References could be made here of two important and well known routes, *Uttrapatha* and *Dakshinapath*. The route *Dakshinapath* was from Rajgriha to Pratisthan on Godavari via Saravasti and Saketa and *Uttrapatha* was from Saravasti to Pataliputra via Mathura across the sandy desert of Rajputana. There were other routes too, like Benaras to Ujjain, Videha via Kashmir to Gandhara etc.

The guilds, specially of merchants and traders contributed a lot in giving better shape to the economy of the country. Rajghat has yielded two interesting Shreni's Sealings Seventeen more Sealings, bearing the Legend of Shreni's, in Gupta character, were unearthed at Basarah in the course of Spooner's excavation. These Seals indicate that mercantile communities issued Seals, through their respective guild, for business transactions. Thus it becomes clear that guilds contributed to the state economy in business transactions and gave as full-fledged commercial pattern of economic development. Apart from these social and economic contribution, different aspects of cultural life of the people were also affected through efforts of the guilds. Disaffection of some mercantile group of people with Brahmanism on account of certain social and religious factors, largely contributed to the development of unorthodox seeks. The traders artisans and other craftsmen showed their interest in Buddhism and Jainism. Therefore religious gifts, donation and assistance rendered by mercantile groups enriched the cultural heritage of both sects. Various references about liberal gifts to Buddhism are recorded in literary sources as well noted from epigraphic records. The guilds also helped in the construction of Buddhist stupas and shrines. Gifts made by ivory workers guilds at Vidisa is well recorded. Similarly another epigraph from Sanchi refers to the gift made by weaver's guilds. People from mercantile group were not only attached with Buddhism but they also extended their support to the cultural heritage of Jainism. A large number of artisans and craftsmen were the follower of this sects. The weavers, potters and blacksmith found favour with Jaina Sramana who frequently took shelter in their shops. The well known trader sada putta was an ardent supporter of Jaina faith. Their adherence and allegiance to this sect testify that artisans, merchants and other workers had embraced Jainism as well as Buddhism. These two sects, specially, helped in their activities by way of creating social and ethical harmonious rules and regulations. If Protestantism in Europe paved the way for commercial resolution in seventeenth century, similarly Buddhism and Jainism levelled the ground for economic and commercial progress of the people in our country.

During the Gupta period and onwards, guild also contributed by way of doing several philanthropic activities. The Mandasore stone inscription of Kumargupta recorded that a Sun temple was built by silk weaver's guild by the wealth they had acquired from trade.The construction of a temple of Shiva by the head of Oil miller is recorded in a Prasasthi of Baijnatha. An inscription of Siladitya also mentions that a temple of Durga was founded at the command of Jentaka, who was an influential merchant. Therefore, contribution of guilds, merchants, artisans, craftsmen and dealers in different commodities, were of immense importance. The guilds affected almost every aspects of human life and promoted a sense of advancement in the field of socio-economic development of the country. Their contribution and importance cannot be rejected even in modern day open economy where production oriented centres and towns are highlighted. Their devotion, dedication in all form and affiliation with different religion brought cultural pluralism which enriched our ancient cultural heritage, to be expressed here in its best form as Unity in Diversity. Tourism potential and cultural expansion would not have been possible, had these guilds not been active, cooperation towards their own creativity and perfection in their profession. Their importance and utility in modern perspective may be judged by keeping in mind the role of FICCI (Federation of Indian Chamber of Commerce and Industries) what, we see today the role of companies and corporation in national economy of our country. Similarly guilds (ancient times) played its multi-functional role and argument that state economy tried to create an atmosphere of homogenity, cultural pluralism and people's advancement in all sphere of life.

HINDU, BUDDHIST AND JAINA SYSTEM OF EDUCATION (ANCIENT INDIA)

The main aim of education in early India was the training of the mind as an instrument of knowledge. It may be called *yoga* or the process of bringing together the individual soul and the Oversoul. The individual is the *adhara* (base) which is vitalized by the cosmic energy *(prakrti, maya or sakti)* pervading the world. When the *adhara* is fully fitted to bear the impact of divine energy, its evolution is complete and the man becomes *siddha,* the fulfilled or perfected soul. The teacher's admission of the pupil was a solemn and sacred ceremony known as *upanayana* or initiation. The ceremony took three days, during which as explained in the *Atharva-Veda,* the teacher held the pupil within him to impart to him a new birth, and the pupil emerged as a *dvija* or twice born. The pupil was to imbibe the inward method of the teacher, the secrets of his efficiency, the spirit of his life and work and these things were too subtle to be taught. The highest knowledge is described as *vidya* or *paravidya* as distinguished from *avidya* or *aparavidya,* which is a body of contigent truths, half truths and fallacies.

Three steps are distinguished in the attainment of supreme knowledge. These are *sravana, manana* and *nididhyasana.*

Three steps are distinguished in the attainment of supreme knowledge. These are *sravana, manana* and *nididhyasana. Sravana* is listening to the words or texts as they are uttered by the teacher. The system of oral tradition, by which knowledge was transmitted from teacher to pupil by *guruparampara* (a succession of teachers) or *sampradaya* (handing down). Such knowledge was imparted in the form known as *mantra or sutra,* by which the maximum of meaning was compressed within the minimum of words. All the learning of the times was thus held between the teacher and the taught, and the teacher was the walking library and source of knowledge. *Sadba* or sound of the sacred word or *mantra* has its own potency and value apart from its sense and its intrinsic and innate implications, its rhythm, its vibrations should be captured. The receiving of this knowledge was to be followed by the process of its assimilation by *manana,* deliberation or reflection on the topic taught. Learning was to be completed by the third step or process, which was technically called *nididhyasana* (meditation), leading to the realization of truth after is intellectual apprehension. A set of external aids to knowledge was also formulated to supplement these inner disciplines and processes and to strengthen the moral foundations for the pursuit of knowledge. The first that the pupil must live with his teacher as a member of his family, so that his education may be a whole time process. Living with his teacher as his *antevasin* (companion), the pupil had to take advantage of the opportunities which opened out before him in such a school. His first duty was to walk to the woods, collect fuel and bring it home for tending the sacred fire.

The pupil's next duty was to tend the teacher's house and cattle. Tending the house was training for him in self help in dignity of labour by manual service for his teacher and the student brotherhood. The pupil's received a valuable training in the love of the cow as the animal most serviceable to man and in the industry of rearing cattle and dairy farming with all the other advantages it gave of outdoor life and robust physical exercise. Another duty of the *brahmacharin* was to go out on a daily round of begging. It was not the selfish begging but for the academic corporation to which he belonged. All these external practices operate as aids to knowledge by strengthening the potency of the mind as an instrument for acquiring knowledge. The aim of education is thus *cittavrtti-nirodha* (control of the mental wages) by which the individual merges in the universal. The different types of institutions by which education was promoted. The first was the *ashrama* or hermitage, a home of learning with an individual teacher as its head, who admitted to his domestic school as many pupils as he found fit and could instruct. In these schools the pupils passed their period of studentship properly *(brahmacharya)*. But there might be pupils who would prefer to continue as students through life, dedicated to the pursuit of learning. Such students are known as *naisthika brahmacharins*. There were also in the country institutions for advanced study known as *parisads*. The most famous *parisad* of the times was the Pancala *parisad,* which was patronized by the philosopher king of the country, Pravahana Jabali, who daily drove out of his palace in his royal chariot to attend its sittings.

Besides these residential schools, academies for advanced study and circles of wandering scholars given to philosophical discussions, there were the assemblies of learned men gathered together by kings at their courts. Such a conference is described in *Brhadaranyaka Upanisad,* stating how Janaka, king of Videha, invited to his court the learned scholars of the Kuru-Panchala country. The procedure adopted by the conference was to make its proceedings as fruitful as possible. Exponents of these schools were selected to present to the conference the doctrines promulgated by each school. Eight such exponents and leading philosophers were thus chosen. They were Uddalaka Aruni, Asvala, Artabhaga, Bhujyu, Usasta, Kahola, Vidagdha Sakalya and Gargi Vacaknavi (the woman philosopher), Uddalaka was very famous who contributed most to the philosophy of the Upanisads. Asvala was the *hotr* priest of King Janaka. Bhujyu was a fellow pupil of Aruni senior. King Janaka announced that he would award the royal prize to the philosopher who answered the most subtle and difficult questions that were put to him. Even the woman philosopher Gargi publicly challenged his wisdom by posing two perplexing problems, but Yajnavalkya successfully answered these questions. From the story of the lady Gargi it appear that women were then considered as equals of men in their eligibility and capacity for achieving the highest knowledge. The Upanisads also tell us the story of Maitreyi, the worthy wife of Yajnavalkya, as his partner in the pursuit of the highest knowledge.

Though the old tradition of the father as the teacher was continued down to the times of Manu and Yajnavalkya, it was the usual practice to send the boys after the ceremony of *upanayana* (investiture with the sacred thread) to live with a teacher. The texts distinguish between two types of teachers, namely the *acharya* (who performs the pupil's *upanayana* and teachers him the whole of the Veda) and the *upadhyaya* (who teaches the pupil only a portion of the Veda or its auxiliaries). The *acharya's* position was very high. The text distinguish between two types of students, namely, the *upakurvana* (one who offers some remuneration to the teacher after completing his studies and leaves to lead a home life) and the *naisthika* (one who lives perpetually with his teacher or in the event of his death with his family). The pupil is to observe the prescribed rules about dress and mode of begging alms as well as about food and drink, he should be restrained in thought and speech and should shun personal adornment and amusements. His behavior should be respectful towards his superiors and guarded in the presence of women. The pupil should pay no fee to his teacher in advance, but at the end of his studies he should offer something according to his means or to the teacher's desire. The scheme of training for a Vedic student may be supplemented by an account of the education of a Kshatriya prince given in Kautilya's *Arthasastra.* After his tonsure ceremony and before reaching his seventh year, he has to learn the alphabet and the account, after the *upanayana* ceremony he has to study the four sciences, namely, *trayi* (the Vedas with their auxiliaries), *anviksiki* (the three schools of philosophy), *varta* (economics), and *danda-niti* (politics). Even after the completion of his studies, and his marriage in his sixteenth year, he has to go through a daily routine of receiving lessons in the art of war and in *Itihasa* (historical traditions). Of the two branches of discipline *(vinaya)* namely, the acquired and the natural, the first, should be imparted only to eager and intelligent pupils.

The *Milindapanha* (the questions of Menander), a celebrated Buddhist literature contains a remarkable account of the current curriculum of studies for a Brahmana and for a prince. The Brahmana studied the four Vedas astronomy and astrology, materialistic philosophy, and the science of omens. By contrast, the prince learnt the arts of managing horses, elephants and chariots of writing and accounts and of waging war. A fresh type of education was developed during this period in the Buddhist monasteries for the training of the newly ordained monks, the rules under this head being laid down in the section of the canon concerned. The monk, to begin with was to place himself under the guidance of a teacher after making a formal application and receiving his tacit consent. The teacher was called *acharya* or *upadhyaya,* the pupil was daily to serve the teacher at his bath, toilette and meals and on his begging tour and nurse him during his illness. The teacher on his side was to give a complete instruction to his pupils to supply their necessaries to nurse them during sickness and so forth. In the *Ramayana* the *ashrama* (hermitage) of Bharadvaja at Prayaga and in the *Mahabharata* the *ashrama* of Saunaka, disktingished as a *kulapati* or teacher of ten thousand pupils, Kanva' was situated esbrama at Naimisa forest on the banks of the Malini river. The *Milindapanha* mentions a number of Buddhist hermitages of this type of Dhammarakkhita at Pataliputta, Ayupala at Sagala, which were visited by Nagasena as a wandering scholar for the purpose of instruction.

The students from distant Mithila and Rajagrha in the east and from Ujjayini in the south, not to speak of those from the Sivi and Kuru kingdoms in Uttarapatha, flocked to Takshasila, capital of the Gandhara kingdom, to complete their education under world renowned teachers. The *Jatakas* also mention Varanasi as a great centre of learning which was established mostly by students trained at Takshasila. The *Ramayana* says that the city of Ayodhya, capital of the Kosala kingdom, is said to have contained schools of Vedic and Puranic learning along with residences of the students. A Jataka tells that how former kings used to send their sons to distant lands for completing their education, so that they might be trained to quell their pride, to endure heat and cold, and to acquire the ways of the world. The condition of medical education during Buddha age of is illustrated by the narrative of the career of Jivaka. He was born as the son of a courtesan at Rajagriha and brought up by prince Abhaya of Magadha. He was sent to study medicine under a world renowned teacher at Takshasila. There he stayed for seven years and completed his training by passing a difficult practical test in the knowledge of medicinal plants. He rose to the position of court physician of Bimbisara, king of Magadha and established a country wide practice in medicine and surgery. A more detailed account in medicine is found in the *Susruta Samhita,* a well known surgical work belonging to the early centuries of the Christian era. The preceptor admitted his pupil by performing a special *upanayana* ceremony, which was open to all the three upper classes and according to some to sudras as well. The students should have proficiency both in theory and practice, failing either of which he would be in the position of a bird clipped of one of its wings. The *Divyavadana* refers to the training of the sons of rich merchants at that time. The list of studies comprised the knowledge of writing, arithmetic, coins, debts and deposits, examination of gems, elephants and horses. Advanced types of educational institutions were continued during the period of the Imperial Guptas and their successors. The child of reaching his eighth or tenth year should be initiated into the vow of studentship and be instructed thereafter in the Vedas as well as in the military science. The high standard of the prince's education is illustrated at its best by the examples of the scholar kings of this period such as Samudragupta, Harsavardhana, Mahendravarman and Yasovarman before A.D. 1000 and Somesvara III, Ballalasena, Bhoja Paramara in the centuries thereafter. Buddhist pilgrim *I-tsing,* belonging to the latter half of the seventh century, gives striking testimony to the continuance of the old type of education in Buddhist monasteries. Among the monasteries of the Gupta period, Nalanda in Magadha attained the highest distinction because of the magnificence of its establishment and the intellectual and moral eminence of its alumni. In the account of I-tsing Nalanda in eastern and Valabhi in western India were the two places in the country that were visited by advanced students for completing their education. During the rule of the Pala kings Bengal, a fresh group of monasteries (namely, those of Vikramasila, Somapuri, jagaddala, and Uddandapura) rose into eminence as great centres of learning. Among the alumni of these monastic universities, special mention may be made of Dipankara Srijnana (Atisa), who the founder of a reformed school of Buddhism in Tibet and Vidyakara, who wrote a great Sanskrit anthology, *Subhasita-ratnakosa.* The *Harsacarita* introduces to a great Buddhist teacher called Divakaramitra, whose hermitage in the depths of the Vindhya forest and it was visited by King Harsa in search of his sister Rajyasri. In the eleventh century the schools of Kashmir were so famous that they drew scholars from distant Gauda (West Bengal) for higher learning.

According to Hiuen Tsang, the children, after mastering a short primer called 'the Twelve Chapters' or 'the *Siddha* composition', were trained in five sciences, namely, grammar, the science of arts and crafts, medicine, the science of reasoning and the science of the internal.

The curriculum of studies, according to I-tsing, comprised in graded sequence like the Panini's grammar with the commentaries, logic and metaphysics in addition to which the Sutras and the Sastras were prescribed for monks. The parallel list of subjects studied at the Nalanda monastery comprised, not only the works of all the eighteen Buddhist schools but also the Vedas, logic, grammar, medicine, the *Artha-vidya,* the Samkhya and so forth. Some light is thrown upon the training of the craftsman's apprentice. The preceptor Marco Polo, who visited the extreme south of India in the closing years of the thirteenth century says that boys of the traders of the Pandya kingdom, on reaching their thirteenth year, were dismissed by their parents with a small pocket money for earning their living by trade. Thus they grew up to be very dexterous and keen traders.

The *Smrti-candrika,* mentions women students into two classes, namely students of the sacred lore *(brahmavadinis)* and those married straightway *(sadyovadhus).* This development is connected with the tendency in the later Smrtis to reduce progressively the marriageable age of girls. The woman of the upper classes enjoyed much opportunities for education in the fine arts that some of them became accomplished poetesses and authorities. Princes Rajyasri and Avantisundari, wife of the dramatist and rhetorician Rajasekhara could be the examples. The story of Princess Kadambari and Mahasveta in Bana's work, Kamandaki in Bhavabhuti's great drama suggest the existence of regular institutions where girls received their training, sometimes in the company of male students. In the stories of the *Upamiti-bhavaprapanca-Katha* a Jaina allegorical work of the tenth century, references are found that how princesses were skilled in the arts of painting, music and versification.

Takshasila University

Takshasila was situated in Gandhar Mahajanpada covering modern western Pakistan to Afganistan region. Takshasila was earliest known University of India. Probably its foundation was laid in eight or nineth century B.C. In the sixth century B.C. it was famous centre of learning. In the fourth century B.C. Kautilya or Chankya was *Kulpati* of this university. The literary evidences show that Takshasila was known for its medical education. The famous physician Jivaka of Magadha was student of this university. Later on he was appointed as royal physician of Bimbasara of Magadha. He was also a physician of Buddha. Kautilya trained Chandragupta Maurya in the Takshasila University in art of warfare and other learnings. The students of Takshasila founded schools of learning in Varanasi. The prominence of Takshasila declined in the later Gupta age.

Nalanda

The first monastery in Nalanda was founded in the age of Asoka but University was founded in the age of Kumar Gupta. Huientsang says that Harsha had allotted the revenue of 100 villages to this institution. It reached the pinnacle of its glory during the reign of Harsha and it enrolled students from different parts of India as also from foreign lands. Huientsang says that only two or three out of ten applicants succeeded in getting through the Entrance

Examination. The strength of the students of this university was ten thousand. It was purely a residential university, all its students being given free lodging and boarding.. Classes were held during the night also. It is also clear that, besides lectures, there were seminars and symposia also. The number of teachers in the university was 1510. This would make, in general, the teacher-student ratio at about 1:6. It had a big library called Dharmayajna which had three sections known as Ratnasagara, Ratnadadhi and Ratnaranjaka. Harsha had built a great *vihara* on the campus. It was 100 ft in height. The University's courses were multidimensional including the tenets of the 18 Buddhist sects, Vedas, Grammer, Yoga, Samkhya, Logic, Tantra and Medical Science etc. It is said that as many as 100 lectures were delivered daily by the experts there. Silabhadra, the Chancellor of that University was called *Pandita.* Its alumni included such renowned scholars as Huientsang, I-tsing, Kamalasila, Kumarajiva, Dharmadeva and Gunavarma who went to Tibet and China as emissaries of Indian learning and culture. Students used to come here from China, Tibet, Korea, Mongolia and other countries in search of knowledge that made the Nalanda University verily the Oxford University of the East.

Varanasi

Varanasi as a pre-eminent centre of learning in the east. This school was founded by the students of Takshila. Brahmanical and Buddhist subjects were thought here. Varanasi was famous to its school of medicine. A new era dawned with the advent of the Mughals and Varanasi regained its position. It began once again to draw scholars from various parts of the country and several learned families returned to it. Dharmadhikari, Bhatta and Mouni were some of the Maharashtrian and Karnataka families which figured prominently for more than three centuries (1500-1800). Nanda Pandit (1570-1630) the author of *Dattaka Mimamsa,* and Khanderaya, the author of *Parasurama Praksa,* both belonged to the Dharamadhikari family. Sankarbhatta, author of *Davitanernya Vratamaynkha* and many other works, Gangabhatta, author of a dozen works on *Mimamsa, Sisavishnu and Chintamani,* and the author of *Rasamanjari Parimala* belonged to the Sesa family. Kabir and Tulsi Das carried on their literary activities there. Raja Jai Singh established a college there for the education of the princes during Akbar's time. Foreign travellers refer to several seminars at Varanasi where the renowned teachers gave lectures on Hindu religion and philosophy. Prince Dara Shikoh also refers to Benaras as the chief centre of Hindu learning in the preface to his famous work, *Sirri-i-Akbar.*

Nadia (Navadvipa)

Nadia in Bengal was an important seat of Hindu learning during the medieval period. It rose in prominence after the destruction of the Buddhist universities of Nalanda and Vikramshila. Its three branches were at Navadvipa, Santipura and Gopalpara. High standards of scholarship were maintained at Navadvipa. There were no less than 150 teachers for 1100 students. Navya Nyaya was the main subject of specialization at Nadia. Sarvabhauma (1450-1525), the great scholar of the sixteenth century, was the founder of this school. However, studies in the *Smritis,* Gita, Bhagvata, Jnana and Bhakti were also pursued. In fact a chair for the studies of the *Smritis* and a chair of logic were created in the sixteenth century. The chair for astronomy was added in 1718 by Ramarudra Vidyanidhi.

Mithila

Mithila in north Bihar was a reputed centre of learning from ancient times. Janak was founder of this learning centre. Under his patronage philosophy was written in his court. It retained its importance throughout medieval times and students from all parts of the country sought admission there for specialized study in logic. It was one of the pupils of Mithila, Raghunandandasa Rai, who performed *dig-vijaya* at the instance of Akbar. The Emperor was so pleased that he gave him the whole town of Mithla as a gift. The obedient pupil in turn offered it to his teacher, Mahesh Thakur. Mithila's reputation as a centre of learning suffered due to the growing importance of Nadia which was visited by some of its scholars to complete their studies.

Islamic System of Education

The Muslims took firm root in India after the Mongols sacked Baghdad and other Muslim cultural centres in AD 1285. A large number of scholars from these lands took refuge in India during Balban's time. The migrant scholars from such far-off lands as Bukhara, Samarqand and Iraq were not able to carry their invaluable collection of books and manuscripts to India with the result that stress was laid only on such branches of learning as poetry, contemporary local history, jurisprudence, grammar etc. The institutions which provided Islamic elementary education were known as *maktabs.* These are generally attached to mosques. The *madrasa* was a school or college of higher learning which a student attended only after he had completed a course of study in a *maktab.* The *bismillah or maktab* ceremony was performed when a child was four years, four months and four days old, usually after circumcision. Its main purpose was the advancement of knowledge, particularly Islamic doctrines and philosophy. A *maktab* was the primary school. He received his first lesson there in the alphabet from a *moulvi* and then practiced combined lettes. Every child had to know the Quran by heart. After finishing the Quran, the students took lessons in Arabic and Persian grammar. Great stress was laid on calligraphy and students were instructed to practice the style of all the best calligraphists in the country. Simple arithmetic was also taught.

Madrasas were secondary schools or colleges of higher learning. Sometimes these were attached to the chief mosque of a city. Some of the famous *madrasas* established during sultanate period were *Madrasa-i-Muizzi* (built by Iltutmisha and named after Shihab-ud-din Ghori also known as Muizz-ud-din Muhammad Ghori), *Madrasa-i-Nasiri* (established by Iltutmish in memeory of his son Nasir-ud-din Mahmud), *Madrasa-i-Firuzshahi* (built by Firoz Tughlaq) at Delhi, the *Madrasa of Bibi Raja Begum of Jaunur, the Madrasas* of Sikandar Lodhi at Agra, Mathura and Marwar, *Bidar Madrasa of Mahmud Gawan, Sher shah's Madrasa at Narnaul, Madrasa of Abul Fazal at Fatehpur Sikri and Madrasa Dar ul Baqa*

(Abode of Eternity) of Shah Jahan at Delhi. *Madrasas* were also established by individual scholars, such as the *Madrasa of Shaikh Wajih-ud-din Alwai* in Gujarat, Zafar Khan's in Bengal, *Khan-i-Khannan* in Delhi, shihab-ud-din Daultabadi's at Jaunur, Qutub-ud-din Sihalwi's at Lucknow.

The method of teaching was more or less similar to that of the Hindus and was based on memorization, discussion and writing out the lessons taught. The average number of pupils to each teacher was usually four or five going upto a maximum of fifteen. A teacher was usually helped by his senior pupils who acted as assistant masters. Classes were held twice a day in the morning and evening. Some interval was allowed in between. No fee was normally charged. The teacher was held in high esteem and was implicity obeyed. There was no system of periodical examinations among the Muslims. The teacher was the sole judge for the promotion of a pupil to the next standard. When the teacher was satisfied, he would confer on him the academic distinction sometimes celebrated as *dastarbandi* or tying of a turban. A solemn function was held and the turban was tied around the head of the pupil by the teacher. A function was held in honour of Nizam-ud-din Auliya, when he completed his education under Maulana ala-ul-din Usuli. Though no regular degrees were awarded, sometimes certificates or diplomas were awarded by renowned scholars of theology.

During the Sultanate peiod the chief centres of Islamic learning were naturally located in the north-west areas of the country in Multan, Sind, Lahore and Delhi. Agra enjoyed a prominent position as an educational centre throughout the Mughal period. Akbar established a big college there. He specially brought scholars from Shiraz to teach there. The *Madrasa-i-Khas* of Maulana Ala-ud-din Lari and the *Madrasa-i-Safawi* of Sayyed Rafi-ud-din Safawi were famous. Delhi kept up its tradition and was the nucleus of important institutions, as already mentioned. Famous among them were *Humayun's Madrasa* and the *Khair-ul-Manzil* built by Maham Anaga, foster mother of Akbar. Shah Jahan also built at Imperial College near Jami masjid. Jaunpur and Gujrat were two other important centres. Jaunpur, called the Shiraz of India, came into prominence during the reign of Ibrahim sharqi (1401-40). Lahore and Sialkot also attracted a large number of scholars. Sialkot's importance also increased as it was a big centre for the manufacture of paper. Stress was laid on traditional subjects such as jurisprudence, theology, the traditions of the prophet, rhetoric, syntax, etymology, literature, medicine and calligraphy. Mathematics was also studied side by side. Philosophy and logic were introduced during the time of Sikandar Lodhi. Humayun laid emphasis on the study of mathematics, astronomy and geography which were the main subjects of study in the *Madrasas* he built in Delhi. Akbar tried to reorient the educational system by laying stress on the study of such secular subjects as mathematics, astronomy, medicine, philosophy and logic. He issued a *farman* making mathematics and astronomy compulsory subjects.The *Dars-i-Nizamiya,* or the syllabus prepared by Nizam-ud-din Sihalwi who lived during Aurangzeb's time and the list of books given in the *Khulasat-ul-Maktib* leave us in little doubt that the traditional medieval system of education continued with few variations. The sciences and particularly geography were completely neglected. Aurangzeb severely reprimanded his teacher for wasting his time in the teaching of Arabic metaphysics instead of geography and politics.

No separate schools seem to have existed for imparting education to girls. Ibn Batuta's reference to *maktabs* for girls in Hinawr in the south-west region of India may be an exception. In their childhood, girls attended schools alongwith boys and learnt the Quran. The rich appointed tutors to teach their daughters at home. The daughters of Rajput chiefs and big *jagirdars* were usually able to read and write. Ratna Wali, the wife of Puranmal and Mirabai, the well known Hindi poetess, may be mentioned in this connection. Special attention was paid to the education of Mughal princesses. Some of them composed verses and were proficient in music. A few specimens of letters written by Mughal princesses exist. The husband of Gulbadan, daughter of Babar, did not even recognize his wife's handwriting. Her *Humayun Nama* abounds in spelling mistakes and clumsy sentences. There were quite a few ladies such as Zeb un Nisa, Zinat un Nisa (daughtes of Aurangzeb), and Rupmati, wife of Baz Bahadur, ruler of Malwa during Akbar's time, who distinguished themselves in the literary sphere. The literacy of the average middle class woman who had sufficient knowledge of either Sanskrit, Persian, Hindi or of a regional language to enable her to study the religious scriptures. Mukundram, a sixteenth century poet, author of the poem *Chandimangal,* throws light on the education of the average Hindu women in those days. Special stress was laid on the education of widows, some of whom even became teachers. Printing was not in vogue in India in the medieval period. Eight calligraphical systems were in vogue and of these *naskh and nastaliq* were the most important. Babar introduced a new style called *khatt-i-babari.* Expert teachers of the above systems were available in India. Rich decorations and binding which were usual in the case of a presentation copy intended for a rich patron greatly enhanced the price of the book. Humayun purchased Mir Ali's *tuhfat-u-salatin* for Rs. 2500. Jahangir purchased a copy of the *yusuf-Zulaikha,* evidently containing a number of illustrations and paintings, for 1000 *mohurs.*

Almost evey *madrasa* possessed a library, big or small. Many *khanqahs* even today posses collections of old manuscripts. There was a rich collection of books in libraries attached to the *khanqahs* of Bhagalpur and *phulwari-sharif* in Bihar. There were also big libraries in such famous *madrasas* as *Madrasa Firozshahi* at Uchh in Sind and *Madrasa Muaizi* and *Nasiri* at Delhi. The big library attached to the *madrasa* at Ahmedabad called *Sham-i-Burhan* was in existence when Akbar conquered Gujarat. The library attached to the college built by Mahmud Gawan at Bidar contained over 5000 works. Big libraries were also attached to the famous seats of Hindu learning at Varanasi, Tirhut, Mithila and Nadia. These libraries had large collections of rare, authentic ancient manuscripts on philosophy, medicine, religion, history and many other sciences. Muhammad Tughluq had a good library to which were added several hundred valuable Sanskrit manuscripts by Firuz Shah Tughluq which came into his possession in the conquest of Kangra. Some of them were even translated into Persian. Humayun's library was located in a special building, known as Sher Mandal in Purana Qila.

The Imperial Library of the Mughals was further enriched during the reigns of Jahangir, Shah Jahan and Aurangzeb. Several boks and manuscripts, now in various libraries in the country such as the Khuda Baksh Library, Patna and the Oriental Public Library Patna, show the seal fo these Emperors and testify to their interest in the building up of the Imperial Library. Jahangir also took pleasure in distributing books among his nobles. After the fall of Bijapur, many rare and precious books of the Adil Shahi library were carried away by Aurangzeb and added to the Imperial Library. A reference may also be made to the libraries maintained by some Mughal ladies who were scholars of repute, such as Gulbadan Begum, Salima Sultana, Nur Jahana and Zeb-un-Nisa. Baba Farid had a very rich collection of books on religion and mysticism. Nazim-ud-din Auliya possessed a good library containing rare works on religion and philosophy. Amir Khusrau's library was also very rich. The rare collection of books of Amir Ghazi Khan, a courtier of Sultan Ibrahim Lodhi, fell into the hands of Babar after the conquest of the Punjab. Maharaja Chhika Deva Raya of Mysore (1672-1704) had gathered rare Sanskrit and historical works in his library which were subsequently destroyed by Tipu Sultan. Maharaj Sawai Jai Singh of Jaipur (1699-1743) possessed a unique library containing all the astronomical treatises.

British and Modern Education

The colonial government selected the education system as the instrument for hitting target. Since 1813, the planned enterprise started and was given a precise dimension, with the formulation of Macaulay's Minute in February 1835. The Minute was an intended mask of general welfare, broadcast under the banner of educational advancement. Minute recommended the advent of Western learning as beneficial: 'For the revival and promotion literature and the encouragement of the learned natives of India and for the introduction and promotion of knowledge of the sciences among the inhabitants of the British territories.' The British were actually looking for services that would not inexpensive, but also efficient. And the suitable ones were the colonized Indians. Macaulay dreaming of breeding an economically flourishing colony, generating enormous wealth as cheap labor. The arrogant and racist Macaulay asserted the British ideology of the superiority of Wetern learning over the oriental reserve of knowledge. The colonial master's urgency for a uniform and proper administration throughout the empire spawned the emergence of a class of clerks and translators. In the major presidencies Bengal, Madras and Bombay, the British government had to rely on the ability of the District Collectors, for handling the administrative affairs, while the native princes functioned on the instructions of the colonial authority. The native reformists performed the feat of pioneering the English Education. The Hindu College in Calcutta, established in the year 1817, authenticated the ushering of the Bengal Renaissance. The foundation committee was presided over by Raja Rammohun Roy. On October, 1853, a proposition was made, that 'It should be open to all youths of every caste, class or creed'. It was renamed Presidency College in 1855. Presidency College has the proud history of permitting access to female students. In fact, the female student joined the institution in 1897. The documents report that the Hindu college celebrated seat of learning, was the right place for the making of the perfect know how for the government assignments of the East India Company. The Christian missionaries marched forward to plant the flag of British Imperial India, under the humanistic camouflage of Educational Campaigns. They circulated the man benefiting western education. Their target was the elite Indian section of the society. It was because many prestigious families were enamored of the newness of English education.

William Carey visited Bengal in 1800 and established the first missionary Srerampore of Bengal. With his two partners, Joshua Marshman (1768-) William (1769-1823) he formed the famous Serampore Trio. The Nathaniel Forsyth London Missionary Society also embarked on their operations from the Dutch town of Chinsura and after the charter of 1813 erased the ban on missionary activities in India, even the christian missionary society came down India to spread its sway. In 1816, the church missionaries, Greenwood and Schroeter, made their way to Calcutta. The Srerampore Trio tried to make education available to the mass thought his adoption of native frameworks. They prescribed a curriculum of arithmetic, preliminary science, synopsis of history, geography, natural philosophy, ethics. The curriculum was expanded to 103 elementary schools constructed for educational development. It was amazing enough, that by 1818, a total of 6703 students studied in these schools. The greatest achievement of the Sererampore Trio is the foundation of the Srerampore college to patronize the proper cultivation of Oriental Literature and western sciences. The Srerampore Trio recommended the modification of some Hindu practices like the demeaning caste system, the inhumanity of sati and Infanticide, to welcome life of non-violence, equality and liberty.

The London Missionary Society also fantastically accomplished in their project under Robe In 1814, 36 primary schools came into existence in Chinsura. The Governor General, Lord Wellesley, carved out the Fort William College in 1800. Along with this over brimming for education, resided the inclination for eminent translations of Bible into the oriental Sanskrit, Oriya, Assamese, Bangla and Marathi. Indian scholars like Ramram basu and vidyalankar, carried out the work with the foreign experts. This path was followed by the Calcutta School – Book Society (1817), which upheld Bengali the helm of affairs. Journalism became a widespread phenomenon. Alexander Duff (1806-1878), the famous Scottish missionary, stepped in May 1830. He was a key factor in the formation of the Scottish Church on July 1830. Female Education however did not raise to that much of prominence. British tried to advertise the importance of the growing 'woman question dealing with the rights of females, the actual scenario was much different. It was the native Pundit Ishwarchandra Vidyasagar who opened 30 schools to boost up female education in Bengal.

The East India Company became a ruling power in Bengal in 1765. The Indian officers of the East India Company urged the Court of Directors to do something for the promotion of learning. Company's Government to foster oriental learning. Warren Hastings, himself an intellectual, set up the Calcutta Madrasa in 1781 for the study and learning of Persian and Arabic. In 1791 the efforts of Jonsthan Duncan the British Resident at Benares, bore fruit and a Sanskrit College was opened at Benares for the cultivation of the laws, literature and religion of the Hindus. Christian missionaries advocated the teaching of western literature and Christian religion through the medium of English. The Fort William College was set up by Lord Wellesely in 1800 for the training of the civil servants of the company, in the languages and customs of India. The college published an English Hindustani Dictionary, a Hindustani grammar and some other books. The Court of Directors ordered the closure of the college in 1802. The Court of Directors made a humble beginning towards the development of education in India in 1813 when the Charter Act (1813) provided for an annual expenditure of one lakh of rupees for the revival and promotion of literature and the encouragement of the learned natives of India and for the introduction and promotion of a knowledge of the sciences among the inhabitants of the British territories.

The main factor which tipped the scale in favour of English language and western literature was the economic factor. Raja Ram Mohan Roy protested against the Government's proposal to strengthen the Calcutta Madrasa, the Benares Sanskrit College and establishment of more oriental colleges in Bengal. He wrote to Lord Amherst in 1823 that Sanskrit education could only be expected to load the minds of youth with grammatical necessities and metaphysical distinctions of life which are of little or no practical use to their possessors or to society. The protests of Raja Ram Mohan Roy did not go unheeded. The government agreed to encourage the study of English as well as college set up in 1817 by enlightened Bengalis which imparted instruction mainly in English language and emphasized the study of western humanities and scienes. The government also set up three Sanskrit colleges one each at Calcutta, Delhi and Agra.

When company started opening of schools, the controversy started over medium of instruction. This controversy is known as Orientalist Vs Occidantalist (Englicist) Controversy. There were two groups, the orientalists led by H T Prinsep who advocated the policy of giving encouragement to oriental literature and the Anglicist or the English party which favoured the adoption of English as a medium of instruction. As a member of the Executive Council, Macaulary wrote his famous minute on educational policy dated 2 February 1835 and placed it before the council. Macaulay favoured the viewpoint of the Anglicist Party. He showed great contempt for Indian customs and literature when he said that a single shelf of a good European library was worth the whole native literature of India and Arabia. Regarding the utility importance and claims of English language he wrote: 'Whoever knows that language has ready access to all the vast intellectual wealth which all the wisest nations of the earth have created and handed in the course of ninety generations. In India, English the language spoken by the ruling class. It is spoken by the higher class of natives at the seats of government. Possibly, Macaulay aimed to create a class of persons who should be Indian in blood and colour, but English in tastes, in opinions, in morals and in intellect. In other words, he sought the production of brown Englishmen to fill the lower cadres in the company's administration. The Macaulayian system was a systematic effort on the part of the British government to educate the upper classes of India through the medium of English language. Education of the masses was not the aim of Macaulay. It is impossible for us wrote Macaulay in 1835, with our limited means to attempt to educate the body of the people. He rather put implicit faith in the infiltration theory. He believed that the English educated persons would act as a class of interpreters and turn enrich vernacular languages and literature and thus the knowledge of western sciences and literature would reach the masses. Thus a natural corollary of Macaulay's theory was the development of vernacular languages as ancillary to the teaching English. The government made half hearted efforts to develop vernacular languages and the development of literature in these languages was left to the genius and needs of the people who spoke these languages. In the North-West provinces (modern UP) Mr. James Thomason Lieutenant governor during 1843-53, made efforts to develop a comprehensive scheme of village education through the medium of vernacular languages. The smaller English schools were abolished and English education confined to colleges. The motivating force behind Thomason's plan was to train personnel for employment in the newly set up Revenue and Public Works Departments of the province.

Sir Charles Wood's Despatch on Education, 1854

Sir Charles Wood, the President of the Board of Control was a firm believer in the superiority of English and sincerely believed that it could serve as a useful model for the world. Charles Wood showed a larger vision about education than most of the zealous educationsts in India. In 1854 Wood prepared his comprehensive dispatch on the scheme of future education in India. The dispatch came to be considered as the Magna Carta of English education in India. The scheme envisaged a co-ordinated system of education on an all India basis. The main recommendations may be summarized thus:

1. It declared that the aim of government's educational policy was the teaching of western education. It will help in expansion of arts, science, philosophy and literature of Europe.
2. As to the medium of instruction, it declared that for higher education English language was the most perfect medium of education. It also emphasized the importance of the vernacular languages, for it was through the medium of the vernacular languages, that European knowledge could infilter to the masses. This policy is known as 'downward infiltration theory'.
3. It proposed the setting up of vernacular primary schools in the villages at the lowest stage, followed by Anglo-Vernacular high schools and an affiliated college at the district level.
4. It recommended a system of grants-in-aid to encourage and foster private enterprise in the field of education. The grants-in-aid was conditional on the institutions employing qualified teachers and maintaining proper standards of teaching.

5. A Department of Public Instruction under the charge of a Director in each of the five provinces of the Company's territories was to review the progress of education in the province and submit an annual report to the government.
6. Universities on the model of the London University were proposed for Calcutta, Bombay and Madras. The constitution of the University provided for a Senate, a Chancellor, a Vice Chancellor and Fellows, all to be nominated by the Government. The universities were to hold examinations and confer degrees. A university might set up professorships in various branches of learning.
7. The dispatch emphasized the importance of vocational instruction and the need for establishing technical schools and colleges.
8. Teachers Training Institutions on the model then prevalent in England were recommended.
9. The despatch gave cordial support for fostering the education of women.

The new scheme of education was a slavish imitation of English models. Almost all the proposals in the Wood's Despatch were accepted. The Department of Public Instruction was organized in 1855 and it replaced the earlier committee of public instruction and council of education. The three universities of Calcutta, Madras and Bombay came into existence in 1857. Mostly due to Bethune's efforts girls schools were set up on modern footing and brought under the government's grant-in-aid and inspection system.

The ideals and methods advocated in Wood's Despatch dominated the field for about five decades. The same period also witnessed a rapid westernization of the educational system in India. The indigenous system gradually gave place to the western system of education. Most of the educational institutions during this period were run by European headmasters and principals under the education department. The missionary enterprise played its own part and managed a number of institutions. Gradually private Indian effort appeared in the field.

The Hunter Education Commission, 1882-83

In 1882 the government appointed a commission under the chairmanship of W.W. Hunter to review the progress of education in the country since the Despatch of 1854. Another reason for the appointment of the commission was the propaganda carried on by the missionaries in England that the education system of India was not carried on in accordance with the policy laid down in Wood's Despatch. The resolution appointing the commission instructed the chairman to reorganize education in India that the different branches of public instruction should, if possible, move forward together and with more equal step than hitherto. The principal object, therefore, of the enquiry of the commission should be the present state of elementary education throughout the Indian Empire and the means by which this can be extended and improved. The commission was not to enquire into the general working of the Indian universities. Thus the commission mostly confined its remarks to secondary and primary education. It visited all the provinces and passed no fewer than 200 resolutions. Its main recommendations were:

1. It emphasized the state's special care for the extension and improvement of primary education. Primary instruction declared the commission, should be regarded as the instruction of the masses through the vernacular in such subjects as will best fit them for their position in life. While private enterprise was to be welcomed at all stages of education, primary education was to be provided without reference to local co-operation. The commission recommended the transfer of the control of primary education to the newly set up district and municipal boards. The local boards were empowered to levy cess for educational purposes.
2. For secondary education, the principle was laid down that there should be two divisions, one, a literary education leading up to the entrance examination of the university and the other of a practical character preparing students for commercial and vocational careers.
3. The commission recommended that an all out effort should be made to encourage private enterprise in the field of education. To achieve that objective, it recommended the extension and liberalization of the grants-in-aid system, recognition of aided schools as equal to government institutions in matters of status, privileges etc. The government should withdraw, it was recommended as early as possible from the direct management of secondary and collegiate education.
4. The education commission drew attention to the inadequate facilities for female education outside the presidency towns and made recommendations for its spread.

The twenty years following the report of the commission saw an unprecedented growth and expansion of secondary and collegiate education. The marked feature of this expansion was the participation of Indian philanthropic activity. Interest was kindled in Indian and oriental studies apart from the pursuit of western knowledge. Another development of the period was the settingup of the teaching cum examining universities. The Punjab University was founded in 1882 as the supreme literary supreme teaching and supreme examining body. The Allhabad University was set up in 1887. Curzon sought to reconstruct education in India. He referred to the poor quality of teachers who were merely the surveyors of certain articles to a class of purchasers and found fault with the examination ridden system of education. His motives were mainly political and only partly educational. Curzon justified the increase of official control over education in the name of quality and efficiency, but actually sought to restrict education and discipline educated mind towards loyalty to the government. The nationalist mind saw in Curzon's policies an attempt to strengthen imperialism and sabotage development of nationalist feelings.

The Indian Universities Act, 1904

In September 1901 Curzon summoned the highest educational officers of the government throughout India and representatives of universities at a round table conference at Simla. The conference adopted 150 resolutions was followed by the appointment of a commission under the presidency of Sir Thomas Raleigh on 27 January 1902 to enquire into the condition and prospects of universities in India and to recommend proposals for improving their constitution and working. Evidently, the commission was precluded from reporting on primary or secondary education. As a result of the report of the recommendations of the commission the Indian Universities Act was passed in 1904. The main changes proposed were as under:

1. The universities was desired to make provision for promotion of study and research, to appoint university professors and lecturers, set up university laboratories and libraries and undertake direct instruction of students.
2. The Act laid down that the number of fellows of a university shall not be less than fifty nor more than a hundred and a fellow should normally hold office for a period of six years instead of for life.
3. Most of the fellows of a university were to be nominated by the government. The elective elemant at universities of Calcutta, Madras and Bombay was to be twenty each and in case of other universities fifteen only.
4. The government control over the universities was further increased by vesting the government with powers to veto the regulations passed by the Senate of the university. The government could also make additions or alterations in the regulations framed by the Senate and even frame regulations itself over and above the head of the Senate.
5. The act increased university control over private colleges by laying down stricter conditions of affiliation and periodical inspection by the Syndicate. The private colleges were required to keep a proper standard of efficiency. The government approval was necessary for grant of affiliation or disaffiliation of colleges.
6. The Governor-general-in-Council was empowered to define the territorial limits of a university or decide the affiliation of colleges to universities.

Mr. G.K. Gokhale described the bill a retrograde measure which cast unmerited aspersion on the educated classes.

The nationalist opinion both inside and outside the Legislative Council opposed the measure. Mr. G.K. Gokhale described the bill a retrograde measure which cast unmerited aspersion on the educated classes. The country was designed to perpetuate the narrow, bigoted and inexpensive rule of experts. The Sadler Commission of 1917 commented that the act of 1904 made the Indian universities among the most complete governmental universities in the world. Indian opinion believed that Curzon sought to reduce the universities to the position of departments of the state and sabotage development of private enterprise in the field of eduction. However, a good outcome of Curzon's policy was the sanction in 1902 of a grant of Rs. 5 lakhs per annum for five years for improvement of higher education and universities. The government grants have become a permanent feature ever since then.

The Sadler University Commission, 1917-19

In 1917 the government of India appointed a commission to study and report on the problems of Calcutta University. Dr. M.E. Sadler, Vice Chancellor of the University of Leeds, was appointed its Chairman. The commission included two Indian members namely Sir Asutosh Mukerji and Dr. Zia-ud-din Ahmad. While the Hunter Commission had reported on problems of secondary education and the university commission of 1902 mainly on the different aspects of university education, the Sadler commission reviewed the entire field from school education to university education. The Sadler commission held the view that the improvement of secondary education was a necessary condition for the improvement of university education. The commission reported that an effective synthesis between college and university was still undiscovered when the reform of 1904 had been worked out to conclusion and the foundation of a sound university organization had not been laid down. The following were the main recommendations:

1. A twelve year school course was recommended. After passing the Intermediate Examination, rather than the Matriculation, the students were to enter a university. The government was urged to create new type of institutions called intermediate colleges. These colleges could either be run as independent institutions or might be attached to selected high schools. For the administration and control of Secondary Education, the commission recommended the setting up of a Board of Secondary and Intermediate Education.
2. The duration of the degree course after the Intermediate stage should be limited to three years. For the needs of abler student provision was to be made for Honours courses as distinct from the pass courses.
3. The commission recommended less rigidity in framing the regulations of universities.
4. The old type of Indian university, with its large number of affiliated and widely scattered colleges should be replaced by centralized unitary residential teaching autonomous bodies. A unitary teaching university was recommended for Dacca to lessen the rush of numbers at the colleges of Calcutta University. Further, colleges in the mofussil should be so developed as to make it possible to encourage the growth of new university centres by concentration of resources for higher education at a few points.
5. It stressed the need for extension of facilities for female education and recommended the establishment of a special Board of Women Education in the Calcutta University.
6. The necessity of providing substantial facilities for training of teachers was emphasized and desirability of setting up the Departments of Education at the Universities of Calcutta and Dacca.
7. The university was desired to provide courses in applied science and technology and also to recognize their systematic and practical study by award of degrees and diplomas. The universities were also to provide facilities for training of personnel for professional and vocational colleges.

Seven new universities came into existence during 1916-21, namely Mysore, Patna, Benaras, Aligarh, Dacca, Lucknow and Osmania. In 1920, the government of India recommened the Sadler Report to provincial governments.

The Hartog Committee, 1929

The quantitative increase of education inevitably led to deterioration of quality and lowering of standards. There was considerable dissatisfaction with the educational system. The Indian Statutory Commission appointed an auxiliary committee under the chairmanship of Sir Philips Hartog to report on the development of education. The main findings of the Hartog Committee were as follows:

1. It emphasized the national importance of primary education, but condemned the policy of hasty expansion or attempt to introduce compulsion in education. The commission recommended the policy of consolidation.
2. For secondary education, the commission reported that the system was dominated by the Matriculation Examination and many undeserving students considered it the path to university education. It recommended a selective system for admission and urged the retention of most of the boys intended for rural pursuits at the Middle Vernacular School stage. After the Middle Stage students should be diverted to diversified courses leading to industrial and commercial careers.
3. The commission pointed out the weaknesses of university education and criticized the policy of indiscriminate admission which led to lowering of standards. It recommended that all efforts should be concentrated in improving university work, in confining the university to its proper function of giving good advanced education to students who are fit to receive.

Sargeant Plan of Education

In 1944 the Central Advisory Board of Education drew up a national scheme of education, generally known as the Sargeant Plan (Sir John Sargeant was the Educational Adviser to the Government of India). This plan envisaged the establishment of elementary schools and high schools (junior and senior basic schools) and introduction of universal free and compulsory education for children between the ages of six and eleventh. The high schools were to be two types: (a) academic and (b) technical and vocational school with different curriculum. The addition of an extra year each at the high school and the college stages. The Sargeant Scheme envisaged a 40 year educational reconstruction plan for the country, which was reduced to 16 years by the Kher Committee.

Radhakrishnan Commission, 1944-49

In November 1948 the government of India appointed a commission under the chairmanship of Dr. Radhakrishnana to report on university education in the country and suggest improvements. The important recommendations of the report submitted in August 1949 were as follows:

1. Twelve years of pre-university educational course.
2. The working days at the university should not be less than 180 days in the year exclusive of examination days. These working days should be divided into three terms each of 11 weeks duration.

3. Higher education to have three main objectives: General Education, Liberal Education and Occupational Education. The first of these was to be specially emphasized for its importance has not been adequately recognized so far. More attention should be paid to subjects such as Agriculture, Commerce, Education, Engineering and Technology, Law and Medicine. The existing engineering and technical institutes should be looked upon as national assets and steps taken to improve them.
4. A university degree should not be considered as essential for the administrative services.
5. As three years are required to qualify for the first degree, it is not desirable that the work during the period should be judged by a single examination. As far as possible, examinations should be held subject-wise at different stages.
6. The examination standards should be raised and made uniform in all the universities and university education placed on the concurrent list.
7. The scales of pay of the university teachers should be raised.
8. A University Grants Commission should be set up to look after university education in the country.

University Grants Commission

In pursuance of the recommendation of the Radhakrishnan Commission, the University Grants Commission was constituted in 1953. The commission was given an autonomous statutory status by an act of Parliament in 1956. Most of the matters connected with the university education including the determination and co-ordination of standards and facilities for study and research have been committed to the care of this body. The Central Government annually places at the disposal of the University Grants Commission adequate funds from which grants are made to different universities and development schemes are implemented.

Yashpal Committee

Yashpal committee was appointed by the Government of India to enquire the status of higher education in India and to give its recommendation to the government. The Yashpal committee gives their recommendations in 2010. The important recommendations of the Yashpal committee are:

Yashpal committee was appointed by the Government of India to enquire the status of higher education in India and to give its recommendation to the government.

1. It should be necessary for all research bodies to connect with universities in their vicinity and create teaching opportunities for their researchers and far all universities to be teaching and research universities.
2. The committee recommends to introduce humanities and other disciplines to expand their scope to widen scope in literature, linguistics and politics.
3. The syllabi are to be designed with a view to induct the student into community of participant citizens, a new kind of institutional culture and ethos. It would include compulsory exposure and engagement with different kinds of work, in the form of

summer jobs or internships and according to circumstances and surroundings of the particular university.

4. There is a need to expose students especially at the undergraduate level to various disciplines like humanities, social sciences, in an integrated manner. This should be irrespective of discipline they would like to specialize in subsequently.
5. It should be mandatory for all universities to have a rich undergraduate programme and undergraduate students must get opportunities to interact with the best faculty.
6. It is necessary that all kinds of documents generated by the university including its syllabi, the papers, books published by its faculty, the assignments submitted by its students and other products such as audio-video material be treated as its knowledge products.
7. Purely private initiatives need a credible corrective mechanism to do away with the ills associated with it currently. All private institutions which seek the status of a university will have to submit a national accreditation system.
8. The primary focus should be on making education affordable either through scholarships or loans. It is duty of the institution and the states.
9. The commission recommended to create an all encompassing National Commission for Higher Education and Research (NCHER), a constitutional body to replace the existing regulatory bodies including the UGC, AICTE, NCTE and DEC.
10. Universities to be made responsible regarding the academic content of all courses and programmes of study including professional courses. The professional bodies like AICTE, NCTE, MCI, BCI COA, INC, PCI etc. to be divested of their academic functions.
11. Undergraduate programmes to be restructured to enable students to have opportunities to access all curricular areas with a fair degree of mobility. It is highly recommended that normally no single discipline or specialized university should be created.
12. The NCHER should also galvanize research in the university system through the creation of a National Research Foundation.
13. New governing structures to be evolved to enable the universities to preserve their autonomy in a transparent and accountable manner.
14. The NCHER should create several inter-university centre (IUCs) in diverse field to attract participation of several institutions of higher learning.
15. Institution of excellence like the IITs and IIMs to be encouraged to diversify and expand their scope to work as full-fledged universities.
16. The NCHER should identify the best 1500 colleges across India to upgrade them as universities and create clustes of other potentially good colleges to evolve as universities.
17. A national testing scheme for admission to the universities on the pattern of GRE to be evolved which would be open to all the aspirants to university education to be held more than once a year.

18. The government should establish a National Educational Tribunal with powers to adjudicate on disputes among state holders with in institution and between institutions to reduce litigation in court.

Development of Women Education

Radhakanta Deb, encouraged female education in Bengal and under his the Calcutta Female Society, came into being in 1819. He was aided by the Christian Missionary organization the Baptists. Miss Mary Cooke a western philanthropic mind, came down to Kolkata in 1821, being beckoned by the School Society. Her assignment was to collect funds and set up schools. Mary Cooke allied with the Church Missionary Society and gave shape to thirty schools for respectable Hindu girls. These schools flourished because of the Hindu social enthusiasts. Brahmin scholars emerged to be the faculty of these educational institutions. The Bethune School, owing its origin to the contribution of the British reformer, J.E. Drinkwater Bethune, reached the acme of perfection under the extraordinary guidance of the outstanding man of letters, Pundit Vidyasagar. The Bengali Medium School imparted secular education. The hallmark was that even the lowest class girls could access knowledge in this school.

By 1854, there were probably 626 girl's schools all over India. As per as the statistics reveal, Bengal was the leading female literate state of the then India, with 228 students. Next, was Madras with a count of 256. Bombay had a small number of only 65, while North West frontier and the Oudh, could project the handful amount of 17. The concerned institutions were invested with diminutive infrastructure. It should be noted, that although people by that time had started harbouring consent for female education, the larger part of the female community could not avail of the right of education, due to restrictions. The British's assertion of the woman question, enlightened society with the fundamental rights of women. The outcome was the influence of this question on the Indian intelligentsia. The inspired Hindu college Foundation Committee and the Hindu College graduates, were eager to enjoy the boon of modernization and to go ahead of their times, by circulating education among women. They understood that an educated woman can expertly handle individual and social matters and can partake of the responsibilities of life with her spouse, efficiently. This ideology probably worked behind the growing demand for educated brides as the right choice.

Keshab Chandra Sen, the new generation reformer of the Brahma Samaj, founded by Raja Rammohan, conducted the first Brahmo widow-remarriage in August 1862. His prime objective was the spread of female education. To take care of this major aspect of his projects, he built his Brahma Bandhu Sabha in 1863. He offered immense support to the arrangers of the *Bamabodhini Sabha* and *Bamabodhini Patrika* and directed the *Bama Hitaisini Sabha* (1871) on the route of the moral and material betterment of the wretched feminine group of society. Finally, the Brahmika Samaj was raised 1865, as the platform for women to share and enhance their religious knowledge, lessons on the art of stitching and discourse on social affairs. However, the sensitive issue of women's well-being caused a rift among the members of the Brahmo Samaj in 1866. Keshab Chandra Sen, distanced himself from the mainstream activities of the Adi Brahma Samaj, supervised by Debendranath

Tagore. Keshab formed his own organization called the *Navabidhan*. He invited Miss Mary Carpenter to Calcutta, to aid him to his mission of female learning. The deficiency of competent teachers attracted her attention. To attain a solution, she made several propositions before the then Govenor-General. This facilitated the spawning of the National Indian Association to usher in a reconcillation between the British authority and the native Indians, with regard to the course of actions to be followed. Dr. Atmaram Pandurang (1823-1898), enthralled by the motivational activities of Keshub Chandra Sen's Brahmo Samaj created the Prarthana Samaj in Bombay or present Mumbai. Prathana Samaj extended its helping hand to women's education. Arrangements of free libraries and classes were the immediate steps taken. Women and stdents associations continued their social revolution in an ordered manner.

In 1871, Keshub Sen and another English woman, Annettee Akroyd, together started a school. But shism in principles sprouted and Akryod joined the Sadharan Brahmo Samaj to open the Hindu Mahila Vidyalaya. Personalities like Brajakishore Basu, Shivanath Shastri, Durga Mohan Das, Dwarkanath Ganguly were the gems of this reputed group. In 1878 this school converged with the Bethune School to turn into Bethune College, affiliated to the educational authority of the Calcutta University. Bethune College provided opportunity to the pride of Indian womanhood, the first female graduates, Kadambini Basu and Chandramukhi Basu. These brilliant women obtained their Bachelors Degree from Bethune College. Kadambani Bose (Kadambini Ganguly, after marriage to the great emancipator, Dwarkanath Ganguly), pursued higher education and emerged to be the first lady doctor of the nation. In Madras, it was the diligent Annie Besent and her Theosophical Society, which proclaimed aloud, the significance of female learning. Annie, a self independent women was very much vocal, about the early Vedic society, when education and free mobility of women, in the spheres of society was the order of the day asserted that in ancient times Hindu women were educated and moved freely in society. She aimed at a revival of this golden age. Besant's campaign for women's suffrage in 1874 here demonstration of New Unionism in her crusade against the misery of the London match-stick factory-girls in 1888, had already won her international acclaim as the Feminist freedom-fighter.

Madame Blavatsky, one of the founders of the Theosophical Society strongly condemned child marriage, child widowhood, as abominable perverted practice of Hindu beliefs. Besant adored Blavatsky as her ideal and stressed her views in the article 'Education of Women' in the Indian Women's Magazine. Besant opined that India would degenerate into a future of bleakness and nothingness, if women remains in ignorance. She modeled Indian womanhood on the iconic female figure of the Goddess Durga. Her ardent fervor got its manifestation in the women's college, that sprung as per as her principles pledged her efforts to this reform and founded a women's college based on these principles.

Arya Samaj directed the course of female education in North India. Its chief was the visionary Swami Dayanand Saraswati. Towards the close of the nineteenth century, the broad-minded Arya Samajists realized the necessity of incorporating female participation in the grave task of reforms. An allied body to the Arya Samaj the Jullandhar Samaj inaugurated the Arya Kanya Pathshala (Girls School) in 1890 with a lady principal to regulate the work-process. It was succeeded by the maing of the Kanya Mahavidyalaya (Girls Higher

School) of Jullandhar. The dormant structures of these academic centers and the elementary girls school were cemented into conspicuous learning sites in 1892 by the benevolent Lala Devraj. Lala Devraj was that true Karma Yogi or selfless worker who gave space for the growth of girls school in his family abode. We are bound to salute him with respect, when we discover that this salvager used to sell waste paper to collect money for running the school. Even the food that he used to provide to the instructors, working in the school was prepared by the equally devoted mother of Lala Devraj. Slowly with time more and more people started responding to the upheaval of women's improvement. And this premier institution became a catalyst for various kinds of change relating to women in Punjab. One must understand that this rising cult of feminity was a vital aspect of Indian nationalist ideology during the freedom struggle. Female education flowered under the increasing impetus generated from the widened mental horizon of the indigenous Mahatmas (great souls), committed to the architecture of a new reformed society, which would pay women the respect and freedom they deserve.

Right of Children to Free and Compulsory Education

The act provides free schooling to children as a fundamental right. The important provision of the Act are:

1. Every child of the age of six to fourteen years shall have a right to free and compulsory education in a neighbourhood school till completion of elementary education.
2. No child shall be liable to pay any kind of fee or charges or expenses which may prevent him or her from pursuing and completing the elementary education.
3. Where a child is required to move from one school to another either within a state or outside for any reason whatsoever, such child shall have a right to seek transfer to any other school.
4. The central government and the state government shall have concurrent responsibility for providing funds for carrying out the provision of this act.
5. The responsibility of the government shall be:
   - (*i*) Provide free elementary education to every child of the age six to fourteen years.
   - (*ii*) Ensure compulsory admission, attendance and completion of elementary education by every child of six to fourteen years.
   - (*iii*) To ensure availability of a neighbourhood school.
   - (*iv*) Ensure that child belonging to weaker section and the child belonging to disadvantaged group are not discriminated against and prevented from pursuing and completing elementary education on any group.
   - (*v*) Provide special training facilities to teachers.
   - (*vi*) Ensure and monitor admission, attendance and complete elementary education to every child.
   - (*vii*) Ensure good quality education.
6. No child shall be subjected to physical punishment or mental harassment.

Suggested Question

1. What are the important features of Varna system? How was it converted into caste system? Define merits and demerits of the caste system.
2. 'The Ashrams are developed on idea of specialization and division of labour'. Define the Ashramas in context of above statement.
3. Samskaras are rituals to guide the human beings social life. Explain.
4. What are the important features of the Guild (shreni) origanisation? How some of its features are relevant for modern economy?
5. The early system of education was developed to provide the holistic approach to human being as a member of society. Explain.
6. The modern education initiated by East India Company was to create a new class of bureaucracy loyal to British. Justify the statement.

References

1. Chopra P.N, Puri B.N. & Das M.N. *A Social, Cultural and Economic History of India*, (3 Vol), Delhi, 1974.
2. Majumdar R.C. (ed) *The Vedic Age*, Bombay, 1954
3. Majumdar R.C. (ed) *The Age of Imperial Unity*, Bombay, 1954
4. Bhattacharya, Haridas, *The Cultural Heritage of India*, (6 Vol.), Calcutta, 1937.
5. Ahuha Ram, *Indian Social System*, New Delhi, 2005.
6. Indradeva & Shrirama, *Society and Culture in India*, New Delhi, 1999.
7. Dubois, A.J.A., *Hindu Manners, Customs & Ceremonies*, Delhi (reprint), 1999.
8. Grover B.L. & Grover S., *A New Book on Modern Indian History*, Delhi,1990.
9. Report of Yashpal Committee, Government of India.
10. Document on The Right of Children to Free and Compulsory Education Act 2009, Government of India, Gazettee.

9 CHAPTER

MODERN SOCIAL INSTITUTIONS IN INDIA

The family, as an institution is *universal*. It is the most permanent and the most pervasive of all social institutions. All societies both large and small, primitive and civilized, ancient and modern have some form of family. The word *Family* has been taken over from Latin word *Famulus* which means a servant. In other way it denotes a group of producers and slaves and other servants as well as members connected by common descent or marriage. Thus, originally, family consisted of a man and a woman with a child or children and servants. The meaning of family can be explained better by the following definition: MacIver says *Family is a group defined by sex relationship sufficiently precise and enduring to provide for the procreation and upbringing of children.*

Family is a group defined by sex relationship sufficiently precise and enduring to provide for the procreation and upbringing of children.

General Characteristics of the Family

A family comes into existence when a man and woman establish relation between them. Wife or husband may be selected by parents or by the elders or the choice may be left to the wishes of the individuals concerned. Various rules govern this selection. The mating relationship is established thought the institution of marriage. Marriage is an institutional arrangement made by the society according to which the individuals establish marital relationships among themselves. Marriage may assume any one of the forms – monogamy, polygamy or group marriage. Every family is known or recognized by a distinctive name. Family requires a home or a household to live in. After the marriage the wife may reside in husband's parental home. *(Patrilocal or Virilocal Residence)* or she may stay in her parental home to which the husband pays occasional visits *(Matrilocal or Uxorilocal Residence)* or both of them may establish a separate home of their own *(Neolocal Residence)*. Family provides for the satisfaction of the economic needs of its members. There is no human society in which some form of the family does not appear nor has there ever been such a society. The family is grounded in emotions and sentiments. It is based on our impulses of mating, procreation, material devotion, fraternal love and parental care. The family is the nucleus of all other social organizations. The family is peculiarly guarded both by social taboo and by legal regulations. The society takes precaution to safeguard this organization from any possible break down by divorce, desertion or separation.

FORMS OF THE FAMILY

Matriarchal Family

The matriarchal family is also known as the mother centred or mother dominated family.

The matriarchal family is also known as the mother centred or mother dominated family. The mother or the woman is the head of the family and she exercises authority. The matriatrchal family has been the earliest type of family. On this basis it is known that matriatchal are the Khasi tribals of India and others. In it descent is traced through the mother. Hence it is *matrilineal descent.* Daughters inherit the property of the mother. Matriarchal family is *matrilocal in residence.* After the marriage the wife stays back in her mother's house. The husband, who normally stays in his sister's house, pays occasional visits to the wife's house. The mother exercises authority and power in the matriarchal family. She is the head of the family and her decisions are final. The maternal family brings together the kinsman (the wife, her mother and grandmother, her children and brothers etc.) and welds them together into a powerful group.

Patriarchal Family

The patriarchal family is also known as father centered or father dominated family.

The patriarchal family is also known as father centered or father dominated family. Here, the father or the eldest man is the head of the family and he exercises authority. These are recognized through the male line. Patriarchal families are *partilineal* in character, because the descent is traced through the male line. Here only the male children inherit the property of the father. Patriarchal family is *Patrilocal* in residence. Sons continue to stay with the father in his own house even after their marriages. Only the wives come and join them. Here the father or the eldest male member of the family is the dominant person. All the member are subordinated to him. He dedicates terms for other members. All the major decisions pertaining to the family affairs are taken by him only.

The Nuclear Family

It can be defined as a small group composed of husband and wife and immature children which constitutes a unit apart from the rest of the community.

It can be defined as a small group composed of husband and wife and immature children which constitutes a unit apart from the rest of the community. Nuclear family is one which consists of the husband, wife and their children. Soon after their marriage, the children leave their parental home and establish their separate household. Nuclear family is an autonomous unit free from the control of the elders. Since there is physical distance between parents and their married children, there is minimum interdependence between them. A nuclear family is mostly independent. The nuclear family is a characteristic of all the modern industrial societies. The nuclear family has been performing the sexual, the economic, the reproductive and the educational functions.

Nuclear Family

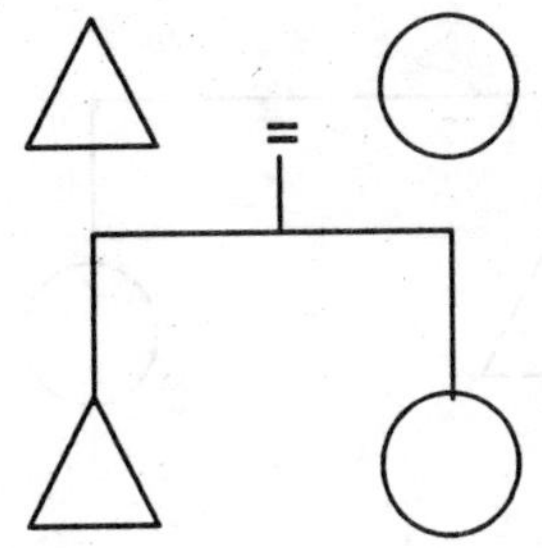

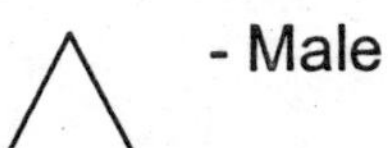

Joint Family

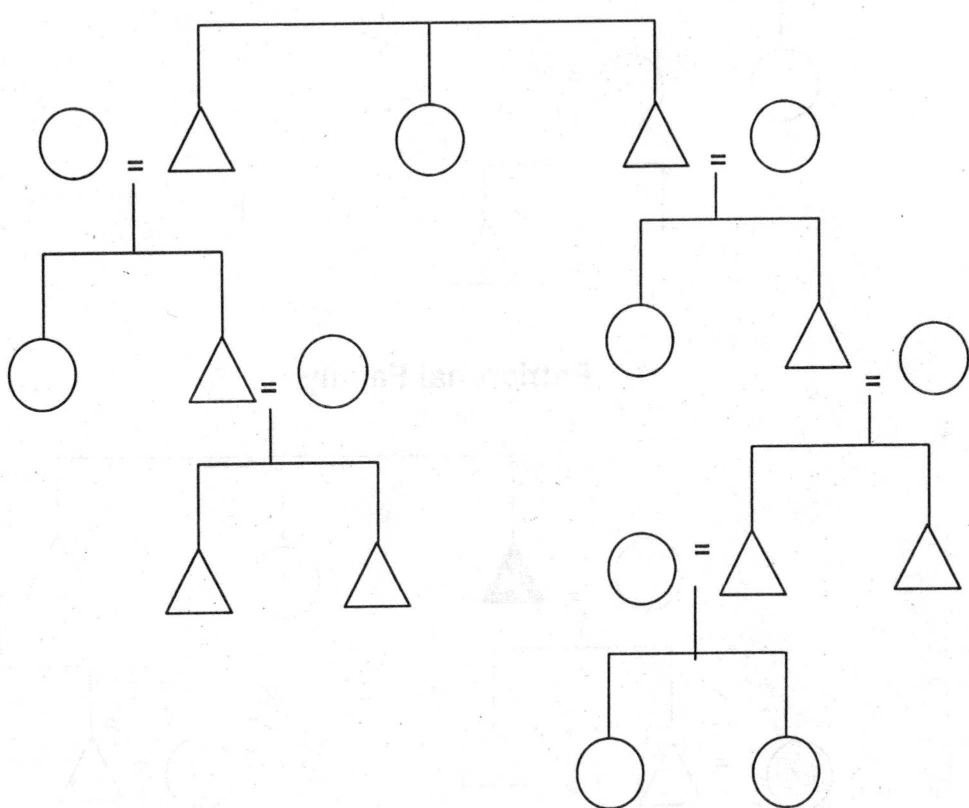

Matriarchal Family

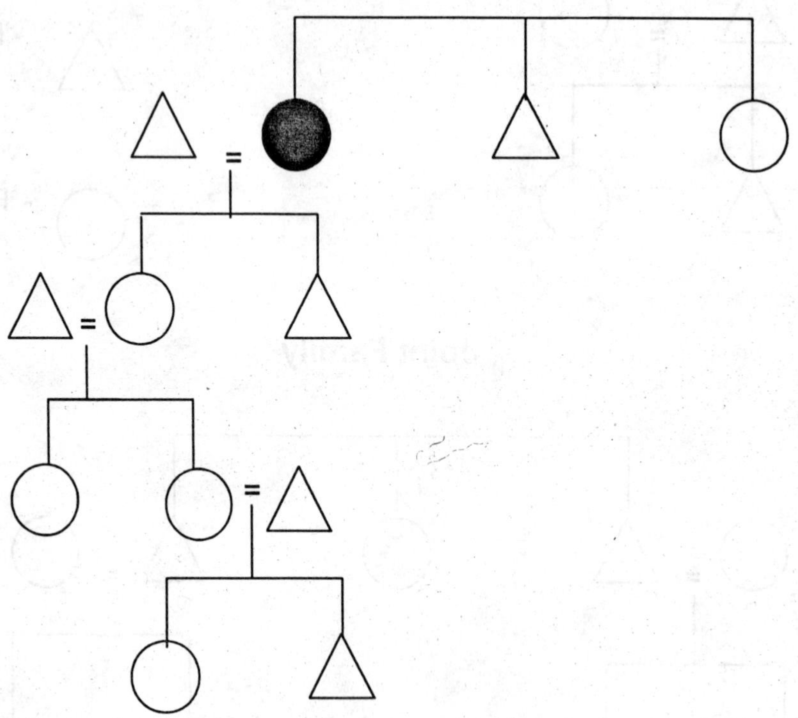

Patriarchal Family

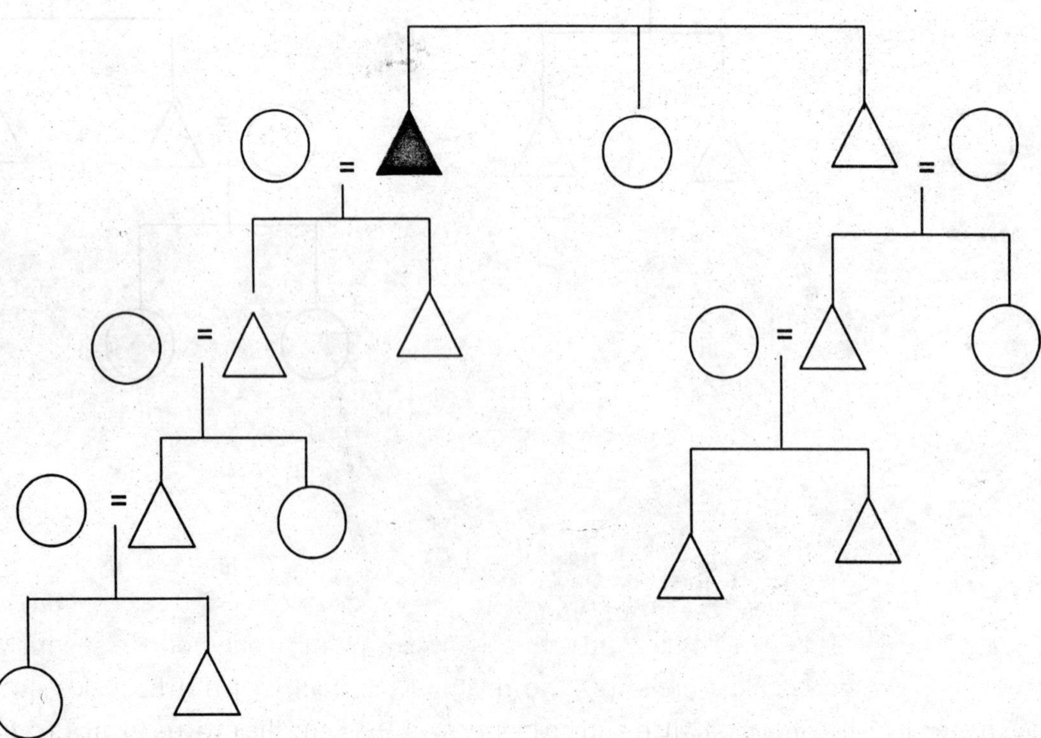

Changing Pattern of Family

Jointness of family in India is not disappearing. Instead of large joint families, there have only locally functioning effective small joint families of two generations or so. A nuclear fissioned family (of husband, wife and unmarried children) will not be totally independent but will be functionally dependent on (i.e., remain joint with) some primary kin like father or brother. The joint relations are mostly confined to parents-children, siblings and uncles and nephews, i.e., lineal relationship is found between father, son and grandson, and the collateral relationship is found between a man and his brothers and uncles. In the rural community, the proportion of joint families is almost the same as that of the nuclear families. Viewed in terms of castes, in villages, higher castes have predominantly joint family while lower castes show a greater incidence of nuclear family. In the urban community, there are more joint families than nuclear families. In the impact villages (i.e. villages within the radius of 7 to 8 km from a town), the family pattern closely resembles the rural pattern and has no correspondence with the urban pattern. Taking all studies on structural changes in family together, it is found:

1. The number of fissioned families is increasing but even living separately, they fulfil their traditional obligations towards their parental families.
2. There is more jointness in traditional (rural) communities and more nuclearity in communities exposed to forces of industralisation, urbanization and westernization.
3. The size of the (traditional) joint family has become smaller.
4. So long the old cultural values persist among people, the functional type of joint family will sustain in our society.
5. Changes from traditional to transitional family include trends toward new-local residence, functional jointness, equality of individuals, equal status for women, increasing opportunity to individual members to achieve their aspirations and the weakening of family norms.

The important values which sustained joint family structure are; (1) Filial devotion of sons (2) Lack of economic viability of some brothers, i.e., their inability to support their children economically (3) Lack of a state organized system of social security for the old age men and women (4) A material incentive for organizing the size of labour unit since it constituted the major share of the capital required for production of goods and services and people had to depend on family labour.

The factors which are now breaking the joint family are : (1) Differential earnings of brothers generating tensions in the family, as the unit of production and service today is predominantly an individual. Up to a point, the values the members inculcate may enable them to subside tension by mutual adjustment and compromise but brothers separate when they focus on the conjugal units. (2) The death of the 'root couple' who holds economic power and inability, incompetence and self interest of sons and their wives to take up the role of 'parental couple'. (3) Incentive of depending on family labour is disappearing with the emergence of a cash nexus. (4) System of social security, savings and extended earning opportunities of the people are leading to nuclearisation of joint family structures. The changes in intra-family relations may be examined at three levels: husband-wife relations, parental-filial relations and relations between daughter-in-law and parents-in-law. In traditional family wife had no voice in family decision-making. But in contemporary family, in budgeting the family expenditure, in disciplining the children, in purchasing goods and giving gifts, the wife now credits herself as equal in power role. Though husband continues to play the *instrumental* role and wife the *expressive* role, yet both often talk things over and consult each other in the process of arriving at a decision. The assumption of economic role and the education of wife has made wives potential equals. The source of power has shifted from culture to resource, where resource is something that one partner may make available to the other helping the latter satisfy his/her needs or attain his/her goals. As such, the balance of power will be on the side of that partner who contributes greater resources to the marriage. It indicated that compared to middle-class families, working class families are more role segregated or autonomic, i.e. working class families have less joint husband-wife activity of all types. It also means that in middle class families, both husband and wife take more active part than the working class families in attempting to direct the behavior of the family group toward solution of the problem.

Emphasising resources factor does not mean that culture has lost its importance. In fact, both factors are important today in conjugal bonds. It may thus be averred that though an average Indian family is husband dominant yet the *ideological* source of power of women is giving place to a *pragmatic* one. In urban areas, wife going with husband for social visits, taking food with husband or even before he does, going together to restaurants and movies etc., indicate increasing companion role of wife. Husband no longer regards his wife as inferior to him or devoid of reasoning but consults her and trusts her in serious matters. As regards closeness of man to his wife and mother, man particularly the educated one, is now equally close to both. The relations between parents *and* children may be assessed in terms of holding authority freedom of discussing problems, opposition of parents by children and modes of imposing penalty. In traditional family, while power and authority was totally vested in the patriarch and he was virtually all powerful who decided everything about education, occupation, marriage and the career of children in the family but in contemporary family, both in nuclear and in joint family, the grandfather has lost his authority. The authority has shifted from patriarch to parents who consult their children on all important issues before taking any decisions about them. Children have also started discussing their problems with parents. They even oppose their parents. Some legislative measures have also given powers to children to demand their rights. Perhaps, it is because of all this that parents do not use old methods of punishing their children. They use economic and psychological methods (denying money, scolding, restricting freedom, reasoning) more than the physical methods. In spite of these changes in relations between parents and children, the children do not think only of their rights and privileges but also of the welfare of parents and siblings. They respect and fear their elders. The relations between *daughter-in-law and parents-in-law* have also undergone change. However, this change is not so significant in daughter-in-law and mother-in-law (DIL-MIL) relations as in daughter-in-law and father-in-law (DIL-FIL) relations. The educated DIL does not observe *purdah* from her FIL and discusses not only the family problems but also the social and even the political issues. Taking all three types of relations (husband-wife, parents-children, and DIL-FIL) together, it may be said: (1) Younger generation now claims more individuality. (2) Consanguineous relationship does not have primacy over conjugal relationship (3) Along with culture and ideological factor the resource factor also affects relations.

Future of Indian Family

The perspective on family in India is usually developed on the conceptual scale of tradition to modernity by undertaking either opinion-surveys of youths or general public belonging to different forms of family structure or making socio-economic surveys of people of different castes and classes in the rural and the urban areas. The two structures (joint and nuclear) will continue to survive. Only the nature of jointness will change from residential to functional one and the size of joint family will shrink to two or three generations. As regards the future of family (as an institution), it may four factors affecting the family: (a) *technological revolution:* access to such conveniences as electricity, piped water in homes, intricate home appliances like gas and fridge, telephone, buses and other vehicles have all changed common man's living and raised his standard of life. Effects of the industrial-technological changes on family are quite evident, like those of productive functions, abandonment of self-sufficiency in family economy, occupational and population mobility, weakening of kinship ties, and so forth (b) *population revolution:* shift from agriculture to manufacturing and service, migration from rural to urban areas, decrease in birth and death rates, increase in average expectation of life and availability of elderly persons in family, replacement of early marriages by post puberty and late marriages etc., have created problems of readjustment, changes in power structure, desire for smaller families and so on (c) *democratic revolution:* ideals of democracy have filtered down to the level of family living. Demand of rights by women, emancipation of children from patriarch's authority, willingness to approach decision making through democratic process and change from familism to individualism may be described as important trends in family and (d) *secular revolution:* there is a shift away from religious values to rational values. Change in wife's attitude towards husband, demand for divorce in case of maladjustment, children's reluctance to support parents in old age, elimination of family worship are all the result of rational thinking and deviation from moral and religious norms. Therefore, several dominant trends in Indian family in the last few decades, as (1) Increasing importance of nuclear family. (2) Transference of some functions e.g., educational, recreational, protective, etc. to some other institutions. (3) Fundamental change in family age structure, i.e., proportionately fewer children to care for and proportionately more elderly persons surviving. (4) Freedom to women due to their education and increasing economic independence. (5) Declining reliance of children upon family controls. (6) Changing values of youth. Though they have respect for and fear of parents yet they want parental support for achieving their individual interests. (7) Liberalisation of attitudes and practices towards sex (8) Change from pre-puberty to post-puberty marriages. (9) Decreasing family size. These characteristics of the present day Indian family point out change in structure and family ties.

These family trends are an ongoing process. The following possible changes in Indian family can be judged:

1. The family will continue to exist. It will not be replaced by state controlled systems of reproduction and child bearing.
2. Its stability will depend more on interpersonal bonds than on social pressures from outside or upon kinship loyalty.
3. It will more depend upon community support and services.
4. With medical advances, the family will have greater control over its biological processes (of separating sexual from reproductive function, controlling sickness or death, and determining sex of the offspring).
5. Remarriage and divorce rates will be high.
6. Parents and grandparents will continue to support their children and grandchildren even after their retirement.
7. Woman's position of power within the family will further improve with increase in gainful employment.
8. Viewed generally, the family will not be equalitarian but will remain husband-dominant family.

STATUS OF WOMEN

The women has been discribed by our holy books, as mothers, as creators and sustainers of life on earth. The women have some special duties to perform, some special paths to follow, some special ideals to strive after. Womens of India have been eternally inspired by the common twin ideals of unity and equality, greatness and fullness, purity and perfection. But inspite of the fact that the fundamental tendencies and strivings have also to recognize individual differences and peculiarities befitting the special inclinations and capacities of different persons. For women also India has recognized two main ideals, viz. that of a *brahmavadini* and that of a *sadyovadhu.* A *brahmavadini* is of an ascetic type, striving for the highest philosophical knowledge: knowledge of Truth, of the Self of Brahman. Thus her ideal of life is spiritual well-being. A *sadyovadhu* is of a domestic type, dedicating herself to the welfare of her family and spending her time mostly in daily domestic duties of an ordinary kind. Each one was great in then own place.

The very high standard of learning culture and all-round progress reached by Indian women during the Vedic Age is a well known fact, the *Rig-Veda* contains hymns *(suktas)* by as many as twenty seven women, called *brahmavadinis* or women seers. Saunaka in his *Brihaddevata* (c. fifth century B.C.), a work on the *Rig-Veda,* has mentioned the names of these twenty seven women seers.The well known Vedic commentrator Sayana has mentioned the names of two more of such seers in addition to the above. During the Vedic Age domestic life was not in any way be inconsistent with spiritual life.

In the Upanisads, *brahmavadini* Gargi had immortal fame, daughter of the Sage Vacaknu, whose highly learned, philosophical discussions with the great sage Yajnavalkya have been recorded twice in the old and celebrated *Brihadaranyaka Upanisad.* The glorious example of a *sadyovadhu* too, is found in the same Upanisad. When the Sage Yajnavalkya on the eve of his retirement from the world desired to divide his property between his two wives Maitreyi and Katyayani, Maitreyi refused to have it with the profound utterance, "What should I do with that through which I cannot be immortal?," Which has really made her immortal. Accordingly, she was given the choicest gift of knowledge by her husband in a most illuminating discourse on the unity of the self. In the Rig-Vedic Grihya-Sutras of Asvalayana and Sankhayana the names of three *brahmavadinis* are mentioned, viz. Gargi Vacakanavi, Vadava Prathitheyi and Sulabha Maitreyi.

The age of Panini (fifth century B.C.) continued the Vedic tradition of culture and education. Those *brahmavadinis* who themselves taught were reverentially called *upadhyaya or upadhyayi and acharya,* while the *sadyovadhus* who were wives of teachers were called *upadhyayani and acharyani.* Women scholars of the Katha School were called *Kathi* of the *Rig-Veda, Bahavrca* Brahmana women scholars of the Grammar of Apisali were called *Apisali* and of the Mimamsa School of Kasakrtsna, Kasakrtsna (Patanjali). Pupils of the woman scholar and teacher Audamedhya were called *Audamedha.* The *Ramayana* and the *Mahabharata* find many instances of the above two types of Indian women, ascetic and domestic. A *brahmavadini* in the *Ramayana* is Anasuya, wife, in the truest sense of the term, of the Sage Atri. Another celebrated woman ascetic of the *Ramayana* is sramani sabari, a low caste. She was the discipline of the great sage Matanga and had her hermitage on the bank of the lake Pampa. The highest manifestation of domestic perfection in the *Ramayana* found in the inimitable personality of Sita, the idol of Indian womanhood throughout the *ages.* Sita as wife, as mother, as one endowed with infinite purity of heart, strength of character, courage and confidence. The *Mahabharata,* too, mentions a galaxy of great women fulfilling their destinies, pursuing their ideals and attaining their ends in different spheres of life in a manner once simple and superb. *Brahmavadinis* of the *Mahabharata* are the daughter of Sandilya described as a *brahmani* who has attained perfection, who has adopted the vow of celibacy and purity, who practices *yoga* who has reached heaven, who has attained perfection in austerity and who is an ascetic. Mention need be made only of Gandhari, Kunti, Draupadi, Savitri, Damayanti, Sakuntala and Satyabhama amongst a great galaxy of noble women who, though housewives, were also reputed scholars and saintly characters. The single case of Gandhari proves what heights of excellence wifehood and motherhood could reach. Her superb injunction: *Yato dharma tato jayah* (Let Victory pertain to the righteous), has become a proverb in India. She was Vidula, who sternly reprimanded her son Sanjaya when he, being defeated by the king of Sind was leading a life of abject dejection. She used the following classic simile: *Muhutam jvalitam sreyali, na tu dhumayitam ciram* (It is far better to blaze up even for a moment than to go on smoking continuously). One of the most celebrated women of the Puranas is Madalasa, the consort of King Ritadhvaja. She was once a great scholar, a saintly woman, a dutiful housewife, and a devoted wife and mother.

The position of women in India gradually deteriorated as the golden Vedic ideals of unity and equality began to fade off. During the period of the Smrtis, women were bracketed with the Sudras and were denied the right to study the Vedas, to utter Vedic *mantras* and to perform Vedic rites. Marriage or domestic life became compulsory for women and unquestioning devotion to and self effacing service of husbands their only duty. A woman is protected by her father during childhood, by her husband during youth and by her sons during old age. She is never fit for freedom. But mothers were honoured, as before, as the very pivots of their famiies and wives as *sahadharminis* or spiritual partners of their spouses. Princess Rajyasri, daughter of Rajyavardhana, king of thaneswar, grew up in the company of friends, expert in song and dance. Girls received their education at home with the help of teachers engaged by their parents. Women, particularly of the middle and upper classes, could read and write.

In A.D. 1058 a lady named Mamaka, wife of Dhanesvara, professing the Mahayana system of Buddhism, caused a copy of the *Astasahasrika* to be written-in the Saddharma-cakra-pravartana Mahavihara at Sarnath Ketaladevi, queen of the Calukya Vikramaditya VI (A.D. 1076-1125) of the Deccan, was called Abhinava Sarasvati for her literary achievement. Silabhattarika composed poems in the Pancali style in which ther is a graceful harmony of sense and sound. The Poetess Vijayanka of Karnata was considered equal to Sarasvati and again as second only to Kalidasa. The poems of Devi, a poetess of Lata (southern Gujarat) are said to have soothed the heart of the people long after her death. Avantisundari, wife of the well known poet Rajasekhara, was a literary critic and also earned reputation as a poetess. Balapandita daughter of the Poet Dhanapala, was a poetess of great merit. About this time a poetess named Sita lived in the court of Paramara Bhoja. She composed songs eulogizing the achievements of Upendra, the founder of the Paramara dynasty. Other poetesses of this age included Bhavadevi, Rajakasarasvati, Sarasvati, Vikatanitamva, Phalguhastini, Marula, Morika and Vijjaka whose poems have been quoted in the anthologies. A lady named Rusa wrote a medical book on the diseases of women, which was translated into Arabic in the eighth century. Tradition relates that Mandana Misra's wife Ubhayabharati (Sarada or Sarasvani) served as an umpire when there was a religious debate between her husband and Sankaracharya.

The marriageable age of a girl as given by Daksa, Angiras, Yama and Parasara varies from eight to twelve. The father of a girl who fails to observe it is deemed to have committed a great sin. Bana relates that King Prabhakaravardhana of Tahaneswar became anxious for the marriage of his daughter when she was nearing maturity. Al Biruni (A.D. 1030) remarks that the Brahmanas in India married girls twelve years old. Mrnalavati, the sister of Taila II (A.D. 997), king of the Deccan, remained unmarried even when she was mature in age. In royal families girls were sometimes given chance to select their husbands in an assembly of kings *(svayamvara-sabha).* The Cahamana Mahendra, king of Marwar, organized a *svayamvara-sabha* for the marriage of his daughter. The Chalukya Vikramaditya VI of the Deccan was selected as her husband by the Silahara princess Chandralekha in such a *sabha.* Ordinarily, the selection of the bridegroom was made by the girl's father, maternal uncle, agnates, or cognates. A girl having no such relatives could according to Narada select a bridegroom of her own choice with the consent of the king. Married women used vermilion. Women also used turmeric, saffron, *kajjala* (lamp black for the eye), betel, auspicious ornaments and articles for keeping the hair in order. Prabhakaravardhana's daughter Rajyasri put on a veil when she met her husband, the Maukhari Grahavarman of Kanauj, for the first time. In the *Kadambari* Patralckha is described as wearing a veil of red cloth. This was, however, not the general custom. Dhoyi, the author of the twelfth century poetical work the *Pavanaduta,* relates that the women of Vijayapura did not observe the *purdah* system. The Arab geographer Abu Zaid (ninth century) reports that most princes in India allow their women to be seen when they hold their court. No veil conceals them from the eyes of the visitors. The contemporary law books and the Pusranas give us pictures of the ideal wife. She was the mainstay of the domestic life and was a source of happiness. She took care of the family deity and entertained the guests. She rose before the others, paid reverence to the elders of the family and prepared food and condiments. She worked hard like a slave, offered food like a mother and gave advice like a counselor in adversity. She was absolutely devoted to her husband. It is stated that as the body is purified by an ablution in the Ganga, so a house is purified by the existence of a *pativrata* (chaste wife). Wives were to be protected by their husbands from evil. The husbands were advised to achieve this end by being devoted to them and not by beating and tyrannizing over them. Women would participate in the religious activities of their husbands. Vilasadevi, queen of Vijayasena (1095-1158) of Bengal, performed in the palace of Vikrampura a homa (offering in the fire) in which gold equivalent to a person's weight was given away. The Gahadavala Govindacandra (A.D. 1114-1156) of Kanauj had a number of queens, of whom two were Buddhists. The Pala king Madanapala (c. A.D. 1150) who was a Buddhist, granted land to the Brahmana Vatesvara Svamin as his fee for reading out the Mahabharata before his queen Chitramatikadevi. Macikabbe the wife of the Ganga Marasimha, who was a Saiva, adopted asceticism and meditating on the Jaina attained salvation by fasting. The Chalukya Jayasimha II Jagadekamalla (A.D. 1015-1043), who was a Jain, is said to have been converted to the Saiva faith by his queen Suggaladevi. Women do not seem to have suffered any religious disabilities. The Princess Pambabbe, sister of the Western Ganga Butuga II (A.D. 971), devoted her life to practicing penance for thirty years. Many women entered the Buddhist church as nuns. The Smrti writers of this period do not advocate the abandoning of the wife by the husband for adultery, but on the contrary allow her to regain all her normal rights after performance of the appropriate penance. The woman was to be abandoned only if she had conceived as the result of the adultery. Some Smrtis and Puranas of this period condemn women for their moral lapses. Women in general, says Varahamihira (c. A.D. 500), are pure and blameless, they deserve the highest honour and respect.

Al Biruni also observes that a woman in India has to choose between two things after the death of her husband, either to burn herself or to remain a widow till her death. The authorities, however, prohibit those wives who have not attained the age of puberty are pregnant or have children very young from becoming a *sati.* Al Biruni similarly reports that women of advanced age and those who had children did not burn themselves. As the merchant Sulaiman (ninth century) says the choice as to whether a woman would burn herself or not lay entirely with her. The practice of the *sati* rite can be traced with the help of historical records throughout this period. The wife of Goparaja, the general of the Gupta king Bhanugupta, is known to have ascended the funeral pyre of her husband in A.D. 510. Queens of Kashmir and Queen Rajyavati of Nepal (eighth century) performed the sati rite. Gundambe, the wife of Nagadeva, a minister of the Calukya Satyasraya of the Deccan (tenth century) burnt herself with her husband, who had lost his life in battle. Harsavardhan's mother Yasomati, however, burnt herself to ashes as soon as it became definite that her husband would be passing away within a short time. The practice of performing the *sati* rite was evidently not universal. Many well-known ladies of this period, such as Prabhavatidevi (of the Vakataka dynasty of the Deccan), Mayanalladevi (mother of Jayasimha Siddharaja of Gujarat), Karpuradevi (mother of the Cahamana Prthviraja III of Ajmer), and Alhanadevi (mother of the Kalacuri Narasimha of Tripuri), did not practice this rite and at the same time were highly esteemed for their devotion to their husbands.

Under the rules of the Smrtis a widow had to lead an austere life. She slept on the floor and was not allowed to use a cot. She did not put on a bodice and dyed garments and did not use collyrium in the eyes and yellow pigment on the face nor any kind of scent. She took only one meal a day. She made oblations every day in memory of her husband and listened to recitations of the Puranas. Bana in his *Harsacharita* refers to the tying of the tuft of hair by the widows. Similarly, a Prathihara inscription of the early tenth century from Pehowa (in the Karnal District of West Punjab), mentions widows having profuse locks of hair. On the other hand, the *Skanda Purana* advocates to tonsuring of widows. The re-marriage of widows is not advocated by the Smrti writers and Puranas. Again, Al Biruni states that in India there is no custom of re-marrying the widow. In Gujarat, up to the middle of the twelfth century, the property of a person dying without a son escheated to the crown, but the Caulukya Kumarapala king of Gujarat, abolished that custom and allowed the sonless widow to inherit her hushand's property.

Women occasionally participated in the public administration as rulers, regents and governors. In the first half of the eighteenth century, the Deccan was ruled by Queen Ratta. About a century earlier, the same country is found to have been administered by Vijayabhattarika of the Calukya dynasty. Sugadha and Didda ruled Kashmir for some time in the tenth century A.D. Tribhuvanamahadevi and her granddaughter Dandimahadevi of the Kara dynasty ruled in Orissa in the eleventh century. The Kakatiya Rudramba occupied the throne of Warangal for some time in the thirteenth century. Marco Polo describes her as a lady of much discretion. She administered her kingdom efficiently, she was a lover of justice, equality and peace. Queen Ballamahadevi ruled the Alupa country (South Kanara) from the capital Varahakanya in the thirteenth century. Queen Mayanalladevi acted as a regent for her son the Caulukya Jayasimha Siddharaja of Gujarat. Karpuradevi, queen of the Cahamana Somesvara of Ajmer, served as a regent for her son Prthviraja III. Nayikadevi carried on the administration of Gujarat as a regent during the infancy of her son, the Caulukya Bhima II. Akkadevi, sister of the Calukya Jayasimha II of the Deccan, acted as the governor of Kisukad. Women also acted as ministers and judges occasionally. Queens Siryadevi and Mahaladevi flourished in Bhor, Bombay, in the last quarter of the eleventh century. A lady named Somanathaiya acted as a minister of Siryadevi and another lady named Balaiya occupied the post of a judge under Mahaladevi. Sometimes women are found leading the army in the battlefield. Akkadevi, is described as fierce in battle and in destroying hostile kings. Some time before A.d. 1047, at the head of an army, she laid siege to the fort of Gokage, modern Gokak, in the Belgaum District. In A.d. 1197 a lady named Umadevi invaded Belagavatti, in the Shimoga District, Mysore, when it was ruled by the feudatory Madhavarasa. Cagaladevi, wife of a feudatory of Toragale, led in person an attack on the town of Nilagunda n the Deccan. In A.d. 1178, when Gujarat was invaded by Mohammed Ghor, Nayikadevi, taking her infant son Caulukya Bhima II in her lap, conducted the army against the invader and inflicted a servere defeat on him.

Ma Twan Lin says that in the houses of the Indians the young girls danced and sang with great skill. The statement of Brhaspati that a woman must avoid dancing when her husband is abroad shows the popularity of this art. Among the festivities at the birth of Harsavardhana, dancing by women of all ranks formed a prominent feature, as described by Bana. Dancing was to the accompaniment of musical instruments, such as tambourines, cymbals, reeds, lutes and *kahalas* (drums) with their brazen sounding boxes. The Ganga Udayaditya's queen was expert in dancing and singing. All the three queens of the Hoysala Ballala I were highly accomplished in dancing. Savaladevi, the queen of the Kalacuri Somadeva of Kalyana, was well known for her skill in music and dancing and is said to have displayed her accomplishments in public. During this period dancing girls known as *devadasis* were engaged for temple services. Four hundred of them were attached to the great temple of Tanjore during the reign of the Cola Rajaraja I. Bhattabhavadev, minister of King Harivarman of East Bengal, gave a hunded dancing girls for the service of the temple of Ananta Vasudeva. About as many were engaged in the temple of Siva at Deopara, in the Rajshahi District, East Bengal during the reign of Vijayasena. Padmavati was the chief of the dancing girls in the temple of Nilakanthesvara at Kalanjara during the reign of the Candella Madanavarman. These girls are generally described as living an immoral life. The dancing girls were known to have enacted dramas occasionally. During the reign of Jatavarman *alias* Vira Pandya of South India, a dancing girl named Virasekharanangai received grants of lands for enacting dramas on festive occasions.

(II)

According to our age-old Indian tradition, there is no distinction between man and women, all being equally Brahman. It is also asserted in some places with due dignity that no *distinction many evils* crept into medieval society and since leadership in the political field had passed into the hands of an alien race, no well-thought out attempt was made. Political and social circumstances compelled a father, at least among the Hindus, to have his daughter married as early as possible. Custom forbade girls to remain the the house of their parents for more than six to eight years from birth. According to Mukundarama, the author of the famous poem *Chandi-mangala,* composed in the sixteenth century, a father who could give his daughter in marriage in her ninth year was considered lucky and worthy of the favours of God. Akbar issued orders that boys were not to marry before the age of sixteen and girls before fourteen, of such early marriages would be weaklings. He was also of opinion that consent of the parents, was essential for the confirmation of a marriage. It was the duty of the *kotwal* to verify and note down the ages of the couple before giving his consent to the marriage.

Inter-caste marriage was quite out of vogue in Hindu society, no attempt was made in the medieval times to reintroduce it. The *Ain-i-Akbari* may be referred to for details regarding caste restrictions. No such restriction existed among the Muslims. Barring some close relations, they had complete freedom in choosing the brides. Akbar, disliked this custom. He allowed marriage between first cousins in special circumstances, when he regarded it as a slight evil for a great good. Polygamy has been prevalent, particularly among the upper and middle-class. The Muslim families, too attracted Akbar's attention. Hindus generally married one wife and never divorce her till death except for the cause of adultery. They could marry a second time only if the first wife proved to be barren. There was no such restriction among the Muslims. Polygamy, naturally, brought many evils in its train. Domestic unhappiness and immorality was the natural consequence. Akbar tried to do away with the evil practice of a young man's marrying an old lady, a practice which was widely prevalent, particularly among the Muslims. The Hindus followed Manu's injunction that a bridegroom should be older than his bride. Quite often a young man, attracted by the wealth of an old lady would marry her disregarding the abnormal difference in age. He further laid down that if a woman happened to be older than her husband by twelve years, the marriage should be considered illegal and annulled.

Akbar was perhaps the only medieval ruler who raised his voice against high dowry, which were prevalent in those days. Sometimes a poor father had not the means to procure even a wedding outfit for his daughter. Tukaram, the greatest of Maharastra saints, could give his daughter in marriage only through the contributions of the villagers. Vallabhacarya was hesitant to let his daughter be engaged to Sri Chaitanya, since he was too poor to pay a handsome dowry. Huge dowries have been referred to in the works of the period, such as *Sursagar, Ramcharitmanas, and Padmavat.* Akbar disapproved of them. The evil of bridal price was wide-spread in the South, particularly among the Brahmanas of the Padaividu kingdom in medieval times. The custom became so coercive that Deva Raya II of Vijayanagara, who ruled in A.D. 1422-49, in consultation with the Brahmanas of all shades of opinion in that division, had to enact a legislation by which all marriages among these Brahmanas were henceforth to be concluded by *kanya-dana* and the father had to give the daughter to the bridegroom with gratitude. Widow Remarriage, except for the lower caste people, had disappeared almost completely in Hindu society during the early medieval age. No efforts were made to reintroduce this custom by any of the mediaeval.Akbar think it advisable to enforce widow remarriage, or he declared it to be lawful. He was of opinion that a young girl who had got no enjoyment from her husband should not be burnt, but if the Hindus took it ill, she should be married to a widower.

Akbar had issued orders that if a young woman was found running about the streets and bazaars of the town, and while, so doing did not veil herself or allowed herself to become unveiled, she was to go to the quarters of the prostitutes and take up the profession. It is, however, to the credit of the saints of the Bhakti movement that they raised their voice against the tyranny of the *purdah.* Pipa (A.D. 1425), a saint of Gagaraungarh advised the queen of Toda, the wife of Sur Sen, that it was not necessary for women to veil themelves in the presene of holy men, while Kabir remonstrated against the observance of *purdah* by his daughter-in-law, saying that it would not be of any avail at the last moment. Though *sati* was only voluntary in the South and not enjoined upon the widows, it is difficult to account for its wide popularity in the Vijayangara empire, whose rulers, however, do not seem to have put any restrictions on its observance. Mohammed-bin-Tughluq was, in all probability, the first medieval ruler who placed restrictions on its observance. A licence had to be obtained before a widow could immolate herself within his dominions. The law was meant to prevent any compulsion or force being used against an unwilling widow. These rules seemed to have continued, as Sidi Ali Reis, who visited India during Humayun's reign, observes that the officers of the Sultan were always present on the scene of *sati* observance. Akbar did not forbid the *sati* altogether, he had issued definite orders to the *kolwals* that they should not suffer a woman to be burnt against her inclination. Din-i-Ilahi, Akbar's new faith, also condemned this practice. Jahangir and Shah Jahan did not make any change in the existing law. The former, when he came to know that in the foothills of the Himalayas Muslim converts had retained the Hindu custom of *sati* and female infanticide, made these a capital offence. Shah Jahan would not allow the burning of widows. Aurangzeb was the only emperor who issued definite orders (1664) forbidding *sati* in his realms altogether, but his orders seem to have had no appreciable effect on the populace, who continued to follow the custom as before.

The efforts at reform, however, were not confined to the kings and emperors in the North. Reforms of the saints of the Bhakti cult like Ramanuja, Madhva, Ramananda, Kabir, Ravidas, Nanak, Tukaram, Purandara Dasa, Sri Chaitanya, Sankara Deva and Dadu, who flourished during this period and covered the whole country. They raised their powerful voice against the vices prevailing in society and made it incumbent on their followers to desist from them. The main results of this movement were the development of the vernacular literature, the modification of caste exclusiveness, the sanctification of family life, the elevation of the status of women, the spread of humaneness and toleration, partial reconciliation with Islam, the subordination of rites and ceremonies, pilgrimages and fasts and learning and contemplation to the worship of God with love and faith, the limitation of the excesses of polytheism, and the uplift of the nation to a high level of capacity both of thought and action. The caste system was a special target of attack for these social reformers, particularly Ramananda, Kabir, Nanak, Tukaram, Sri Chaitanya, and Dadu, who have declared caste distinctions of the Hindus to be vain. Guru Nana described caste rules to be a folly, while Ramananda applied himself to the study of the Sastras to prove that the observance of caste rules was unnecessary for anyone who sought the service of God. Ravidas and Dadu condemned caste distinctions in unequivocal terms, while Sri Chaitanya went a step further and said that if a man ate from the plate of a Dom, he regarded it as most pleasing to God. The main contention of these reformers, a saint of Maharastra, puts it, was fought against the rigidity of the caste-system and untouchability is related by Telugu and Karnataka poets like Sarvajna, Danaka Dasa, Kapilar and Vemana in their compositions. An inscription (A.D. 1632) of the reign of Sriranga Deva, a Vijayangara king, refers to an undertaking. It was due to the preachings and efforts of the Vaisnava reformers, like Ramanuja, Madhva, Sri Chaitanya, Vallabha and others in later times, who placed absolute emphasis on the self-sufficiency of the path of devotion, that the last vestiges of bloodshed connected with human or animal sacrifices were practically done away with. Madhva could not enjoin their complete abolition, which is indeed impossible for anyone who bases his teachings on the authority of the srutis, but he substituted a lamb made of rice flour for one of flesh and blood as a sacrificial offering to the gods. The Sikh gurus resolutely set themselves against the practice of infanticide. It was one of the obligations imposed on neophytes, at the time of their admission to the *pahul* or Sikh baptism. The Gurus also tried to elevate the position of women and remonstrated with those who reveled the female sex.

(III)

During the British rule, a number of changes were made in the economic and the social structures of our society. Some substantial progress was achieved in eliminating inequalities between men and women in education, employment, social rights and so forth. The economic changes during the British period were perhaps the most decisive. The economic structure established by the British was not devised for the love of the country or in the interest of the people. It was primarily meant to exploit Indian resources for the profit of the ruling class. But industrialization led to many changes like mobility of the people, growth of means of transport and communication, weakening of the *jajmani* system, availability of some new opportunities of work to people and so forth. All these created new values and behavior pattern. The idea of imparting education to women emerged in the British period. Christian Missionaries took interest in the education of girls. A girl's school was started for the first time in Bombay in 1824. Lord Dalhousie also declared that no single change in the habit of the people is likely to lead to more important and beneficial consequences than the introduction of education for their family children. The Hunter Commission too emphasized on the need for female eduation in 1882. The Calcutta, Bombay and Madras universities did not permit admission to girls up to 1875. It was only after 1882 that girls were allowed to go for higher education. Since then, there has been a continuous progress in the extent of education among females.

Raja Ram Mohan Roy, who played an important role in getting the *sati* system abolished, raised voice against child marriage and *purdah* system and fought for the right of inheritance for women. Ishwar Chandra Vidyasagar launched a movement for the right of widows to remarry and also pleaded for educating women. Mahrishi Karve took up the problems of widow remarriage and education of women. He established the SNDT Univesity in Maharashtra in 1916. Maharaja Sayaji Rao Gaekwar, ruler of Baroda State, worked for preventing child marriages, polygamy and getting the right of education to women and the right of remarriage to widows. Swami Vivekanand, Swami Dayanand Sarsvati, Annie Besant and Mahatma Gandhi also took interest in the social and the political rights of women. Gandhiji was in favour of treating daughters and sons on a footing of perfect equally.

Some women's organizations like the Banga Mahila Samaj and Theosophical Society functioned at local levels to promote modern ideals for women. Of these, five important national organizations were: Bharat Mahila Parishad, Bharat Stri Mahamandal (founded in 1910), Women's Indian Association (started in 1917 by Annie Besant), National Council of Women in India (founded in 1925 by Lady Aberden and Lady Tata) and All India Women's Conference (established in 1927 thought the efforts of Margaret Cousins and others). These organizations took up issues like women's education, abolition of social evils (such as *purdah* and child marriage), Hindu law reforms, moral and material progress of women, equality of rights and opportunities and women's suffrage. It could be said that the Indian women's movement worked for two goals: (i) uplift of women, that is, reforming social practices so as to enable women to play a more important and constructive role in society and (ii) equal rights for men and women, that is, extension of civil rights enjoyed by men in the political, economic and familial spheres to women also. The factors that provided the required incentive to Indian women's movement were: effect of western education on the concept of complementary sex roles, leadership provided by educated elite women, interest of male social reformers in changing social practices sanctioned by religion, changing socio-religious attitudes and philosophies and decreasing social hostility and opposition of males to women's associations engaged in self-help activities, and benevolent attitude of political nationalist leaders towards the fledging women's movement and their enthusiastic support to certain women campaigns. The Ministry of Welfare, Government of India, too gives grants of voluntary organizations for activities like construction of hostels for working women in cities. The state governments have also schemes of sanctioning money for running Mahila Mandals. Grih Kalyan Kendras and functional literacy centres, organizing camps for the training of rural women with public co-operation and running of co-operative societies exclusively with women membership.

The enacted laws pertaining to women relate to (a) marriage, (b) property and (c) employment. The marriage laws concentrate on age of marriage, remarriage, dissolution of marriage, form of marriage, and freedom in mate selection. The important legislations enacted are: the Child Marriage Restraint Act, 1929, the Hindu Marriage Act, 1955 and the Special Marriage Act, 1954. The property laws enacted are: Hindu Law of Inheritance, 1929, Hindu Women's right to Property Act, 1939, and the Hindu Succession Act, 1956. The laws pertaining to employment are: the Factory Act, 1948, the Employees State Insurance Act, 1948, and the Maternity Benefit Acts. The 1948 Factory Act focuses on working hours, equal wages, load to be carried, sanitational facilities, crèches, and so forth. The Employees State Insurance Act provides five benefits: sickness, maternity, disability, dependent, and medical.

The low status of women in India had mainly stemmed from illiteracy, economic dependence, religious prohibitions, caste restrictions, lack of female leadership and apathetic and callous attitude.

The low status of women in India had mainly stemmed from illiteracy, economic dependence, religious prohibitions, caste restrictions, lack of female leadership and apathetic and callous attitude. The caste system imposed many restrictions on the involvement of women in public affairs. It prescribed an early marriage for girls and on the other, it prohibited widow remarriage and prescribed the practice of *sati*. The patrilineal joint family system curbed women's freedom and contributed to their low status in the family by assigning status based on age, sex and kinship. Woman attempts and succeeds in merging her working role with the general roles of mother and wife. The high satisfaction implies being happy with the performance of both the workers and home makers roles, moderate satisfaction implies marginal balance in the equilibrium of the two roles. Conflict between the new economic and the traditional domestic roles results in the compartmentalization of activities of women at least in the initial phases of their marital lives. This compartmentalization is short lived, because the competing demands of the occupational and domestic worlds will make it impossible for many women to address such demand equitably. The working women have to adjust themselves in home as well as working place. Adjustment is smooth switch-over from one status to other status. Role adjustment depends upon role demands and role performance. A working woman has to face innumerable problems. The home life has to be adjusted with the office routine. The house-work has to be organized on lines different from the traditional.

In a society where about half of the total population and three fifths of the females are illiterate orthodox and tradition-bound beliefs and practices cannot be stuffed overnight. Legislation does make some impact. The important rights assured by the constitution of India to women, like men are:

1. Right to equality, i.e. equality of opportunity, equality before law, equal protection of the laws, not discriminating against any person on grounds of sex, and not discriminating against in matters of public employment on the gender grounds.

2. Right to freedom, i.e. freedom of speech, expression, residence, occupation and mobility.
3. Right against exploitation, i.e. freedom of speech, expression, residence, occupation and mobility.
4. Right to freedom of religion, i.e. professing, practicing and propagating religion freely.
5. Right to constitutional remedies, i.e. approaching courts for enforcing fundamental rights.

The major issues relevant to women and relating to social laws are: marriage, adoption, guardianship and abortion. The important issues pertaining to marriage are: (a) mate selection (b) age at marriage (c) polygamy (d) invalid marriage (e) defective or void marriage (f) divorce (g) restitution of conjugal rights (h) alimony and maintenance (i) custody of child (j) dowry, and (k) remarriage. The important laws, pertaining to these issues are: the Hindu Marriage Act, 1955, the Special Marriage Act, 1954, and the Widow Remarriage Act, 1856. Abortion was legally treated as a criminal offence till 1970. In 1971, the Medical termination of Pregnancy act was passed which legally permitted both pregnant woman and abortionist to cause miscarriage. The legislation, which came into force in April 1972, permits the termination of pregnancy by a registered doctor if it does not exceed twelve weeks. The right to property of a woman refers to her right as a daughter, as a wife, as a widow, and as a mother. According to the Hindu Succession Act, 1956, not only a daughter is given a right in her father's property equal to her brothers, but a widow also gets a share in her deceased husband's property equal to her sons and daughters. The Equal Remuneration Act, 1976 does not permit wage discrimination between male and female workers. The legislation prescribes penalties for those employees who disobey the rules. A very small number of woman (less than one-fifth) have political awareness. Of the women having franchise, about three-fourths exercise it. Interestingly enough, a sense of an outing rather than a real interest in politics motivates women to vote. Voting behavior of women is neither linked with political mobilization nor with political socialization but with their husbands' political beliefs and attitudes. The liberal theory of elections emphasizing the rational choice or preference of the candidate or the party for which an individual voter votes is not valid in describing the voting behavior of women. Justice to women has to be recognized publicly so that human service professionals could respond with proper action. In the first decade after independence, gender equality was recognized as a significant problem and a greater amount of effort went into assuring that exploitation of women would be identified and responded to with proper measures. Social remedies include women welfare services, encouraging the establishment of voluntary organizations and legal literacy of women through mass media. The voluntary organizations have to identify women in need of services. The help of the neighbours has to be sought in reporting cases of abused women to human service agencies. The public education and awareness programmes will help women in taking injustice to them seriously and seeking the help of social work and women's organizations in getting their due rights. Education and vocational training for women will enable them to seek jobs and become economically independent. The independence will reduce their stress, bring fundamental changes in their values and beliefs and make them bold enough to demand and stand-up for their rights.

MODELS OF SOCIAL CHANGE

Sanskritisation

The term *Sanskritisation* was introduced by Prof. M N Srinivas. M N Srinivas in his study of the Coorg in Karnataka found that lower castes, in order to raise their position in the caste hierarcy, adopted some customs and practices of the Brahmainas, and gave up some of their own which were considered to be *impure* by the higher castes.

The term *Sanskritisation* was introduced by Prof. M N Srinivas. M N Srinivas in his study of the Coorg in Karnataka found that lower castes, in order to raise their position in the caste hierarcy, adopted some customs and practices of the Brahmainas, and gave up some of their own which were considered to be *impure* by the higher castes. They gave up habit of meat-eating, drinking liquor and animal sacrifice to their deities. By doing this, within a generation or so they could claim higher positions in the hierarchy of castes. In the beginning, M N Srinivas used the term *Brahminisation* in hood (*Religion and Society Among the Coorgs*). Later on, he replaced it by from Sanskritisation. Sanskritisation means not only the adoption of new customs and habits, but also exposure to new ideas and values which have found frequent expression in the vast body of Sanskrit literature sacred as well as secular *Karma, Dharma, Papa, Maya, Samsara and Moksha* are examples of some of the most comman Sanskritic theological ideas and when people become Sanskritised, these words occur frequently in their talk.

Srinivas explains this by evolving another concept of dominant caste lower castes frequently try to attain the social status of the local dominant caste. The concept of Sanskritization has probably invited much more criticism than it deserves. Many of the limitations of the concept have already been accepted by the author of the concept. The term Sanskritization tends to confuse laymen because of its phonetic similarities with Sanskrit and sansakriti. At many places lower castes chose to imitate the ritual elements of a higher caste while at other places secular elements were borrowed. Also as Srinivas himself has pointed out Sanskritization is a valid explanation of the process of social change in the Hindu society of the times when the society was relatively closed. Today because of many factors revivalism in the lower caste is seen. It is not a major process of social change. Even in terms of traditional Hindu society and the changes therein the concept has outrightly ignored the contribution of Buddhism, Jainism, Islam etc. in bringing social change. The concept is silent about the reverse of Sanskritization especially in terms of tribalisation. Also structural changes in Indian society can never be explained by this process. At places lower castes may never leave their beliefs, rituals etc. rather Sanskritic elements may be added to the non-Sanskritic ones without actually replacing them. In terms of comparative evaluation the concepts given by Redfield and Srinivas, Yogendra Singh comments: 'The concepts of universalization and parochialisation also describe the processes of cultural change implied by Sanskritization, especially universalization comes very close to this concept. Parochialisation, however, refers to an inverted form of Sanskritization or de-Sanskritisation, a connotation which escaped the formulation of Srinivas.

M N Srinivas, Sanskritisation, he described it as, 'the process of mobility of lower castes by adopting vegetarianism and teetotalism to move in the caste hierarchy in a generation or two', he redefined it as 'a process by which a low caste or a tribe or other group changes its customs, rituals, ideology and way of life in the direction of a high and frequently, twice-born caste', (M N Srinivas in his *Social Change in Modern India* – 1971).

Sanskritisation denotes the process in which the lower castes try to imitate the life styles of upper castes in their attemapt to raise their social status. The process seems to be associated with the role of local dominant caste. Sanskritisation denotes the process of upward mobility. A caste is trying to increase its position in the caste hierarchy not at once, but over a period of time. It would take, a period of one or two generations. Mobility that is involved in the process of Sanskritisation results only in positional changes. Sanskritisation is not a new phenomenon as Sanskritisation has been a major process of cultural change in Indian history and it has occurred in every part of the Indian sub continent. The castes which enjoyed higher economic and political power but rated relatively low in ritual ranking went after Sanskritisation for they felt that their claim to a higher position was not fully effective. The three main aspects of power in the caste system are the ritual, the economic and the political ones. Economic betterment is not a necessary pre-condition to Sanskritisation, nor economic development must necessarily lead to Sanskritisation. Sometimes a group (caste, tribe) may start by acquiring, political power and this may lead to economic development and Sanskritisation. Economic betterment, the acquisition of political power, education, leadership and a desire to move up in the hierarchy, are all relevant factors in Sanskritisation. Sanskritisation is not necessarily confined to the castes within the Hindu community, it is found in tribal communities also. The Bhils of Western India, the Gonds and Oraons of Middle India have come under the influences of Sanskritisation. The process of Sanskritisation serves as a reference group. Caste group tries to orient its beliefs, practices, values, attitudes and life styles in terms of another superior or dominant group. Sanskritisation does not take place in the same manner in all the places. Studies have revealed that in most of the cases the lower castes tend to imitate the upper castes particularly the Kshatriya and Brahmin castes. The British rule in India provided a favourable atmosphere for Sanskritisation to take place. Political independence has weakened the trend towards this change. Sanskritisation serves to reduce or remove the gap between the ritual and secular rnaking. It immediately starts imitating the so called status-symbols of the customs, rituals, ideals, beliefs, values, life-styles, etc. of the upper caste communities. Sanskritisation has often been construed as a kind of protest against the traditional caste system in which the status is ascribed or predetermined. Sanskritisation does not denote a basic change in the structure of the Hindu society. It should not be construed that through this process any kind of social change can be brought about in the caste-ridden society.

Westernisation

Westernization is a simple concept. It is defined by Srinivas as 'the changes brought about in Indian Society and culture as a result of over 150 years of British rule, the term assuming changes occurring at different levels, technology, institutions, ideology and values'. Emphasis on humanitarianism and rationalism is a part of Westernization which led to a series of institutional and social reforms in India. Establishment of scientific technological and

Westernization is a simple concept. It is defined by Srinivas as 'the changes brought about in Indian Society and culture as a result of over 150 years of British rule.

educational institution, rise of nationalism, new political culture and leadership in the country are all by products of westernization. According to Srinivas, the increase in Westernization does not retard the process of Sanskritization, both go on simultaneously and to some extent, increase in westernization accelerates the process of Sanskrtization. For instance, the postal facilities, railways, buses and newspaper media which are the western impact on India render more organized religious pilgrimages, meetings, caste solidarities etc. possible now than in the past.

During the nineteenth century the British slowly laid the foundation of a modern state by surveying land, settling the revenue, creating a modern bureaucracy, army and police, instituting law courts codifying the law, developing communications, railways, post and telegraph, roads and canals, establishing schools and colleges and so. The British brought with them the printing press which led to many sided changes. Books and journals made possible the transmission of modern as well as traditional knowledge to large number of Indians. Newspapers helped the people living in the remote corners of the country to realize their common bonds and to understand the events happening in the world outside. More than any other thing the western education had an impact on the style of living of people.

Westernisation is a simpler concept. As it is already made clear. *M N Srinivas* defends the usage of the term when he says that there is need for such a term when analyzing the changes that a non-western country undergoes as a result of prolonged contact with a Western one. Westernisation implies, *certain value preferences.* It implies an active concern for the welfare of all human beings irrespective of caste, economic position, religion, age and sex. Westernisation not only includes the introduction of new institutions (for example, newspaper, elections, Christian missionaries) but also fundamental changes in old institutions. *For example,* India had schools long before the arrival of the British. The form and pace of westernization of India varied from region to region and from one action of population to another. One group of people became westernised in their dress, diet, manners, speech, sports, while another absorbed western science, knowledge and literature, remaining relatively free from certain other aspects. Brahmanas accepted the western dress habits and educational systems and also used gadgets such as radio, relevision, car, telephone etc. But they did not accept British diet, dancing, huntng and such other habits. This distinction only relative and not absolute. Westernisation pervades political and cultural fields also. He writes westernization has given birth not only to nationalism but also to revival of communalism, casteism, heightened linguistic consciousness and regionalism.

The process of Sanskritisation implies mobility within the framework of caste, while westernization implies mobility outside the framework of caste. The concept has its own limitation. The concept will be of little use in explaining the nature of social change taking place in post-Independent India.

Modernisation

Daniel Learner introduced the term *Modernisation* for the first time in his study of the Middle Eastern societies, to refer to the changes brought about in a non western country by contact, direct or indirect with a western country. Modernisation is the current term for an old process of social change whereby less developed societies acquire the characteristics common to more developed societies. The key to understanding Modernisation lies in thinking of it as a set of change that affects the whole society. Modernisation involves a transformation of social, political and economic organizations.

The process has its economic, political, educational, technological, military, administrative, cultural and other faces. The concept has been used in a very diffused manner. It involves a change from simple, traditional techniques such as hand weaving towards the use of scientific knowledge and technology, for example, powerlooms. Agricultural shifts from subsistence farming to commercial farming on a larger scale. This means growing cash crops, buying non-agricultural products in the markets on a large quantity and often hiring people to do farm work. In industry there is a movement away from the use of human and animal power and towards the use of machinery driven by non-human power. For example, ploughs pulled by oxen are replaced by tractors driven by hired hands. Traditional religious systems tend to lose influences. Powerful non-religious ideologies such as patriotism, nationalism, democracy, secularism, etc. arise. In education, the literacy rate increases greatly and formal educational institutions become widespread. Mass media also serves the purpose of educational resource and information channel. New form of administrative organization such as bureaucracies develop in the political, economic, educational and other fields. Modernisation includes such specific aspects of changes as:

1. Industralisation of economy and adopting scientific technology in industry, agriculture, dairy farming, etc., to make them highly productive
2. Secularization of ideas, i.e. a diffusion of secular, rational norms in culture
3. A remarkable increase in geographic and social mobility which includes occupational mobility
4. A spread of scientific and technical education
5. A transition from ascribed to achieved status
6. An increase in material standard of living
7. High proportion of working force employed in secondary and tertiary rather than primary production, that is, manufacturing and services as opposed to agriculture and fishing
8. An increment of mobility in the society, understood in terms of urbanization, spread of literacy and media participation
9. High expectancy of life at birth
10. Relatively greater measure of public participation in the polity, or at least democratic representation in defining and choosing policy alternatives.

Modernization in India started mainly with the western contact, especially through the establishment of the British. This contact brought about many far reaching changes in culture and social structure of India. The growth of this process was very much selective and partial,

It never encompassed the micro structures of Indian society such as family, caste, kin group and village community. But at the macro level, the components of modernization such as a universal legal system, expansion of western form of education, urbanization and industrialization, spread of new means of communication and transport and social reforms, led the way in the transformation of Indian society. Along with these aspects of structural modernization such as, rational bureaucratic systems of administration and judiciary, army and industrial bureaucracy, new classes of business elite and entrepreneurs, came into being. There was the emergence of political elite and a nationalist leadership. These modernizing structures had a uniform character throughout the country. Modernization process in India has undergone a basic change from its colonial pattern. Discontinuity in modernization between macro-structures and micro-structures slowly disappeared. Introduction of adult franchise and federal parliamentary form of political structure have carried new political values to all the sections of the population. Planned legal reforms in Hindu marriage and inheritance laws have tremendously influenced the Hindu family system. Community development projects and the Panchayat Raj System created political awareness and participation in local level management and administration of justice. Caste too has undergone radical transformation making lot of compromises with the changed conditions. There were people to support the cause of modernism and there were also people to cling on to the traditional way of life. Thus people had to tolerate the coexistence of tradition with modernism. But, coexistence cannot last long in all the areas. Because, many a time, traditional ethos and values become nonconcilable. Thus confronation starts with the practical problem of either sticking on to tradition or to go on the path of modernization.

Five main problems of modernization are : (1) Modernisation demands that society must change in all ways at once. But such a regular and co-ordinated pattern of growth cannot be planned and materialized. Some amount of social interest hence is bound to be there. (2) Modernisation of social and economic institutions may create conflicts with the traditional ways of life. *(3)* Another problem is that, most often roles adopted by the people are modern, but their values continue to be traditional. New Business firms and industrial establishments and shops etc. are either opened or inaugurated as per the dictates of the traditional Muhurtam. *(4)* Yet another problem is that there is lack of cooperation among agencies those modernize and among those institutions and systems which are already modernized. (5) Though modernization raises the aspirations of people, the social system does not provide enough chances to materialize them. This creates frustration, disappointment and social unrest.

Suggested Question

1. Under impact of industralisation and urbanization the tradition family structure has been changed. Explain.
2. Discuss the socio-economic status of women in modern India. What are the important factors changing the position of women?

3. The sanskritisation and modernization are models of socio-economic changes in the Indian society. Define with examples.
4. Write Short Notes:
   (i) Westernisation
   (ii) Dominant Caste
   (iii) Joint Family
   (iv) Nuclear Family
   (v) Matriarchal Family
   (vi) Patriarchal Family

References

1. Indra Deva & Shrirama, *Society & Culture of India,* Delhi, 1999.
2. Rao, C N S, *Sociology: Principles of Sociology with an Introduction to Social Though,* New Delhi, 2005.
3. Kolenda. P, *Caste in Contemporary India,* Delhi.
4. Srinivas M.N, *Caste in Modern India and other Essays,* Delhi.
5. Pandey V.C. & Anup Pandey, *A New History of Ancient India,* Delhi, 1998.

10
CHAPTER

OVERVIEW OF CROSS-CULTURAL MANAGEMENT

Anthropological Meaning of Culture

Culture as 'a complex whole which includes knowledge, belief, art, morals, laws, customs and any other capabilities and habits acquired by man as a member of society'.

Tylor was the first anthropologist to provide a scientific definition of culture. In his book *Primitive Culture* (1871), he defines culture as 'a complex whole which includes knowledge, belief, art, morals, laws, customs and any other capabilities and habits acquired by man as a member of society'. Malinowski says that culture is total way of life and it includes all the mental, social and physical means those make life run its course'. Bidney in his book, '*Theoretical Anthropology*' holds that culture of a people may be defined as the some total of material and intellectual equipment, whereby they satisfy their biological and social needs and adopt themselves to their environment. E.A. Hobel in his book, '*Man in Primitive World* (1958:7), has defined culture as the sum total of integrated behavior patterns, which are characteristics of the members of a society and which are therefore not the result of biological inheritance. Culture is not determined by heredity, but it is a result of total social inventions. Culture is invention of man for the fulfillment of social needs. It is transferred from one generation to another through socialization process and exchange of ideas. Herskovits, an American anthropologist, in his book *Man and His Work* has defined culture as the man-made part of environment. Environment is of two type: (i) natural environment and (ii) social environment. The total social environment of man is his culture, because it is made by man himself.

Culture is invention of man for the fulfillment of social needs.

Exhibit

In Japan, Procter & Gamble (P&G) used an advertisement for Camay soap in which a man meeting a woman for the first time compared her skin to that of a fine porcelain doll. Although the ad had worked well in South America and Europe, it insulted the Japanese. "For a Japanese man to say something like that to a Japanese woman means he's either unsophisticated or rude," said an advertising man who worked on the account. Interestingly, P&G used the ad despite the warning from the advertising agency.

Another Camay ad that failed in Japan showed a Japanese woman bathing when her husband walks into the bathroom. She begins to tell him about her new beauty soap, but the husband, stroking her shoulder, hints that suds are not what are on his mind. Although it was well received in Europe, it failed badly in Japan, where it is considered bad manners for a husband to intrude on his wife.

P&G also erred because it lacked knowledge about the business culture. The company introduced Cheer detergent by discounting its price, but this lowered the soap's reputation. Said a competitor, 'Unlike in Europe and the United States, once you discount your product here, it's hard to raise the price again'. Wholesalers were alienated because they made less money due to lower margins. Moreover, apparently P&G did not realize that Japanese house wives shop in the 50000 or more neighborhood convenience stores close to home. These small retailers, who sell 30 percent of all the detergent bought in Japan have limited shelf space and thus do not like to carry discounted products because of the lower profit earned.

Although acquiring knowledge about Japanese culture was both time consuming and expensive, evidently P&G was a good learner. Eight years after its difficulties with Cheer detergent, the company reentered the soap market, which was then controlled by two powerful Japanese consumer products concerns, Kao and Lion Corporation. Just two years later P&G held 20 percent of the market. What did it do differently this time?

When the home office told the Japanese affiliate to find new markets for products in which the firm was strong elsewhere in the world, P&G Japan sent researchers to study Japanese dishwashing habits. They found that Japanese homemakers used much more detergent than was needed. This indicated that consumers wanted a more powerful soap, which P&G's laboratory created. The marketing message was simple: A little bit of Joy cleans better yet is easier on the hands. This message hit home. Said a Japanese homemaker who, after seeing the pilot commercials, rushed to buy a bottle, Grease on Tupperware, that's the toughest thing to wash off, I had to try it.

Retailers wanted the product because P&G did the things it hadn't done with Cheer. For example, this time the profit margins for the retailers were high. P&G also exploited a weakness in the competing Japanese products: Their long necked bottles wasted space, but Joy bottles were compact cylinders that took up less space in stores, warehouses and delivery trucks. A buyer for a large Japanese store chain estiamated that the bottle improved the efficiency of the store's distribution by 40 percent.

Source

International Business, Tata Magraw Hill, Delhi, 2010

Donal A Bal, W H Macctalprik, M S Minor, J M Gerenger, J M Mac Nett

When people work in societies and cultures different from their own the problems encounter in dealing with a single set of cultures are multiplied by the number of cultural sets they find in each of their foreign markets. How do international business people learn to live with other cultures? The first step is to realize that there are cultures different from their own.

Then they must go on to learn the characteristics of those cultures so that they may adapt to them. The experts seem to agree on a number of characteristics of culture such as the following:

1. **Culture is learnt:** Culture is not inherited. It is acquired through experience and learning.
2. **Culture is shared:** Culture is not specific to single individuals but is shared by people who are members to particular groups, organizations and societies.
3. **Culture is trans-generational:** Culture is passed on, in a cumulative process, from one generation to the next.
4. **Culture is symbolic:** Culture depends on the individual's human capacity to symbolize or to use one thing to represent another.
5. **Culture is patterned:** Culture possesses structure and is integrated. Change in one aspect of culture causes changes in another.
6. **Culture is adaptive:** Culture depends on the human capacity to adapt to change.
7. **Culture is descriptive:** Culture defines the boundaries of different groups.

Culture depends on the human capacity to adapt to change.

Universals of Cross-cultural Business

Each culture is composed of cultural universals, or the critical characteristics of the total way of life of that group of people. The major cultural universals are language, religion, material elements, customs, temporal factors, aesthetics, societal organization, education, age, gender, and common interests.

Cross- Cultural Universals

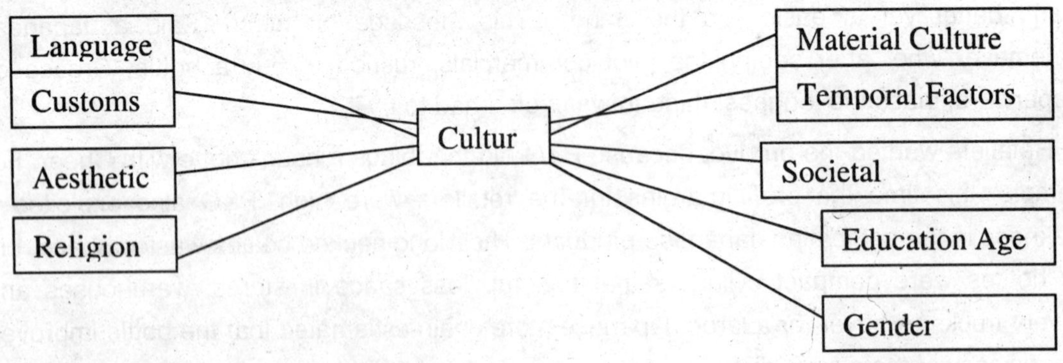

Culture determines the use of language in each of its main forms – spoken language and unspoken language.

1. Language

The most obvious cultural distinction is probably that of language and communication. A languae is the mirror of a culture. Culture determines the use of language in each of its main forms – spoken language and unspoken language. Spoken language actually splits some nations into more than one culture. There are two cultures in Switzerland matching its two languages – German and French. Canada is currently experiencing serious political pressure to split the nation into two separate countries – one that speaks English and one that speaks

French. In the world of business, the spoken language is critical for four reasons. First, language can be essential in the process of collecting and evaluating information. Knowledge of the local business environment should not be totally dependent upon the opinions of outsiders. A manager with the ability to analyse the business situation first hand, through knowledge of the language, has a tremendous market advantage. Second, a manager needs to communicate with other members of the local society. Internal company communications with non English speaking employees cannot be accomplished effectively through interpreters. Language goes beyond the pure technical skills to help the manager understand the nuances and context within which languaging takes place. The different cultural pattern can be learnt by following examples:

manager with the ability to analyse the business situation first hand, through knowledge of the language, has a tremendous market advantage.

(*i*) Kellogg had to rename its Bran Buds in Sweden because the brand name was translated as burned farmer.

(*ii*) In Chinese, Coca-Cola means Bite the head of a dead tadpole.

(*iii*) Because the Japanese have trouble pronouncing snap, crackle and pop, Kellogg advertises its Rice Krispies in Japan with the caricatures, patchy, pitchy and putchy.

(*iv*) A Romanian hotel posted a notice to its English speaking guests that the elevator was not working the notice read, the lift is being fixed. For the next few days, we regret that you will be unbearable.

(*v*) Making a circle with the finger and thumb to signify 'OK' can get you into serious trouble all around the globe:

- In France and Belgium, this symbol means that you are worth zero
- In Japan, it means that you are asking for a bribe
- In Brazil, the gesture is grossly insulting
- Americans and most Europeans understand the thumbs-up gesture, but in Southern Italy and Greece, it sends the message that we transmit with the middle finger.

Unspoken language, sometimes referred to as non-verbal language, is an effective way of communicating our beliefs, values, and attitudes as well as augmenting our verbal messages. The following examples are most widely recognized-facial expressions, walking, posture, hand gestures, colour symbolism, proxemics, touching, eye contact, olfaction (smells), artifacts (jewellery), clothing hairstyles, cosmetics and silence. Hand gestures can be very expressive in some cultures, but they often have different or even contradictory meanings. Colour symbolism can be very confusing for the international manager. The colour green, for example, is popular in Muslim countries, but it symbolizes disease in most jungle covered countries. The colour red symbolizes royalty or masculinity in Great Britain, but red is blasphemous in most of Africa.

Unspoken language, sometimes referred to as non-verbal language, is an effective way of communicatin g our beliefs, values, and attitudes as well as augmenting our verbal messages.

2. Aesthetics

Aesthetics pertains to a culture's sense of beauty and good taste and is expressed in its art, drama, music, folklore and dances.

Art

Colors, especially can be deceptive because they mean different things to different cultures. The colour of mourning is black in the United States and Mexico, black and white in the Far East and purple in Brazil.

Of particular interest to international business people are the formal aspects of art, colour and form because of the symbolic meanings they convey. Colors, especially can be deceptive because they mean different things to different cultures. The colour of mourning is black in the United States and Mexico, black and white in the Far East and purple in Brazil. Green is a propitious colour in the Islamic world, and any advertisement or package featuring green is looked at favorably there. While in the United States mints are packaged in blue or green paper, in Africa the wrapper is red. So marketers must be careful to check whether colours have any special meanings before using them for products, packages, or advertisements. Be careful of symbols, too. The number seven signifies good luck in the United States but the opposite in Singapore, Ghana and Kenya. In Japan, the number four is unlucky. If you are giving a Japanese client golf balls, make sure there are more or less than four in the package. Also, in general, avoid using a nation's flag or any symbols connected with religion.

Nike, the athletic shoe maker, recalled 38000 pairs of shoes carrying the word air written in flaming letters because, according to Muslims, it resembles the word Allah in Arabic. Another 30000 pairs were diverted from Arabian countries to less sensitive countries. Recently, protests in Europe followed the publication in Denmark of cartoons showing Mohammed wearing a turban shaped like a bomb. It is also important to learn whether there are local aesthetic preferences for form that could affect the design of products, packaging, or even the building in which the firm is located. The American style of steel and glass in the midst of oriental architecture will be a constant reminder to the local population of the outsider's presence. Feng Shui – In Asia it is often believed that if buildings, furniture, roads and other human made objects are placed in harmony with nature, they can bring good fortune. If they are not they will cause a disaster. Before building a house, scheduling a funeral, or making an investment, a master of feng shui (pronounced 'fung shway') is called in to give a seal of approval.

Music and Folklore

Musical commercials are generally popular worldwide, but tastes vary and the marketer must know what kind of music each market prefers. Thus, a commercial that used a ballad in the United States might be better received to the tune of a holero in Mexico or a samba in Brazil. However, if the advertiser is looking to the youth market with a product that is patently American, then American music will help reinforce its image. And singers like Shakira appeal to both markets.

Those who wish to steep themselves in a culture find it useful to study its folklore, which can disclose much about a society's way of life. The incorrect use of folklore can sometimes cost the firm a share of the market. For example, associating a product with the cowboy would not obtain the same results in Chile or Argentina as in the United States, because in those countries the cowboy is a far less romantic figure – it's just a job. On the other hand, Smirnoff's use of an image of late revolutionary leader Ernesto 'Che' Guevara in an advertisement for spicy vodka sparked controversy in Cuba, where Guevara is a national hero. As another instance a US company might be paying handsome royalties to use American cartoon characters in its promotion, only to find they are considerably less important in foreign markets. In Mexico, songs of the 'Singing Cricket' are known to all youngsters and their mothers and a commercial tie-in with that character would be as advantageous to the firm as its use of Peanuts or Mickey Mouse. In many areas, especially where nationalistic feeling is strong, local firms have been able to compete successfully with foreign affiliates by making use of indigenous folklore in the form of slogans and proverbs. Tales and folklore are valuable in maintaining a sense of group unity. Knowing them is an indication that one belongs to the group, which recognizes that an outsider is unfamiliar with its folklore.

3. Material Culture

The technology of a society is the mix of the usable knowledge that the society applies and directs toward the attainment of cultural and economic objectives, it exists in some form in every cultural organization. It is significant in the improvement of living standards and a vital factor in the competitive strategies of multinational firms. Technological superiority is the goal of most companies, of course, but it is especially important to international companies for a number of reasons:

The Korean firm Samsung was once known for cheap and unappealing electronics. But its skills in the design of sleek, attractive products have made it a leader in cell phones and it tops global markets for color television, flash memory and LCD panels. Samsung's elegant experience showroom in New York city draws 1500 visitors on a typical Saturday.

(*i*) It enables a firm to be competitive or even attain leadership in world markets. The Korean firm Samsung was once known for cheap and unappealing electronics. But its skills in the design of sleek, attractive products have made it a leader in cell phones and it tops global markets for color television, flash memory and LCD panels. Samsung's elegant experience showroom in New York city draws 1500 visitors on a typical Saturday.

(*ii*) It can be sold (via licensing or management contract), or it can be embodied in the company's products.

(*iii*) It can give a firm confidence to enter a foreign market even when other companies are already established there.

(*iv*) It can enable the firm to obtain better than usual conditions for a foreign market investment because the host government wants the technology that only the firm has (for example, permission for a wholly owned subsidiary in a country where the government normally insists on joint ventures with a local majority).

(*v*) IBM, confident of its superior technology, insisted on and obtained permission from the Mexican government to set up a wholly owned subsidiary when other computer manufacturers were forced to accept local partners.

(*vi*) It can enable a company with only a minority equity position to control a joint venture and preserve it as a captive market for semiprocessed inputs that it – but not the joint venture – produces.

(*vii*) It can change the international division of labour. Some firms that moved production overseas where labour was cheaper have returned to their home countries because production methods based on new technology have reduced the direct labour content of their products. With labour costs as low as 5 percent of total production costs going overseas to save 30 to 40 percent in labour costs, for example, produces only about a 2 percent cost saving. This may be more than offset by the transportation costs to bring the finished merchandise to the United States. Fender Musical Instruments Co. makes Fender guitars in both Ensenada, Mexico and Corona, California and sales of guitars from both locations are about even.

(*viii*) It is causing major firms to form competitive alliances in which each partner shares technology and the high costs of research and development. This is known as strategic technology leveraging, which is the concept of using external technology to complement rather than substitute for internal technology.

Technology's cultural aspects are certainly important to international managers, because new production methods and new products often require that people change their beliefs and ways of living. A self employed farmer may find that factory work is unappealing. If workers have been accustomed to the conditions of cottage industries in which each individual performs all the operations, they find it difficult to adjust to the monotony of tightening a single bolt. The throw away instead of repair philosophy behind the design of many new products necessitates a change in the use habits of people who have been accustomed to repairing something to keep it operating until it is thoroughloy worn out. Generally, the greater the difference is between the old and the new method or product, the more difficult it is for the firm to institute a change.

4. Societal Organization

Local personnel managers are prone to fill the best jobs with family members, regardless of their qualifications.

Every society has a structure or an organization that is the patterned arrangement of relationships defining and regulating the manner by which its members interface with one another. Anthropologists generally study this important aspect of culture by breaking down its parts into two classes of institutions, those based on kinship and those based on the free association of individuals. The family is the basic unit of institutions based on kinship. Unlike the American family, which is generally composed of the parents and their children, families in many nations – especially the developing ones – are extended to include all relatives by o and by marriage. For the foreign firm, the extended family is a source of employees and business connections. The trust that people place in their relatives, however distant, may motivate them to buy from a supplier owned by their cousin's cousin, even thought the price is higher. Local personnel managers are prone to fill the best jobs with family members, regardless of their qualifications. Although the extended family is large, each member's feeling of responsibility to it is strong. An individual's initiative to work is discouraged if he or she is asked to share personal earnings with unemployed extended family members no matter what the kinship is. Responsibility to the family is frequently a cause of high absenteeism in developing countries, where the worker is often called home to help with the harvest. Managements have spent large sums to provide comfortable housing for workers and their immediate familes, only to find them living in crowded conditions after members of their extended families have moved in.

5. Religion

Religion, an important component of culture, is responsible for many of the attitudes and beliefs affecting human behavior.

Protestant

The protestant religion is outcome of renaissance which divided the christianits into Roman catholics and the Protestants. Protestants initiated new work approach based on virtue and liberty. Europeans and Americans are believed to view work as a moral virtue. This view may stem in part from the Protestant work ethic and expressed by Luther and Calvin, who believed it was one's duty to glorify God by hard work and the practice of thrift.

Protestants initiated new work approach based on virtue and liberty.

Hinduism

Hinduism does not have a single founder or a central authority but is practiced by more than 80 percent of India's population. Although there is great diversity among regions and social classes, Hinduism has certain characteristic features. Most Hindus believe that everything in the world is subject to an eternal process of death and rebirth (samsara) and that individual souls (atmans) migrate from one body to another. They believe one can be liberated from the samsara cycle and achieve eternal bliss (nirvana) through (1) yoga (purification of mind and body) (2) devout worship of the gods or (3) good works and obedience to the laws and customs (dharmas) of one's caste.

They believe one can be liberated from the samsara cycle and achieve eternal bliss (nirvana) through (1) yoga (purification of mind and body) (2) devout worship of the gods or (3) good works and obedience to the laws and customs (dharmas) of one's caste.

A knowledge of the caste system is important to managers because the castes are the basis of the social division of labour. The highest caste, the Brahmins or priesthood, is followed by the Kshatriyas, the merchants, the peasants etc. An individual's position in a caste is inherited, as is that person's job within the caste and movement to a higher caste can be made only in subsequent lives. The government of India has outlawed discrimination based on the caste system and has worked to improve the situation of those in the lower castes, such discrimination still exists. Indian newspapers usually carry a classified section for those seeking marriage partners, and ads are often explicit about the caste of the ad buyer and the caste requirement of the marriage partner.

In Japan a somewhat similar system existed up to 17th century, when the feudal Tokugawa regime imposed a rigid social pecking order. The warrior administrator samurai were at the top. Below them were farmers and artisans, then merchants, and, at the bottom, those with occupations considered dirty and distasteful, such as slaughterers, butchers and tanners. As in India, where discrimination against untouchables is illegal, all natives of Japan who are of Japanese descent are legally equal. However, the descendants of the lowest Japanese class remain trapped in their ghettos, working in small family firms that produce knitted garments, bamboo wares, fur and leather goods, shoes and sandals.

Buddhism

Gautama taught that by extinguishing desire, his followers could attain englightenment and escape the cycle of existence into nirvana.

Buddhism began in India to reform of Hindusim. At the age of 29, Prince Gautama renounced his wife, son, and wealth and set out to solve the mysteries of misery, old age, and death. After six years of experimenting, he suddenly understood how to break the laws of *karma* and the cycle or rebirth (samsara). Gautama emerged as the Buddha (the Enlightened One). He renounced the austere self discipline as well as the extremes of self indulgence, both of which depended on a craving that locked people into the cycle of rebirth. Gautama taught that by extinguishing desire, his followers could attain englightenment and escape the cycle of existence into nirvana. By opening his teaching to everyone, he opposed the caste system. Buddhism is the most flourishing religion of South East Asia.

Jainism

Their greatest impact on Indian culture is manifested in the wide spread acceptance of their doctrine of nonviolence, which prohibits animal slaughter, war, and even violent thoughts.

The Jain religion was founded by Mahavira, a contemporary of Buddha. Jain doctrine teaches that there is no creator, no god and no absolute principle. Through right faith, correct conduct and knowledge of the soul, Jains can purify themselves, become free of samsara and achieve Kaivalya. Although relatively few in number, Jains are influential leaders in commerce and scholarship. Their greatest impact on Indian culture is manifested in the wide spread acceptance of their doctrine of nonviolence, which prohibits animal slaughter, war, and even violent thoughts.

Sikhism

Sikhism is the religion of an Indian ethinic group, a military brotherhood, and a political movement that was founded by Nanak. Sikhs believe there is a single god but they also accept the Hindu concepts of samsara, karma and spiritual liberation. More than 80 percent of Sikhs live in the state of Punjab. In Canada they have sizable presence. Here number of schools are opened for learning of Punjabi language.

Confucianism

Jen, the cultivation of which is its own reward. A second principle, *li*, prescribes a gentle decorum in all actions and may account for the Chinese emphasis on politeness and deference to eldes.

The name of Confucius is inseparable from Chinese culture and civilization, which were already well developed when he set out to transform ancient traditions into a system capable of guiding personal and social behavior. Confucianism may be considered a religion since Confucius built his philosophy on the notion that all reality is subject to an eternal mandate from heaven. Confucius taught that each person bears within himself or herself the principle of unselfish love for others, Jen, the cultivation of which is its own reward. A second principle, *li*, prescribes a gentle decorum in all actions and may account for the Chinese emphasis on politeness and deference to eldes.

Taoism

Taoism is a mystical philosophy founded by Lao-tzu, a contemporary of Confucius. It is just as likely that he never existed, and that the Lao Tzu is an anthology. Taoism, which means philosophy of the way, holds that each of us mirrors the male and the female energies (yin and yang) that govern the cosmos. The aim of Taoist meditation and rituals is to free the self from distractions and become empty to allow the cosmic forces to act.

Shintoism

Shintoism is the indigenous religion of Japan. Shinto legends define the founding of the Japanese empire as a cosmic act, and the emperor was believed to have divine status. As a part of the World War II settlement, the emperor was forced to renounce such a claim. Shintoism has no elaborate theology or weekly workship. Many homes contain a small Shinto shrine.

Islam

Islam accepts as God's eternal word the *Quran*, a collection of Allah's (God's) revelations to Muhammad, who is viewed by Muslims as the messenger of God. Muhammad was not only the prophet of God, but also led the Islamic state. The basic spiritual duties of all Muslims consist of the five pillars of faith: (1) accepting the confession of faith and Muhammad is the messenger of god (2) making the five daily prayers while facing Mecca (Muhammad's birthplace) (3) giving charity (4) fasting during the daylight hours of Ramadan, a 29 or 30 day month in Islam's lunar calendar and (5) making a pilgrimage to Mecca at last once in a person's lifetime.

6. Customs

Every culture maintains critical and unique standards over certain customs, manners and ways of doing things. Customs and manners are especially important in negotiating business agreements in other cultures. For instance, in Asian cultures it is common practice to answer any question with the word, 'yes' with the actual answer to be given later. American negotiators tend to assume that the first word, 'yes' signifies agreement and move on to the next point to be negotiated. That is why so many western managers accuse Asians of changing their minds after agreements have been reached. Another problem experienced by Americans operating in Asian cultures is the custom on the part of Asians to never call attention to their own achievements. Thus, when interviewing a prospective Asian for a position in a US firm, questions regarding the applicant's past successes will probably fail to elicit the desired information. In the same vein, it is the American custom to reward and to expect workers, especially professionals and managers to be self starters. However, in much of Europe, South America and parts of Asia employees believe that acting independently is a breach of authority. Another way in which local customs impact on business activities is the use of colour symbolism.

Temporal Factors

Two diverse approaches to time-monochronic time and polychromic time. Monochronic time represents the ordered, precise, schedule driven view of time.

Polychromic time is the view that time is a vague element that is caught up in the multiple, cyclical, and concurrent involvement of different people.

Attitudes toward time cause serious cross cultural problems. To better understand the potential dangers involved with temporal factors, managers should become familiar with two diverse approaches to time-monochronic time and polychromic time. Monochronic time represents the ordered, precise, schedule driven view of time. In America and much of Western Europe, this attitude towards time is reflected by our motivation to make precise appointments, keep a tight calendar, be prompt, stick to the schedule, and never waste time. On the other hand, polychromic time is the view that time is a vague element that is caught up in the multiple, cyclical, and concurrent involvement of different people. If an American makes a time specific appointment in an Arabic country, for example, there may be an hour or two's wait in the outer office only to find out that the other person is out of town. Similarly, when an American conducts business in Latin America, he or she must understand that manana does not really mean tomorrow-it usually means at some point in the future.

7. Age

Marketers have long practiced the art of segmenting a market by age groups, to better identify potential products, packaging, advertising and other marketing factors. A culture's age structure is especially important to the distributors of such products as atheletic equipment, designer clothes, denims, VCR's video tapes, compact disks, and compact disk players.

8. Gender

One of the keys to market analysis is the relative equality between the sexes. In nations where women have few rights and little input into major family purchasing decisions, traditional female-oriented products and modern household appliances may not be readily marketable. Also of interest to the international firm is the gender make-up of the workforce. Usually, as a nation becomes industrialized, more women enter the job market and begin to exercise greater influence on the culture.

9. Education

A major element of a culture is education – both formal and informal. Researchers tend to assess a culture's education level by its literacy rate and by enrollment numbers in both secondary and higher education. Enrollment numbers, alone, may not help define the quality of a culture's education. The literacy rate is used by some firms to determine the sophistication of its advertising and the nature of its human resource recruitment and training policies. Countries with low literacy rates are found to be limited with respect to trained personnel, suggesting that the firm amy have to transfer key personnel from other locations. International managers are also concerned with a culture's educational mix in order to identify those areas of important education concentration. In this regard, most of Europe has recently adopted the advanced management education being offered in US business schools. The brain drain often results when highly educated people emigrate to other countries to seek more appropriate opportunities. Some nations have over educated their workforce without providing commensurate job opportunities, so some of those people will have to either take domestic jobs below their skill level or seek opportunity elsewhere. In other cases, brain drain has been caused by governmental wage controls. For example, in highly socialized countries where the salaries of health care professionals are capped by government decree, many of those professionals have emigrated to countries that welcome their skills and do not attempt to limit their earning capacity. After undergoing a severe brain drain for over a quarter of a century, some nations-principally Taiwan and South Korea-have implemented reverse brain drain programmes that offer new rewards to entice those emigrants to return to their native lands.

Cross-Cultural Diversity

In addition to learning to manage cultural diversity, the successful manager of the future must also develop skills in the management of individual diversity. Within each culture, there will still be many ways in which each individual will be uniquely different. The skilled manager will carefully and individual will be uniquely different. The skilled manager will carefully and selectively apply the ethics and different strokes for different folks. So critical elements of a well developed program for the improved management of diversity will include the following:

(*i*) Strong and visible support from top management

(*ii*) Continuous effort to assess the diversity management programme

(*iii*) Flexible programmes for the recruitment, training, retention and upward mobility of a diverse workforce.

(*iv*) Programmes to accommodate family needs, such as day care and care for the elderly

(*v*) Alternative work schedules, including part time work, job sharing, compressed work weeks, flextime etc.

(*vi*) Telecommuting opportunities for non conventional workers and foreign workers who do not wish to immigrate

(*vii*) Diversity training

(*viii*) Language training

(*ix*) Mentoring, or the use of high level manages to guide high potential women, minorities and other diverse employees

(*x*) Support groups that can help build minority networks for the support and guidance of applicable employees

(*xi*) Career development and promotions to maximize the upward mobility of diverse employees to overcome the glass ceilings that tend to hold them back.

Indian Panorama

First of all, the Indian manager is not burdened with the aging workforce that confronts managers in most of the world. The Indian workforce is young, with some 40 percent of the population below the age of 14 years. This assures a large pool of applicants from which to select and train new workers. They tend to demonstrate a high power distance position. This means that they tend to accept the fact that managers make decisions and their right to do so is not questioned. Indian workers reflect a low uncertainty avoidance, demonstrating low levels of stress, low levels of anxiety, and a greater willingness to take business risks. They are strong individualists with high levels of initiative, autonomy and achievement orientation. Indian workers are found to manifest the qualities of masculinity, aggressiveness and assertiveness. Indian managers reflect a number of positive characteristics: (1) they demonstrate a high moral orientation (2) they are highly individualistic and (3) they have a strong leaning toward organization compliance and competence. Indians expressed for the following values they wished to inculcate in their children:

Indians expressed for the following values they wished to inculcate in their children: 1. Good manners/politeness 2.Value for learning 3.Sense of responsibility

1. Good manners/politeness
2. Value for learning
3. Sense of responsibility
4. Tolerance and respect for others
5. Consciusness at work
6. Independence
7. Loyalty
8. Ability to communicate

Cross-Cultural Business Pattern

	North Americans	Arabs	Russians
1. Primary Negotiating style and Process	Factual: appeals made to logic	effective: appeals made to emotions	Axiomatic: Appeals make to ideals.
2. Conflict: Opponent's arguments countered with	Objective facts	Subjective feelings	Asserted ideals
3. Making Concessions	Small concessions made early to establish relationship	Concessions made through out as a part of the bargaining	A few, if any small concessions made
4. Response to opponent's concessions	Usually reciprocate opponent's concessions	Almost always reciprocates opponent's concessions	Opponent's concessions are viewed as weakness and almost never reciprocated
5. Relationship	Short term	Long term	No continuing relationship limited
6. Authority	Short term	Broad	
7. Initial Position	Moderate	Extreme	Extreme
8. Deadlines	Very Important	Casual	Ignored

Source: International Journal of Intercultural Relations, vol. 1, E.S. Glenn, D. Wilmeyers, and K.A. Stevenson, Cultural styles of persuasion.

Negotiation Styles from a Cross-cultural Perspective

Japanese	America	Latin America
1. Emotional sensitivity highly valued. Hiding of emotions.	Emotional sensitivity is not highly valued straight forward or impersonal dealings.	Emotional sensitivity valued, passionate.
2. Subtle power plays, conciliation	Litigation, not as much as conciliation	Great power plays, Use of weakness
3. Loyalty to employer, Employer takes care of employees	Lack of commitment to employer, breaking of ties by either if necessary	Loyalty to employer, Who is often a family
4. Group decision making by consensus	Teamwork provides input to decision maker	Decisions made by one individual
5. Face saving crucial, Decisions often made on basis of saving someone from embarrassment	Decisions made on cost benefit basis, face saving does not always matter.	Face saving crucial in decision making to preserve honour dignity
6. Decision makers openly influenced by special interests	Decision makers influenced by special interests but often not considered ethical	Execution of special interests of decision maker expected and condoned
7. Not argumentative, quiet when right	Argumentative when right or wrong, but impersonal	Argumentative when right or wrong, passionate
8. What is in writing must be accurate, valid	Great importance given to documentation as proof	Impatient with documentation, seen as obstacle to general principles
9. Step by step approach to decision making	Methodically organized decision making	Impulsive, spontaneous decision making
10. Good of group is the ultimate aim	Profit motive or good of individual ultimate aim	What is good for the individual is good for the group
11. Cultivate a good emotional social setting for decision making, to know decision makers	Decision making impersonal, avoid involvements, conflict of interest	Personalised approach necessary for good decision making

Source: Casse, P. training for the Multicultural manager. A practical and cross-cultural approach to management of people, society for intercultural education & training.1982.

CROSS-CULTURAL BUSINESS ZONES

1. Japan

Japan is a relationship focused formal, monochromic and reserved culture.

Japan is a relationship focused formal, monochromic and reserved culture. The Japanese negotiation process is based on maintaining harmony in relationships. Open conflict is avoided. Differences are resolved through cooperation and persistence. The Japanese strive for long term relationship based on trust. Negotiations are conducted by teams and not by individuals. Communication is reserved and self controlled. The context is highly complex. Spoken word is only one part, the total picture and the message may convey several levels of meaning. Much is expected to be understood without words. A lot can be achieved working behind the scenes where neither party is in danger of loosing face. The Japanese place more emphasis on exchanging extensive and detailed information. A meeting that might take three days in the west will probably take two weeks in Japan. Not being hasty is a sign of wisdom and sincerity. Further, consensus building (ringi seido) is valued. But, once decisions are taken Japanese will implement it faster than in the west, in fact, total time taken for negotiation and implementation would be less in Japan. The Japanese make life long commitments. Contracts are not important, they can be changed as and when problems arise. Bottom up planning ensures broad participation. The Japanese do not believe in bargaining and every rise in price has to be justified with facts and figures. They are conservative in approach, formal and observe certain rituals seriously. China, Korea, Tiawan and Singapore also follow this model.

The Japanese do not believe in bargaining and every rise in price has to be justified with facts and figures.

2. Germany

Germany is a deal focused moderately formal, monochromic and reserved culture.

Germany is a deal focused moderately formal, monochromic and reserved culture. Germans are planned and well organized negotiators. Conflict is seen as dysfunctional and a symptom of being unprepared. Direct in their approach, they pride themselves on speaking their mind. Clarity of understanding is the prime goal of communication and they readily get to point. They like to examine every small detail thoroughly. They tend to be uncomfortable with the effusive compliments that are common in some other cultures. Visitors should use pleasantries such as 'danke' (thanks) and 'bitte' (please) liberally.

Non verbal cues and signals are not widely used and eye contact is important.

Germany is a strongly monochromic culture i.e. 'punktlichkeit' (punctuality) is very important. Their protocol is formal and they give attention to procedural aspects. Conservative in dress, they don't like anything too flashy or fashionable, these indicate lack of seriousness and discipline. The Germans are team oriented and their goal is to further the interests of the organization and government. They tend to keep a distance between themselves and their counterparts, as they feel the closeness might interfere with the negotiating process. Germans use low context communication. Non verbal cues and signals are not widely used and eye contact is important. They trust past performance to judge the individual rather than their intuition. Agreements are written and respected. They are risk averse and less short term oriented than their American counterparts. Decision making is centralized and flows from top. They like to be addressed by designations or achievements. UK, Denmark, Finland, Netherlands, Czech Republic also follow their approach.

3. France

France is a moderately deal focused, formal, variably expressive and monochromic culture. As people, the French constitute the most brilliant and the most dangerous nation of Europe and the best qualified in turn to become an object of admiration, hatred, pity or terror but never of indifference Alexis de Toque Ville said. The French are proud, at times displaying supremacy. They are rational about individual achievements are care little what others think of them.

In negotiations, the French follow their own logic based on previously established principles. They are thoroughly prepared and expect the same from other side. They believe that conflict can be constructive and help progress. They expect direct and honest arguments and due authority on the other side. Status conscious, social class is a key factor in selection of negotiators. The French are extremely formal and their attention to manners and respect is paramount in all business situations, even with friends in business. Negotiation issues are more important than relationships. The French tend to remain guarded about their personal lives and relationships. They quickly get down to business without wasting time. They are not receptive to hard sell tactics and like to have a detailed contract to be signed, written in French. The French motivation to work is different from any other nation in the world. To the French, the only thing that really matters is the quality of life (qualite de la vie), the french work to live, do not live to work. Belgium, Italy, Spain, Hungry follow France.

In negotiations, the French follow their own logic based on previously established principles.

4. Russia

Russia is a relationship focused, formal, polychromic and expressive culture. Speaking with the experience of 35 visits to markets in Russia, Jenn Jensen managing director of the Danish firm F. Uhren Roll Meat A/s, emphasizes that 90 percent of business in Russia is done fact to face. You build your business on relationships. For Russians, negotiation is a competitive process in which their aim is to maximize their gains at the other side's loss. All Russian executives are trained in the art of conducting negotiations. They can be confrontational, blunt and combative negotiators and the process can be very slow or made slow. The decision making is centralized and their approach is highly individualistic.

Russians are conscious of protocol and enjoy certain formalities like an after dinner. They like to be addressed by their complete names. Hard bargainers, they use premeditated tactics to achieve the best alternative. They are cautious because they avoid uncertainties. Russians generally insist on formal signing of agreement and it is not uncommon for agreement to be renegotiated. Unlike east and south Asians, they are direct, saying what they mean and meaning what they say. In Russia, expect meetings to start a little late and run well beyond the scheduled time. Senior officials will keep several conversations going simultaneously. The Russians are quite and restrained at the beginning of a negotiation, but can display emotions and temper at critical moments. Winston Churchill rightly described Russia as a riddle wrapped in a mystery inside an enigma. Poland, Rumania follow Russia.

Russians are conscious of protocol and enjoy certain formalities like an after dinner. They like to be addressed by their complete names. Hard bargainers, they use premeditated tactics to achieve the best alternative.

5. Brazil

Brazil is a relationship focused, formal, polychromic and expressive culture. Initial correspondence with the Brazilians should be in their national language Portuguese or Spanish. Establishing an atmosphere of trust is a precondition to a successful business relationship. Topics for small talks include football, Brazilian history and places to visit. Brazilians value deep, long lasting relationships. In southern Brazil, people value firm schedules and time, but in other parts of the country, clocks tick at different speeds. Waiting for an hour is not too long. Status is highly valued, and therefore your dress and the hotel you stay in count. Warm and friendly, Brazilians tend to be talkative, and openly show emotions in public.

Conversational overlap is not considered rude. Brazil is definitely a high context culture. As a sign of friendliness, they stand close maintaining physical and eye contact while talking. Brazilians are widely known as tough bargainers.

Conversational overlap is not considered rude. Brazil is definitely a high context culture. As a sign of friendliness, they stand close maintaining physical and eye contact while talking. Brazilians are widely known as tough bargainers, not afraid to turn down offers rather bluntly. Negotiation process can be very lengthy and they expect their counterparts to offer concessions. Wining and dining is expected and encouraged for establishing trust and relationship. When arguing, Brazilians appeal to one's sensibilities and emotion. Arguments are persuasive, not because they are based on statistics and figures but because they are based on apparent common sense and are made with ferour and sincerity. Inference, assumptions and tradition are likely to play a part in persuasion. Brazilian society is highly bureaucratic, hierarchical and class conscious with centralized decision making. Argentina, Maxico and other Latin American countries follow its business practice.

6. Arab World

The Arab countries are relationship focused, polychromic and expressive culture. The Arab world is conservative, traditional and strongly influenced by Islam, which pervades every aspect of life.

The Arab countries are relationship focused, polychromic and expressive culture. The Arab world is conservative, traditional and strongly influenced by Islam, which pervades every aspect of life. One must learn Arab customs, practices and taboos. An Arab's honour, dignity and reputation are precious to him and are protected at all cost. Loyalty to the family is a paramount value, family needs often come before individual needs. Arabs readily express emotion and their language is marked by frequent exaggeration. They make use of elaborate and ritualized forms of greeting and leave talking. They avoid confrontation and saying no. Time is flexible. When a meeting is in progress, people will come and go freely and telephone calls will be attended to. Arabs attach a great deal of importance to status and rank. In meetings, respect should be shown to senior most person. It is also important not to criticize any person publicly. Mutual respect is to be shown at all times. Arabs often act on the basis of emotion rather than logic. They believe that everything happens by the will of Allah. Most of the work is done through administrative channels and high contacts are useful. Decision making is slow and most business is done face to face. Arab negotiators tend to be enthusiastic bargainers and expect their counterparts to grant major concessions. It is wiser to build a wide margin into initial offer, leaving room for manoeuvre during the lengthy negotiating process. Entertaining and being entertained are essential parts of building a close relationship. Arabs will press you to eat more than you want. Similarly, when hosting Arabs you must keep them pushing to eat and drink. Egypt, and other Middle Eastern countries follow their approach.

Arabs will press you to eat more than you want. Similarly, when hosting Arabs you must keep them pushing to eat and drink.

7. Australia

Australia is a deal focused, informal, monichronic and variable expressive culture. Australians are more reserved than their counterparts in southern Europe or Latin America. But they are more direct and straight forward in their speech than the Germans, Dutch or Americans. Aussies are known for vociferous argument and even confrontations or open disagreements. Negotiators from Arab world or Japanese might consider this behavior as hostile, while the latter's polite and mild behavior is considered by Australians as an attempt to mislead or confuse them. Australians are one of the most egalitarian and informal society in the world, surprising even the Americans. They consider Americans overly concerned with status, degrees, wealth or position in the corporate hierarchy. Visiting negotiators are advised to avoid impressing Australians by their titles or accomplishments. However their egalitarianism does not extend to women in business. As regards their orientation to time, they are somewhat less monochromic than Germans or Americans. With regard to space bubble, they prefer an arm's distance like English or Americans and also direct eye contact. The best policy for success in sales presentations is moderation and soft selling. Instead of over emphasizing your company's name, let your documentation, testimonials and third party reports speak for you.

Somewhat less monochromic than Germans or Americans. With regard to space bubble, they prefer an arm's distance like English or Americans and also direct eye contact.

References

1. Donald A. Bal, W.H. Macctal Prick, M.S. Minar, J.M. Gerenger, J.M. Mae Nelt,
2. *International Business,* Tata Macgraw Hill, Delhi, 2010
3. E.S. Glenn, D.Wilmeyers, K.A. Stevenson, *Cultural Styles of Persuation,* International Journals of Inter-cultural Relations, Vol. 1.
4. Richard Mead, *International Management: Cross Cultural Dimension,* Black well, Delhi, 2005.

EXHIBITS AND CASE STUDIES

EXHIBIT No. 1

Genetically Modified Food: Ethical and Unethical Issues

The term GM foods or GMOs (genetically modified organisms) is most commonly used to refer to crop plants created for human or animal consumption using the latest molecular biology techniques. These plants have been modified in the laboratory through non conventional breeding. GM foods are resistant to insects and viruses and more able to tolerate herbicides. Governments around the world are hard at work to establish a regulatory process to monitor the effects of and approve new varieties of GM plants. Yet depending on the political, social and economic climate within a region or country, different governments are responding in different ways. Food regulatory authorities require that GM foods receive individual pre-market safety assessments. A GM food will only be approved for sale if it is safe and as nutritious as its conventional counterparts. The safety of GM foods is still being debated. The possible monopolization of the world food market by large multinational companies that control the distribution of GM seeds is a possible fear. Using genes from animals in plant foods may pose ethical, philosophical or religious problems. Animal welfare could be adversely affected more readily. New GM organisms could be patented so that life could become commercial property through patenting.

Critics have objected to GM foods on several grounds, including possible safety issue like environmental hazards in the form of unintended harm to other organisms, reduced effectiveness of pesticides, human health risks involving, effect on digestive tract, moreover there is a need to bring fresh seeds each year involving greater costs. From the time when the earliest pioneers of medicine took the Hippocratic Oath, the importance of ethical considerations in relation to actions affecting living entities has been recognized by professionals. The general principles are still of fundamental importance: respect for life and the need for a balance of benefit over harm resulting from any intervention. Ethics is all about what we can do and what we should do. It's about the diffence between the good and bad – the right and the wrong. It is undoubtedly in the genetic engineering of animals that the unnaturalness of this technology is creating much public unease: for instance, the transfer of human genes into an animal, which reflects the fact that the new transgenic organism contains copies of the gene originally obtained from this source. Genetic engineering of animals may also meet severe moral oppositions if there are instances of animals suffering as a result of this process. Already there is evidence of animals suffering severe arthritis following application of transgenic growth hormones to improve their meat quality. A UK report (by the committee on the Ethics of Genetic Modification and Food Use, 1993) identified some of the main ethical concerns relating to the food use of certain transgenic organisms:

1. Transfer of human genes to food animals (eg. Transfer into sheep of the human gene for Factor IX, a protein involved in blood clotting)
2. Transfer of genes from animals whose flesh is forbidden for use as food by certain religious groups to animals that they normally eat (eg. Pig genes into sheep would affect Jews and Muslims)
3. Transfer of animal genes into food plants that may be of particular concern to some vegetarians.
4. Use of organisms contains human genes as animal feed.

Many bioethicists have called for a ban on species altering technologies. People tend to ask whether scientists are playing God when they tamper the natural characteristics of a plant/animal. Will these interventions redefine what it means to be normal? If they are later found to be harmful, we won't be able to do anything about it and the damage can spread if the plants and organisms multiply.

EXHIBIT No. 2

Ethical Issues Regarding Cloning Technology

Today, cloning is not a new concept in modern science. There have been a lot of different opinions for or against. Cloning can be regarded as an unethical issue and it might lead to some unpredictable problems in near future.

The first and foremost reason to oppose cloning is the uncertainty of using clones for transplant purpose. For instance, Dolly was a successful case of animal cloning in India, but she aged much more quickly than the donor. Similarly aging could happen in human organ clones if they were used for transplanting and cause side effects as well as bad reactions to human body. Consequently, this phenomenon might create a lot of medical risks.

Another reason to question is that the organ cloning process may be applied for the process of cloning babies. Therefore, procedures of cloning can easily lead to baby cloning which is illegal at the present. As the consequence, cloning babies would be carried out by some people without control, catering for bad purpose, which would seriously mess up our simple life.

The final reason to oppose cloning is the ethical issue. Imagine that human cloning became easy to work out, there would be a trend that people create their clones as fashion. This problem is really inhuman. Once human cloning was developed, there would be a black market where infertile couples could buy a cloned embryo that was stolen or was to be discarded in order to have a child. Additionally cloning to make human copies is sometimes as similar as producing machines, which is extremely condemned by many people, organizations, and religions. In such condition, cloning is considered to be unethical because of its bad effect on human life. In the future cloning needs more researches, experiment as well as governmental supervision to cope with some unpredictable trouble.

However ethical objections to human cloning are more philosophical than they are practical. The very idea of cloning assumes that our individuality can be understood so well that we can duplicate it. If human cloning ever become a reality, that this is not true would become evident. After all, we are more than a mere collection of genes. The American Medical association holds some points of reason why cloning should not take place. They are:

- There are unknown physical harms introduced by cloning.
- Unknown psychological harms introduced by cloning, including violations of autonomy and privacy.
- Impact on familial and societal relations.
- Potential effects on the human gene pool.

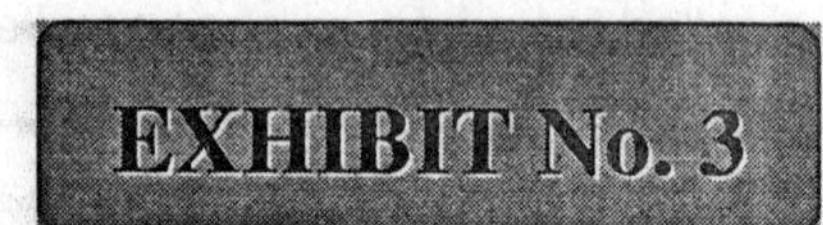

Petroleum Industry: Ethical Concerns

The petroleum companies have been established:

- To promote the general welfare of the petroleum business.
- To advance the use of petroleum and petroleum equipment through means consistence with the public interest.
- To develop and maintain relationship with refineries, produces, marketees transportation groups, government and legislative bodies that will maintain a standard of excellence in delivering, manfacturing, blending, producing, packaging, promoting and marketing petroleum products and services.
- Maintain and service all accounts efficiently and professionally.
- Recognise the need to store, transport, distribute and retail energy products in environmentally responsible, safe and secure manner with the highest regard for the safety and health of our work force and of the communities in which we operate.
- Respect the rights and interests of competitors.
- Monitor technological developments to assure avail ability of the highest quality products and service and imposition of the most stringent standard within the petroleum industry.
- Always be guided by a spirit of justice, honour, and fairness within their communities and in all dealings with other members of the petroleum industry and with associated industries.

Unethical Practices in Petroleum Trade: Case of BP (British Petroleum)

BP have recently begun to receive criticism for many of their activities. The most recent (August) criticism for their exploration in the arctic. Green Peace Foundation has heavily opposed this and the ecological zone was nearly forced into bankruptcy through an injunction served on them by BP. Like Shell, BP pays the military cell of other countries to protect their interest which is against the rights and interests of the local people. The physical environment is being manipulated and often results in the deaths of those who dare to protest. A leaked colonial report shows BP paying the military and supplying them with details of peasant trade union and environmental activists. BP has caused large scale environmental destruction in Alaska which is now leading to the development of the Atlantic frontier, a highly sensitive ecosystem and important expansion area of the oil industry. Also questionable are the developments in Peru and Angola. BP has been criticized a number of times in the past for its mineral operations on tribal people lands. The company has now pulled out of minerals. It does however continue to search for oil.

Patent Law: Ethical and Unethical

There is an inherent conflict between the property ownership mechanism of the patent system and the free dissemination of knowledge that has been a hallmark. The patent system was enacted to promote discovery and innovation. There is a legal assertion of right within patent either in the field of medical development or any other proposed procedure. There is currently so much flexibility and leeway in the law that it allows attorney to act in ways that essentially subvert the stated goals of the patent system.

In addition to this patents also need to recognize their ethical obligation to the public as well as their clients. Patent law is different from many areas of the law, in that the system was founded on altruistic goals of saving the public interest and promoting the development of technologies for the good of society and the property of the country. The system itself implies an ethical duty to society and the single minded advocacy of the client by entering patent law. Attorneys need to recognize that they bring upon themselves the need for a higher ethical consciousness. The patent law ethical obligation proposed one step which would clarify the unique ethical obligation that patent attorneys need to recognize. It would also start a dialogue within the patent community which would clarify the obligation.

Example of Ethical Violation: Brazil vs US, March 19, 2010

"Brazil plan to break I P rights on American drugs, music, software and movies as retaliation for its cotton subsidies," said by Latha Jishnu. At the recent UNDP consultation on access to affordable medicines, they were struck by the presentation made by Juliana Borges Vallini, a young woman from Brazil. Vallini is the head of Intellectual property for the ministry of health programme on HIV/AIDS and hepatitis, and her job is to ensure that the ministry has access to the most affordable drugs needed to treat Brazilians suffering from either of these conditions.

Health is fundamental right in Brazil, and the country guarantees universal access to treatment in 2008. It spent as much as 4640 million just for treating its 19000 AIDs patient. Affordable drugs are key to this programme and the country has not baulked at tough patent battles with the global pharmaceuticals giant in an effort to get them to reduce the steep prices for life saving medicines. Quite often, the mere threat of breaking the patents on the drug has worked for Brazil – as it has with Thailand.

The one time that Brazil did break the patent was in 2007 when it issued a compulsory license – an option provided by the World Trade Organization (WTOs) agreement on IP rights or TRIPS as it is called for Efavirenz, which is used to treat HIV/AIDS.

The same clarity and firmness of purpose are evident in the way Brazil has handled its trade dispute with the US over its legal cotton subsidies. Its decision on 14th July 2010 to apply sharply jacked up tariffs on 102 American products along with the plans to retaliate against US IPRs, has the world riveted. The eight year dispute centers on the illegal cotton subsidies given by the US government to its cotton farmers to protect them against price downturns and after the long drawn out case, brazil was awarded the right to apply up to $829 million in the higher tariffs and cross retaliation panel the first time the WTO had allowed a country to make retaliatory measures In sectors other than in the one that had been caused injury.

The measures announced by Brasilia boiled down to a simple fact that Pharmaceuticals, biotechnology and chemicals apart from Hollywood films, American software, music and books will lose their IP protection. A range of option will be used against American IP owners from reducing the term of IP protection to licensing technology without the authorization of the right holder (with or without remuneration) suspending a patent holder's exclusive right of importation and assessing taxes on royalty payments. The US has been dismissive on the trade row and even last week it had spoken slightingly of the issue when secretarial state Hillary Clinton told a press conference that 'I feel like, I have walked into a movie that has been going on for years'. That film may have started jump now since Brazil has changed the script rather dramatically.

Case Study No. 1 : Bhopal Disaster

The Bhopal Gas Tragedy is the world's worst industrial catastrophe occurred on the night of December 2-3, 1984 at the Union Carbide India Limited (UCIL) pesticide plant in Bhopal, India. UCIL was the Indian subsidiary of Union Carbide Corporation. In 1994, Supreme Court of India allowed UCC the sale of 50.9 percent of its assets in India. The Bhopal plant was sold to McLeod Russel (India) Ltd. Union Carbide Corporation (UCC), is now a subsidiary of Dow Chemical Company. Around midnight on December 2-3, 1984, there was a leak of methyl isocyanate (MIC) gas and other substances from the plant, resulting in the exposure of several thousands of people.

Over two decades since the tragedy, certain civil and criminal cases remain pending in the United States District Court, Manhattan and the District Court of Bhopal, India, against Union Carbide with an Indian arrest warrant also pending against Warren Anderson, CEO of Union Carbide at the time of the disaster. Greenpeace asserts that as the Union Carbide CEO, Anderson knew about a 1982 safety audit of the company's identical plant in the US. In June 2010, seven ex-employees, including the former chairman of UCIL, were convicted in Bhopal of causing death by negligence and sentenced to two years imprisonment and a fine of about $2000 each, the maximum punishment allowed by law.

The Chairman and CEO of Union Carbide, Warren Anderson, had been arrested and released on bail by the Madhya Pradesh Police in Bhopal on December 7, 1984. The arrest, which took place at the airport, assured Anderson would meet no harm by the Bhopal community. Anderson was taken to Union Carbide's house after which he was released six hours later on $2100 bail and flown out on a government plane. It is claimed by the then Deputy Chief of Mission of the US embassy in New Delhi, that communications between the Government of India and himself relating to the release of Warren Anderson to return to the US went through the erstwhile foreign secretary.

The Dow Chemical Company purchased Union Carbide in 2001 for $10.3 billion in stock and debt. Dow has publicly stated several times that the Union Carbide settlement payments have already fulfilled Dow's financial responsibility for the disaster. However, Dow did not purchase UCC's Indian subsidiary, Union Carbide India. That was sold in 1994 and renamed Eveready Industries India Limited. The acquisition has gained criticism from the International Campaign for Justice in Bhopal, as it is apparently contrary to established merger law in that Dow denies any responsibility for Carbide's Bhopal liabilities. According to the Bhopal Medical Appeal, Carbide remains liable for the environmental devastation as environmental damage was not included in the 1989 settlement, despite ongoing contamination issues. In August 2010 one of the assistants of Borak Obama mailed Montek Singh Ahluwalia, the Depty Chairman of Planning Commission to go slow on Dow chemical case if India wants US help to get World Bank Loan. Lack of political willpower has led to a stalemate on the issue of cleaning up the plant and its environs of hundreds of tones of toxic waste, which has been left untouched. Environmentalists have warned that the waste is a potential minefield in the heart of the city, and the resulting contamination may lead to decades of slow poisoning, and diseases affecting the nervous system, liver and kidneys in humans.

Questions

1. Can Warren Anderson's behaviour be called as socially responsible?
2. What were his responsibilities towards the society as a CEO?
3. Was Indian Government right in helping Anderson escape owing to his own personal safety?

Case Study No. 2

Indian culture is unique. It believes in universalism. For an Indian the whole world is a family of his own. Our culture asks us to behave with others as we behave with our family members. Our culture has love and respect for all cultures. Learning, here, starts from birth and continues till death. We are always open to learn from others. Our values of tolerance and learning from others have insulated our culture intact. The institution of Indian family is also unparallel. Family is formed on the basis of sacrifice. Normally, father is an earning member and mother is to manage the family expenditure with that earning. Father and mother sacrifice their all comforts for growth and development of their children. In poor families, parents may remain hungry and make all out effort to properly rear their children. When parents become old, their sons and daughters have to take their care as they had done in their childhood. Parents are treated as deities and are virtually worshipped by their sons, daughters in law as also by their grandsons and granddaughters. With the majority of women taking up outside jobs, the parents look after their grandsons and granddaughters. Parents are to be obeyed always. If someone disobeys his parents, he is likely to be expelled from the community and the close relatives.

Dr. Mishra is working as an Incharge Medical Officer at a Primary Health Centre situated at a block of Unnao district. He is in UPPMS and holds a degree of MD in Medicine. He has inherited a grand house from his father who died four years back. His mother is alive. Dr. Mishra is a married man and has his wife and two children (one daughter and one son aged 8 & 2 years respectively). His house is located in a private colony of Lucknow city. The colony is occupied by middle class people belonging to different castes, communities, religions and states. In spite of all variations, people meet together on various festivals. Dr. Mishra, being a good physician keeps himself available for people of the colony round the clock. He has earned a good name as a doctor.

When people live together, at occasions, they happen to have infighting also. It was four years back that some neighbor of Dr. Mishra had a fight with his father subsequently, his father died and his mother attributed cause the death to that quarrel. From that time onward, there was no relationship between the two families, even they stopped speaking to each other. Thereafter, Dr. Mishra's mother asked him not to attend to any medical emergency of that family to which Dr. Mishra gave his acceptance.

It was around 2.30 a.m. in December, 2009 when a phone call from that family came to Dr. Mishra that one member of their family has suddenly become unconscious and that no doctor is becoming available and that he is requested to kindly attend to the patient. His mother, wife and children wake up and he informed about the phone call. His mother demanded that he should not go there at any cost. Dr. Mishra took his car out and went to attend the patient disobeying his mother's instructions. Not only this, when the patient showed no improvement, he took him to medical university and returned from the university at about 10.00 a.m. His mother got angry and did not touch food for one day in protest. Dr. Mishra became late for his own duty.

Questions

1. What are the characteristics of Indian culture as given in this case of which of them can be integrated in modern business?
2. Was Dr. Mishra's mother right in not allowing his son to attend patient? Give your agreement or disagreement with justification.
3. Was the doctor right in attending the patient and becoming late for his own duty? If so, justify the case.

Case Study No. 3

Lucknow University MBA (LUMBA), Department of Business Administration has distinguished itself right from its inception in late 70's till date in inviting scholars from academics as well as from industries, corporate sector and government sector for sharing their experiences with students of MBA. This has enabled the department to earn name and fame not only in India but also in various developing and developed countries through its students. They are given immense opportunities for learning and experiencing. Some of them had brought their companies to heights. Not only this, LUMBA has produced a number of great scholars and great administrators.

It was in early 1980's when the department had no building of its own. It was organizing its classes in whatever rooms were found vacant. It was running under the Department of Commerce. It was taking help from various institutions like Indian Statistical Institute, Calcutta (Kolkata) and Psycho Technical Cell of RDSO, Lucknow etc. in holding admission tests and interviews. Since, MBA was a rare degree at that time; very bright students joined this course. Some of them were getting placements in the companies, some were opening institutions of management and some of them preferred Indian Administrative Services also. The faculties extended invitations to various dignitaries of government sector so that students could get some clues to compete in their respective jobs. RDSO (Research, Designs and Standard Organization) Lucknow is taken to be brain of Indian Railways. It is distinguished for keeping on its role a very large number of class-I officers. During the period of early 1980's, RDSO got on IRTS officer posted as director traffic and psycho technical cell. He had done his Ph.D in English literature from the University of Gauhati and was in touch with head of Department of English, Lucknow University. He was very fond of inviting academicians to RDSO and being invited by various academic forums in Lucknow. As some of the students of MBA were from RDSO, they mentioned the name of the said director to their head and this gentleman was invited to deliver a talk on Business Forecasting with special reference to traffic forecast on Indian Railways.

It was afternoon time when the said director from RDSO along with one assistant officer as well as two traffic inspectors came to deliver the talk. He was welcomed by the then working head of the department and other faculty members. In welcome 10 to 15 minutes were devoted. Then he first of all, highlighted his profile in which he spent 15 minutes time. Then he started speaking on contributions of English literature, poets like Shakespeare, Milton, Keats, Shelley and TS Elliot. He spoke so nicely that students kept pin-drop silence. He spoke in the last hardly in about 15 minutes on the topic and finished his lecture. He showed his inability to speak further because he had some other pre-occupations. The head of LUMBA thanked him for addressing the students. However students got frustrated because they could not learn anything new on the topic and wanted to ask questions on the topic which he did not allow for lack of time. While he went to RDSO along with his team, he asked them as to how he spoke. While, the inspectors offered all praise, the assistant officer who was promoted from inspectors rank to the rank of class-II officer and was working on ad hoc basis, pointed out that he did not do justice to the topic and that he could not satisfy the students. This angered the director who reprimanded the assistant officer in various ways for speaking the truth.

Questions

1. Was the director right to devote all the time in showing his knowledge of English literature and pay scant attention to the topic. How will you distribute time given to you for your business assignment?
2. Was the assistant officer right to point out the lacking of his boss. Write your comments in favour or against of it.
3. Was the director right or wrong to scold his assistant officer? Give your answer with justification. Can it be a model in a business organization?
4. Will you leave your professional ethics to gain favour in such cases?

Case Study No. 4

Tropicana was founded in Bradenon, Florida USA in 1947. Over last 50 years of expansion, it became one of the most respected beverage brands. Its presence is felt in 63 countries and it is now world's no. one juice brand owned by Pepsico Inc. It sells two type of juices as Tropicana and Tropicana 100%.

In India Tropicana juice product has been endorsed by Indian Medical Association (IMA) as a health drink (28-08-10 Times of India, Lucknow Edition). But the ethics committee of Medical Council of India (MCI) issued notice to IMA for endorsering products like Tropicana as a health drink. Dr. Dharma Prakas, Secretary IMA confirmed that they had received show cause notice by MCI. He said that 'we have not endorsed any product in the last two years 2009 and 2010. And whatever endorsement were done before that will be coming to an end in 2011'. As a policy IMA has decided that it will not be doing any more endorsement.

He further said that commitments IMA had made before the law against endorsements came into force in December 2009 will have to be completed.

Questions

1. Has IMA right to issue such endorsements contrary to ethical norms of advertisement.
2. Define advertisement ethics in view of above case study.
3. What are the key ethical concerns that bodies like MCI and IMA should focus on while endorsing a product?

Case Study No. 4

ITC Limited is one of leading companies of India. ITC ensures that its corporate system should be managed to meet share holder's aspirations and also social expectations. Its corporate governance model is based on two core principles i.e. the management should have executive freedom to ensure growth of the company and that freedom should be based on effective accountability. To implement this policy ITC adopted the policy of trusteeship, transparency, empowerment and accountability. The company believes that the practice of such adaptation lead to the right corporate culture.

The structure of the company carries out the task of strategic supervision as trustee of shareholders in a manner that impart objectivity and services accountability from the management. The Board of Director of the company has constituted five committees of the board for audit, the compensation, the investor service, the nomination and safety committee. ITC's remuneration policy is based on attaining and retaining high caliber talent. There was investor grievance committee to redress the problems of share holder, investors etc. The nomination committee is primarily concerned with making recommendations to the board regarding top level succession and appointments. The legal and safety committee ensures compliance with statutory requirements and safety standards.

By possessing such structure ITC's corporate governance policy reinforce and realize the company's belief in ethical corporate citizenship both within the organization as well as in external relationship.

Questions

1. How has ITC evolved it ethical policy of corporate governance?
2. What are the ways in which organizations can instill objectivity and accountability in their functioning?
3. Has ITC been able to meet the expectations of all its stakeholders through its corporate governance policy?

Index

A

Action, 20
Adam Smith, 43
Adhikara, 94
Advantage, 9
Aesthetics, 294
Africa,166
Aggression,158
Agni, 223
Ahimsa, 49
Ajiva, 67
Akbar, 280
Akkadevi, 279
Alexandria, 165
Amanusya, 207
Anger Management, 48
Anicca, 67
Annals, 9
Annaprasana, 223
Annie Besant, 98
Antevasin, 243
Anteyesti, 226
Anuloma, 226
Anuvrata, 78
Anxiety, 303
Apad dharma, 240
Aparavidya, 243
Aparigraha, 261
Aptech mode, 118
Arab, 308
Aristotile, 28
Arjuna, 64
Arsha, 226
Aryan, 208
Ashrama, 228
Astanga, 160
Australia, 309
Autonomy, 151
Avantika, 241

B

Bandha, 54
Bhagvadgita, 62
Bharucha, 241
Brahmacharya, 228
Brazil, 308
Bruno, 2
Buddha, 69
Buddhist, 66
Business Zones, 306

C

Calcutta Madras, 253
Capitalism, 110
Career, 67
Caste, 216
Chaitanya, 281
Chamber, 223
Champa, 241
Chandragupta Maurya, 247
Charler wood, 225
China, 248
Chorus, 5
Christian, 2
Christianity, 32
Chronic, 149
Chuda Karma, 223
Civil, 217
Clone, 311
Coca-Cola, 168
Cognitive, 157
Colonial system, 14
Communication, 151
Communist Manifesto, 35
Conflict, 47
Confucianism, 300
Constantinople, 1
Constitution, 196
Constitutional remedies, 199
Constructive, 47
Constructive, 47
Contract, 158
Copernicus, 2
Coping, 157
Copy Right, 174
Corporate Governance, 121
Culture, 292
Custom, 301

D

Daiva, 92
Dakshinapath, 241
Damayanti, 55
Dan Quixote

Danda, 224
Dandaniti, 56
Dantapura, 237
Dante, 3
Denial, 159
Destructive, 148
Development, 2
Dharma, 46
Dhyana, 62
Dialectic, 24
Directive Principle, 200
Displacement, 159

E

Ecology, 164
Egypt, 191
Emile Durkhem, 40
Emile, 40
Emotional, 150
Epidemic, 165
Equality, 197
Ethics, 20
Eustress, 148
Exchange, 164
Exhibit, 292
Exogamy, 204

F

Factor, 253
Factory, 13
Family, 243
Federation, 242
Folk Love, 296
France, 307
Free Trade, 185
Fundamental duties, 202

G

Gandhi, 102
Garbhadhana, 222
Gayatri, 210
Gender, 294
Germany, 306
Globalization, 164
Gold Standard, 188
Grhastha, 230
Guild, 234
Gunas, 46
Gunavarma, 248

H

Hanumana, 46
Harsha, 247
Hartog Commission, 260
Harvard, 43
Hetuvada, 70
Himsa, 54
Hinduism, 299
Hiranyagarbha, 222
Horizontal, 219
Hunter Commission, 256

I

Immanual Kant, 39
Industrial Revolution, 7
Infosys, 118
International Monetary Fund, 188
Investment, 170
Islam, 301

J

Jainism, 78
Japan, 306
Jat Karman, 223
Jati, 216
Jen, 300
Jiva, 78
Jivaka, 247
Jnana, 249
John Calvin, 17
Joint Family, 76
Judicial, 83
Justice, 94

K

Kabir, 281
Kadambari, 277
Kaivalya, 300
Kala, 78
Karl Marx, 35
Karma, 47
Karmayoga, 62
Karnabheda, 225
Kautilya, 82
Kesant, 225
Kosala, 49
Krishna, 50
Kshatriya, 299

L

Language, 249
Liberty, 12
Liverpool, 8
Lokachara, 53

M

Madhva, 283
Mahabharata, 245
Mahavastu, 235
Mahavira, 234
Mahayana, 276
Maitrevi, 244

Maktab, 249
Management Ethics, 120
Manana, 302
Manchester, 8
Mandasore, 242
Manu, 92
Mara, 71
Market, 129
Material Culture, 297
Materialism, 132
Mathura, 241
Matriarchal, 268
Maurya, 234
Max Weber, 16
McDonald, 169
Mechanism, 313
Megasthenese, 234
Middlepath, 66
Modernisation, 288
Moksha, 54
Montaigne, 4
Mudita, 53

N

Nadia, 248
Nalanda, 247
Nam karna, 223
Narada, 235
Narendra Nath, 97
Nastika, 205
Negotiation, 305
Newton, 32
Nibbana, 71
Nigama, 58
Niruddha, 161
Nirvana, 299
Niskramana, 223
Niyama, 95
Non Tariff, 187
Non-Aryan, 204
Nuclear family, 268

O

Occupation, 217
Optimism, 151
Organization, 45
Overload, 152

P

Padmavat, 281
Page, 216
Paisacha, 95
Pakka, 218
Panchala, 209
Pani, 207
Panini, 275
Panorama, 303
Papal, 1
Paramount, 307
Patanjali, 275
Patent, 313
Pativrata, 237
Patriarchal, 268
Pepsi, 168
Personality, 150
Petrarch, 3
Phallus, 206
Pieta, 5
Plato, 23
Politics, 27
Polychromic, 302
Polygamy, 267
Prajapatya, 226
Pranayama, 161
Pratiloma, 226
Pravara, 204
Prayaga, 245
Preamble, 183
Preyas, 52
Primitive Communism, 18
Primitive Culture, 292
Proctor & Gamble, 292
Production, 57
Protestant, 299
Ptolemy, 2
Pudgala, 78
Puga, 235
Puja, 95
Pumsavana, 222
Purana, 206
Purshottoma, 49
Purus sukta, 207
Purusa, 208
Purusartha, 204
Pushkalavati, 241

R

Rabelais, 4
Railway, 288
Raka, 222
Ram Mohan Roy, 254
Rama, 45
Ramananda, 282
Ramanuja, 282
Ramayana, 245
Ramcharitmanas, 281
Ratanasagara, 248
Rationalisation, 159
Ravana, 243
Ravidas, 282
Reddy, 219
Regression, 159

Religion, 33
Renaissance, 6
Republic, 25
Revolution, 2
Ricardo, 12
Right against exploitation, 199
Right to Equality, 197
Right to freedom of religion, 199
Right to freedom, 198
Rigveda, 51
Rishi, 108
Robert Boyle, 3
Romeo, 4
Rousseau, 32
Russia, 307

S

Sadler Commission, 258
Sagotra, 226
Sakti, 84
Samadhi, 67
Samata, 75
Samavartan, 225
Samba, 296
Samdhya, 230
Samhita, 209
Samkhya, 210
Sampradaya, 243
Samsara, 299
Samskara, 220
Samsung, 297
Samvidapatra, 234
Sananda, 162
Sanchi, 236
Sangha, 234
Sannyasa yoga, 232
Sanskrit, 207
Sanskritsation, 286
Sapinda, 226
Saptapadi, 204
Sarnath, 66
Sarthvaha, 236
Sasmita, 162
Sastra, 232
Satapatha Brahmana, 209
Sati, 253
Satya, 51
Satyagraha, 104
Seal, 296
Secular, 67
Security Council, 190
Segment, 216
Selye, 155
Settlement, 208
Shintoism, 301
Shiraz, 251
Shreni, 47
Shreyas, 52
Siddha, 243
Sikhism, 300
Sila, 69
Silk road, 165
Simantonayana, 222
Sita, 276
Smrti, 276
snata, 225
Social Responsibility, 112
Socialism, 12
Socialist, 193
Societal Organisation, 295
Socrates, 23
Solidarity, 219
Soma, 221
Sparsa, 225
Sraddha, 223
Sravana, 243
Sresthi, 211
Stability, 67
Stress, 147
Sublimation, 159
Sudra, 276
Sukta, 275
Sulka, 87
Supra, 162
Sursagar, 281
Susruta, 223
Svadharma, 63
Svastika, 223
Swaraj, 104
Syadvada, 81
Syllogism, 29
Symbolism, 65

T

Takshasila, 247
Tamasika, 55
Taoism, 301
Tapas, 161
Team Management, 50
Teetotalism, 286
Temporal, 294
Theosophical society, 283
Time Management, 48
Tisya, 222
Toyota, 169
Trade Barrier, 187
Trade in services, 180

Trusteeship, 110
Typhus, 14

U

Uddalaka, 244
Ujjain, 241
Underload, 152
Uniform Civil Code, 201
University Grant commission, 261
Untouchable, 218
Upanayana, 224
Upanishad, 228
Upanita, 225
Upasana, 260
Urbanization, 235
USA, 318
Utilitarianism, 142
Utopia, 67

V

Vaikhanasa, 220
Vaisali, 241
Vaisya, 207
Valabhi, 246
Vallabhacarya, 281
Value, 271
Vanik, 207
Vanprastha, 231
Varaha, 278
Varanasi, 248
Varna, 206
Varta, 245
Vartani, 87
Veda, 51
Vedanta, 97
Vedarmbha, 225
Vertical, 219
Vibhisana, 46
Vibhuti, 54
Videha, 241
Vidisa, 241
Vidyarmbha, 224
Vihara, 248
Vishnu, 80
Vishti, 86
Vivekananda, 97
Voltaire, 31
Vrata, 78
Vyaji, 60

W

Welfare, 310
Westernization, 287
William carey, 253
Withdrawal, 158

Y

Yajnavalkya, 275
Yajnopavita, 209
Yama, 95
Yana, 84
Yang, 301
Yashpal Committee, 261
Yin, 301
Yoga, 62
Yudhisthira, 55

Z

Zend-Avesta, 207